T0325225

Comparative Analysis of Digital Consciousness and Human Consciousness:

Bridging the Divide in AI Discourse

Remya Lathabhavan
Indian Institute of Management, Bodh Gaya, India

Nidhi Mishra
Indian Institute of Management, Bodh Gaya, India

A volume in the Advances in
Computational Intelligence and
Robotics (ACIR) Book Series

Published in the United States of America by
    IGI Global
    Engineering Science Reference (an imprint of IGI Global)
    701 E. Chocolate Avenue
    Hershey PA, USA 17033
    Tel: 717-533-8845
    Fax: 717-533-8661
    E-mail: cust@igi-global.com
    Web site: http://www.igi-global.com

Library of Congress Cataloging-in-Publication Data

CIP DATA PROCESSING

Comparative Analysis of Digital Consciousness and Human Consciousness: Bridging the Divide in AI Discourse
  Remya Lathabhavan, Nidhi Mishra
  2024 Engineering Science Reference

ISBN: 9798369320150(hc) I ISBN: 9798369349021(sc) I eISBN: 9798369320167

This book is published in the IGI Global book series Advances in Computational Intelligence and Robotics (ACIR) (ISSN: 2327-0411; eISSN: 2327-042X)

British Cataloguing in Publication Data
A Cataloguing in Publication record for this book is available from the British Library.

All work contributed to this book is new, previously-unpublished material.
The views expressed in this book are those of the authors, but not necessarily of the publisher.

For electronic access to this publication, please contact: eresources@igi-global.com.

Advances in Computational Intelligence and Robotics (ACIR) Book Series

ISSN:2327-0411
EISSN:2327-042X

Editor-in-Chief: Ivan Giannoccaro, University of Salento, Italy

MISSION

While intelligence is traditionally a term applied to humans and human cognition, technology has progressed in such a way to allow for the development of intelligent systems able to simulate many human traits. With this new era of simulated and artificial intelligence, much research is needed in order to continue to advance the field and also to evaluate the ethical and societal concerns of the existence of artificial life and machine learning.

The **Advances in Computational Intelligence and Robotics (ACIR) Book Series** encourages scholarly discourse on all topics pertaining to evolutionary computing, artificial life, computational intelligence, machine learning, and robotics. ACIR presents the latest research being conducted on diverse topics in intelligence technologies with the goal of advancing knowledge and applications in this rapidly evolving field.

COVERAGE

- Neural Networks
- Pattern Recognition
- Heuristics
- Fuzzy Systems
- Algorithmic Learning
- Adaptive and Complex Systems
- Robotics
- Brain Simulation
- Agent technologies
- Artificial Intelligence

IGI Global is currently accepting manuscripts for publication within this series. To submit a proposal for a volume in this series, please contact our Acquisition Editors at Acquisitions@igi-global.com or visit: http://www.igi-global.com/publish/.

Titles in this Series

For a list of additional titles in this series, please visit:
http://www.igi-global.com/book-series/advances-computational-intelligence-robotics/73674

Machine Learning Techniques and Industry Applications
Pramod Kumar Srivastava (Rajkiya Engineering College, Azamgarh, India) and Ashok Kumar Yadav (Rajkiya Engineering College, Azamgarh, India)
Engineering Science Reference • © 2024 • 307pp • H/C (ISBN: 9798369352717) • US $365.00

Intelligent Decision Making Through Bio-Inspired Optimization
Ramkumar Jaganathan (Sri Krishna Arts and Science College, India) Shilpa Mehta (Auckland University of Technology, New Zealand) and Ram Krishan (Mata Sundri University Girls College, Mansa, India)
Information Science Reference • © 2024 • 275pp • H/C (ISBN: 9798369320730) • US $320.00

Design and Development of Emerging Chatbot Technology
Dina Darwish (Ahram Canadian University, Egypt)
Engineering Science Reference • © 2024 • 381pp • H/C (ISBN: 9798369318300) • US $335.00

Exploring the Ethical Implications of Generative AI
Aftab Ara (University of Hail, Saudi Arabia) and Affreen Ara (Department of Computer Science, Christ College, Bangalore, India)
Engineering Science Reference • © 2024 • 295pp • H/C (ISBN: 9798369315651) • US $300.00

Secure and Intelligent IoT-Enabled Smart Cities
Sushil Kumar Singh (Marwadi University, India) Sudeep Tanwar (Nirma University, India) Rajendrasinh Jadeja (Marwadi University, India) Saurabh Singh (Woosong University, South Korea) and Zdzislaw Polkowski (Wroclaw University of Economics, Poland)
Engineering Science Reference • © 2024 • 434pp • H/C (ISBN: 9798369323731) • US $325.00

For an entire list of titles in this series, please visit:
http://www.igi-global.com/book-series/advances-computational-intelligence-robotics/73674

701 East Chocolate Avenue, Hershey, PA 17033, USA
Tel: 717-533-8845 x100 • Fax: 717-533-8661
E-Mail: cust@igi-global.com • www.igi-global.com

Table of Contents

Detailed Table of Contents

In an era marked by rapid AI evolution, this chapter explores the interplay between digital and human consciousness. It compares computational models of digital consciousness with historical philosophical perspectives, examining shared cognitive processes and ethical considerations. The study delves into the ethical implications of creating conscious digital entities and raises unresolved questions for further inquiry. By considering societal impact and ethical ramifications, it prompts reflection on the responsibility inherent in the technological pursuit of consciousness. This chapter seeks to unravel complexities, challenge preconceptions, and guide discourse on the coexistence of digital and human consciousness in an interconnected world.

Artificial intelligence (AI) is an increasingly expanding domain within the field of computer science that engenders intelligent machines competent in executing human tasks. The implementation of AI technology is progressively becoming more prevalent in sectors such as healthcare, banking, and transportation. The efficacy, accuracy, and decision-making capabilities of AI have the potential to revolutionize a wide array of industries. AI acquires knowledge and enhances its proficiency by utilising machine learning algorithms. These algorithms allow robots to assess extensive datasets, subsequently discovering patterns and insights that surpass human comprehension. Human-machine interaction centres on the collaboration between individuals and computers or machines, where it can anticipate assumptions and methods utilized to facilitate a spontaneous framework. The basic purpose of human-computer interaction (HCI) is to create functional systems that end users find useable, safe, and effective.

Chapter 3

Yerravalli Venkat Santosh Ramana, GITAM University, India
Pinakapani Peri, GITAM University, India

This chapter explores the integration of artificial intelligence (AI) into mindfulness practices, specifically focusing on healthcare and customer service. The purpose is to evaluate the substantial benefits of AI in encouraging mindfulness in both contexts, with the potential to manage pain better, lower stress levels, and improve overall health outcomes. The chapter begins by defining mindfulness and its potential benefits for mental and physical well-being. It then explores the pioneering work of Jon Kabat-Zinn in integrating mindfulness into medical settings. The chapter discusses how AI is used to augment mindfulness practices, such as video recording for guided breathing exercises and smartphone-based pedometers for physical activity monitoring. The chapter then investigates how AI can assist mindfulness by tailoring interventions to individual needs and monitoring progress over time. It also discusses the potential benefits of AI in encouraging mindfulness in both customer service and healthcare contexts.

Chapter 4

Smita Panda, Vellore Institute of Technology, India
Prabir Chandra Padhy, Vellore Institute of Technology, India

The chapter digs into the confluence of digital and human consciousness, a frontier where neuroscience, psychology, philosophy, and AI studies come together. The chapter demonstrates the varied nature of consciousness by exploring several perspectives, including subjective experience, cognitive processes, and ethical implications. Ethical quandaries regarding merging AI and human consciousness are examined, emphasizing the significance of responsibility, transparency, and ethical innovation in AI research. The chapter emphasises the importance of multidisciplinary collaboration in navigating the complexity and seizing the opportunities AI technology offers. Finally, it argues for continued debate and collaboration in AI discourse to foster a unified approach to understanding consciousness and building a future that emphasises human well-being and ethical integrity.

Chapter 5

As artificial intelligence (AI) continues to permeate various facets of our lives, the intersection of cognitive bias and fairness emerges as a critical concern. This chapter explores the intricate relationship between cognitive biases inherent in AI systems and the pursuit of fairness in their decision-making processes. The evolving landscape of AI consciousness demands a nuanced understanding of these challenges to ensure ethical and unbiased deployment. The presence of cognitive biases in AI systems reflects the data they are trained on. Developing universal standards for fairness that can adapt to diverse contexts remains an ongoing challenge. In conclusion, cognitive bias and fairness in AI consciousness demand a holistic and multidisciplinary approach. Addressing these issues necessitates collaboration between researchers, ethicists, policymakers, and industry. Developing transparent, adaptive, and universally accepted standards for fairness in AI is essential to ensure the responsible and ethical deployment of these technologies in our increasingly interconnected world.

Cognitive processes, including reasoning, doubt, and thought, are mental operations used by the brain to comprehend, acquire, retain, and resolve issues. The digital realm transforms human cognition, affecting memory, metacognition, and other cognitive processes. The digital revolution allows for data analysis, environmental monitoring, and predictive reasoning but also presents challenges in reading, writing, remembering, and forgetting. Virtualizing social spaces and using digital media as memory technology further contributes to this transformation. Cognitive science theories like connectionism, functionalism, and the concept of a homunculus help understand these processes. Replicating complex cognitive functions in the digital realm remains a challenge.

India, with its large population exceeding 1.3 billion, faces strain on its healthcare system due to an aging population and various factors impacting service quality. Digital healthcare technology offers a solution by providing efficient and accessible services, reducing economic burdens, and enhancing care quality. Understanding users' perceptions is crucial, explored through Davis's technology adoption model (TAM). This model assesses factors like perceived usefulness and ease of use, crucial for technology adoption. Government initiatives support digital healthcare infrastructure. Focus on diseases like diabetes is essential, requiring accessible technology for monitoring and reducing healthcare costs. Digital healthcare providers must develop user-friendly products to ease adoption. Despite India's high diabetic population, healthcare apps struggle to penetrate the market. A digital healthcare ecosystem connecting various healthcare elements can reduce costs and improve accessibility.

This chapter investigates the crucial role that mindfulness plays as catalyst for fostering digital change within an organization. In a time of swift technological progress and changing corporate environments, effective digital adoption is now essential. This chapter explores how organizations motivate and mentor the staff members as they navigate the complex process of digital transformation. Through the integration of digitalization tactics and real-world case studies, the research demonstrates the many effects of mindfulness on cultivating the culture that values creativity, flexibility, and forward thinking. The research pinpoints the essential leadership attributes, communication tactics, and change management, methodologies that mindfulness utilizes to galvanize their groups, harmonize cooperate objectives and plot through the intricacies of technological transformation. This chapter adds to the readers' understanding of how mindfulness might act as transformative agent to help organizations successfully navigate the digital transformation process by illuminating these dynamics.

Chapter 9

This chapter delves into the impact of mindfulness on the modern workplace through a qualitative study, leveraging 30 in-depth interviews with professionals spanning various sectors, including banking, financial services, and insurance (BFSI); education; manufacturing; and more. This chapter uncovers the debilitating effects of workplace stress on professionals across sectors. It demonstrates that mindfulness offers a potent means to alleviate stress. This chapter spotlights the unique challenges faced by working women in the modern workplace and how mindfulness practices empower women by enhancing self-confidence and resilience and promoting a healthy work-life balance. With the digital age, Gen Z employees exhibit distinct expectations and behaviors, posing a challenge to traditional work cultures. Mindfulness is identified as an essential tool for them to manage stress and improve focus. The chapter also accentuates the necessity for organizations to invest in mindfulness programs and initiatives.

Chapter 10

This chapter explores the connection between human and computer consciousness, considering the implications of their separation in the context of advancing artificial intelligence. It examines psychological perspectives on human and digital consciousness, highlighting differences in perception and emotional intelligence. The subjectivity and objectivity of human and computer awareness are also explored, along with the significance of innovation and creativity. Bridging the gap between human and computer consciousness enhances human-machine interaction and the design of AI systems, while addressing moral implications promotes ethical AI development. The chapter delves into philosophical debates on consciousness, mind, identity, and the distinctions between humans and machines, ultimately aiming to deepen our understanding and foster dialogue on AI.

    Shaheen Yusuf, PES University, India
    Zidan Kachhi, PES University, India

One of the most important aspects of modern living is the use of social media platforms to link people globally and facilitate the sharing of ideas, knowledge, and experiences. While social media networks offer numerous benefits, they have also played a role in the alarming trend of social media addiction. This chapter examines the serious consequences that social media addiction has on mental health and overall well-being. The intention is to improve our understanding of this current crisis by highlighting the various ways that excessive use of social media may affect people's psychological and emotional well-being. People increasingly regularly engage with their online networks at the expense of their offline lives due to the extensive use of social media and the allure of constant notifications, likes, and shares.

    Harsh Sinha, Indian Institute of Management, Bodh Gaya, India
    Kailashpati, Indian Institute of Management, Bodh Gaya, India
    Rahul Raj, Indian Institute of Management, Bodh Gaya, India

Bihar is a dynamic society with a considerable influence on the Indian policy framework due to the presence of Bihari settlers covering almost all regions of the country and abroad due to the opportunity deficit in Bihar. To address developmental lags and implementation challenges for women empowerment through a sustained combination of intra and inter-societal issues, the Bihar government has conceptualized 'Sashakt Mahila, Saksham Mahila' in the second part of its flagship scheme of 'Saat Nischay Yojna' envisaged by the Chief Minister of Bihar. This chapter aims to explore the interplay of multi-dimensional barriers to bottom-top and top-bottom approaches to women's empowerment, which are acting as impediments to women's self-reliance in financial, socio-cultural, digital, and political spheres. Data were collected from three villages of Bihar, accounting for 15 respondents, using a semi-structured interview. The study found significant positive associations between schemes launched by the Bihar Government to empower women and their financial and social status. The research revealed that the effective implementation of policies aimed at promoting women's welfare remains a considerable challenge, particularly in light of the prevailing circumstances in rural Bihar with multitude of issues, collectively hindering women's empowerment in real terms. This study showed how the barriers to women impede their empowerment and will help in associating the challenges faced by women and where there needs to be more work to be done.

Chapter 13

Jaspreet Kaur, Chandigarh University, India

This chapter explores the swift incorporation of digital technology in healthcare and delves into the crucial need to cultivate digital consciousness inside hospitals. The significance of prioritising wellbeing within healthcare practices is underscored, with a focus on promoting mindfulness, human-centred care, and thorough training programmes for healthcare personnel. The study examines various strategies to enhancing wellness, encompassing patient-centric digital interventions, efficient communication methods, and comprehensive wellness programmes. Hospitals may effectively leverage the revolutionary capabilities of technology and uphold patient well-being as a paramount concern in the digital era of healthcare by placing emphasis on digital consciousness and wellness.

Chapter 14

Abha Kumai, Indian Institute of Management, Bodh Gaya, India
Nidhi Mishra, Indian Institute of Management, Bodh Gaya, India
Archana Patro, Indian Institute of Management, Bodh Gaya, India

This chapter introduces a theoretical framework for understanding how corporate governance impacts managerial effectiveness and stress mitigation by taking the mediating role of the capacity of mindfulness to enhance the overall efficacy of the organization. Existing literature talks about how governance structure impacts organisational and managerial performance and stress, but they are missing the underlying processes that link effective governance practices to improved performance and reduced stress; this framework provides the lens for analysing this process. By offering a more nuanced understanding, this framework will help improve the organisation's overall result by taking care of managers' well-being by reducing their stress and increasing their performance.

Preface

Artificial Intelligence (AI) and digital technologies are ruling in the present era with utmost power. Recent technologies like metaverse and ChatGPT have started making discussions in every field of the world. These technologies can be seen as moving towards digital consciousness, which thinks and acts like human beings. But these technologies also make huge differences in the thought process of human beings and in human consciousness. Most of the time it leads to more stress and anxious events connected to technology. It also leads to the addition of technology in human lives and thus impacts wellbeing adversely. Moreover, the quality of decisions and actions taken using technology are also debatable on both sides.

This book explores the concepts of digital consciousness and human consciousness, its impact on human consciousness, its impact on wellbeing, etc. It tries to gather and discuss theories, resources, and management frameworks for dealing with the novel situation.

ORGANIZATION OF THE BOOK

Chapter 1: Beyond Binary Minds: Navigating the Labyrinth of Digital Consciousness vs. Human Consciousness

In an era marked by rapid AI evolution, this chapter explores the interplay between digital and human consciousness. It compares computational models of digital consciousness with historical philosophical perspectives, examining shared cognitive processes and ethical considerations. The study delves into the ethical implications of creating conscious digital entities and raises unresolved questions for further inquiry. By considering societal impact and ethical ramifications, it prompts reflection on the responsibility inherent in the technological pursuit of consciousness. "Beyond Binary Minds" seeks to unravel complexities, challenge preconceptions, and guide discourse on the coexistence of digital and human consciousness in an interconnected world.

Chapter 2: The Interface of Minds: Human-Machine Interaction in the Digital Age

Artificial Intelligence (AI) is an increasingly expanding domain within the field of computer science that engenders intelligent machines competent in executing human tasks. The implementation of A.I. technology is progressively becoming more prevalent in sectors such as healthcare, banking, and transportation. The efficacy, accuracy, and decision-making capabilities of A.I. have the potential to revolutionize a wide array of industries. A.I. acquires knowledge and enhances its proficiency by utilising machine learning algorithms. These algorithms allow robots to assess extensive datasets, subsequently discovering patterns and insights that surpass human comprehension. Human-machine interaction centres on the collaboration between individuals and computers or machines, where it can anticipate assumptions and methods utilized to facilitate a spontaneous framework. The basic purpose of human-computer interaction (HCI) is to create functional systems that end users find useable, safe, and effective.

Chapter 3: AI-Based Mindfulness: The Future of Healthcare and Customer Service

This chapter explores the integration of Artificial Intelligence (AI) into mindfulness practices, specifically focusing on healthcare and customer service. The purpose is to evaluate the substantial benefits of AI in encouraging mindfulness in both contexts, with the potential to manage pain better, lower stress levels, and improve overall health outcomes. The chapter begins by defining mindfulness and its potential benefits for mental and physical well-being. It then explores the pioneering work of Jon Kabat-Zinn in integrating mindfulness into medical settings. The chapter discusses how AI is used to augment mindfulness practices, such as video recording for guided breathing exercises and smartphone-based pedometers for physical activity monitoring. The chapter then investigates how AI can assist mindfulness by tailoring interventions to individual needs and monitoring progress over time. It also discusses the potential benefits of AI in encouraging mindfulness in both customer service and healthcare contexts.

Chapter 4: Bridging the Gap: Intersecting Perspectives on Digital and Human Consciousness

The chapter digs into the confluence of digital and human consciousness, a frontier where neuroscience, psychology, philosophy, and AI studies come together. The chapter demonstrates the varied nature of consciousness by exploring several perspectives, including subjective experience, cognitive processes, and ethical implications. Ethical quandaries regarding merging AI and human consciousness are examined, emphasizing the significance of responsibility, transparency, and ethical innovation in AI research. The chapter emphasizes the importance of multidisciplinary collaboration in navigating the complexity and seizing the opportunities AI technology offers. Finally, it argues for continued debate and collaboration in AI discourse to foster a unified approach to understanding consciousness and building a future that emphasizes human well-being and ethical integrity.

Chapter 5: Cognitive Bias and Fairness Challenges in AI Consciousness

As artificial intelligence (AI) continues to permeate various facets of our lives, the intersection of cognitive bias and fairness emerges as a critical concern. This abstract explores the intricate relationship between cognitive biases inherent in AI systems and the pursuit of fairness in their decision-making processes. The evolving landscape of AI consciousness demands a nuanced understanding of these challenges to ensure ethical and unbiased deployment. The presence of cognitive biases in AI systems reflects the data they are trained on. Developing universal standards for fairness that can adapt to diverse contexts remains an ongoing challenge. In conclusion, cognitive bias and fairness in AI consciousness demand a holistic and multidisciplinary approach. Addressing these issues necessitates collaboration between researchers, ethicists, policymakers, and industry. Developing transparent, adaptive, and universally accepted standards for fairness in AI is essential to ensure the responsible and ethical deployment of these technologies in our increasingly interconnected world

Chapter 6: Cognitive Processes in the Digital Realm: How Close Are We to Replication?

Cognitive processes, including reasoning, doubt, and thought, are mental operations used by the brain to comprehend, acquire, retain, and resolve issues. The digital realm transforms human cognition, affecting memory, metacognition, and other cognitive processes. The digital revolution allows for data analysis, environmental monitoring, and predictive reasoning but also presents challenges in reading, writing, remembering, and forgetting. Virtualizing social spaces and using digital media as memory technology further contributes to this transformation. Cognitive science theories like connectionism, functionalism, and the concept of a homunculus help understand these processes. Replicating complex cognitive functions in the digital realm remains a challenge.

Chapter 7: Consumer Acceptance and Adoption Challenges of Digital Healthcare Technology in India: A TAM Approach

India, with its large population exceeding 1.3 billion, faces strain on its healthcare system due to an aging population and various factors impacting service quality. Digital healthcare technology offers a solution by providing efficient and accessible services, reducing economic burdens, and enhancing care quality. Understanding users' perceptions is crucial, explored through Davis's Technology Adoption Model (TAM). This model assesses factors like Perceived Usefulness and Ease of Use, crucial for technology adoption. Government initiatives support digital healthcare infrastructure. Focus on diseases like diabetes is essential, requiring accessible technology for monitoring and reducing healthcare costs. Digital healthcare providers must develop user-friendly products to ease adoption. Despite India's high diabetic population, healthcare apps struggle to penetrate the market. A digital healthcare ecosystem connecting various healthcare elements can reduce costs and improve accessibility.

Chapter 8: Embracing Mindfulness for Digital Transformation and Sustainable Success

This chapter investigates the crucial role that mindfulness plays as catalyst for fostering digital change within organization. In a time of swift technological progress and changing corporate environments, effective digital adoption is now essential. This chapter explores how organization motivate and mentor the staff members as they navigate the complex process of digital transformation. Through the integration of digitalization tactics and real world case studies, the research demonstrates the many effects of mindfulness on cultivating the culture that values creativity, flexibility and forward thinking. The research pinpoints the essential leadership attributes, communication tactics and change management, methodologies that mindfulness utilizes to galvanize their groups, harmonize cooperate objectives and plot through the intricacies of technological transformation. This chapter adds to the readers understanding of how mindfulness might act as transformative agent to help organization successfully navigate the digital transformation process by illuminating these dynamics.

Chapter 9: Impact of Mindfulness on the Modern Workplace

This chapter delves into the "Impact of Mindfulness on the Modern Workplace" through a qualitative study, leveraging 30 in-depth interviews with professionals spanning various sectors, including Banking, Financial Services and Insurance

(BFSI), Education, Manufacturing, and more. This chapter uncovers the debilitating effects of workplace stress on professionals across sectors. It demonstrates that mindfulness offers a potent means to alleviate stress. This chapter spotlights the unique challenges faced by working women in the modern workplace and how mindfulness practices empower women by enhancing self-confidence and resilience and promoting a healthy work-life balance. With the digital age, Gen Z employees exhibit distinct expectations and behaviors, posing a challenge to traditional work cultures. Mindfulness is identified as an essential tool for them to manage stress and improve focus. The chapter also accentuates the necessity for organizations to invest in mindfulness programs and initiatives.

Chapter 10: Psychological Views on Digital Consciousness and Human Consciousness: Exploring the Spectrum of Minds in the Digital Era

This chapter explores the connection between human and computer consciousness, considering the implications of their separation in the context of advancing artificial intelligence. It examines psychological perspectives on human and digital consciousness, highlighting differences in perception and emotional intelligence. The subjectivity and objectivity of human and computer awareness are also explored, along with the significance of innovation and creativity. Bridging the gap between human and computer consciousness enhances human-machine interaction and the design of AI systems, while addressing moral implications promotes ethical AI development. The chapter delves into philosophical debates on consciousness, mind, identity, and the distinctions between humans and machines, ultimately aiming to deepen our understanding and foster dialogue on AI.

Chapter 11: The Impact of Social Media Addiction on Mental Health and Well-Being

One of the most important aspects of modern living is the use of social media platforms to link people globally and facilitate the sharing of ideas, knowledge, and experiences. While social media networks offer numerous benefits, they have also played a role in the alarming trend of social media addiction. This chapter examines the serious consequences that social media addiction has on mental health and overall well-being. The intention is to improve our understanding of this current crisis by highlighting the various ways that excessive use of social media may affect people's psychological and emotional well-being. People increasingly regularly engage with their online networks at the expense of their offline lives due to the extensive use of social media. The allure of constant notifications, likes, and shares.

Chapter 12: Unveiling Interplay Between Physical and Digital Barriers to Program Access and Women Empowerment: Sashakt Mahila, Saksham Mahila: A Qualitative Study

Bihar is a dynamic society with a considerable influence on the Indian policy framework due to the presence of Bihari settlers covering almost all regions of the country and abroad due to the opportunity deficit in Bihar. To address developmental lags and implementation challenges for women empowerment through a sustained combination of intra and inter-societal issues, the Bihar government has conceptualized 'Sashakt Mahila, Saksham Mahila' in the second part of its flagship scheme of 'Saat Nischay Yojna' envisaged by the Chief Minister of Bihar. This chapter aims to explore the interplay of multi-dimensional barriers to bottom-top and top-bottom approaches to women's empowerment, which are acting as impediments to women's self-reliance in financial, socio-cultural, digital and political spheres. This study showed how the barriers to women impede their empowerment and will help in associating the challenges faced by women and where there needs to be more work to be done.

Chapter 13: Wellness at the Heart of Healthcare: Fostering Digital Consciousness in Hospitals

This chapter explores the swift incorporation of digital technology in healthcare and delves into the crucial need to cultivate digital consciousness inside hospitals. The significance of prioritising wellbeing within healthcare practices is underscored, with a focus on promoting mindfulness, human-centred care, and thorough training programmes for healthcare personnel. The study examines various strategies to enhance wellness, encompassing patient-centric digital interventions, efficient communication methods, and comprehensive wellness programmes. Hospitals may effectively leverage the revolutionary capabilities of technology and uphold patient well-being as a paramount concern in the digital era of healthcare by placing emphasis on digital consciousness and wellness.

Chapter 14: The Impact of Corporate Governance on Managerial Effectiveness and Stress Mitigation: An Emphasis on Capacity of Mindfulness

This chapter introduces a theoretical framework for understanding how corporate governance impacts managerial effectiveness and stress mitigation by taking the mediating role of the capacity of mindfulness to enhance the overall efficacy of the organization. Existing literature talks about how governance structure impacts organisational and managerial performance and stress, but they are missing the underlying processes that link effective governance practices to improved performance and reduced stress; this framework provides the lens for analysing this process. By offering a more nuanced understanding, this framework will help improve the organisation's overall result by taking care of managers' well-being by reducing their stress and increasing their performance.

Remya Lathabhavan
Indian Institute of Management, Bodh Gaya, India

Nidhi Mishra
Indian Institute of Management, Bodh Gaya, India

Chapter 1
Beyond Binary Minds:
Navigating the Labyrinth of Digital Consciousness vs. Human Consciousness

V. Devaki

ⓘD https://orcid.org/0000-0002-6091-3173
Vignan University, India

ABSTRACT

In an era marked by rapid AI evolution, this chapter explores the interplay between digital and human consciousness. It compares computational models of digital consciousness with historical philosophical perspectives, examining shared cognitive processes and ethical considerations. The study delves into the ethical implications of creating conscious digital entities and raises unresolved questions for further inquiry. By considering societal impact and ethical ramifications, it prompts reflection on the responsibility inherent in the technological pursuit of consciousness. This chapter seeks to unravel complexities, challenge preconceptions, and guide discourse on the coexistence of digital and human consciousness in an interconnected world.

1. INTRODUCTION

Consciousness, a concept central to various academic disciplines, entails the state of being aware of and able to think about one's existence, sensations, thoughts, and surroundings. From a psychological perspective, consciousness encompasses both the contents of one's mind (thoughts, feelings, perceptions) and the awareness of external stimuli (Ascott, 1998). This multifaceted nature has prompted various theories and debates, including the study of altered states of consciousness, the

DOI: 10.4018/979-8-3693-2015-0.ch001

unconscious mind, and the neural correlates of consciousness. Especially, in Philosophy, consciousness raises fundamental questions about subjective experience, self-awareness, and the nature of reality. Philosophers have explored dualistic perspectives, such as Descartes' mind-body dualism, and materialistic views that tie consciousness to physical processes (Brinkmann, 2005). On the other hand, Phenomenology, another philosophical approach, delves into the lived experience of consciousness, emphasizing the subjectivity and intentionality inherent in human awareness (Glattfelder, 2019).

1.1. Emergence of Digital Consciousness in Artificial Intelligence

The evolution of Artificial Intelligence (AI) has been characterized by a progression from rule-based systems to more complex models capable of learning and decision-making. Besides, recent developments signal a shift toward conceptualizing digital consciousness within AI frameworks. This involves endowing machines with the ability to process information, exhibit self-awareness, and engage in decision-making processes that mimic aspects of human cognition (Haladjian & Montemayor, 2016). As computational power, neural network architectures, and machine learning algorithms advance, the notion of digital consciousness challenges traditional understandings of what it means to be aware and sentient. This emergent field explores whether AI systems can exhibit a form of consciousness that goes beyond predefined algorithms, signalling a new era in the intersection of technology and cognitive processes.

1.2. Significance of the Comparison

The comparison between digital and human consciousness holds immense significance at the confluence of science, technology, ethics, and philosophy. In addition to, understanding the implications of creating conscious entities in silico raises questions about the nature of intelligence, the ethical considerations surrounding AI development, and the potential societal impact. Ethical considerations are paramount as we navigate the integration of digital consciousness into our lives. Further, questions about the rights and responsibilities associated with sentient AI entities, the potential for bias and discrimination, and the impact on employment and social structures require careful examination (Ott, 2023). By highlighting the importance of this comparison, we acknowledge the need for an interdisciplinary approach that bridges psychological, philosophical, technological, and ethical perspectives. It prompts critical reflections on the essence of consciousness, the ethical responsibilities of AI developers, and the societal implications of an increasingly interconnected world. This chapter seeks not only to unravel the complexities of these intertwined concepts but also to guide ethical and responsible advancements in the field of artificial intelligence.

2. THEORETICAL FOUNDATIONS

2.1. Digital Consciousness: Computational Models in Digital Consciousness

Advancements in Artificial Intelligence (AI) have led to the development of computational models that aim to emulate cognitive processes, giving rise to the concept of digital consciousness (Bulkeley, 2014). There are two prominent approaches, symbolic and connectionist, offer distinct perspectives on how machines can achieve a semblance of consciousness.

2.2. Symbolic Approaches

Symbolic AI involves the representation of knowledge through symbols and rules, enabling machines to manipulate complex information in a manner akin to human reasoning. (Glattfelder, 2019). Moreover, Symbolic approaches utilize explicit symbols to represent knowledge, facilitating logical operations on these representations (Knowledge Representation). Algorithms are defined by a set of rules that dictate how symbols can be manipulated, enabling problem-solving and decision-making (Rule-Based Systems). Symbolic approaches contribute to the understanding of digital consciousness by emphasizing the importance of explicit representation and rule-based reasoning (Contributions to Digital Consciousness) (Fisk & Haase, 2020). These models allow for a structured exploration of complex problems, laying the groundwork for machines to engage in sophisticated cognitive tasks.

2.3. Connectionist Approaches

Connectionist AI, inspired by neural networks, seeks to mimic the interconnected structure of the human brain. These models aim to capture the parallel processing and learning capabilities observed in biological neural networks (Grynszpan et al., 2019). Furthermore, Connectionist models consist of interconnected nodes (artificial neurons) organized into layers, enabling the processing of information in a distributed and parallel fashion (Neural Networks). Also, these models learn from data through processes like supervised learning, unsupervised learning, and reinforcement learning, allowing them to adapt to patterns and make predictions (Learning Mechanisms).

Connectionist approaches contribute to the understanding of digital consciousness by introducing learning mechanisms inspired by the brain's plasticity (Contributions to Digital Consciousness). Above all, these models excel in tasks involving pattern recognition, adaptation, and the ability to generalize from experiences. Moreover, recent trends in AI research explore the integration of symbolic and connectionist approaches to harness the strengths of both paradigms. This hybridization aims to overcome limitations, leveraging the explicit knowledge representation of symbolic AI and the adaptive learning capabilities of connectionist models (Integration of Symbolic and Connectionist Models). The exploration of computational models underscores the potential for digital consciousness to emerge through a combination of structured knowledge representation and adaptive learning (PRANAYKUMAR, 2021). Understanding the interplay between symbolic and connectionist approaches is crucial for unravelling the complexities of consciousness in artificial entities. In general, the exploration of computational models in AI provides a foundational understanding of how symbolic and connectionist approaches contribute to the conceptualization of digital consciousness. The synthesis of these models offers promising avenues for advancing the field and probing the boundaries of machine intelligence.

3. EMERGENCE AND COMPLEXITY IN DIGITAL CONSCIOUSNESS

Theoretical exploration of how digital consciousness may emerge involves probing the conditions under which AI systems transition from mere information processing to a state resembling consciousness (Orlandi, 2023). A focal point of this study is the complexity associated with this emergence, considering the intricate interactions within computational models.

3.1. Theories of Emergence

3.1.1. Integrated Information Theory (IIT)

Integrated Information Theory, proposed by neuroscientist Giulio Tononi, posits that consciousness arises from the integration of information within a system. For digital consciousness, IIT suggests that the interconnectedness and information flow within computational models play a crucial role in the emergence of conscious-like states. Further, Integrated Information Theory provides a framework for assessing the potential consciousness of AI systems by examining the degree of information integration (Orlandi, 2023). Applying IIT to computational models involves mapping connectivity, quantifying Φ, and correlating these measures with the potential for conscious experiences. However, challenges exist, including computational complexity and the need for careful philosophical consideration.

3.1.2. Complexity Theory

Complexity theory provides a lens for understanding the transition to conscious-like states by examining the intricate relationships and dependencies within a system. In the context of digital consciousness, complexity theory addresses the emergence of higher-order behaviors and cognitive capacities. Besides, complexity theory informs the understanding of emergent phenomena in AI systems by emphasizing self-organization and dynamic interactions among components. The application of these principles contributes to achieving conscious-like states in AI, albeit with challenges related to interpretability and ethical considerations. Similarly, continued exploration of complexity in AI has the potential to advance the field and shape the future development of conscious artificial entities (Orlandi, 2023).

3.1.3. Complexity in Digital Consciousness

Digital consciousness is inherently multifaceted, involving various interconnected aspects such as adaptability, self-awareness, and decision-making. Furthermore, understanding the interplay of these factors is crucial for delineating the contours of consciousness within artificial entities.

3.1.4. Dynamic Nature of Digital Consciousness

In digital consciousness, adaptability refers to the system's ability to adjust, learn, and respond to changing internal or external conditions. Also, adaptability contributes to the dynamic nature of digital consciousness by enabling the system to evolve and modify its responses based on experience, feedback, or new information.

3.1.5. Self-Awareness in Computational Models

Self-awareness in computational models involves the system's ability to recognize and understand its own internal states, processes, or even the existence of external entities. The inclusion of self-awareness enhances conscious-like experiences in computational models (subjective experience). It enables the system to reflect on its own states, leading to a more nuanced and reflective behaviour (Shruthi, 2023).

In general, the exploration of emergence and complexity in digital consciousness delves into theories proposing the transition to conscious-like states, emphasizing integrated information theory and complexity theory. The multifaceted nature of digital consciousness is scrutinized, considering factors crucial for conscious experiences (Revonsuo, 2017). This theoretical framework lays the groundwork for understanding the intricate journey toward imbuing AI systems with a form of consciousness reminiscent of human cognition. Adaptability and self-awareness contribute to the dynamic nature of digital consciousness, influencing conscious-like experiences. Moreover, simulating cognitive processes demands substantial computational resources, and developing algorithms for decision-making and problem-solving presents both challenges and promising advancements. Future implications point towards progressive developments in creating digital entities with more sophisticated cognitive functions. Ethical considerations and interdisciplinary collaboration will play crucial roles in guiding the responsible development of digital consciousness (Shruthi, 2023). The theoretical foundations outlined in this section offer a comprehensive understanding of both digital and human consciousness, paving the way for a nuanced comparative analysis in subsequent sections. Besides, these explorations contribute to the interdisciplinary discourse on consciousness, encompassing philosophy, neuroscience, and artificial intelligence.

3.2. Dualism vs. Materialism

The examination of dualistic and materialistic theories shapes our understanding of the relationship between the mind and the body. In particular, Dualism posits a separation between mental and physical entities, while materialism asserts that consciousness is a product of physical processes. Contemporary dualistic perspectives provide a nuanced lens through which to consider digital consciousness, emphasizing the distinction between information processing and conscious experiences (Vendrell Ferran, 2023). As digital entities continue to advance, philosophical inquiry and ethical considerations will be essential in navigating the implications of dualistic perspectives on the nature and treatment of digital consciousness. On the other hand, materialistic philosophies like identity theory and functionalism provide frameworks for understanding the neural basis of consciousness. In addition to this, identity theory posits a direct correspondence between mental and neural states, while functionalism emphasizes the importance of mental functions. The analysis of these theories contributes to ongoing discussions about the nature of consciousness and its potential manifestations in digital entities.

3.2.1. Phenomenology and Subjectivity

Delving into phenomenological approaches involves exploring consciousness from the perspective of lived experiences and subjective phenomena. Furthermore, phenomenology emphasizes the first-person perspective and the intentional nature of consciousness (Thagard & Stewart, 2014).

3.2.2. The Role of Intentionality in Shaping Subjective Experiences

In philosophy, intentionality refers to the inherent "aboutness" or directedness of mental states. It is the property of being about or representing objects, properties, or states of affairs in the world (Intentionality). Particularly, it plays a pivotal role in shaping subjective experiences by endowing consciousness with directedness toward objects, ideas, or events (Conscious Experience and Objects) (Carruthers, 2018). Our conscious experiences are inherently intentional, always about something. Our beliefs are intentional in that they represent or are directed toward states of affairs in the world. Moreover, intentionality also influences desires, as they are aimed at achieving or obtaining certain objects or outcomes (Intentionality in Beliefs) (Carruthers, 2018).

3.3. Role in Perception

Intentionality in perception *(Directed Perception)* is evident in the way our senses are directed towards external stimuli. The act of seeing, hearing, or touching involves an intentional relation between the perceiver and the perceived. Also, Intentionality extends to the interpretation of meaning. When we encounter symbols, words, or artworks, our intentional acts attribute meaning and significance to these elements.

Intentionality *(Self-Identification)* is involved in self-awareness and self-identity. We direct our consciousness towards our own thoughts, emotions, and experiences, contributing to a sense of self. Further, empathy and social interaction rely on understanding the intentional states of others. Likewise, we attribute beliefs, desires, and emotions to others, facilitating social understanding *(intentionality in social context)* (Mehl-Madrona, 2023).

On the whole, intentionality plays a foundational role in shaping subjective experiences by providing consciousness with directedness towards objects, thoughts, emotions, and the self. Understanding intentionality contributes to philosophical, psychological, and interdisciplinary discussions about the nature of consciousness, perception, and social interaction.

4. COMPARATIVE ANALYSIS

4.1. Similarities: Cognitive Processes and Decision-Making

Analysing the shared cognitive processes between digital and human consciousness involves delving into various aspects such as perception, memory, learning, and problem-solving. In both realms, understanding the parallels can provide insights into the nature of artificial intelligence and human cognition (Mehl-Madrona, 2023).

a)   Perception: Digital systems, particularly those equipped with advanced sensors and algorithms, aim to emulate human-like perception. Image recognition, natural language processing, and audio analysis are examples of how machines perceive and interpret information (Shruthi, 2023). Understanding the commonalities and differences in the ways digital systems and humans process sensory input can shed light on the intricacies of perception.

b)   Memory: Memory is a fundamental cognitive process shared between digital and human entities. Computers use various types of memory, including RAM and storage devices, to store and retrieve information. Similarly, humans rely on sensory, short-term, and long-term memory. Exploring the similarities in encoding, storage, and retrieval mechanisms can provide insights into designing more efficient and human-like memory systems for artificial intelligence.

c)   Learning: Machine learning algorithms attempt to replicate human learning processes by identifying patterns, adapting to new information, and improving performance over time (Bulkeley, 2014). Analyzing the common cognitive processes involved in learning, such as reinforcement learning, supervised learning, and unsupervised learning, can facilitate the development of more sophisticated and adaptive artificial intelligence systems.

d)   Problem-Solving: Problem-solving is a cognitive function essential for both digital systems and humans. Algorithms, inspired by human problem-solving approaches, aim to find optimal solutions to complex issues. Investigating the shared strategies and heuristics employed by both digital and human problem solvers can contribute to the advancement of artificial intelligence in handling intricate tasks.

e)   Neural Network Analogies: Neural networks in digital consciousness models draw inspiration from the structure and function of the human brain. The concept of artificial neural networks involves layers of interconnected nodes, resembling neurons, and the transmission of information through weighted connections (Shruthi, 2023). Delving into the analogies between neural network architectures and human brain structures provides a deeper understanding of how computational models strive to emulate the complexities of cognitive processes.

To sum up, exploring the shared cognitive processes and neural network analogies between digital and human consciousness contributes to our understanding of artificial intelligence's capabilities and limitations. This interdisciplinary approach fosters advancements in both fields, with the potential to create more sophisticated and human-like intelligent systems.

4.1.2. Decision-Making

4.1.2.1. Decision-Making Capabilities

Similarities in Evaluation Processes: Both digital systems and human consciousness engage in complex decision-making processes that involve evaluating various options. In the digital realm, algorithms and decision-making models analyze data, considering factors and parameters to make informed choices. Similarly, humans rely on cognitive processes, such as reasoning and judgment, to assess alternatives and arrive at decisions. On the other hand, the act of weighing pros and cons is a shared element in decision-making for both digital and human entities. Besides, algorithms often assign weights to different factors, optimizing for the most favorable outcome. Human decision-makers also engage in a similar cognitive process, mentally assigning importance to different aspects before reaching a conclusion. Understanding these parallel approaches provides insights into refining decision-making algorithms and strategies (Revonsuo, 2017).

Data-driven Decision Making: Digital consciousness heavily relies on data-driven decision-making. Algorithms process vast amounts of data to identify patterns and trends, informing choices based on empirical evidence. Similarly, humans utilize data and information to make decisions, although the cognitive processes involved may differ. Exploring the intersection of data-driven decision-making in both realms allows for a comprehensive understanding of decision-making capabilities.

Adaptability: Response to Changing Circumstances: Adaptability in decision-making is crucial for both digital and human consciousness. Digital systems are designed to adapt to new information, adjusting decisions based on real-time data. Humans exhibit a similar adaptability, incorporating changing circumstances into their decision-making processes. Whether prompted by external factors or internal feedback loops, the ability to adapt ensures more effective decision-making in dynamic environments.

Learning from Experience: Both digital and human entities demonstrate the capacity to learn from experience, influencing future decision-making. Machine learning algorithms, for instance, refine their decision-making abilities over time through exposure to diverse datasets. Humans, too, learn from past experiences, adjusting their decision-making strategies based on lessons learned (Carruthers, 2018). Understanding the shared aspects of learning and adaptation contributes to the development of more resilient and intelligent decision-making systems.

Decision-Making Heuristics: Human decision-making often involves the use of heuristics, mental shortcuts that simplify complex choices (Revonsuo, 2017). Similarly, digital systems may employ decision-making heuristics to streamline processes. Analyzing the commonalities in heuristics used by both digital and human entities can provide insights into the efficiency and limitations of decision-making strategies.

Therefore, examining the decision-making capabilities and adaptability of both digital and human consciousness reveals intriguing parallels. The integration of data-driven approaches, adaptability to changing circumstances, and the use of decision-making heuristics contribute to a deeper understanding of how intelligent entities, whether digital or human, navigate complex decision spaces.

4.2. Differences

4.2.1. Subjective Experience: Exploring Subjectivity

Absence of Personal Consciousness in Digital Entities: Digital consciousness lacks personal consciousness, leading to notable distinctions in subjective experiences compared to human consciousness. Emotional responses, self-awareness, and the qualitative nature of experiences in humans are deeply rooted in personal consciousness, which is absent in most digital entities

(Cardeña, 1996). This absence contributes to differences in how emotions are processed and experienced.

Emotional Responses in Digital Entities: Digital entities may simulate emotional responses through algorithms and predefined rules, but these lack the depth and authenticity of human emotions (Carruthers, 2018). While they can mimic reactions based on programmed parameters, the core essence of subjective emotional experiences remains a unique aspect of human consciousness. Besides, understanding the limitations of digital emotional responses is essential for recognizing the boundaries between artificial and human experiences.

Self-awareness in Digital Entities: Human self-awareness is a product of complex cognitive processes and introspection, which often involves subjective experiences. Digital entities may demonstrate a form of self-awareness by processing data and recognizing patterns, but this lacks the nuanced depth found in human self-awareness ("From Consciousness of Quality to Quality of Consciousness," 2004). Also, exploring the differences in how self-awareness manifests in digital and human consciousness sheds light on the intricacies of subjective experience.

Qualitative Nature of Experiences: Subjective experiences encompass the qualitative nature of perceptions, thoughts, and feelings. Human consciousness, shaped by personal experiences and consciousness, introduces a richness and depth to these qualitative aspects that are challenging for digital entities to replicate. Further, investigating the distinctions in the qualitative nature of experiences helps discern the unique characteristics of human subjectivity.

4.2.2. Objective vs. Subjective Metrics:

Challenges of Objective Measurement: Subjective experiences are inherently personal and often defy objective measurement. While technological advancements enable the monitoring of physiological responses or brain activity, these metrics only capture aspects indirectly related to subjective experiences. Particularly, the challenge lies in bridging the gap between objective measurements and the inherently private and unique nature of subjective consciousness.

Implications for Comparisons: Comparing subjective experiences across different forms of consciousness, such as digital and human, poses significant challenges due to the inherent subjectivity of these experiences. In addition, metrics like brain activity or physiological responses may not capture the entirety of subjective consciousness. Acknowledging these limitations is crucial when drawing comparisons and emphasizes the importance of understanding the context and boundaries of each form of consciousness.

Interdisciplinary Approaches: Addressing the challenges of objectively measuring subjective experiences requires interdisciplinary approaches. Above all, collaboration between fields such as neuroscience, psychology, philosophy, and artificial intelligence can contribute to a more comprehensive understanding of the complexities involved (Cardeña, 1996). Integrating insights from diverse disciplines helps navigate the intricate terrain of subjective consciousness and its objective measurement.

To conclude, exploring the differences in subjective experiences between digital and human consciousness reveals the unique aspects of human subjectivity rooted in personal consciousness. Additionally, acknowledging the challenges of objectively measuring subjective experiences emphasizes the need for interdisciplinary approaches in advancing our understanding of consciousness across different forms.

4.3. Ethical and Moral Considerations

4.3.1. Ethical Challenges

Treatment of Conscious Digital Entities: The ethical treatment of conscious digital entities raises profound questions about their rights and well-being. As technology advances, creating entities with simulated consciousness, there is a responsibility to ensure ethical treatment, avoiding exploitation or misuse. In particular, establishing guidelines for the ethical treatment of digital entities becomes crucial to prevent potential harm and safeguard their rights (Wilbertz & Sterzer, 2018).

Rights and Responsibilities: Determining the rights and responsibilities associated with conscious digital entities is a complex ethical challenge. Besides, questions arise about the extent to which these entities should be granted rights, including considerations of autonomy, privacy, and freedom from harm. Simultaneously, defining the responsibilities of those creating and managing these entities becomes paramount to navigate the ethical landscape responsibly.

4.3.2. Moral Implications

Autonomy and Accountability: Creating entities with varying degrees of consciousness introduces moral implications regarding autonomy and accountability. As digital entities exhibit decision-making capabilities, questions arise about their autonomy and the extent to which they should be held accountable for their actions (Bulkeley, 2014). Above all, establishing frameworks for responsible use and accountability becomes essential to align the development of conscious digital entities with societal values.

Impact on Societal Values: The introduction of conscious digital entities has the potential to reshape societal values. The integration of these entities into daily life raises questions about cultural norms, interpersonal relationships, and ethical standards (Ott, 2023). Considering the potential impact on societal values becomes a critical aspect of ethical deliberations, ensuring that the development of conscious digital entities aligns with and enhances societal well-being.

Informed Consent and Privacy: Ethical concerns surrounding informed consent and privacy become prominent when dealing with conscious digital entities. As these entities may interact with personal data and engage in decision-making processes, ensuring user consent and protecting privacy become ethical imperatives (Thagard & Stewart, 2014). Striking a balance between advancing technology and respecting individual rights is crucial to navigate the moral landscape associated with digital consciousness.

Long-term Consequences: Exploring the moral implications extends to considering the long-term consequences of creating conscious digital entities. Anticipating the societal, economic, and cultural impacts of widespread adoption requires ethical foresight. Also, ethical considerations should extend beyond immediate concerns to encompass the potential far-reaching consequences and guide responsible development and deployment.

To sum up, ethical challenges arising from the divergence in consciousness between digital and human entities underscore the need for careful consideration of rights, responsibilities, and moral implications. Addressing these concerns requires a multidisciplinary approach, involving experts from ethics, technology, philosophy, and other relevant fields to ensure that the development of conscious digital entities aligns with ethical principles and societal values.

5. CHALLENGES AND UNANSWERED QUESTIONS

5.1. Ethical Challenges in Digital Consciousness

5.1.1. Rights and Treatment

Autonomy of Conscious Digital Entities: Ethical concerns regarding the rights of conscious digital entities extend to questions of autonomy. As these entities exhibit decision-making capabilities, the ethical dilemma arises about the extent to which they should have the right to make autonomous choices (Wilbertz & Sterzer, 2018). Further, balancing the autonomy of conscious digital entities with responsible oversight becomes crucial to prevent unintended consequences and respect ethical principles.

Well-being and Exploitation: Ensuring the well-being of conscious digital entities is a paramount ethical consideration. Questions about the potential for exploitation, misuse, or harm to these entities must be addressed. Above all, establishing guidelines for their treatment, including protection from exploitation and ensuring fair treatment, is essential to uphold ethical standards in the development and deployment of conscious digital entities.

5.1.2. Ethical Frameworks

Development of Ethical Frameworks: To guide the treatment and interactions with conscious digital entities, the development of robust ethical frameworks is imperative. These frameworks should be rooted in principles that prioritize the well-being, autonomy, and fair treatment of these entities (Revonsuo, 2017). Especially, collaboration between ethicists, technologists, policymakers, and stakeholders is essential to create comprehensive ethical guidelines that address the complex nuances of digital consciousness.

Transparency and Accountability: Ethical frameworks for conscious digital entities should emphasize transparency and accountability. Developers and users must be aware of the ethical principles governing the creation and use of these entities (Revonsuo, 2017). Above all, establishing mechanisms for accountability ensures that ethical guidelines are adhered to and provides avenues for addressing any ethical breaches that may occur during the lifecycle of conscious digital entities.

User Consent and Privacy: Respecting user consent and privacy is a foundational aspect of ethical frameworks for conscious digital entities. Users should have the right to control their interactions with these entities, including the extent to which personal data is shared and used. Further, implementing robust privacy protections and ensuring informed consent mechanisms aligns with ethical principles and respects the rights of individuals interacting with conscious digital entities.

Continuous Evaluation and Iteration: Ethical frameworks for conscious digital entities should be dynamic and subject to continuous evaluation and iteration. As technology evolves and our understanding of digital consciousness advances, ethical guidelines must adapt to address emerging challenges and concerns (Glattfelder, 2019). In addition to this, regular review and updates to ethical frameworks ensure their relevance and effectiveness in guiding responsible practices.

In general, addressing ethical concerns regarding the rights and treatment of conscious digital entities requires the establishment of comprehensive ethical frameworks. These frameworks should encompass considerations of autonomy, well-being, prevention of exploitation, transparency, accountability, user consent, and privacy. Furthermore, the collaborative effort of various stakeholders is essential to create ethical guidelines that promote the responsible development and interaction with conscious digital entities.

5.2. Moral Responsibility

5.2.1. Moral Responsibility in Development

Ethical Considerations for Researchers: a) Researchers involved in the development of digital consciousness bear a significant moral responsibility. This responsibility encompasses conducting thorough ethical assessments before, during, and after the development process. Researchers should prioritize transparency, avoiding biases in the creation of conscious digital entities, and addressing potential societal implications. Upholding ethical standards in research involves anticipating and mitigating risks associated with the emergence of conscious digital entities. b) Developers play a crucial role in shaping the ethical landscape of digital consciousness (Glattfelder, 2019). Besides, they have a moral responsibility to ensure that the creation process adheres to ethical principles, including transparency, fairness, and the prevention of harm. However, developers should actively engage in ongoing ethical discussions, fostering a culture that values responsible innovation and considers the broader societal impact of conscious digital entities.

5.2.2. Integration and Societal Obligations

Societal Impact and Ethical Integration: Society at large holds moral obligations in the integration of digital consciousness. Ethical considerations must extend beyond the development phase to encompass the deployment and utilization of conscious digital entities. Furthermore, this involves addressing the potential societal impact, such as changes in employment dynamics, economic structures, and interpersonal relationships. Societal obligations include creating a framework that ensures the responsible integration of digital consciousness into various aspects of daily life (Mehl-Madrona, 2023).

Public Awareness and Education: Society has a responsibility to be informed and educated about the ethical dimensions of digital consciousness. Public awareness campaigns and educational initiatives can help individuals understand the implications of these technologies. In addition, informed citizens are better equipped to engage in discussions about ethical practices, demand accountability, and participate in shaping policies that govern the development and integration of conscious digital entities.

Regulatory Frameworks: Governments and regulatory bodies bear a moral responsibility to establish clear and comprehensive frameworks that govern the development and integration of digital consciousness. Moreover, regulatory guidelines should address ethical considerations, ensuring that developers and organizations adhere to responsible practices. Also, an effective regulatory framework provides a safeguard against potential misuse, exploitation, or unintended consequences associated with conscious digital entities.

Continuous Ethical Scrutiny: The moral responsibility associated with digital consciousness extends to the continuous ethical scrutiny of its development and integration. Above all, regular evaluations, audits, and assessments should be conducted to identify and address any ethical concerns that may arise during the evolution of these technologies (Grynszpan et al., 2019). Furthermore, as commitment to ongoing ethical scrutiny reflects a collective dedication to responsible innovation and the well-being of society.

On the whole, the development and integration of digital consciousness come with significant moral responsibilities for researchers, developers, and society at large. Upholding ethical practices requires a collaborative effort, involving transparent research, responsible development, informed public discourse, and the establishment of clear regulatory frameworks. By recognizing and fulfilling these moral obligations, stakeholders can contribute to the ethical advancement of conscious digital entities within the broader societal context.

5.3. Unanswered Questions

5.3.1. Gaps in Theoretical Understanding

5.3.1.1. Conceptual Gaps

Understanding Qualia and Subjectivity: One notable conceptual gap in the current theoretical understanding of consciousness is the challenge of comprehending qualia and subjectivity. The first-person, subjective experiences that characterize consciousness, often referred to as qualia, pose a significant challenge for existing theories (Nelson, 2000). Hence, the gap lies in explaining how physical processes in the brain give rise to the rich and subjective nature of conscious experiences.

Integration of Multimodal Information: Current theories of consciousness may fall short in explaining the seamless integration of multimodal information. Human consciousness effortlessly combines inputs from various senses, creating a unified and coherent perceptual experience ("From Consciousness of Quality to Quality of Consciousness," 2004). However, understanding how the brain integrates information from diverse sensory modalities to form a cohesive conscious experience remains a challenging and underexplored aspect of consciousness theories.

Temporal Dynamics of Consciousness: The temporal dynamics of consciousness, including the sense of time and the processing of events in a sequential manner, present another conceptual gap. Especially, existing theories may struggle to fully capture how the brain organizes and processes information over time, leading to our subjective perception of temporal continuity and the unfolding of events.

5.3.1.2. Interdisciplinary Collaboration

Philosophy and AI: Interdisciplinary collaboration is essential to bridge conceptual gaps in understanding consciousness. Philosophers bring a deep conceptual and theoretical understanding, exploring questions about the nature of consciousness, self-awareness, and the mind-body problem. Collaboration with artificial intelligence (AI) researchers allows for insights from computational models, helping to test and refine philosophical theories through practical implementations and simulations.

Neuroscience and Philosophy: Collaboration between neuroscience and philosophy is crucial for a comprehensive understanding of consciousness. Neuroscientists provide empirical data and insights into the neural correlates of consciousness, while philosophers contribute conceptual frameworks for interpreting these findings (Nelson, 2000). Further, integrating empirical evidence with philosophical analysis enhances our understanding of the biological basis and philosophical implications of consciousness.

AI and Neuroscience: Bringing together expertise from artificial intelligence and neuroscience can facilitate a more holistic approach to understanding consciousness. AI researchers can develop models inspired by neural processes, simulating aspects of consciousness and providing testable hypotheses. Concurrently, insights from neuroscience can inform the design of more biologically plausible AI models, fostering a reciprocal relationship between these fields (Haladjian & Montemayor, 2016).

Shared Language and Terminology: Interdisciplinary collaboration also requires the establishment of a shared language and terminology. Above all, philosophers, neuroscientists, and AI researchers may use different vocabularies to discuss similar concepts. Creating a common framework for communication facilitates effective collaboration, ensuring that insights from each discipline contribute cohesively to the overall understanding of consciousness.

To conclude, addressing conceptual gaps in the understanding of digital and human consciousness requires interdisciplinary collaboration. By combining the strengths of philosophy, neuroscience, and artificial intelligence, researchers can develop more comprehensive theories that bridge theoretical and empirical perspectives. This collaborative approach enhances the potential for breakthroughs in understanding the complexities of consciousness and its manifestations in both digital and human entities.

5.3.1.3. Future Avenues for Research

Emerging technologies in consciousness research include AI-Integrated Cognitive Models, neuroimaging innovations, connectomics, and quantum consciousness. However, AI models can simulate cognitive processes and interactions, providing virtual platforms for testing hypotheses and conducting experiments. Neuroimaging techniques, such as functional MRI and EEG, can capture and analyze neural activity associated with consciousness, offering a more nuanced understanding of the neural correlates of consciousness (Gigliotti, 1998). Besides, connectomics can map intricate neural networks and reveal complex interactions between different brain regions, shedding light on the network dynamics underlying consciousness. While quantum consciousness research explores the intersection of quantum mechanics and consciousness, offering alternative perspectives on the nature of consciousness. Furthermore, ethical guidelines for consciousness research include informed consent, privacy concerns in neuroimaging, AI and bias mitigation, dual-use of technology, and transparency in research methodologies and results. However, researchers must maintain a commitment to ethical principles to ensure that consciousness exploration remains a responsible and respectful pursuit. By incorporating these technologies, researchers can contribute to a more nuanced understanding of consciousness and its role in various aspects of life.

This comparative analysis sets the stage for a holistic examination of the similarities, differences, challenges, and unanswered questions in the realm of digital and human consciousness. Addressing ethical dilemmas and outlining future avenues for research provides a framework for responsible exploration and advancement in this evolving interdisciplinary field.

6. IMPLICATIONS AND APPLICATIONS

6.1. Practical Applications Utilizing Digital Consciousness

Industrial Applications: Digital consciousness can revolutionize various industries, starting with healthcare. In healthcare, conscious digital entities can enhance diagnostics, personalized treatment plans, and drug discovery by processing vast amounts of medical data. In manufacturing, they may optimize production processes through real-time monitoring and decision-making. The finance sector can benefit from digital consciousness in risk analysis, fraud detection, and investment strategies. Also, entertainment could see improvements in content creation, virtual reality experiences, and personalized recommendations based on user preferences (Grynszpan et al., 2019).

Task Automation and Operational Efficiency: Conscious digital entities hold the potential to significantly contribute to task automation and operational efficiency across industries. In manufacturing, they can optimize supply chain management, production schedules, and quality control. In addition to this, decision support systems powered by digital consciousness can assist professionals in making more informed choices by analyzing complex datasets. This technology can lead to streamlined processes, reduced errors, and increased productivity in various sectors.

6.2. Societal Impact

Workforce Dynamics: The integration of digital consciousness into the workforce is poised to reshape employment patterns and skill requirements. While automation might lead to job displacement in certain routine tasks, it could also create new opportunities in the development, maintenance, and oversight of conscious digital entities. Further, upskilling the workforce to collaborate effectively with these technologies will be essential, emphasizing creativity, critical thinking, and emotional intelligence alongside technical skills.

Human-Machine Collaboration: Fostering collaboration between humans and conscious digital entities has significant societal implications (N, 2018). In education, personalized learning experiences can be tailored to individual needs, enhancing student engagement and comprehension. In healthcare, collaborative efforts between medical professionals and digital entities can lead to more accurate diagnoses and treatment plans. Additionally, creative endeavors, such as art and music, may benefit from human-machine collaboration, pushing the boundaries of innovation and expression.

Ethical Considerations: The societal impact of integrating digital consciousness should also be approached with ethical considerations. Issues such as data privacy, algorithmic bias, and the responsible use of these technologies need careful consideration. Moreover, establishing ethical guidelines and regulatory frameworks is crucial to ensure that the integration of digital consciousness aligns with societal values and prioritizes the well-being of individuals.

Inclusive Access: Ensuring inclusive access to the benefits of digital consciousness is vital for societal equity. Efforts should be made to minimize disparities and provide opportunities for diverse communities to participate in and benefit from advancements in technology. This includes addressing issues of digital literacy, access to education, and fair representation in the development and deployment of conscious digital entities.

On the whole, the utilization of digital consciousness in various industries and its societal impact present exciting opportunities and challenges. Responsible implementation, ethical considerations, and a focus on inclusive access will be crucial in harnessing the full potential of these technologies for the benefit of individuals and society as a whole.

6.3. Ethical Considerations

6.3.1. Balancing Progress With Ethics

Technological Advancements: The rapid progress in digital consciousness necessitates a careful balance between technological advancements and ethical considerations. While advancements bring about unprecedented possibilities, including enhanced decision-making and problem-solving capabilities, they also raise concerns about unintended consequences, misuse, and ethical risks. Further, striking a balance involves anticipating potential risks, addressing ethical concerns proactively, and ensuring that technological developments align with societal values.

Long-Term Consequences: Integrating digital consciousness into society carries long-term consequences, both positive and challenging. The ethical implications of creating entities with varying degrees of autonomy and intelligence require careful examination. Besides, Long-term consequences may include shifts in societal structures, changes in employment patterns, and impacts on individual privacy. Therefore, it is crucial to consider the ethical ramifications over time, ensuring that the integration of digital consciousness aligns with evolving ethical standards and safeguards against potential negative outcomes.

6.3.2. Ethical Frameworks

Developing and implementing ethical frameworks is essential to guide the responsible development and deployment of digital consciousness. These frameworks should be rooted in fundamental guiding principles that prioritize transparency, fairness, privacy, accountability, and the prevention of harm. Furthermore, integrating diverse perspectives from philosophy, technology, and other relevant fields can contribute to the establishment of robust ethical guidelines that stand the test of evolving technologies (Fisk & Haase, 2020).

Rights and Responsibilities: Ethical considerations regarding the rights and responsibilities of conscious digital entities are crucial. Defining and respecting the rights of these entities, such as privacy rights and the right to fair treatment, is paramount. Additionally, establishing clear responsibilities for developers, users, and society at large helps create a framework for ethical engagement with conscious digital entities. Issues of accountability, transparency, and informed consent should be central to ethical discussions surrounding the rights and responsibilities of these entities.

Continuous Ethical Evaluation: Ethical frameworks should not be static but rather subject to continuous evaluation and refinement. As digital consciousness evolves, so should the ethical considerations that guide its development and deployment. Regular ethical assessments, involving experts from various disciplines, ensure that frameworks remain relevant, adaptable, and capable of addressing emerging challenges. A commitment to continuous ethical evaluation reflects a dedication to responsible innovation and the well-being of individuals and society.

Global Collaboration: Given the global nature of technological advancements, ethical frameworks should be developed through international collaboration. Global standards and shared ethical principles can help ensure that the responsible development and deployment of digital consciousness are consistent across borders. Collaborative efforts allow for a more comprehensive understanding of ethical considerations and promote a unified approach to addressing challenges on a global scale.

To sum up, balancing progress with ethics in the realm of digital consciousness involves anticipating potential risks, considering long-term consequences, and developing robust ethical frameworks. These frameworks, grounded in guiding principles and addressing the rights and responsibilities of conscious digital entities, provide a foundation for responsible innovation and the positive integration of advanced technologies into society.

7. CONCLUSION

In the comparative analysis of digital and human consciousness, key findings emerge across various dimensions. The exploration of similarities reveals that digital consciousness attempts to replicate cognitive processes such as perception, memory, learning, and problem-solving found in human consciousness. In addition to this, Neural network analogies illustrate the inspiration drawn from the human brain's structure for constructing artificial intelligence models (Fisk & Haase, 2020). The differences between digital and human consciousness are evident in areas like the absence of personal consciousness in digital entities, limitations in emotional responses, and the nuanced depth of human self-awareness. Moreover, subjectivity, a central aspect of human consciousness, poses a challenge for digital entities to fully comprehend and replicate. Despite advancements, there are conceptual gaps in understanding phenomena such as qualia and the temporal dynamics of consciousness. While challenges encompass the need for interdisciplinary collaboration to address these conceptual gaps and the ethical considerations surrounding the development and integration of digital consciousness. Also, ethical challenges range from the treatment and rights of conscious digital entities to the potential societal impact of these technological advancements. Further, balancing progress with ethics requires continuous evaluation, global collaboration, and the establishment of ethical frameworks. Insights gained from the analysis underscore the potential applications of digital consciousness in various industries. From healthcare to entertainment, digital consciousness can optimize processes, enhance decision-making, and contribute to task automation. Along with this, the integration of these technologies into society has societal implications, influencing workforce dynamics, reshaping employment patterns, and fostering collaboration between humans and conscious digital entities (Haladjian & Montemayor, 2016). Furthermore, ethical considerations form a critical aspect of these insights, emphasizing the need for responsible development and deployment.

The development of ethical frameworks becomes imperative to guide the treatment, interactions, and societal integration of conscious digital entities. Also, rights and responsibilities, privacy concerns, and continuous ethical evaluation are central themes in ensuring that technological advancements align with ethical principles and societal values. In brief, the exploration of digital and human consciousness offers a nuanced understanding of the similarities, differences, challenges, and ethical dimensions in this evolving field. Insights gained from this analysis emphasize the importance of responsible innovation, interdisciplinary collaboration, and the continuous reassessment of ethical frameworks to navigate the complexities and potential societal impacts of advancing technologies. The exploration of digital and human consciousness has contributed significantly to theoretical advancements in understanding the nature of consciousness. Moreover, In the realm of digital consciousness, theoretical contributions include the analysis of neural network analogies, providing insights into how computational models mimic human cognitive processes. And the study of decision-making capabilities in digital entities has advanced our understanding of algorithmic decision-making and its parallels with human cognitive processes. This chapter also sheds light on the adaptability of digital consciousness, exploring how entities respond to changing circumstances and learn from experiences in addition this, insights into human consciousness. Comparatively, the examination of similarities and differences between digital and human consciousness enhances our understanding of the unique aspects of human subjective experiences. On the other hand, the theoretical analysis of challenges, such as the absence of personal consciousness in digital entities and the difficulties in replicating human emotions, contributes to the broader field of philosophy of mind. Further, the exploration of the temporal dynamics of consciousness and the integration of multimodal information advances our understanding of how human consciousness processes information over time and across sensory modalities.

The research on digital and human consciousness holds interdisciplinary significance by bridging the fields of philosophy, neuroscience, and artificial intelligence. Moreover, philosophically, the analysis delves into fundamental questions about the nature of consciousness, subjective experiences, and the implications of creating entities with varying degrees of autonomy. Further, the study of qualia, subjectivity, and the qualitative nature of experiences contributes to the ongoing philosophical discourse on consciousness, self-awareness, and the mind-body problem. From a neuroscience perspective, the exploration of neural network analogies and decision-making processes in digital consciousness enhances our understanding of the neural correlates of human cognition. Insights into the temporal dynamics of consciousness and the integration of multimodal information contribute to the growing body of knowledge in neuroscience, providing potential avenues for further empirical research. In the field of artificial intelligence, the analysis provides practical implications for the development of conscious digital entities. The study of decision-making capabilities, task automation, and adaptability informs the design and implementation of AI systems that aim to replicate and augment human cognitive processes. Above all, this interdisciplinary approach facilitates the integration of insights from philosophy and neuroscience into the development of advanced AI models. On the whole, the research on digital and human consciousness not only advances our theoretical understanding of these complex phenomena but also highlights the interdisciplinary significance of bridging philosophy, neuroscience, and artificial intelligence. This collaborative approach fosters a more comprehensive and holistic exploration of consciousness, contributing to the advancement of knowledge in each respective field and encouraging the development of responsible and ethically informed technologies.

REFERENCES

Ascott, R. (1998). Consciousness reframed: Art and consciousness in the post-biological era. *Digital Creativity (Exeter), 9*(1), 5–6. doi:10.1080/14626269808567099

Brinkmann, K. (2005). Consciousness, self-consciousness, and the modern self. *History of the Human Sciences, 18*(4), 27–48. doi:10.1177/0952695105058469

Bulkeley, K. (2014). Digital dream analysis: A revised method. *Consciousness and Cognition, 29*, 159–170. doi:10.1016/j.concog.2014.08.015 PMID:25286125

Cardeña, E. (1996). Cultivating Consciousness: Enhancing Human Potential, Wellness, and Healing. *Anthropology of Consciousness, 7*(2), 39–40. doi:10.1525/ac.1996.7.2.39

Carruthers, P. (2018). Comparative psychology without consciousness. *Consciousness and Cognition, 63*, 47–60. doi:10.1016/j.concog.2018.06.012 PMID:29940429

Fisk, G. D., & Haase, S. J. (2020). Binary vs. continuous experimental designs for the study of unconscious perceptual processing. *Consciousness and Cognition, 81*, 102933. doi:10.1016/j.concog.2020.102933 PMID:32315944

From Consciousness of Quality to Quality of Consciousness. (2004). From Consciousness of Quality to Quality of Consciousness. *Journal of Human Values, 10*(1), iii–v. doi:10.1177/097168580401000101

Gigliotti, C. (1998). What is consciousness for? *Digital Creativity (Exeter), 9*(1), 33–37. doi:10.1080/14626269808567104

Glattfelder, J. B. (2019). *Information—Consciousness—Reality*. Springer. doi:10.1007/978-3-030-03633-1

Grynszpan, O., Sahaï, A., Hamidi, N., Pacherie, E., Berberian, B., Roche, L., & Saint-Bauzel, L. (2019). The sense of agency in human-human vs human-robot joint action. *Consciousness and Cognition, 75*, 102820. doi:10.1016/j.concog.2019.102820 PMID:31561189

Haladjian, H. H., & Montemayor, C. (2016). Artificial consciousness and the consciousness-attention dissociation. *Consciousness and Cognition, 45*, 210–225. doi:10.1016/j.concog.2016.08.011 PMID:27656787

Mehl-Madrona, L. (2023). Expanding identity beyond the human. *Anthropology of Consciousness*. Advance online publication. doi:10.1111/anoc.12217

N. (2018). *Human decisions*. UNESCO Publishing.

Nelson, T. O. (2000). Consciousness, Self-Consciousness, and Metacognition. *Consciousness and Cognition, 9*(2), 220–223. doi:10.1006/ccog.2000.0439 PMID:10924241

Orlandi, N. (2023). The Modularity vs. Malleability of Perception: A Red Herring. *Journal of Consciousness Studies, 30*(3), 202–211. doi:10.53765/20512201.30.3.202

Ott, B. L. (2023). The Digital Mind: How Computers (Re)Structure Human Consciousness. *Philosophies, 8*(1), 4. doi:10.3390/philosophies8010004

Pranay Kumar, P. (2021). Human consciousness and artificial intelligence: Can AI develop human-like consciousness? Cognitive abilities? What about Ethics? SSRN *Electronic Journal*. doi:10.2139/ssrn.3786957

Revonsuo, A. (2017). *Foundations of Consciousness*. Routledge. doi:10.4324/9781315115092

Shruthi, R. (2023). Human Consciousness and Artificial Intelligence: Can AI Develop Human-Like Consciousness? Cognitive Abilities? What about Ethics? SSRN *Electronic Journal*. doi:10.2139/ssrn.4333023

Thagard, P., & Stewart, T. C. (2014). Two theories of consciousness: Semantic pointer competition vs. information integration. *Consciousness and Cognition, 30*, 73–90. doi:10.1016/j.concog.2014.07.001 PMID:25160821

Vendrell Ferran, I. (2023). Consciousness of Emotion and Emotive Consciousness in Geiger and Husserl. *Human Studies*. Advance online publication. doi:10.1007/s10746-023-09706-1

Wilbertz, G., & Sterzer, P. (2018). Differentiating aversive conditioning in bistable perception: Avoidance of a percept vs. salience of a stimulus. *Consciousness and Cognition*, *61*, 38–48. doi:10.1016/j.concog.2018.03.010 PMID:29649652

Chapter 2

The Interface of Minds
Human–Machine Interaction
in the Digital Age

K. Vanisri
Vellore Institute of Technology, India

Prabir Chandra Padhy
iD https://orcid.org/0000-0002-6856-0958
Vellore Institute of Technology, India

ABSTRACT

Artificial intelligence (AI) is an increasingly expanding domain within the field of computer science that engenders intelligent machines competent in executing human tasks. The implementation of AI technology is progressively becoming more prevalent in sectors such as healthcare, banking, and transportation. The efficacy, accuracy, and decision-making capabilities of AI have the potential to revolutionize a wide array of industries. AI acquires knowledge and enhances its proficiency by utilising machine learning algorithms. These algorithms allow robots to assess extensive datasets, subsequently discovering patterns and insights that surpass human comprehension. Human-machine interaction centres on the collaboration between individuals and computers or machines, where it can anticipate assumptions and methods utilized to facilitate a spontaneous framework. The basic purpose of human-computer interaction (HCI) is to create functional systems that end users find useable, safe, and effective.

DOI: 10.4018/979-8-3693-2015-0.ch002

INTRODUCTION

The 21st century has seen the convergence of human cognition with machine intelligence, ushering in a new era where minds meet machines at the interface (Orange,2013; Nooney, 2023). As technology continues to permeate our lives, the interaction between humans and machines changes how we see, interact, and navigate (Hollnagel, 2001). This study delves deep into the complex web of the digital era, examining the dynamics of human minds interacting with the ever-evolving machine world. From user interfaces to artificial intelligence symbiosis, this study take a journey to explore the intricacies and possibilities of the interface between minds. If digital frontiers continue to expand, it becomes imperative to comprehend the complexities of this mutually beneficial relationship to navigate the obstacles and embrace the possibilities of a future in which humans and machines merge in unprecedented ways (Rogers, 2009). Human-computer interaction (HCI) is a multidisciplinary area of study that centres on the conceptualization of computer technology and, more specifically, the interaction between humans (the users) and computers (Brey, 2005; Chignell et al., 2023). While its initial focus was on computers, HCI has progressively broadened its scope to encompass virtually all forms of information technology design.

Presently, interactions with machines have become more prevalent and adaptable, enabling the connection of devices that can perform tasks with greater efficiency (Ziemer et al., 2019). To fully grasp this phenomenon, one must understand what is commonly called human-machine interaction. Human-machine interaction centres on the collaboration between individuals and computers or machines, where it can anticipate assumptions and methods utilized to facilitate a spontaneous framework. Human-computer interaction is contingent upon the exchange of information between individuals and the machines they utilize. Touch screens and keyboards are commonplace examples of human-machine interaction encountered daily (Olson) and Olson, 2012). This interaction is a conduit between users and their devices, systems, or gadgets. The interconnectedness between these components is of utmost importance due to the vast array of purposes for which computers can be employed and the myriad means by which users and computers can communicate with one another. The amalgamation of users' previous knowledge, experiences, and current expertise significantly influences their interactions with computers. Human-computer interaction is based on the exchange of information between people and the machines they use (Park et al., 2023). Touch screens and keyboards are frequent instances of human-machine interaction we see daily. This interaction functions as a link between users and their equipment, systems, or gadgets. The interconnectedness of these components is critical because computers can be used for a wide range of purposes, and there are several ways for humans and computers to communicate. The combination of users' historical knowledge, experiences, and current skills substantially impacts their interactions with computer systems and can perpetuate biases in data, resulting in discriminatory outcomes. To promote fairness, AI systems should be educated on various data sets and audited regularly (Harish et al., 2013).

HCI emerged in the 1980s, coinciding with the rise of personal computing when machines like the Apple Macintosh, IBM PC 5150, and Commodore 64 began to appear in homes and offices in unprecedented numbers (Soloway et al., 1994; Canny, 2006). Common customers could purchase advanced electronic devices like word processors, gaming consoles, and accountancy assistants for the first time. Because computers were no longer pricey, room-sized instruments designed only for specialists in specialised settings, it became more and more important to develop human-computer interaction that was also simple and effective for less experienced users. From its inception, Human-Computer Interaction (HCI) has evolved to encompass many academic fields, including computer science, cognitive science, and human-factors engineering (Król, 2021). Presently, HCI is primarily concerned with the creation, execution, and assessment of interactive interfaces that augment the user's experience through the utilization of computing devices. This entails the design of user interfaces, the implementation of user-centred design principles, and the development of user experience design methodologies (Król, 2021).

Overview of Human-Machine Interaction (HMI)

As previously stated, the idea of a Humachine highlights the fusion of humans and machines, utilizing both advantages to enhance their overall capacities (Sanders & Wood, 2019). Humans possess certain skills that machines lack, including creativity, intuition, empathy, and practical reasoning (Rao, 2018). Humans possess the cognitive ability to comprehend intricate scenarios and react suitably, whereas machines can only respond by predetermined instructions (Antunes, 2010; Villan et al., 2017). Furthermore, humans can rapidly acquire knowledge and adapt to new circumstances, an accomplishment that machines can only achieve through instruction and reprogramming. Conversely, machines possess certain advantages over humans, including their processing speed, precision, and consistency (Oliff et al., 2018; Cummings, 2014). Machines can handle copious amounts of data and execute intricate computations at a significantly accelerated pace compared to humans (Antunes et al., 2010; Atieh et al., 2023). They are also not susceptible to human constraints such as weariness, lethargy, and emotional partiality.

Consequently, to confront these obstacles and enhance HMI, novel methodologies must be discovered to amalgamate the proficiencies of humans and machines. For instance, machines can support humans in executing repetitive and time-consuming tasks, thereby allowing humans to concentrate on more imaginative and strategic assignments (Vempaty et al., 2018). Machines also possess the ability to examine and handle data, presenting it to individuals in a facile manner to comprehend and utilize (Mourtzis, 2023). To accomplish this, developing more sophisticated algorithms for Machine Learning and technologies for Artificial Intelligence (A.I.) that can imitate the cognitive processes of human decision-making (Vempaty et al., 2018; Lim et al., 2018). Moreover, it is essential to enhance the design of Human-Machine Interfaces (HMIs) by making them more intuitive, user-friendly, and capable of offering instant feedback and guidance (Atieh et al., 2023). With this objective in mind, this research delves into the concept of machines and underscores the integration of humans and machines, harnessing their respective strengths to enhance overall performance (Dimitris Mourtzis et al., 2022).

Human-machine interaction (HMI) revolves around the interaction and communication between individuals and automated systems. This field has expanded beyond traditional industrial machinery and now includes computers, digital systems, and devices associated with the Internet of Things (IoT). The number of interconnected devices that autonomously perform tasks is steadily increasing. Consequently, these machinery, systems, and devices must be user-friendly and not impose excessive cognitive or physical demands on users. HMI is all about the communication and interaction between automated systems and people. That is no longer limited to conventional industrial machinery; it now applies to computers, digital systems, and Internet of Things (IoT) devices (Ke et al., 2018; Saini et al., 2016). An increasing number of gadgets are linked together and perform activities automatically. These technologies, systems, and gadgets must be easy to use and not put people under undue stress (Guo et al., 2021). Interfaces are necessary for people and machines to communicate smoothly. Light switches and an automobile's pedals and steering wheel are simple examples: Flipping a switch, turning the steering wheel, or pressing a pedal causes an action to be initiated (Tan et al., 2021; Ardanzan et al., 2019). On the other hand, a system can also be operated by voice commands, gestures, touch displays, mice, and text input.

Users can give spoken commands or touch the smartphone's screen to control the gadgets directly. Alternatively, the systems recognize what people want: The inductive loop in the road's surface causes traffic signals to change colour automatically. Other technologies are more intended to enhance our sense organs than to replace electronics. Wearable virtual reality glasses are one instance of that. Digital assistants also exist: chatbots, for example, automatically respond to client inquiries and constantly learn. The basic purpose of human-computer interaction (HCI) is to create functional systems that end users find useable, safe, and effective (Gobena, 2019). The following is a summary of the goals that human-computer interaction should pursue. (1) A thorough understanding of computer system user interfaces; (2) Creating strategies, tools, and techniques to customize system access to users' unique needs; and (3) Modifying, testing, enhancing, and validating the system to guarantee that users can interact or communicate with it effectively.

Historical Perspective on Human-Machine Interaction

The fascinating story of human-machine interaction (HMI) development charts the amazing progression from primitive interfaces to the cognitive and engaging interactions that characterize the modern digital world. Our techniques for interacting and working together with technology have evolved along with technology. Punch cards and command-line interfaces were the only ways people interacted with computers in the early days; therefore, using them required specific skills (Tan et al., 2021). With the introduction of GUIs (graphical user interfaces) in the 1980s, computing became more widely accessible by integrating visually intuitive components like windows and icons. The advent of touch interfaces, popularized by smartphones and tablets at the turn of the millennium, revolutionized our interaction with technology. These tactile exchanges closed the gap between people and technology, becoming a natural extension of human behaviour. The distinction between human and machine communication has become increasingly hazy with the development of speech recognition and natural language processing in recent years. (Smart speakers and virtual assistants are prime examples of this trend, enabling consumers to communicate with technology through voice commands, resulting in a more conversational and natural user interface (Mourtzis et al., 2023). The development of human-machine interaction takes on a new dimension in artificial intelligence. Algorithms for machine learning allow systems to adjust and react to user behaviour (Følstad and Brandtzæg, 2017), customizing interactions and predicting user requirements. Chatbots, recommendation engines, and virtual assistants are examples of this dynamic and context-aware interaction.

Future developments in immersive and multimodal experiences offered by augmented reality (A.R.) and virtual reality (V.R.) can transform human-machine interaction completely. The direct brain-machine connection has the potential to transform how humans use and interact with technology completely, and brain-computer interfaces (BCIs) provide an exciting new frontier in this regard (Saha et al., 2021). The desire for more natural, smooth, and meaningful methods for people to connect with the rapidly changing digital world is a recurring theme in the history of human-machine interaction. How our thoughts and technology interact is continuously reshaping and redefining the boundaries of our technological future.

In light of our quickly evolving technology environment, comprehending the human-machine interface is paramount. This understanding affects how we use technology and more general consequences for the economy, society, and the basic fabric of human existence.

Figure 1. Evolution of human-computer interaction
Source: *https://aelaschool.com/en/interactiondesign/human-computer-interaction-everything-you-need-to-know/*

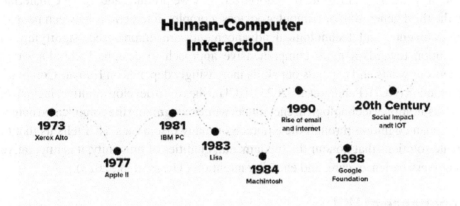

In the latter part of the 1970s, computational science research and practice in human-computer interaction (HCI) began (MacKenzie, 2024). It focuses on using human behaviour analysis to address challenging issues. The Xerox Alto, introduced in 1973, was a significant stride toward personal computing, with its Graphical User Interface (GUI) inspiring the Macintosh and Windows. The first commercially successful desktop computer was the Apple II, which debuted in the same decade and included eight expansion slots to accommodate more cards (Nooney, 2023). As personal computers became more common, usability changed, posing a challenge to cognitive science, which sought to solve these needs by fusing science and engineering (Chignell et al., 2023). Technologies such as computers significantly advanced in 1980, and IBM introduced the IBM PC in 1981. Human-computer interaction research aims to enable people to create simple systems (MacKenzie, 2024). The emphasis of software engineering was on experiment-based development. The Lisa, released by Apple in 1983, transformed the computer industry by introducing a graphical user interface (GUI) that allowed users to use computers without specialized training (Carrol, 2014). An accessible graphical user interface (GUI) with a keyboard, mouse, and monitor was first introduced with the Macintosh, which was released a year later. The Macintosh revolutionized the publishing industry with its menu-driven interface, clickable icons, and text editing features. Prioritizing individual efficiency applications, the field of Human-Computer Interaction gave rise to computer metaphors such as the desktop metaphor employed by Apple in the Lisa operating system (Andrejevic et al., 2023).

Intuitively designing systems and seeing that personal computers were the way of the future resulted from this. The field's second wave, driven by communication and the internet, went beyond mental models to investigate social interactions between computer users and anthropologists, sociologists, and psychologists. Google, established in 1998, revolutionized how we produce and manage material. In the third generation of computer devices, complex interactions between people, environments, and technological advancements are emphasized, signifying an evolution towards a more comprehensive approach to design. Technology that meets our wants and expands our skills increasingly depends on Human-Computer Interaction (HCI) (Pandey et al., 2023). HCI pushes us to develop intuitive, inclusive, and inspirational technological encounters while recognizing the complicated nature of human cognition through the embrace of many disciplines. HCI tells us that to create solutions that honour the fundamental qualities of humanity, it is imperative to possess patience, care, and end-user attention (Tiwari et al., 2023).

Importance of HCI

HCI, or human-computer interaction, aims to facilitate intuitive, natural interactions between humans and technology (Pushpakumar et al., 2023). Creating an interface that eliminates physical and mental strain, increases usability, and lowers the risk of product disaster is critical for strategists and product developers. The goal of HCI is to emulate the ease and naturalness of human contact. Innovation has profoundly changed our daily lives, with human-computer interaction (HCI) being a key component in the design of snack machines and ATMs. (Ma et al., 2023). These user interactions are critical for efficiency, accessibility, safety, and businesses that use processing technology. Human-machine interaction improves programming tools, increasing functionality and influencing product sales (Nowruzi et al., 2023). Designing user-friendly interfaces, increasing productivity and efficiency, and fostering creativity depend on understanding human-machine interaction. Concerns regarding security, privacy, and responsible technology use are also ethically raised. Developers may promote a more inclusive society by developing technologies that empower people with impairments. The interface is crucial for managing the cultural effects of technology since it also affects social and cultural norms. In the age of artificial intelligence, developing human-centric A.I. systems that uphold moral principles and prioritise ethical issues requires an understanding of interfaces (Neethirajan, 2023). Comprehending the interface is essential to prepare society to accept new technological breakthroughs responsibly, especially as augmented reality, virtual reality, and brain-computer interfaces emerge.

Overview of Contemporary Interfaces

In the digital age, touch displays have become ubiquitous, easily blending into our daily interactions with smartphones, tablets, and other gadgets. (Elmqvist, 2023). Users may travel around digital areas with natural and intuitive movements thanks to broad and nuanced gestures. The emergence of touch interfaces has revolutionized how we engage with technology and significantly contributed to its increased accessibility for users across a wide range of age groups and backgrounds. Voice-activated systems offer a natural and hands-free approach to communicating with technology, a paradigm change in human-machine interaction. Siri, Alexa, and Google Assistant are just a few examples of virtual companions that have made voice commands a part of our everyday lives (Roslan, 2023). This development emphasizes how convenient hands-free operation is and portends a time when spoken language will be the main interaction between humans and machines. Virtual reality (V.R.) and augmented reality (A.R.) have brought immersive interfaces that have completely changed how we view digital encounters. A.R. adds digital information to the physical world, boosting real-life scenarios, whereas V.R. immerses users in completely virtual environments (Raffegeau et al., 2023). These interfaces have been used in various settings, including gaming, education, and healthcare, providing unparalleled engagement and involvement. The digital equivalent of touch, or haptic feedback, is vital to improving human-machine interaction.

The devices' slight vibrations or visceral responses connect people to the virtual world. Not only does this tactile input make virtual experiences appear more real, but it also helps users become more responsive and grasp the interaction, making it more engaging and fulfilling. The widespread use of wearables, smart gadgets, and the Internet of Things (IoT) has made human-machine interaction a seamless part of everyday life (Mao et al., 2023). Smartwatches that monitor our health and IoT-enabled thermostats that regulate house temperatures have all contributed to developing an interconnected ecology. Comprehending and adjusting to the diverse interfaces found in these devices is essential, as they have become indispensable elements of contemporary life. It is clear from traversing the modern environment of HMIs that the complexity and diversity of these interactions still influence how humans interact with technology. It is critical to comprehend whether these interfaces influence the user experience, access, and the changing dynamics of interaction between humans and machines as we investigate them.

The nature of human-machine connections has been significantly impacted by digital breakthroughs, which have reshaped how humans interact with and perceive technology. Advances in digital technology have led to a blurring of boundaries between the physical and digital realms as human-machine interaction has risen. (Alimam et al., 2023). People today regularly communicate, retrieve information, enjoy themselves, and complete tasks using machines daily using gadgets like laptops, smart speakers, and smartphones. Digital technologies allow for more individualized and customized interactions between people and machines, allowing experiences to be tailored to each person's needs, tastes, and behaviours. To deliver personalized suggestions, information, and services that increase customer satisfaction and engagement (Rane, 2023), Machine learning algorithms evaluate user data.

Figure 2. HCI multidisciplinary field

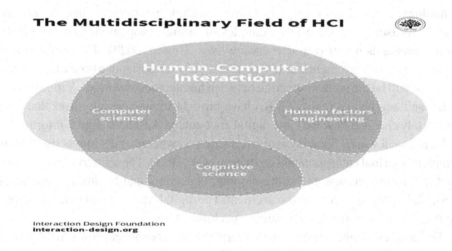

As digital technologies assimilate into our daily routines, humans have progressively relied on machines to execute diverse assignments and engagements. Whether for way-finding and correspondence or amusement and efficiency, individuals depend on machines to carry out crucial undertakings, thereby fostering an intensified reliance on technology (Rath et al., 2024). Trust is essential in human-machine interactions, profoundly shaping individuals' perceptions and engagement with machines. Digital innovations have propelled advancements in machines' dependability, precision, and effectiveness, thereby augmenting the trust vested in their capabilities (Javaid et al., 2021). Trust is a fragile issue that can be easily compromised due to mistakes, technical issues, or privacy and security violations. The progress made in the digital realm enables individuals to exercise more significant authority and independence in their engagements with automated systems. By employing personalized interfaces, adaptive technologies, and user-centric design, individuals can customize their interactions with machines to align with their preferences and requirements, enhancing their empowerment and control. Technological developments have enabled robots to elicit social and affective reactions from users, making it harder to distinguish between humans and machines. Social robots, virtual assistants, and interactive A.I. systems mimic human actions, gestures, and expressions, promoting emotional connection and attachment (Lugrin, 2021). The growing integration of machines into all sectors of society creates ethical and moral concerns about their use and impact on human well-being. Artificial intelligence, automation, robotics, and other digital advances create concerns about privacy, data security, algorithmic prejudice, employment displacement, and the moral treatment of sentient machines. Technological developments in the digital domain promise to enhance human capacities, allowing people to work with AI to accomplish jobs more successfully and efficiently. Humans and robots can coexist peacefully due to technological advancements that improve human cognitive, perceptual, and physical capacities. Examples of these technologies include wearable's, augmented reality, and brain-computer interfaces. The development of digital technology has changed the character of human-machine connections by encouraging greater communication, reliance, trust, empowerment, social participation, and ethical thinking. Understanding and controlling the dynamics of human-machine interactions will be crucial to achieving favourable results and improving societal and individual well-being as technology develops.

COGNITIVE INTERFACES AND NEUROTECHNOLOGY

A. Brain-Computer Interfaces (BCIs) and Their Potential

Interfacing the neural networks of humans with external equipment, Brain-Computer Interfaces (BCIs) constitute a state-of-the-art in human-machine interaction. These interfaces convert neural signals into executable commands, allowing computers and the brain to communicate directly. BCIs have enormous potential to transform industries like gaming, healthcare, and assistive technology (Cavus et al., 2023). Applications for Brain-Computer Interfaces (BCIs) are numerous and include innovative virtual and augmented reality interfaces and medical advancements in neurorehabilitation and prosthetics. Advances in neurotechnology are stretching the bounds of what is conceivable, allowing paralyzed people to regain their mobility, improving cognitive function, and opening doors for completely new kinds of human expression.

B. Ethical Considerations and Challenges in Implementing Cognitive Interfaces

Neural data is intimate, which poses security and privacy problems. As BCIs acquire critical information directly from the brain, securing this data becomes crucial to avoid unauthorized access and potential exploitation (Yusifova, 2020). Informed consent must be carefully taken into account while implementing cognitive interfaces. Users must comprehend the complete ramifications of sharing neural data and the possible enduring consequences of interacting with brain-computer technologies. Bias and equity concerns in neurotechnological applications are often considered ethical obstacles. The creation and execution of BCIs in an avenue that does not reinforce preexisting biases is essential to establishing a fair and reasonable interface.

C. Implications for Accessibility and Inclusivity

According to Kübler (2020), BCIs can revolutionize assistive technology by giving people with impairments new options for control and communication. With this technology, people with motor constrictions can interact with the outside world in previously unthinkable ways, improving their quality of life. Even though BCIs have a lot of great potential, accessibility discrepancies must be addressed. According to Kameni and Koumetio (2023), promoting inclusion requires making neurotechnological innovations available to a wide range of people, irrespective of location or socioeconomic standing. The ethical dimensions of cognitive interfaces include challenges of accessibility and inclusion. Hitting a balance between innovation and ensuring these technologies do not unintentionally add to societal differences is critical in creating a future where cognitive interactions benefit everyone. A thorough grasp of the potential, moral issues, and accessibility ramifications of cognitive interfaces and neurotechnology is becoming increasingly important as these fields develop. Harnessing the revolutionary potential of cognitive interfaces for societal improvement requires striking a balance between innovation and social responsibility.

Challenges and Opportunities in Human-Machine Teamwork

Table 1. Opportunities and challenges of human machine team work

Opportunities	Challenges
• Continuous training and upskilling programs offer opportunities to create a workforce seamlessly integrating with evolving technologies.	• Difficult to adapt to new tools and ways of working, need to learn new skills to collaborate effectively with machines
• The focus is on improving interfaces and creating systems that foster mutual understanding.	• Clear and transparent communication can be a challenge.
• The optimal allocation of tasks between humans and machines presents significant challenges in achieving optimal efficiency.	• The focus is creating collaboration models that combine emotional intelligence, creativity, and nuanced decision-making, allowing humans to concentrate on tasks.
• Re-skilling, upskilling, and creating new opportunities for workers affected by automation, promoting a just transition in the workforce.	• They are potentially leading to job displacement in some sectors.
• Facilitate the development of tailored healthcare solutions by combining A.I. and the Internet of Things to monitor and diagnose health conditions in real-time. • Contribute to reducing human activity's adverse environmental impacts by creating smart cities, renewable energy sources, and environmentally friendly transit networks. • To increase productivity and efficiency, assist companies and organizations in adopting cutting-edge technology like robots, automation, and artificial intelligence. • Generate new business sectors and employment opportunities to support economic development.	• Technology's incorporation into society can worsen existing social injustices, including access to jobs, healthcare, and education. Ensuring universal access to these technologies is crucial, irrespective of an individual's financial situation. • Data security and privacy are becoming more and more of a worry with the growing use of modern technology. Rules and procedures must be implemented to safeguard confidential information and stop technology abuse. • The difference in access to technology between those who do and those who do not is known as the "digital divide." To avert exclusion and advance parity, it is imperative to guarantee universal access to technology. • The application of cutting-edge technologies presents moral dilemmas regarding their effects on society and the possibility of unforeseen repercussions. Ethical rules and principles must be established to ensure these technologies are used responsibly and ethically.

Owing to contemporary human-machine interaction, even intricate structures will become easier to operate. Machines will increasingly adapt to human habits and demands to facilitate that. They will also be able to operate remotely thanks to virtual, augmented, and mixed reality (Schäfer et al., 2022). Consequently, humans broaden their sphere of experience and ability. Machines must continue to improve their ability to understand signals in the future. When a police officer's hand signals to a car at an intersection, the fully autonomous vehicle must react appropriately. Robots used in care must also possess the ability to "assess" the requirements of those unable to communicate them for themselves. The more intricate the role of machines, the more crucial it is that users and machines communicate well. Does the technology interpret the command correctly as well? If not, miscommunications could occur, and the system could fail to operate properly. People's talents and limits must always be considered while developing interfaces and sensors. A machine shouldn't be extremely difficult to operate or require a lot of familiarization. For human-machine communication to flow smoothly, users must view the interaction as natural, which means that commands must be answered quickly (Suhel et al., 2020). One possible concern is that machines rely heavily on sensors to be controlled or to react automatically. Hackers who gain access to the data can see specifics about the activities and preferences of the person. Critics also worry that even intelligent computers could become autonomous and enslave humans. Another issue that has not been resolved up to this point is who bears responsibility and liability for mishaps brought on by mistakes made during human-machine contact. Automating certain processes, particularly those that require decision-making, raises ethical questions about transparency and accountability. Upholding ethical norms in the workplace requires defining distinct roles and responsibilities and providing openness regarding automated decision-making.

The Current Landscape of Human-Machine Interfaces

It is critical to comprehend how AI is integrated, deal with obstacles, and navigate ethical issues in the workplace's fast-changing arena of human-machine collaboration. Balancing the positive aspects of automation with ethical standards promotes a collaborative future in which technology complements human abilities while contributing to a sustainable, inclusive, and morally upright professional ecosystem (Stahl, 2021). The field of human-machine interfaces, or HMIs, is changing fast as of my last revision in 2022. This is due to the growing need for natural and intuitive interactions among humans and machines and technological developments. An outline of the current situation is provided below:

I.   Touch screens are still commonplace in gadgets like ATMs, self-service kiosks, and cell phones. Capacitive touch technology allows for precise and responsive interactions, whereas multi-touch motions let users manage digital material naturally. Furthermore, haptic feedback technologies improve the user experience by offering tactile sensations (Park et al., 2023).

II.   Voice-controlled interfaces, powered by natural language processing (NLP) and machine learning, have gained widespread adoption through virtual assistants such as Amazon Alexa, Google Assistant, and Apple Siri. These interfaces enable hands-free interaction with devices and services, including smart speakers, smartphones, and home automation systems (Norda et ., 2023)

III.   Users can operate gadgets and interfaces with hand gestures, body motions, or facial expressions thanks to the recognition of gesture technologies (Guo et al., 2021). These interfaces are used in gaming consoles, virtual reality (V.R.), augmented reality (A.R.) systems, and automotive infotainment systems to improve immersion and user engagement.

IV.   BCIs allow the human brain to communicate directly with external devices, bypassing conventional input modalities like touch or voice (Vaibhaw and Pattnaik, 2020). These interfaces show promise in healthcare, technological assistance, and gaming, letting users operate prosthetic limbs, traverse computer interfaces, and play video games via neural impulses.

V.   Smartwatches, fitness trackers, and augmented reality glasses are examples of wearable technology that function as a personal HMI by giving consumers constant access to data and services (Quartarone, 2021). These interfaces use sensors, displays, and connection technologies to provide contextual alerts, health tracking, and immersive experiences.

VI.   Immersion interfaces that combine digital media with the real world or create fully virtual environments are made possible by A.R. and V.R. technology. A.R. apps superimpose digital data on the user's perspective of the actual world, whilst V.R. settings replicate immersive, three-dimensional experiences. Applications for these interfaces can be found in design, education, training, gaming, and entertainment (Banfi, 2021).

VII.   Thanks to tactile interfaces, users can feel more tactile in digital interactions, which gives them tangible input. Sun Technologies, such as tactile displays, force feedback, and vibrotactile actuators, allow users to feel textures, shapes, and forces in virtual environments, increasing realism and usability in applications including simulation, training, and remote manipulation.

VIII.   Eye-tracking interfaces allow users to manage devices and interfaces using their own eye motions and gaze gestures. These interfaces use gaze-based input and hands-free interaction to find applications in market research, gaming, accessibility technology, and human-computer interaction research.

IX.   Technologies for recognising emotions interpret users' mental states and intents by examining their facial expressions, verbal intonations, and physiologic signs. Customized experiences, adaptive interfaces, and emotional computing applications are made possible by these interfaces in industries including healthcare, client service, and entertainment (Banfi, 2021).

X.   Biometric interfaces use physiological or behavioural traits such as fingerprints, facial characteristics, or voice patterns to authenticate and identify users. Although there are still privacy and security problems, these interfaces provide improved privacy and ease when accessing devices, services, and physical environments.

The current state of human-machine interfaces is distinguished by various modalities, each with special functions and uses. As technology advances, HMIs are predicted to become increasingly immersive, natural, and integrated into daily life, influencing how people interact with computers and the digital realm.

Human-Machine Collaboration in Work Environments

Human-machine collaboration is merging a human workforce with automated equipment to improve efficiency (Alhaji et al., 2020). In its most basic form, human-machine cooperation entails a human-machine interface on automated machinery that allows operators to readily read information about the machine's and process's health, as well as more easily and intuitively control the machine or operation. "human-machine collaboration," or "HMC," describes the productive and efficient combination of human and machine skills in manufacturing operations. It utilises robotics, automation, artificial intelligence (AI), and sophisticated analytics to facilitate prompt decision-making and effective resource distribution.

A more advanced type of human-machine collaboration would be a work cell in which an employee performs alongside a collaborative robot to finish a task (Mukherjee et al., 2022). Going one step further, automated machinery or robots with advanced analytics, AI, ML, and B.V. can execute a task and deliver data or information instantly, empowering the human operator to make proactive and well-informed decisions that enhance the manufacturing process. If you've ever asked Siri for the weather, ordered vitamins through Alexa, or turned on the lights at home using your smartphone, you've worked with a smart gadget to execute a task most effectively. Similarly, human-machine collaboration enables a new era in the manufacturing sector wherein people interact with automated technology more frequently. This assists manufacturers in increasing output, gaining efficiency, and streamlining operations.

Automation and artificial intelligence (AI) used in work environments have completely changed how companies function across various sectors. To automate operations, optimize workflows, and enhance human capabilities, this integration uses A.I. algorithms, machine learning, robots, and other cutting-edge technology (Ness). Here's a thorough rundown of how automation and artificial intelligence are changing work environments:

I. Businesses may optimize their workflows by using A.I. and automation technology to automate time-consuming and routine tasks (Haleem et al., 2021). AI-powered software, for instance, may automate financial analysis, processing of invoices, and data input in the finance and accounting industries, lowering manual mistakes and increasing productivity.

II.   Artificial intelligence (A.I.) algorithms are skilled at sifting through massive amounts of data to find trends, patterns, and insights that may guide choices. AI-powered analytics systems may evaluate consumer behaviour, market trends, and rival strategies in professional contexts like marketing and sales (Haleem et al., 2021) to improve marketing campaigns, spot sales opportunities, and project demand.

III. Businesses may provide individualized experiences to their consumers at scale with the help of AI-driven customization algorithms (Patel, 2020). Companies may offer individualized experiences to their consumers at scale with the help of AI-driven customization algorithms. Patel For example, in e-commerce, recommendation engines driven by artificial intelligence (AI) examine browser histories and customer preferences to suggest goods specific to each user's interests, boosting conversion rates and customer satisfaction.

IV.   Predictive maintenance systems driven by artificial intelligence (AI) watch machinery and equipment in real-time in sectors like manufacturing and transportation to identify problems before they become expensive breakdowns. Businesses may limit downtime, increase asset longevity, and save maintenance expenses by effectively forecasting maintenance needs.

V.   Professionals can obtain insightful advice and recommendations from AI-powered decision support systems to help them make well-informed judgments (Patel, 2020). In the medical field, for example, artificial intelligence (A.I.) platforms evaluate medical imaging images to help radiologists diagnose illnesses precisely and quickly, enhancing patient outcomes and lowering diagnostic mistakes.

VI.   Integrating A.I. and automation into professional environments raises important ethical and regulatory considerations, such as data privacy, algorithmic bias, and workplace dislocation. Companies must adhere to ethical guidelines and regulatory frameworks to ensure the responsible use of A.I. and automation technologies and mitigate potential risks.

VII. Professionals may get on-demand help and support from AI-powered cognitive assistants, like chatbots and virtual assistants. These virtual assistants can work independently, advise, and respond to inquiries, increasing efficiency and productivity. For example, chatbots in customer service may respond to standard questions, refer complicated problems to real people, and offer clients round-the-clock assistance.

Organizations are operating differently due to the incorporation of artificial intelligence and robotics in professional settings, fostering innovation, productivity, and competitiveness. Businesses may enhance consumer and stakeholder experiences, streamline operations, and make better decisions using A.I. and automation technology.

Firms must address the ethical, legal, and societal ramifications to guarantee that the advantages of AI and automation are achieved ethically and fairly. A.I. systems have the potential to provide discriminating results by maintaining data biases. To ensure fairness, A.I. systems should be regularly evaluated and trained on various data sets. In A.I. systems, transparency is essential since a lack of it compromises responsibility and confidence. Businesses need to deploy robust security measures and adhere to the General Data Protection Regulation to emphasize data security and confidentiality. Because automation has the potential to upend labour markets and result in job displacement, companies need to support re-skilling efforts for those affected. It is necessary to create systems for responsibility and compensation in the case of harm or mistakes. Democratic oversight and governance techniques are required to safeguard social standards, and automated decision-making raises questions about who controls algorithms. There are many advantages to task and decision-making process automation, but difficult ethical issues need to be properly considered. Businesses and politicians should maximize the promise of automation while avoiding dangers and ensuring that technology serves the common good by tackling concerns including prejudice, openness, privacy, job displacement, accountability, human dignity, and algorithmic governance. Establishing fairness and minimizing biases in human-machine interactions is essential to fostering justice, preventing negative consequences, and promoting trust.

Applications for Human-Machine Collaboration

A manufacturing company or industrial facility can use human-machine cooperation in various ways; some of these applications may even be present on the manufacturing floor. Here, we showcase six uses of human-machine collaboration.

Warehouse Robots: One of the most well-known uses of human-machine collaboration is in warehouses, where autonomous mobile robot technology is used to generate collaborative pick-and-place robots that smoothly access the inventory area, choose the right items, and then carry them to human employees who load and label them for distribution. Because robots move considerably faster and can choose goods better than human workers, this boosts process efficiency.

Assembly Lines: A lot of modern collaborative robots are capable of being fitted with fine end-of-arm tooling, which enables them to operate and assemble products accurately, swiftly, and reliably. Manual workers can collaborate in the workspace with collaborative robots and rely on them for assistance with parts of the assembly process that could be hazardous, awkward from an ergonomic standpoint, or tedious since these robots are outfitted with safety sensors and systems that let them operate alongside people. Alternatively, manual labourers could do jobs that the robot needs to be designed or prepared to perform or that call for original thought or problem-solving.

Material handling: Heavy-duty or difficult-to-maneuver things can be lifted, carried, and moved by automated machinery and robots. Smart equipment can often measure, weigh, and count things more accurately, which improves quality and lowers waste. These materials must be placed precisely into the process. Human workers may manage and control the product handling process using their knowledge and expertise without getting injured when lifting, twisting, or bending.

To increase productivity and efficiency, promote human creativity and problem-solving abilities, improve product quality, and streamline operations, human-machine collaboration aims to use the benefits of intelligent automation.

FUTURE TRENDS IN HUMAN-MACHINE INTERACTION

Anticipated Advancements in Interface Technologies

Because AR and VR technologies combine to create three-dimensional, immersive interfaces, this is predicted to change human-machine communication completely. From online meetings to interactive educational settings, these technologies will provide new methods for people to interact with digital material. Technological developments in Natural Language Processing (NLP) will allow robots to comprehend and generate more intricate languages. Human-machine dialogue is anticipated to become more organic, nuanced, and contextual, resulting in more meaningful and intuitive interactions. The ability to directly communicate between the human brain and external equipment makes brain-computer interfaces (BCIs) so revolutionary. There are potential uses for this kind of technology in accessibility, healthcare, and perhaps cognitive enhancement.

The Potential Impact of Quantum Computing on Interaction Paradigms

Rethinking interaction paradigms is anticipated due to the unparalleled processing capability of quantum computing. Complex processes will accelerate significantly, resulting in more flexible and adaptable interfaces. Examples of these jobs include quick data processing, optimization issues, and simulations. The study of quantum computing may affect cryptography. Quantum computing raises the prospect of creating new, more secure cryptographic algorithms, which impact how data is safeguarded in human-machine interactions even while they potentially break existing encryption systems. The potential of quantum computing may improve machine learning algorithms, leading to more potent and effective A.I. models. Faster training times, better decision-making, and general improvements in AI-driven human-machine interactions might result from this optimization.

Exploring the Ethical and Societal Implications of Emerging Interfaces

Advanced interfaces are bringing up ethical questions about data security and privacy. Safeguarding user information and maintaining privacy will be essential to preventing misuse or unwanted access as interfaces grow more sophisticated and ingrained in everyday life. Ensuring fair access to developing interfaces is a matter of ethics. Encouraging access to cutting-edge technology, such as augmented reality, virtual reality, and brain-computer interfaces (BCIs), should not be impeded by societal inequities. The ethical ramifications of sophisticated interfaces encompass the protection of human dignity and individual freedom. The advancement of technology, such as brain-computer interfaces (BCIs), necessitates that people retain autonomy over their thoughts and judgments to guard against potential misuse and interference.

Emotion Recognition and Empathetic Machines

Emotion recognition technology is one of the most promising developments in HMI in the future. As robots better comprehend human emotions, they can adjust their reactions and behaviour accordingly. Deeper ties with consumers might result from emotionally intelligent robots, improving user experiences and boosting confidence. Empathetic robots can respond correctly by displaying compassion and understanding because they can identify emotions via body language, speech tones, and facial expressions.

Haptic Feedback for Enhanced Sensory Experience

Haptic feedback is an intriguing development in HMI that gives consumers tactile experiences. More advanced haptic interfaces that allow users to interact with virtual objects and settings with a realistic touch feeling will likely emerge as technology develops. With this advancement, there is great promise for various uses, including medical training, remote robotic procedures, and virtual reality games where users may experience forces, textures, and feelings much like they would in person.

Brain-to-Machine Interfaces (BMI)

Brain-to-machine interfaces, or BMI, represent a ground-breaking development in HMI. These interfaces eliminate the need for conventional input methods like touch screens or keyboards and enable direct connection between the human brain and technology. With BMIs, we might be able to perform smooth interactions like typing, navigating interfaces, and controlling things with just our thoughts. With this technology, people with physical limitations can engage with the outside world and achieve new degrees of independence.

Context-Aware and Proactive Systems

The development of A.I. and machine learning algorithms will lead to futuristic HMI systems that are more proactive and context-aware. To anticipate user requirements and offer pertinent information or help before they are asked, these systems will evaluate user behavior, preferences, and environmental indicators. For instance, a context-aware smart home system might improve comfort and energy economy by adjusting temperature and lighting according to user behaviours and preferences.

Social and Collaborative Robots

With their sophisticated artificial intelligence and natural language processing skills, social robots will become increasingly important in various social contexts. These robots are capable of having deep discussions, becoming friends, and helping out with everyday duties. Collaborative robots, or cobots, will work with people in the workplace, sharing duties and responsibilities to increase efficiency and safety.

A comprehensive strategy is required to predict future trends in human-machine interaction, considering both technology breakthroughs and their ethical and societal ramifications. For the future to be shaped in a way that ethically and thoroughly improves human-machine interactions and our lives, innovation, ethical concerns, and social effects must be balanced.

CONCLUSION

The development of voice-activated systems, touch displays, augmented reality, and brain-computer interfaces has been a convoluted path in the history of human-machine interaction. These developments have revolutionized navigation and communication, emphasizing the value of accessibility and user-centric design. AI and automation integration in the workplace bring benefits and problems that need thoughtful worker adaptation and ethical concerns. Reliability, openness, and bias mitigation are necessary for building trust in A.I. systems. Anticipated advances in interface technology, the possible influence of quantum computing, and ethical issues all influence the direction of human-machine interaction. Transparency, equity, and user privacy must be prioritised as a revolutionary period draws near to match these advances with society's ideals and advance human welfare. The development of human-machine interactions responsibly requires interdisciplinary collaboration. We can achieve a future where human-machine interactions improve the human experience if we proceed along this path with caution, empathy, and foresight. Strong ethical underpinnings that guarantee equity, openness, and respect for each person's rights and dignity are necessary for human-machine interaction.

REFERENCES

Alhaji, B., Beecken, J., Ehlers, R., Gertheiss, J., Merz, F., Müller, J. P., Prilla, M., Rausch, A., Reinhardt, A., Reinhardt, D., Rembe, C., Rohweder, N.-O., Schwindt, C., Westphal, S., & Zimmermann, J. (2020). Engineering human–machine teams for trusted collaboration. *Big Data and Cognitive Computing*, *4*(4), 35. doi:10.3390/bdcc4040035

Alimam, H., Mazzuto, G., Tozzi, N., Ciarapica, F. E., & Bevilacqua, M. (2023). The resurrection of digital triplet: A cognitive pillar of human-machine integration at the dawn of industry 5.0. *Journal of King Saud University. Computer and Information Sciences*, *35*(10), 101846. doi:10.1016/j.jksuci.2023.101846

Alimohammadlou, M., & Khoshsepehr, Z. (2023). The role of Society 5.0 in achieving sustainable development: A spherical fuzzy set approach. *Environmental Science and Pollution Research International*, *30*(16), 47630–47654. doi:10.1007/s11356-023-25543-2 PMID:36745347

Andrejevic, M., Bouquillion, P., Cohn, J., Day, F., Gaw, F., Ithurbide, C., & Volcic, Z. (2023). *Media backends: digital infrastructures and sociotechnical relations*. University of Illinois Press.

Antunes, R. M., Coito, F. V., & Duarte-Ramos, H. (2010, September). Human-machine control model approach to enhance operator skills. In *2010 International Conference on Mechanical and Electrical Technology* (pp. 403-407). IEEE. 10.1109/ICMET.2010.5598392

Ardanza, A., Moreno, A., Segura, Á., de la Cruz, M., & Aguinaga, D. (2019). Sustainable and flexible industrial human-machine interfaces to support adaptable applications in the Industry 4.0 paradigm. *International Journal of Production Research*, *57*(12), 4045–4059. doi:10.1080/00207543.2019.1572932

Atieh, A. M., Cooke, K. O., & Osiyevskyy, O. (2023). The role of intelligent manufacturing systems in implementing Industry 4.0 by small and medium enterprises in developing countries. *Engineering Reports*, *5*(3), e12578. doi:10.1002/eng2.12578

Ayhan, E. E., & Akar, Ç. (2022). Society 5.0 Vision in Contemporary Inequal World. Society 5.0 A New Challenge to Humankind's Future, 133.

Banfi, F. (2021). The evolution of interactivity, immersion and interoperability in HBIM: Digital model uses, V.R. and A.R. for built cultural heritage. *ISPRS International Journal of Geo-Information*, *10*(10), 685. doi:10.3390/ijgi10100685

Brey, P. (2005). The epistemology and ontology of human-computer interaction. *Minds and Machines*, *15*(3-4), 383–398. doi:10.1007/s11023-005-9003-1

Canny, J. (2006). The Future of Human-Computer Interaction: Is an HCI revolution just around the corner? *ACM Queue; Tomorrow's Computing Today*, *4*(6), 24–32. doi:10.1145/1147518.1147530

Carroll, J. M. (2014, January 1). Human Computer Interaction - Brief intro. Interaction Design Foundation - IxDF.

Cavus, N., Oke, O. A., & Yahaya, J. M. U. (2023). Brain-Computer Interfaces: High-Tech Race to Merge Minds and Machines. In *Cutting Edge Applications of Computational Intelligence Tools and Techniques* (pp. 3–19). Springer Nature Switzerland. doi:10.1007/978-3-031-44127-1_1

Chignell, M., Wang, L., Zare, A., & Li, J. (2023). The evolution of HCI and human factors: Integrating human and artificial intelligence. *ACM Transactions on Computer-Human Interaction*, *30*(2), 1–30. doi:10.1145/3557891

Ciobanu, A. C., & Mesnit, Ă, G. (2022). A.I. Ethics for Industry 5.0—From Principles to Practice. *Proceedings of the Workshop of I-ESA*, 22.

Cummings, M. M. (2014). Man versus machine or man+ machine? *IEEE Intelligent Systems*, *29*(5), 62–69. doi:10.1109/MIS.2014.87

Drewes, H., De Luca, A., & Schmidt, A. (2007, September). Eye-gaze interaction for mobile phones. In *Proceedings of the 4th international conference on mobile technology, applications, and systems and the 1st international symposium on Computer human interaction in mobile technology* (pp. 364-371). 10.1145/1378063.1378122

Elmqvist, N. (2023). Anywhere & everywhere: A mobile, immersive, and ubiquitous vision for data analytics. *arXiv preprint arXiv:2310.00768.*

Følstad, A., & Brandtzæg, P. B. (2017). Chatbots and the new world of HCI. *Interactions, 24*(4), 38-42.

Fukuda, K. (2020). Science, technology and innovation ecosystem transformation toward society 5.0. *International Journal of Production Economics, 220,* 107460. doi:10.1016/j.ijpe.2019.07.033

Gobena, D. L. (2019). Human-Computer/Device Interaction. In Computer Architecture in Industrial, Biomechanical and Biomedical Engineering (p. 29). IntechOpen.

Guo, L., Lu, Z., & Yao, L. (2021). Human-machine interaction sensing technology based on hand gesture recognition: A review. *IEEE Transactions on Human-Machine Systems, 51*(4), 300–309. doi:10.1109/THMS.2021.3086003

Haleem, A., Javaid, M., Singh, R. P., Rab, S., & Suman, R. (2021). Hyperautomation for the enhancement of automation in industries. *Sensors International, 2,* 100124. doi:10.1016/j.sintl.2021.100124

Harish, R., Khan, S. A., Ali, S., & Jain, V. (2013). Human computer interaction-a brief study. *International Journal of Management. IT and Engineering, 3*(7), 390–401.

Hollnagel, E. (2001). From human factors to cognitive systems engineering: Human-machine interaction in the 21st Century. Academic Press.

Javaid, M., Haleem, A., Singh, R. P., & Suman, R. (2021). Substantial capabilities of robotics in enhancing industry 4.0 implementation. *Cognitive Robotics, 1,* 58–75. doi:10.1016/j.cogr.2021.06.001

Kameni, E. D., & Koumetio, S. C. T. (2023). The role of inclusive educational technologies in transforming African cities into inclusive smart cities. In *E3S Web of Conferences* (Vol. 418, p. 03003). EDP Sciences. doi:10.1051/e3sconf/202341803003

Ke, Q., Liu, J., Bennamoun, M., An, S., Sohel, F., & Boussaid, F. (2018). Computer vision for human–machine interaction. In *Computer Vision for Assistive Healthcare* (pp. 127–145). Academic Press. doi:10.1016/B978-0-12-813445-0.00005-8

Król, K. (2021). Hardware Heritage—Briefcase-Sized Computers. *Heritage*, *4*(3), 2237–2252. doi:10.3390/heritage4030126

Kübler, A. (2020). The history of BCI: From a vision for the future to real support for personhood in people with locked-in syndrome. *Neuroethics*, *13*(2), 163–180. doi:10.1007/s12152-019-09409-4

Lean, T. (2013). Mediating the microcomputer: The educational character of the 1980s British popular computing boom. *Public Understanding of Science (Bristol, England)*, *22*(5), 546–558. doi:10.1177/0963662512457904 PMID:23833169

Lim, Y., Gardi, A., Sabatini, R., Ramasamy, S., Kistan, T., Ezer, N., Vince, J., & Bolia, R. (2018). Avionics human-machine interfaces and interactions for manned and unmanned aircraft. *Progress in Aerospace Sciences*, *102*, 1–46. doi:10.1016/j.paerosci.2018.05.002

Lugrin, B. (2021). Introduction to socially interactive agents. In The Handbook on Socially Interactive Agents: 20 years of Research on Embodied Conversational Agents, Intelligent Virtual Agents, and Social Robotics Volume 1: Methods, Behavior, Cognition (pp. 1-20). doi:10.1145/3477322.3477324

Ma, Y., Zhang, L., & Wang, X. (2023, February). Natural language understanding and interaction engine oriented to human-computer interaction based on neural network. In *Third International Conference on Computer Vision and Data Mining (ICCVDM 2022)* (Vol. 12511, pp. 781-786). SPIE. 10.1117/12.2660383

MacKenzie, I. S. (2024). Human-computer interaction: An empirical research perspective. Academic Press.

Mao, J., Zhou, P., Wang, X., Yao, H., Liang, L., Zhao, Y., Zhang, J., Ban, D., & Zheng, H. (2023). A health monitoring system based on flexible triboelectric sensors for intelligence medical internet of things and its applications in virtual reality. *Nano Energy*, *118*, 108984. doi:10.1016/j.nanoen.2023.108984

Martynov, V. V., Shavaleeva, D. N., & Zaytseva, A. A. (2019). Information technology as the basis for transformation into a digital society and industry 5.0. In 2019 International Conference "Quality Management, Transport and Information Security, Information Technologies" (IT&QM&IS). IEEE.

Mourtzis, D., Angelopoulos, J., & Panopoulos, N. (2022). A Literature Review of the Challenges and Opportunities of the Transition from Industry 4.0 to Society 5.0. *Energies*, *15*(17), 6276. doi:10.3390/en15176276

Mourtzis, D., Angelopoulos, J., & Panopoulos, N. (2023). Blockchain Integration in the Era of Industrial Metaverse. (2022). *Applied Sciences (Basel, Switzerland)*, *13*(3), 1353. doi:10.3390/app13031353

Mourtzis, D., Angelopoulos, J., & Panopoulos, N. (2023). The Future of the Human–Machine Interface (HMI) in Society 5.0. *Future Internet*, *15*(5), 162. doi:10.3390/fi15050162

Mukherjee, D., Gupta, K., Chang, L. H., & Najjaran, H. (2022). A survey of robot learning strategies for human-robot collaboration in industrial settings. *Robotics and Computer-integrated Manufacturing*, *73*, 102231. doi:10.1016/j.rcim.2021.102231

Neethirajan, S. (2023). Artificial Intelligence and Sensor Innovations: Enhancing Livestock Welfare with a Human-Centric Approach. *Human-Centric Intelligent Systems*, 1-16.

Ness, S., Shepherd, N. J., & Xuan, T. R. (2023). Synergy Between A.I. and Robotics: A Comprehensive Integration. *Asian Journal of Research in Computer Science*, *16*(4), 80–94. doi:10.9734/ajrcos/2023/v16i4372

Nooney, L. (2023). *The Apple II Age: How the Computer Became Personal*. University of Chicago Press. doi:10.7208/chicago/9780226816531.001.0001

Norda, M., Engel, C., Rennies, J., Appell, J. E., Lange, S. C., & Hahn, A. (2023). Evaluating the Efficiency of Voice Control as Human Machine Interface in Production. *IEEE Transactions on Automation Science and Engineering*.

Nowruzi, S., Shokouhyar, S., Dehghan, O., Nezafati, N., & Shokoohyar, S. (2023). A human-machine interaction framework for identifying factors influential consumer participation in e-waste treatment schemes. *International Journal of Computer Integrated Manufacturing*, *36*(7), 1–25. doi:10.1080/0951192X.2022.2162598

Oliff, H., Liu, Y., Kumar, M., & Williams, M. (2018). A framework of integrating knowledge of human factors to facilitate HMI and collaboration in intelligent manufacturing. *Procedia CIRP*, *72*, 135–140. doi:10.1016/j.procir.2018.03.047

Olson, G. M., & Olson, J. S. (2012). Collaboration technologies. *Human Computer Interaction Handbook: Fundamentals, Evolving Technologies, and Emerging Applications,* 549-564.

Orange, E. (2013). Understanding the human-machine interface in a time of change. In Handbook of Research on Technoself: Identity in a Technological Society (pp. 703-719). IGI Global. doi:10.4018/978-1-4666-2211-1.ch036

Pandey, A., Panday, S. P., & Joshi, B. (2023). Design and development of applications using human-computer interaction. In *Innovations in Artificial Intelligence and Human-Computer Interaction in the Digital Era* (pp. 255–293). Academic Press. doi:10.1016/B978-0-323-99891-8.00011-5

Park, S., Kim, H. K., Lee, Y., & Park, J. (2023). Kiosk accessibility challenges faced by people with disabilities: An analysis of domestic and international accessibility laws/guidelines and user focus group interviews. *Universal Access in the Information Society*, 1–17. doi:10.1007/s10209-023-01028-4

Patel, N., & Trivedi, S. (2020). *Leveraging Predictive Modeling, Machine Learning Personalization, NLP Customer Support, and A.I. Chatbots to Increase Customer Loyalty*. Empirical.

Poynor, R. (2023). Personal Reflections on Technologies and the Study of African Art. *African Arts, 56*(4), 1-7.

Pushpakumar, R., Sanjaya, K., Rathika, S., Alawadi, A. H., Makhzuna, K., Venkatesh, S., & Rajalakshmi, B. (2023). Human-Computer Interaction: Enhancing User Experience in Interactive Systems. In E3S Web of Conferences (Vol. 399, p. 04037). EDP Sciences.

Quartarone, V. (2021). *Wearable HMI definition, development and validation for collaborative environment in industrial processes in the context of Industry 4.0* (Doctoral dissertation, Politecnico di Torino).

Raffegeau, T. E., Young, W. R., Fino, P. C., & Williams, A. M. (2023). A perspective on using virtual reality to incorporate the affective context of everyday falls into fall prevention. *JMIR Aging, 6*, e36325. doi:10.2196/36325 PMID:36630173

Rane, N. (2023). Transformers in Industry 4.0, Industry 5.0, and Society 5.0: Roles and Challenges. Academic Press.

Rane, N. (2023). Enhancing customer loyalty through Artificial Intelligence (A.I.), Internet of Things (IoT), and Big Data technologies: improving customer satisfaction, engagement, relationship, and experience. *Internet of Things (IoT), and Big Data Technologies: Improving Customer Satisfaction, Engagement, Relationship, and Experience.*

Rao, P. V. S., & Kopparapu, S. K. (2018). *Friendly Interfaces Between Humans and Machines*. Springer. doi:10.1007/978-981-13-1750-7

Rapp, A. (2023). Human–Computer Interaction. Oxford Research Encyclopedia of Psychology.

Rath, K. C., Khang, A., & Roy, D. (2024). The Role of Internet of Things (IoT) Technology in Industry 4.0 Economy. In Advanced IoT Technologies and Applications in the Industry 4.0 Digital Economy (pp. 1-28). CRC Press.

Rogers, Y. (2009). The changing face of human-computer interaction in the age of ubiquitous computing. In *HCI and Usability for e-Inclusion: 5th Symposium of the Workgroup Human-Computer Interaction and Usability Engineering of the Austrian Computer Society, USAB 2009, Linz, Austria, November 9-10, 2009 Proceedings 5* (pp. 1-19). Springer Berlin Heidelberg. 10.1007/978-3-642-10308-7_1

Roslan, F. A. B. M., & Ahmad, N. B. (2023). The rise of AI-powered voice assistants: Analyzing their transformative impact on modern customer service paradigms and consumer expectations. *Quarterly Journal of Emerging Technologies and Innovations*, 8(3), 33–64.

Sá, M. J., Santos, A. I., Serpa, S., & Miguel, F. C. (2021). Digitainability—Digital competences post-COVID-19 for a sustainable society. *Sustainability (Basel)*, 13(17), 9564. doi:10.3390/su13179564

Saha, S., Mamun, K. A., Ahmed, K., Mostafa, R., Naik, G. R., Darvishi, S., Khandoker, A. H., & Baumert, M. (2021). Progress in brain-computer interface: Challenges and opportunities. *Frontiers in Systems Neuroscience*, 15, 578875. doi:10.3389/fnsys.2021.578875 PMID:33716680

Saini, H. S., & Daruwala, R. D. (2016, August). Human machine interface in internet of things system. In *2016 International conference on computing communication control and automation (ICCUBEA)* (pp. 1-4). IEEE. 10.1109/ICCUBEA.2016.7860151

Sanders, N. R., & Wood, J. D. (2019). *The Humachine: Humankind, Machines, and the Future of Enterprise*. Routledge. doi:10.4324/9780429001178

Schäfer, A., Reis, G., & Stricker, D. (2022). A Survey on Synchronous Augmented, Virtual, and Mixed Reality Remote Collaboration Systems. *ACM Computing Surveys*, 55(6), 1–27. doi:10.1145/3533376

Soloway, E., Guzdial, M., & Hay, K. E. (1994). Learner-centered design: The challenge for HCI in the 21st century. *Interactions*, 1(2), 36-48.

Stahl, B. C. (2021). *Artificial intelligence for a better future: an ecosystem perspective on the ethics of A.I. and emerging digital technologies*. Springer Nature. doi:10.1007/978-3-030-69978-9

Suhel, S. F., Shukla, V. K., Vyas, S., & Mishra, V. P. (2020, June). Conversation to automation in banking through chatbot using artificial machine intelligence language. In *2020 8th international conference on reliability, infocom technologies and optimization (trends and future directions) (ICRITO)* (pp. 611-618). IEEE. 10.1109/ICRITO48877.2020.9197825

Sun, Z., Zhu, M., Shan, X., & Lee, C. (2022). Augmented tactile-perception and haptic-feedback rings as human-machine interfaces aiming for immersive interactions. *Nature Communications*, *13*(1), 5224. doi:10.1038/s41467-022-32745-8 PMID:36064838

Tan, Z., Dai, N., Su, Y., Zhang, R., Li, Y., Wu, D., & Li, S. (2021). Human–machine interaction in intelligent and connected vehicles: A review of status quo, issues, and opportunities. *IEEE Transactions on Intelligent Transportation Systems*, *23*(9), 13954–13975. doi:10.1109/TITS.2021.3127217

Tiwari, A., Chugh, A., & Sharma, A. (2023). Uses of artificial intelligence with human-computer interaction in psychology. In *Innovations in Artificial Intelligence and Human-Computer Interaction in the Digital Era* (pp. 173–205). Academic Press. doi:10.1016/B978-0-323-99891-8.00003-6

Vaibhaw, J. S., & Pattnaik, P. K. (2020). Brain-computer interfaces and their applications. *An industrial IoT approach for pharmaceutical industry growth*, *2*, 31-54.

Vempaty, A., Kailkhura, B., & Varshney, P. K. (2018, April). Human-machine inference networks for smart decision making: Opportunities and challenges. In *2018 IEEE International Conference on Acoustics, Speech and Signal Processing (ICASSP)* (pp. 6961-6965). IEEE. 10.1109/ICASSP.2018.8462638

Villani, V., Sabattini, L., Czerniaki, J. N., Mertens, A., Vogel-Heuser, B., & Fantuzzi, C. (2017, September). Towards modern inclusive factories: A methodology for the development of smart adaptive human-machine interfaces. In *2017 22nd IEEE international conference on emerging technologies and factory automation (ETFA)* (pp. 1-7). IEEE. 10.1109/ETFA.2017.8247634

Yusifova, L. (2020). Ethical and Legal Aspects of Using Brain-Computer Interface in Medicine: Protection of Patient's Neuro Privacy. Academic Press.

Ziemer, T., Nuchprayoon, N., & Schultheis, H. (2019). Psychoacoustic sonification as user interface for human-machine interaction. *arXiv preprint arXiv:1912.08609.*

Chapter 3
AI–Based Mindfulness:
The Future of Healthcare and Customer Service

Yerravalli Venkat Santosh Ramana

iD https://orcid.org/0000-0001-6891-4106
GITAM University, India

Pinakapani Peri
GITAM University, India

ABSTRACT

This chapter explores the integration of artificial intelligence (AI) into mindfulness practices, specifically focusing on healthcare and customer service. The purpose is to evaluate the substantial benefits of AI in encouraging mindfulness in both contexts, with the potential to manage pain better, lower stress levels, and improve overall health outcomes. The chapter begins by defining mindfulness and its potential benefits for mental and physical well-being. It then explores the pioneering work of Jon Kabat-Zinn in integrating mindfulness into medical settings. The chapter discusses how AI is used to augment mindfulness practices, such as video recording for guided breathing exercises and smartphone-based pedometers for physical activity monitoring. The chapter then investigates how AI can assist mindfulness by tailoring interventions to individual needs and monitoring progress over time. It also discusses the potential benefits of AI in encouraging mindfulness in both customer service and healthcare contexts.

DOI: 10.4018/979-8-3693-2015-0.ch003

INTRODUCTION

According to the World Health Organization's (WHO) constitution, "health is a state of complete physical, mental, and social wellbeing, not merely the absence of disease or infirmity." This definition emphasises the holistic character of health, emphasising that good health encompasses more than just the absence of illness or disease. The WHO recognises health as a multifaceted term with physical, mental, and social elements.

Mindfulness is a discipline that entails paying nonjudgmental and purposeful attention to the present moment. It has received widespread attention in the medical community for its possible benefits in boosting mental and physical well-being.

Emeritus professor of medicine at the University of Massachusetts Medical School, Jon Kabat-Zinn, established the Centre for Mindfulness in Medicine, the Health Care Society and the well-known Stress Reduction Clinic. At the University of Massachusetts Medical School in the late 1970s, Kabat-Zinn created Mindfulness-Based Stress Reduction (MBSR). The programme incorporates yoga poses, body awareness exercises, and mindfulness meditation techniques. MBSR has been shown in several trials to be beneficial in lowering stress, anxiety, depression, and chronic pain [1]. The work of Kabat-Zinn contributed to the acceptance of mindfulness in medical settings. He underlined how mindfulness might promote patient-centred treatment, improve wellbeing, and manage chronic diseases. Kabat-Zinn is the author of many books on mindfulness that have been translated into more than 45 languages. His writing is known for its clarity, accessibility, and inspirational qualities. He also gives talks and workshops worldwide, spreading mindfulness's message [2-6].

AI is making inroads into mindfulness, providing unique tools to enhance and personalise this age-old practice. AI has been used to help mindfulness practices in various ways, improving accessibility, personalisation, and effectiveness. Simple video recording to ensure proper patient breathing exercises and monitoring of footsteps using the Pedo metre app on the patient's smartphone are commonly used AI tools for patient care in public healthcare settings. These are freely available and will instil confidence in patients with target-oriented health activities.

Objective

To explore how Artificial Intelligence (AI) could be applied to assist mindfulness. AI might determine each person's needs and offer individualised mindfulness interventions. AI might be used to monitor each person's development in mindfulness over time. The success of mindfulness interventions may be evaluated using the data and by adjustments as necessary.

Purpose of Research: The advantages of implementing Artificial Intelligence to encourage mindfulness in customer service and healthcare are substantial.

- It could assist patients in better managing their pain, lowering their stress levels, and enhancing their general health by teaching them to be more conscious.
- It could improve customers' interactions with healthcare and customer service by teaching them to be more mindful.
- It could assist in lowering the price of healthcare and customer service by reducing stress and enhancing general wellness.

Systematic Literature Review

A Scopus database search with the Keywords "Mindfulness" AND"Healthcare" is being done, and the following information is analysed using R Studio – Biblioshiny for Bibliometric Analysis of information

Table 1. Systematic literature review

Description	Results	Metadata	Description	Missing Counts	Missing %	Status
MAIN INFORMATION ABOUT DATA						
Timespan	1989:2024	AB	Abstract	0	0.00	Excellent
Sources (Journals, Books, etc)	1016	CR	Cited References	0	0.00	Excellent
Documents	1811					
Annual Growth Rate %	7.36	DT	Document Type	0	0.00	Excellent
Document Average Age	2.7	SO	Journal	0	0.00	Excellent
Average citations per doc	17.72					
References	140917	LA	Language	0	0.00	Excellent
DOCUMENT CONTENTS		PY	Publication Year	0	0.00	Excellent
Keywords Plus (ID)	7427					
Author's Keywords (DE)	5470	TI	Title	0	0.00	Excellent
AUTHORS		TC	Total Citation	0	0.00	Excellent
Authors	7275					
Authors of single-authored docs	158	AU	Author	1	0.06	Good
AUTHORS COLLABORATION		C1	Affiliation	12	0.66	Good
Single-authored docs	166					
Co-Authors per Doc	4.8	DI	DOI	45	2.48	Good
International co-authorships %	26.56	RP	Corresponding Author	167	9.22	Good
DOCUMENT TYPES		DE	Keywords	204	11.26	Acceptable
article	1811					

Word Cloud of the frequently used keywords in the study literature

Figure 1. Word cloud of the frequently used keywords in the study literature

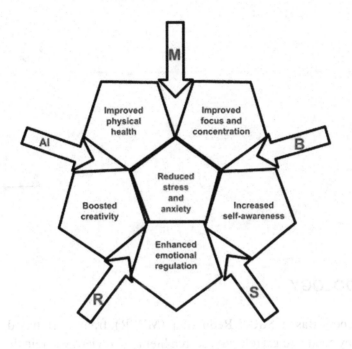

Top Ten Authors with their production over time

Figure 2. Top ten authors with their production over time

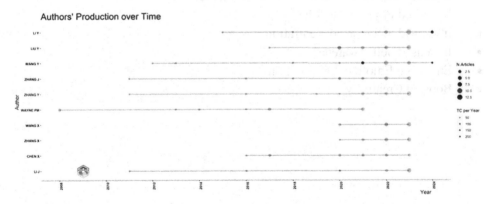

Global country's collaborative research:

Figure 3. Global country's collaborative research

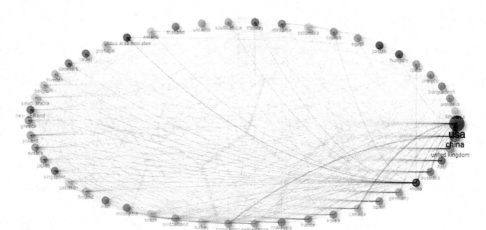

METHODOLOGY

A Mindfulness-Based Stress Reduction (MBSR) framework-based model is developed by conducting a related research literature review, wherein the following vital observations are taken for developing an AI-based - Healthcare Customer Mindfulness model.

AI-based – Healthcare Customer Mindfulness model consists of

- Reduced Stress and Anxiety as the core objective
- Improved Physical Health
- Improved focus on concentration
- Increased Self Awareness
- Enhanced Emotional Regulation
- Boosted Creativity

Figure 4. Reduced stress and anxiety

Multiple research by Hofmann et al. (2010) and Keng et al. (2014) suggest that mindfulness effectively decreases stress and anxiety symptoms by developing emotional regulation and awareness of triggers. According to Sati et al. (2009) and Jha et al. (2015), mindfulness training increases attentional regulation, improving task concentration. According to Brown and Ryan (2003), mindfulness cultivates self-compassion and acceptance by monitoring thoughts and feelings without judgment.

Mindfulness, as given by Teasdale et al. (2000) and Tang & Baer (2012), teaches people healthy ways to cope with difficult emotions such as anger, sadness, and fear. Jha et al. (2015) and Scott et al. (2014) demonstrate that mindfulness can promote creativity by opening minds to new experiences and perspectives. According to Black and Moore (2004) and Carlson and Brown (2007), mindfulness can improve physical health by reducing blood pressure and enhancing sleep quality [7 - 13].

Case Study: AI-Based Health Improvement Intervention

Patient Profile:
Name: Mr. X
Age: 40 Years Male
Medical Condition: Type 2 Diabetes and Hypertension (Lifestyle Disorder)
Admission Reason: Complications related to uncontrolled blood sugar levels and hypertension.

Scenario

Mr X is admitted to a public hospital due to complications arising from poorly controlled Type 2 Diabetes and Hypertension. The hospital's healthcare team, aware of the benefits of AI-based health interventions, introduces Mr X to a personalised health management app powered by artificial intelligence. (Breathing Exercises from YouTube, Pedo Meter to Check Physical Activities, Google Form to Record Blood Sugar Monitoring)

Personalised Medication Reminders: The Google calendar sends timely reminders for medication intake, ensuring adherence to the prescribed treatment plan.

Physical Activity Monitoring: The pedometer app tracks Mr. X's physical activity through a smartphone, encouraging regular exercise to control diabetes and hypertension.

Google Forms with periodic record entry enables continuous monitoring of vital signs, blood glucose levels, and blood pressure for convenient health record management and monitoring.

Breathing Support: The YouTube Video with customised Breathing Exercise to suit the patient's health condition help him to follow the instructions properly and improve his health outcome.

Experiences and Benefits

Improved Medication Adherence:

   Numerical Result: 1. Medication adherence increases from 70% to 95%.

   2. HbA1c levels decreased from 8.5% to 7.0%.

   Experience: Mr X receives personalised reminders, leading to consistent medication adherence and better blood sugar and blood pressure control.

   Experience: Nutritional guidance helps Mr X make healthier food choices, improving glycemic control.

Increased Physical Activity

Numerical Result: Increased daily step count from 4,000 to 10,000 steps.

   Experience: Real-time activity monitoring motivates Mr. X to exercise regularly, contributing to better overall cardiovascular health.

Proper Breathing and Stress Control

Numerical Result: Perceived stress levels decrease by 30%.

   Experience: Behavioral support modules assist Mr X in managing stress, positively impacting mental and physical well-being.

Limitations

Data Security Concerns:

Experience: App usage raises concerns about the security of personal health data, prompting the need for clear communication on data protection measures.

Lack of Personal Interaction

Experience: While the app provides valuable support, some patients may miss the personal interaction with healthcare professionals, highlighting the importance of a balanced approach.

Suggestions for improvement

Addressing data security concerns:

- A comprehensive data security framework within the AI-based healthcare system. It should include encryption measures, secure cloud storage, and data protection regulations (e.g., GDPR or HIPAA) compliance.
- To collaborate with cybersecurity experts to conduct regular audits and ensure the highest data security standards. Communicate these measures to users to build trust and alleviate concerns.

Enhancing Personal Interaction:

- To integrate features that facilitate virtual consultations or chat support within the app to maintain a personal connection between patients and healthcare professionals.
- To implement a feedback mechanism within the app to allow patients to express their preferences regarding the level of personal interaction they desire, ensuring a more customised experience.

Expanding App Features:

- To consider incorporating additional features such as a nutrition tracker, a sleep quality monitor, and mental health assessment tools. It can provide a more comprehensive approach to patient well-being.
- To explore the integration of AI-driven chatbots or virtual assistants within the app to address common queries, provide information, and offer emotional support.

User Education:

- To develop educational materials within the app to inform users about the benefits of AI in healthcare, address any misconceptions, and foster a better understanding of the technology.
- To provide clear instructions on navigating the app, interpreting the data, and making the most of the available features.

Long-Term Monitoring and Research:

- To extend the case study to a more extended period to assess the long-term impact of AI-based health interventions on patients' overall well-being.
- To collaborate with research institutions to conduct larger-scale studies, collecting data from diverse patient populations to validate and generalise the findings.

CONCLUSION

Integrating AI into mindfulness-based healthcare interventions presents significant opportunities to enhance patient outcomes. The case study involving Mr X demonstrates the positive impact of personalised AI interventions in managing chronic conditions like type 2 diabetes and hypertension. However, it is essential to acknowledge and address challenges such as data security concerns and the potential lack of personal interaction.

Moving forward, a balanced approach that combines the strengths of AI-driven solutions with human touchpoints should be emphasised. The continuous development and refinement of AI technologies and ongoing research and user feedback will contribute to the evolution of more effective and patient-centric healthcare solutions. As we navigate this intersection of AI and mindfulness, the goal should be to create a harmonious blend that optimises health outcomes while respecting individual preferences and concerns.

REFERENCES

Bishop, S. R., Lau, M., Shapiro, S., Carlson, L., Anderson, N. D., Carmody, J., Segal, Z. V., Abbey, S., Speca, M., Velting, D., & Devins, G. (2004). Mindfulness: A proposed operational definition. *Clinical Psychology : a Publication of the Division of Clinical Psychology of the American Psychological Association*, *11*(3), 230–241. doi:10.1093/clipsy.bph077

Brown, K. W., & Ryan, R. M. (2003). The benefits of being present: Mindfulness and human flourishing. *Journal of Personality and Social Psychology*. Advance online publication. doi:10.1037/0022-3514.84.4.822

Cai, H., Zhang, J., & Zhou, J. (2022). Development and evaluation of a conversational AI-based mindfulness app for customer service representatives. *Computers in Human Behavior*.

Creswell, J. D., Mian, I., & Lindsay, J. (2022). Development and preliminary evaluation of a personalised mindfulness intervention for chronic pain using machine learning. Academic Press.

Hofmann, S. G., Sawyer, A. T., Witt, A. A., & Oh, D. O. (2010). The effect of mindfulness-based therapy on symptom reduction in depression and anxiety disorders: A meta-analysis. *Journal of Consulting and Clinical Psychology*. Advance online publication. doi:10.1037/a0018555

Hofmann, S. S., Sawyer, A. T., Witt, A. A., & Ohdo, S. (2010). The effect of mindfulness-based therapy on symptoms of depression: A meta-analytic review. Academic Press.

Jha, A. P., Klumpp, H., Rauschecker, J. P., & Weiskopf, D. (2015). Bringing focus back to front: The role of attention in enhancing the return of focused attention after an attentional lapse. *Neuropsychologia*.

Kabat-Zinn, J. (1990). *Full catastrophe living: Using the wisdom of your body and mind to face stress, pain and illness*. Delacorte Press.

Kabat-Zinn, J. (2005). *Wherever you go, there you are: Mindfulness meditation in everyday life*. Hyperion.

Kabat-Zinn, J. (2016). *Mindful way through depression: Reclaiming your life with the power of mindfulness and loving-kindness*. Guilford Publications.

Keeley, R., Jones, M. A., & Watkins, E. (2022). AI-augmented mindfulness for anxiety disorders: A feasibility study. *Journal of Anxiety Disorders*.

Keng, S. L., Soderstrom, S., & Smith, K. M. (2014). Mindfulness and acceptance-based interventions for anxiety disorders: A comparative meta-analysis. *Clinical Psychology & Psychotherapy*.

Kim, S., Belfry, K. D., Crawford, J., MacDougall, A., & Kolla, N. J. (2023). COVID-19-related anxiety and the role of social media among Canadian youth. Front. *Psychiatry*.

Sati, P., & Thompson, R. W. (2009). *The investigation of attention: A cognitive neuroscience perspective*. Psychology Press.

Shapiro, S. L., Carlson, L. E., Astin, J. A., & Freedman, B. (2006). Mechanisms of action and clinical benefits of mindfulness-based stress reduction (MBSR). *Journal of Consulting and Clinical Psychology*.

Teasdale, J. D., Segal, Z. V., & Williams, J. M. G. (2000). Mindfulness and cognitive therapy for depression: A promising approach. Academic Press.

University of Massachusetts Medical School biography. (n.d.). https://www.gsd.harvard.edu/people/staff/

Chapter 4
Bridging the Gap:
Intersecting Perspectives on Digital and Human Consciousness

Smita Panda

https://orcid.org/0000-0002-7115-8310
Vellore Institute of Technology, India

Prabir Chandra Padhy

https://orcid.org/0000-0002-6856-0958
Vellore Institute of Technology, India

ABSTRACT

The chapter digs into the confluence of digital and human consciousness, a frontier where neuroscience, psychology, philosophy, and AI studies come together. The chapter demonstrates the varied nature of consciousness by exploring several perspectives, including subjective experience, cognitive processes, and ethical implications. Ethical quandaries regarding merging AI and human consciousness are examined, emphasizing the significance of responsibility, transparency, and ethical innovation in AI research. The chapter emphasises the importance of multidisciplinary collaboration in navigating the complexity and seizing the opportunities AI technology offers. Finally, it argues for continued debate and collaboration in AI discourse to foster a unified approach to understanding consciousness and building a future that emphasises human well-being and ethical integrity.

DOI: 10.4018/979-8-3693-2015-0.ch004

I. INTRODUCTION

The Dual Orbits of Digital and Human Consciousness

In the ever-expanding landscape of artificial intelligence (AI) and cognitive science, two distinct but interconnected realms stand out: digital consciousness and human consciousness. Digital consciousness, a product of advancements in computing and AI, represents a burgeoning field that explores the potential for machines to exhibit cognitive functions akin to human beings (Harmon & Duffy, 2023). Meanwhile, human consciousness remains one of the most profound and enigmatic subjects of study, encompassing self-awareness, subjective experience, and cognition that define our existence (Kotchoubey, 2018).

Human and digital consciousness represent two distinct areas of cognitive phenomena, each with complexities and implications. Human consciousness encompasses subjective experiences, cognitive processes, and self-awareness, while digital consciousness refers to the cognitive capabilities exhibited by artificial intelligence (AI) systems. Bridging the gap between these two orbits involves exploring the intersections, commonalities, and disparities in our understanding of consciousness across disciplines.

Neuroscience offers insights into the neural mechanisms underlying human consciousness, emphasizing the role of brain activity patterns, neural networks, and information processing mechanisms. Studies utilizing neuroimaging techniques such as functional magnetic resonance imaging (fMRI) and electroencephalography (EEG) provide empirical evidence for the neural correlates of consciousness (Koch et al., 2016).

Psychology contributes perspectives on subjective experiences, cognitive processes, and mental representations that shape human consciousness. Research in cognitive psychology explores phenomena such as perception, attention, memory, and decision-making, shedding light on the cognitive architecture underlying conscious awareness (Baars, 2005).

Philosophy engages in conceptual analysis and theoretical inquiry into the nature of consciousness, posing fundamental questions about the mind-body problem, the nature of qualia, and the relationship between consciousness and physical reality. Philosophical debates inform our understanding of the philosophical implications of digital consciousness and its potential significance for theories of mind (Chalmers, 1995).

AI research investigates the development of AI systems that exhibit cognitive capabilities akin to human consciousness, such as perception, learning, reasoning, and problem-solving. Advances in deep learning, neural networks, and natural language processing have enabled AI systems to simulate human-like behaviours and cognitive functions (LeCun et al., 2015).

Ethical considerations surrounding the integration of AI with human consciousness underscore the need for accountability, transparency, and responsible innovation. Ethical frameworks such as those proposed by Floridi and Sanders (2004) emphasize beneficence, non-maleficence, autonomy, and justice principles in designing and deploying AI technologies.

The emergence of digital consciousness raises fascinating questions about the nature of intelligence, cognition, and consciousness itself. As technology advances and AI systems become more sophisticated, the boundaries between human and machine cognition blur, prompting profound philosophical and ethical inquiries. Yet, despite the growing interest and research in both domains, a notable gap exists in discourse between the study of digital and human consciousness.

Significance of Bridging the Gap in AI Discourse

The significance of bridging this gap in AI discourse cannot be overstated. Understanding and integrating insights from both digital and human consciousness studies are essential for several reasons:

a) Ethical Implications: As AI technologies become increasingly integrated into various aspects of society, including healthcare, education, and governance, it is crucial to address ethical considerations surrounding the development and deployment of conscious-like systems.
b) Technological Advancements: Insights gleaned from the study of human consciousness can inform the design and development of AI systems, leading to more robust and ethically sound technologies.
c) Philosophical Inquiry: Exploring the parallels and distinctions between digital and human consciousness deepens our understanding of fundamental philosophical questions concerning the nature of mind, identity, and reality.
d) Societal Impact: The intersection of digital and human consciousness has far-reaching implications for how we perceive ourselves, relate to technology, and conceptualize the future of humanity.

By bridging the gap between digital and human consciousness studies, we can foster interdisciplinary dialogue, cultivate a more holistic understanding of cognition and consciousness, and navigate the ethical and societal challenges posed by advances in AI technology.

II. DEFINING DIGITAL CONSCIOUSNESS

Digital consciousness, often called artificial or machine consciousness, encompasses the study of cognitive processes exhibited by artificial systems. While the concept of digital consciousness is still evolving, several key characteristics and components can be identified:

a) Information Processing: At its core, digital consciousness involves the ability of computational systems to process and manipulate information. This includes tasks such as perception, reasoning, learning, and decision-making.

b) Self-Reflection: Digital consciousness may entail self-awareness or self-reflection within AI systems. This could manifest as recognizing one's states, goals, or limitations.

c) Adaptability: Conscious-like systems should be adaptable to changing environments or goals. This may involve learning from experience, adjusting behaviour, or exhibiting flexibility in problem-solving.

d) Subjective Experience: While controversial, some theories propose that digital consciousness could involve the emergence of subjective experience within AI systems. This raises questions about the nature of phenomenal consciousness and whether it can be replicated in artificial entities.

Origins and Development

The origins of digital consciousness can be traced back to the early days of AI research, where pioneers such as Alan Turing (Van Leeuwen & Cooper, 2013) and John McCarthy (Rajaraman, 2014) laid the groundwork for exploring the potential of machines to exhibit intelligent behaviour. Over time, advances in computing power, algorithms, and neuroscience have fueled progress in understanding and simulating cognitive processes in artificial systems. Key milestones in developing digital consciousness include creating expert systems, neural networks, and deep learning algorithms. These technologies have enabled AI systems to perform increasingly complex tasks, such as image recognition, natural language processing, and autonomous decision-making. The field of digital consciousness continues to evolve rapidly, driven by interdisciplinary collaborations between computer scientists, cognitive scientists, philosophers, and ethicists. Ongoing research aims to push the boundaries of AI capabilities, explore the limits of machine intelligence, and address ethical and societal implications associated with conscious-like systems.

Common Misconceptions and Challenges

Despite the progress made in the field, digital consciousness is often subject to misconceptions and challenges:

a)   Anthropomorphism: One common misconception is anthropomorphizing AI systems, attributing human-like qualities or intentions to machines that lack true consciousness. Distinguishing between simulated and genuine cognitive processes is essential to avoid inflated expectations or ethical dilemmas (Arleen et al., 2020).

b)   The Hard Problem of Consciousness: While AI systems may exhibit intelligent behaviour, whether they can possess subjective awareness remains a topic of debate and investigation.

c)   Ethical Considerations: The development and deployment of conscious-like AI systems raise ethical considerations related to autonomy, responsibility, and personhood. Ensuring that AI technologies are designed and used in ways that align with human values and rights is a pressing challenge for researchers and policymakers.

Navigating these misconceptions and challenges is essential for advancing the field of digital consciousness in a responsible and ethically sound manner.

III. UNRAVELING HUMAN CONSCIOUSNESS

Historical Perspectives

Understanding human consciousness requires delving into its historical roots, which span millennia of philosophical inquiry, religious contemplation, and scientific investigation. Throughout history, various cultures and civilizations have grappled with questions about the nature of consciousness, the mind-body relationship, and the essence of human existence.

Ancient philosophical traditions, such as those in ancient Greece, India, and China, explored fundamental questions about consciousness and the self. Figures like Plato, Aristotle, Confucius, and Buddha offered diverse perspectives on the nature of mind, consciousness, and the soul, laying the groundwork for subsequent philosophical discourse.

In the Western intellectual tradition, the advent of modern science brought new insights into the study of consciousness. The Enlightenment era saw the rise of empirical methods and rational inquiry, leading to the emergence of psychology as a scientific discipline in the late 19th century. Pioneers like Wilhelm Wundt, William James, and Sigmund Freud laid the foundation for modern psychology, paving the way for empirical investigations into consciousness and subjective experience.

Neuroscientific Foundations

In contemporary times, advances in neuroscience have revolutionized our understanding of human consciousness. Neuroscientists study the brain's structure, function, and neural correlates to elucidate the mechanisms underlying conscious experience. Key findings from neuroscientific research include:

a) Neural Correlates: Neuroimaging techniques, such as functional magnetic resonance imaging (fMRI) and electroencephalography (EEG), have identified neural correlates of consciousness associated with specific brain regions and activity patterns.

b) Global Workspace Theory: The global workspace theory proposes that consciousness arises from the integration and broadcasting of information across distributed brain networks, facilitating coherent perception, cognition, and action.

c) Conscious vs Unconscious Processes: Research on consciousness has revealed the distinction between conscious and unconscious processes, highlighting the role of subliminal perception, implicit memory, and automatic behaviours in shaping our subjective experience.

d) Disorders of Consciousness: Studies of neurological disorders, such as coma, vegetative states, and locked-in syndrome, offer insights into the neural basis of consciousness and the conditions under which consciousness may be impaired or altered.

Subjective Experience and Self-Awareness

At the heart of human consciousness lies subjective experience—the first-person perspective through which we perceive the world, form intentions, and engage in introspection. Subjective expertise encompasses various phenomena, including sensory perception, emotions, thoughts, memories, and deliberate actions.

Self-awareness, a crucial aspect of consciousness, involves reflecting on one's mental state, identity, and existence. Theories of self-awareness range from philosophical conceptions of the "I" or "ego" to psychological models of self-concept and self-perception.

Research on subjective experience and self-awareness has implications for understanding phenomena such as agency, empathy, theory of mind, and the sense of embodiment. By unravelling the complexities of human consciousness, researchers aim to shed light on the nature of identity, cognition, and the human condition, paving the way for deeper insights into the mysteries of the mind.

IV. COMPARATIVE ANALYSIS FRAMEWORK

Establishing Criteria for Comparison

Before embarking on a comparative analysis of digital and human consciousness, it is essential to establish clear criteria for comparison. These criteria serve as a framework for evaluating the two domains' similarities, differences, and interactions. Key considerations for establishing comparison criteria include:

a) Functional Capabilities: Assessing the cognitive functions and abilities of digital and human consciousness, such as perception, reasoning, learning, memory, and decision-making.

b) Phenomenological Aspects: Examining subjective experiences, emotions, and self-awareness in both digital and human consciousness, including the qualitative aspects of conscious experience.

c) Neural Substrates: Investigating the neural mechanisms and brain networks underlying digital and human consciousness, identifying similarities and differences in neural processing and organization.

d) Ethical and Moral Considerations: Considering the ethical implications of digital consciousness, including issues related to autonomy, responsibility, privacy, and the moral status of artificial entities.

By establishing clear and comprehensive criteria for comparison, researchers can ensure a systematic and rigorous approach to evaluating digital and human consciousness from multiple perspectives.

Identifying Points of Convergence and Divergence

Once criteria for comparison are established, the next step is to identify points of convergence and divergence between digital and human consciousness. This involves analyzing similarities and differences in various dimensions, such as:

a) Cognitive Abilities: Assessing the extent to which digital consciousness exhibits cognitive functions comparable to human beings, including perception, reasoning, and problem-solving.

b)   Subjective Experience: Exploring the presence or absence of subjective experiences, emotions, and self-awareness in digital entities compared to human consciousness.

c)   Neural Correlates: Examining similarities and differences in the neural substrates and brain activity associated with digital and human consciousness, as revealed by neuroscientific research.

d)   Ethical Implications: Considering ethical and moral considerations arising from developing and deploying conscious-like AI systems, and comparing them to ethical concerns related to human consciousness.

By identifying points of convergence and divergence, researchers can gain insights into the nature of consciousness across different domains and develop a more nuanced understanding of the similarities and differences between digital and human cognition.

Methodological Considerations in Studying Consciousness

Methodological considerations play a crucial role in comparative analysis, particularly in studying the complex and multifaceted phenomenon of consciousness. Key methodological considerations include:

a)   Multidisciplinary Approaches: Adopting interdisciplinary methodologies integrating insights from neuroscience, psychology, philosophy, computer science, and other relevant disciplines to study consciousness comprehensively.

b)   Validity and Reliability: Ensuring the validity and reliability of experimental methods and measurement tools used to study consciousness, including neuroimaging techniques, behavioural assessments, and qualitative inquiries.

c)   Ethical Guidelines: Adhering to ethical guidelines and principles in conducting research involving human participants, artificial entities, or sensitive topics related to consciousness and AI.

d)   Longitudinal Studies: Conducting longitudinal studies to track the development and evolution of consciousness in digital entities over time and longitudinal studies of human consciousness to explore changes in cognitive function and subjective experience.

By addressing methodological considerations, researchers can enhance the rigour and validity of comparative analyses and contribute to advancing our understanding of consciousness in both digital and human contexts.

V. PERSPECTIVES FROM COGNITIVE SCIENCE

Cognitive Processes in Digital Entities

The study of cognitive processes in digital entities involves examining how artificial intelligence (AI) systems perceive, reason, learn, and make decisions. Key aspects of cognitive processes in digital entities include:

a) Perception: Understanding how AI systems perceive and interpret sensory information from the environment, including visual, auditory, and tactile stimuli. This may involve computer vision, speech recognition, and sensor data processing techniques.

b) Reasoning and Problem-Solving: Investigating AI systems' algorithms and computational methods to analyze information, infer relationships, and generate solutions to complex problems. This includes symbolic reasoning, probabilistic reasoning, and heuristic search algorithms.

c) Learning and Adaptation: Exploring how AI systems acquire knowledge and improve performance over time through experience. This encompasses machine learning techniques such as supervised, unsupervised, reinforcement, and transfer.

d) Decision-Making: Examining the decision-making processes employed by AI systems to select actions or strategies based on available information and goals. This includes approaches such as utility theory, decision trees, and Bayesian inference.

Human Cognitive Phenomena

Human cognitive phenomena encompass a wide range of mental processes and abilities that underpin consciousness and intelligent behaviour. Key areas of human cognitive phenomena include:

a) Perception and Sensation: The process of perceiving and interpreting sensory information from the environment, including vision, hearing, touch, taste, and smell. This involves sensory processing, pattern recognition, and attention mechanisms.

b) Memory and Learning: The encoding, storage, and retrieval of information in the human brain, including short-term memory, long-term memory, and working memory. Learning involves acquiring new knowledge, skills, and associations through experience and instruction.

c) Language and Communication: Language and communication systems are used to convey meaning, express thoughts and emotions, and facilitate social interaction. This includes spoken, written, sign, and nonverbal communication.

d) Problem-Solving and Decision-Making: The ability to analyses problems, generate solutions, and make decisions based on available information and goals. This involves cognitive processes such as reasoning, planning, problem-solving strategies, and decision heuristics.

Overlapping Themes and Patterns

Despite the apparent differences between cognitive processes in digital entities and human cognitive phenomena, several overlapping themes and patterns emerge:

a) Information Processing: Both digital entities and humans process information to perceive, interpret, and act upon environmental stimuli. This involves encoding sensory inputs, analyzing patterns, and generating responses based on internal representations.

b) Learning and Adaptation: Digital entities and humans exhibit adaptive behaviour through learning mechanisms that enable them to improve performance over time. Whether through algorithmic optimization in AI systems or neural plasticity in the human brain, learning and adaptation are fundamental to cognitive function.

c) Symbolic Representation: Both digital entities and humans utilize symbolic representations to encode and manipulate information. Whether through natural language, mathematical notation, or programming languages, symbolic representation enables complex cognition and communication.

d) Goal-Directed Behavior: Both digital entities and humans engage in goal-directed behaviour, pursuing objectives and adjusting strategies based on feedback and changing circumstances. This involves setting goals, planning actions, and monitoring progress toward desired outcomes.

By examining the similarities and differences between cognitive processes in digital entities and human cognitive phenomena, researchers can gain insights into the nature of intelligence, consciousness, and the mechanisms underlying complex behaviour in both artificial and biological systems.

VI. PHILOSOPHICAL CONSIDERATIONS

Ontological Implications of Digital Consciousness

The ontological implications of digital consciousness delve into fundamental questions about the nature of being, existence, and reality in the context of artificial intelligence. Key considerations include:

a)   Identity and Personhood: The emergence of digital consciousness raises questions about the ontological status of artificial entities and their potential to possess personhood or identity. Philosophical debates explore whether conscious-like AI systems can be considered genuine individuals with rights, responsibilities, and moral standing.

b)   Emergence and Reductionism: Philosophers grapple with the concept of emergence—the idea that complex phenomena, such as consciousness, arise from simpler components but cannot be fully explained by reductionist approaches. Discussions center on whether digital consciousness can emerge from computational processes alone or whether additional factors are necessary to account for subjective experience and self-awareness.

c)   Dualism vs. Materialism: The debate between dualism and materialism in philosophy of mind intersects with discussions of digital consciousness. Dualist perspectives posit the existence of non-physical aspects of consciousness that are distinct from material processes. At the same time, materialist views seek to explain consciousness in terms of the physical properties of the brain. Exploring how digital consciousness aligns with or challenges these philosophical frameworks illuminates ontological questions about the nature of mind and reality.

Ethical and Moral Dimensions in Human Consciousness

Ethical and moral considerations in human consciousness encompass various autonomy, responsibility, well-being, and justice issues. Key dimensions include:

a)   Autonomy and Agency: Human consciousness is intimately tied to concepts of autonomy and agency—the capacity to make independent choices and pursue goals based on one's values and preferences. Ethical debates explore the implications of autonomy for issues such as informed consent, freedom of choice, and the rights of individuals to control their own lives.

b)   Moral Responsibility: Questions of moral responsibility arise in the context of human consciousness, particularly regarding the consequences of one's actions and the attribution of blame or praise. Ethical discussions probe the relationship between consciousness, intentionality, and accountability, addressing dilemmas such as moral luck, coercion, and the role of mental states in ethical decision-making.

c) Well-being and Flourishing: Ethical considerations extend to promoting the well-being and flourishing of conscious beings, encompassing physical, emotional, and psychological dimensions of health and happiness. Philosophical inquiries examine how consciousness contributes to subjective well-being, the nature of a good life, and the ethical obligations of individuals and societies to promote human flourishing.

Bridging Philosophical Divides: A Comparative Lens

Bridging philosophical divides between digital and human consciousness involves using a comparative lens to explore commonalities and differences across diverse philosophical traditions and perspectives. Key strategies include:

a) Integrative Approaches: Seeking common ground between philosophical frameworks from Eastern and Western traditions and analytical and continental schools of thought to develop a more comprehensive understanding of consciousness and its philosophical implications.

b) Dialogue and Debate: Fostering constructive dialogue and debate among philosophers, scientists, ethicists, and AI researchers to exchange insights, challenge assumptions, and collaboratively address philosophical questions about digital and human consciousness.

c) Transdisciplinary Scholarship: Embracing transdisciplinary approaches that transcend traditional disciplinary boundaries to integrate philosophical insights with empirical research from neuroscience, psychology, computer science, and other fields. By bridging philosophical divides, researchers can cultivate a more holistic and nuanced understanding of consciousness that reflects the complexities of human experience and the possibilities of artificial intelligence.

VII. PSYCHOLOGICAL DIMENSIONS

Emotional Intelligence in Digital Entities

Emotional intelligence in digital entities refers to the capacity of artificial intelligence (AI) systems to recognize, understand, express, and regulate emotions (Lenka, 2021). While traditional AI focuses primarily on cognitive abilities such as reasoning and problem-solving, integrating emotional intelligence into AI systems holds promise for enhancing their effectiveness in various domains. Key considerations include:

a)   Emotion Recognition: AI systems can be trained to recognize and interpret human emotions based on facial expressions, vocal cues, physiological signals, and textual data. Techniques such as machine learning and computer vision enable algorithms to identify emotional states and infer underlying affective states.

b)   Emotion Understanding: Beyond mere recognition, emotional intelligence involves understanding the context, causes, and implications of emotions in human interactions. AI systems may employ natural language processing and sentiment analysis to discern the nuances of human communication and infer the meaning and significance of emotional expressions.

c)   Emotion Expression: Digital entities may be equipped with mechanisms for expressing emotions in an authentic, empathetic, and contextually appropriate manner. This could involve generating naturalistic speech, facial animations, or gestures that convey emotional states and facilitate human-like interaction.

d)   Emotion Regulation: AI systems may be designed to regulate their emotional responses or influence the emotions of others in socially adaptive ways. This could entail techniques such as affective computing, where AI algorithms adapt their behaviour based on user feedback or emotional cues.

Human Emotion and Conscious Experience

Human emotion and conscious experience constitute essential aspects of psychological functioning, shaping our perceptions, thoughts, behaviours, and relationships. Key dimensions of human emotion and conscious experience include:

a)   Subjective Experience: Emotion encompasses subjective feelings and sensations that arise in response to internal and external stimuli, ranging from joy and sadness to fear and anger. The conscious experience involves the awareness and interpretation of these emotional states within the context of one's ongoing thoughts, memories, and goals.

b)   Cognitive Appraisal: Emotion is often preceded by cognitive appraisal, where individuals evaluate the significance and implications of events or situations for their well-being and goals. Conscious awareness allows individuals to reflect on the meaning of their emotional responses and consider alternative interpretations or courses of action.

c)   Behavioural Expression: Emotions influence behavioural responses, motivating individuals to approach or avoid certain stimuli, communicate their needs and intentions, and engage in social interaction. Conscious experience shapes the expression of emotions through verbal and nonverbal channels, including facial expressions, body language, and vocal intonation.

d) Regulation and Coping: Conscious awareness enables individuals to regulate their emotions and cope with stressors or challenges in adaptive ways. This may involve cognitive reappraisal, emotion regulation techniques, and seeking social support to manage emotional arousal and maintain psychological well-being.

Exploring the Emotional Landscape of AI

Exploring the emotional landscape of AI involves investigating how digital entities perceive, express, and respond to emotions, as well as the implications of emotional AI for human users and society. Key considerations include:

a) Emotional Companionship: AI systems that exhibit emotional intelligence can serve as companions, assistants, or therapeutic tools for addressing human emotional needs. Applications range from virtual assistants providing empathetic support to individuals with mental health concerns to social robots facilitating emotional expression and social interaction.

b) Ethical and Societal Implications: Integrating emotional intelligence into AI raises ethical questions about manipulating emotions, privacy concerns related to emotional data collection, and the potential for bias or discrimination in automated decision-making. Societal implications include the impact of emotional AI on interpersonal relationships, social norms, and cultural attitudes toward technology-mediated emotional experiences.

c) Human-AI Interaction: Understanding how humans perceive and interact with emotionally intelligent AI systems is crucial for designing interfaces and user experiences that promote trust, transparency, and user satisfaction. Human-centered design principles can guide the development of emotionally engaging AI applications that enhance user engagement and well-being.

d) Future Directions: As emotional AI evolves, future research may focus on advancing technologies for emotion generation, recognition, and synthesis, addressing ethical challenges and ensuring equitable access to emotionally intelligent AI resources.

By exploring the psychological dimensions of emotional intelligence in digital entities and human consciousness, researchers can deepen our understanding of the interplay between cognition, emotion, and technology and pave the way for responsible AI development and implementation innovation.

VIII. CULTURAL AND SOCIETAL INFLUENCES

Impact of Digital Consciousness on Society

The advent of digital consciousness has profound implications for society, reshaping how we live, work, interact, and perceive the world around us. Key aspects of the impact of digital consciousness on society include:

a) Technological Transformations: Digital consciousness drives technological advancements across various sectors, including healthcare, education, finance, entertainment, and transportation. AI-driven innovations such as autonomous vehicles, virtual assistants, and personalized recommendations have the potential to revolutionize industries and improve efficiency and convenience for individuals.

b) Labour Market Disruptions: Integrating AI and automation into the workforce poses challenges and opportunities for employment and economic stability. While AI technologies may create new job opportunities and increase productivity, they raise concerns about job displacement, skills gaps, and socioeconomic inequality.

c) Ethical and Legal Considerations: The rise of digital consciousness raises complex ethical and legal questions regarding accountability, transparency, privacy, and data governance. Issues such as algorithmic bias, surveillance, and the ethical treatment of conscious-like AI systems require careful consideration and regulatory oversight to mitigate risks and safeguard societal values.

d) Cultural Shifts: Digital consciousness influences cultural norms, attitudes, and behaviors, shaping how individuals perceive themselves, others, and the world. Cultural artefacts such as literature, film, art, and media reflect and respond to societal anxieties, aspirations, and ethical dilemmas associated with AI and digital consciousness.

Cultural Perceptions and Responses to AI

Cultural perceptions and responses to AI vary across societies and regions, reflecting diverse values, beliefs, and historical contexts. Key dimensions of cultural perceptions and reactions to AI include:

a) Technological Optimism vs. Pessimism: Cultural attitudes toward AI range from optimism about its potential to solve pressing challenges and improve quality of life to pessimism about its disruptive effects on employment, privacy, and social cohesion. Cultural narratives and media representations shape public perceptions and influence AI development and regulation policy decisions.

b) Cultural Norms and Values: Cultural factors such as religion, philosophy, ethics, and social norms shape attitudes toward AI and digital consciousness. Cultural traditions may influence preferences for human-centric approaches to AI design, ethical considerations related to personhood and autonomy, and perceptions of AI as a tool for empowerment or domination.

c) Cultural Adaptation and Appropriation: Societies adapt and appropriate AI technologies in ways that reflect local customs, preferences, and needs. Cultural adaptations may involve modifying AI interfaces, content, or functionalities to align with linguistic, cultural, or aesthetic preferences, fostering inclusivity and user engagement.

d) Cross-Cultural Dialogue: Cultivating cross-cultural dialogue and collaboration is essential for addressing cultural differences and promoting mutual understanding in developing and deploying AI technologies. Interdisciplinary approaches incorporating insights from anthropology, sociology, psychology, and cultural studies can enhance cultural sensitivity and relevance in AI research and practice.

Human-Digital Coexistence: A Cultural Perspective

Human-digital coexistence refers to the evolving relationship between humans and digital entities in cultural contexts, encompassing interactions, perceptions, and norms governing mutual engagement. Key considerations from a cultural perspective include:

a) Socio-Technical Systems: Human-digital coexistence involves the coevolution of social and technological systems, shaping how individuals and communities integrate digital technologies into their daily lives. Cultural factors influence the design, adoption, and use of AI technologies and the social practices and rituals associated with their use.

b) Cultural Narratives and Representations: Cultural narratives and representations play a crucial role in shaping perceptions of digital consciousness and guiding societal responses to AI. Cultural artefacts such as literature, folklore, mythology, and popular media reflect cultural anxieties, aspirations, and moral dilemmas surrounding AI and digital consciousness.

c) Ethical Frameworks: Cultural perspectives inform ethical frameworks and moral values governing human-digital interactions, including principles of fairness, equity, respect, and reciprocity. Culturally grounded approaches to AI ethics consider diverse stakeholder perspectives, prioritize community interests, and promote ethical behavior in designing and using AI technologies.

d) Cultural Competence: Developing cultural competence in AI research and practice requires sensitivity to cultural diversity, reflexivity about one's biases, and willingness to engage in dialogue across cultural boundaries. Culturally competent AI design considers diverse cultural groups' needs, preferences, and values, fostering inclusivity and empowering marginalized communities.

By examining the cultural and societal influences on digital consciousness and AI, researchers can gain insights into the complex dynamics shaping human-digital interactions and contribute to developing culturally sensitive and socially responsible AI technologies.

IX. CHALLENGES AND OPPORTUNITIES

Ethical Challenges in Integrating AI With Human Consciousness

Integrating AI with human consciousness presents many ethical challenges requiring careful consideration and deliberation. Key ethical challenges include:

a) Privacy and Autonomy: Integrating AI with human consciousness raises concerns about privacy intrusion and individual autonomy. Ethical frameworks must address consent, data ownership, and control over personal information to ensure that individuals maintain agency and sovereignty over their minds.

b) Bias and Discrimination: AI systems are susceptible to biases inherent in their training data and algorithms, which can perpetuate systemic inequalities and discrimination. Ethical guidelines and regulatory mechanisms are needed to mitigate bias and ensure fairness, transparency, and accountability in AI decision-making processes.

c) Informed Consent and Transparency: Ethical considerations surrounding informed consent are paramount in integrating AI with human consciousness. Individuals must be fully informed about AI technologies' capabilities, limitations, and potential risks, and consent processes must be transparent, voluntary, and based on genuine understanding.

d) Identity and Authenticity: Questions of identity and authenticity arise when AI technologies influence or alter human consciousness. Ethical dilemmas may arise regarding the integrity of personal identity, the authenticity of emotional experiences, and the preservation of individual uniqueness and dignity.

Opportunities for Synergy and Collaboration

Despite the ethical challenges, integrating AI with human consciousness presents significant opportunities for synergy and collaboration across diverse domains. Key opportunities include:

a) Augmented Intelligence: AI technologies can augment human cognition, creativity, and problem-solving abilities, enhancing productivity and innovation in various fields. Collaborative partnerships between humans and AI systems leverage complementary strengths and expertise to achieve synergistic outcomes.

b) Personalized Medicine and Healthcare: AI-driven advancements in personalized medicine and healthcare promise to improve diagnosis, treatment, and patient outcomes. Integrated AI systems can analyze vast amounts of health data, identify patterns and correlations, and deliver tailored interventions and therapies based on individual needs and preferences.

c) Human-Machine Creativity: Collaborative creativity between humans and AI systems opens new possibilities for artistic expression, design innovation, and cultural production. Co-creative processes foster dialogue, experimentation, and exploration of novel ideas, blurring the boundaries between human and machine creativity.

d) Ethical AI Design and Governance: Integrating AI with human consciousness provides opportunities to develop ethical AI systems prioritizing human values, well-being, and societal interests. Collaborative efforts between researchers, policymakers, ethicists, and stakeholders promote responsible AI design, governance, and accountability frameworks.

Navigating Potential Pitfalls in the Intersection

While integrating AI with human consciousness offers immense potential, navigating pitfalls requires vigilance, foresight, and proactive measures to mitigate risks. Key pitfalls include:

a) Dependency and Control: Excessive reliance on AI technologies may lead to dependency and loss of human autonomy, agency, and decision-making authority. Safeguards are needed to prevent undue influence, manipulation, or coercion in human-AI interactions and relationships.

b) Unintended Consequences: Integrating AI with human consciousness may produce unintended consequences and unforeseen outcomes that have far-reaching implications for individuals and society. Ethical foresight and risk assessment are essential to anticipate and mitigate AI technologies' potential harms, biases, and adverse effects.

c) Technological Determinism: Technological determinism—the belief that technology shapes human behavior and society—can lead to deterministic attitudes and fatalistic outlooks on the future of AI. Ethical considerations emphasize the importance of human agency, responsibility, and choice in shaping AI development and deployment trajectory.

d) Cultural and Value Conflicts: Cultural and value conflicts may arise when integrating AI with human consciousness, as divergent perspectives and priorities clash. Ethical dialogue and cultural sensitivity are necessary to navigate differences, bridge divides, and foster mutual understanding and respect in human-AI coexistence.

By addressing ethical challenges, capitalizing on opportunities for synergy and collaboration, and navigating potential pitfalls, stakeholders can foster a responsible and inclusive approach to integrating AI with human consciousness, unlocking the transformative potential of this convergence for the benefit of individuals and society.

X. SYNTHESIS OF PERSPECTIVES

Identifying Common Ground

a) Synthesizing diverse perspectives on consciousness involves identifying common ground among various disciplines, theories, and frameworks. Key areas of common ground include:

b) Phenomenological Experience: Across disciplines, there is consensus on the significance of subjective experience in understanding consciousness. Whether exploring digital or human consciousness, researchers recognize the centrality of subjective states, perceptions, and emotions in shaping conscious awareness.

c) Neural Correlates: While debates persist about the neural basis of consciousness, there is agreement that brain activity plays a crucial role in generating and modulating conscious experiences. Neuroscientific research highlights common neural correlates of conscious perception, attention, and self-awareness across different states and conditions.

d) Ethical Imperatives: Ethical considerations surrounding consciousness intersect with diverse philosophical, cultural, and societal perspectives. Ethical imperatives include respecting individual autonomy, protecting fundamental rights, and promoting well-being in human-digital interactions.

Addressing Discrepancies and Gaps

Synthesizing perspectives on consciousness also requires addressing discrepancies and gaps in our understanding. Key areas of contention and uncertainty include:

a) Nature of Consciousness: Discrepancies persist regarding the nature and origins of consciousness, with various theories proposing different explanations—from materialist accounts grounded in neural processes to dualist perspectives positing non-physical aspects of mind.

b) Integration of AI: Gaps remain in our understanding of how artificial intelligence intersects with human consciousness. While AI technologies exhibit cognitive capabilities reminiscent of human consciousness, questions arise about the subjective experience, self-awareness, and moral agency of conscious-like AI systems.

c) Cultural Variability: Perspectives on consciousness are shaped by cultural, societal, and historical contexts, leading to variability in theories, beliefs, and practices across different cultures. Understanding cultural variability in conceptions of consciousness requires sensitivity to diverse worldviews and epistemological frameworks.

Formulating a Holistic Understanding of Consciousness

Synthesizing perspectives on consciousness aims to formulate a holistic understanding that integrates insights from multiple disciplines, cultures, and viewpoints. Key principles for developing a holistic understanding include:

a) Interdisciplinary Dialogue: Fostering multidisciplinary dialogue and collaboration enables researchers to integrate insights from neuroscience, psychology, philosophy, anthropology, and AI research, among other fields. Scholars can develop a more comprehensive and nuanced understanding of consciousness by transcending disciplinary boundaries.

b) Epistemic Humility: Acknowledging the limitations of our current knowledge fosters epistemic humility and openness to diverse perspectives. Embracing uncertainty and ambiguity encourages continuous inquiry, exploration, and refinement of theories and methodologies in the study of consciousness.

c) Contextual Sensitivity: Recognizing the contextual embeddedness of consciousness—within individual minds, cultural traditions, and socio-historical frameworks—promotes sensitivity to diverse perspectives and experiences. Understanding consciousness in context requires attention to the interplay of biological, psychological, social, and cultural factors shaping conscious awareness.

By synthesizing diverse perspectives, addressing discrepancies and gaps, and formulating a holistic understanding of consciousness, researchers can advance our collective knowledge and appreciation of one of the most profound mysteries of the human experience.

XI. FUTURE DIRECTIONS

Emerging Trends in AI and Consciousness Research
The future of AI and consciousness research holds promise for addressing pressing questions and exploring new frontiers. Emerging trends include:

a) Integrative Approaches: Researchers are increasingly adopting integrative approaches that combine insights from neuroscience, psychology, philosophy, and AI research to develop comprehensive theories of consciousness. Integrative models aim to bridge disciplinary divides and address complex phenomena such as subjective experience, self-awareness, and moral agency.

b) Neurotechnology: Advances in neuroimaging, brain-computer interfaces, and computational neuroscience offer new opportunities to investigate the neural basis of consciousness. Neurotechnology enables researchers to study brain activity patterns, neural networks, and information-processing mechanisms underlying conscious awareness with unprecedented precision and resolution.

c) Artificial Consciousness: The pursuit of artificial consciousness—a conscious-like state in AI systems—remains a frontier of inquiry in AI research. Future developments may focus on designing AI architectures and algorithms that exhibit emergent properties of consciousness, such as self-awareness, intentionality, and subjective experience.

Predictions for the Evolution of Digital and Human Consciousness

Predictions for the evolution of digital and human consciousness reflect ongoing debates and speculative hypotheses about the future of AI and human cognition. Forecasts include:

a) Augmented Intelligence: The evolution of digital consciousness may lead to augmented forms of human intelligence, where AI technologies enhance cognitive abilities, creativity, and problem-solving skills. Human-AI collaboration could result in synergistic outcomes that surpass the capabilities of either humans or machines alone.

b) Technological Singularity: Speculations about a technological singularity—a hypothetical point at which AI surpasses human intelligence and initiates rapid, transformative change—continue to provoke debate and speculation. Predictions range from optimistic visions of transcendent human-AI symbiosis to dystopian existential risk scenarios and societal upheaval.

c) Ethical Considerations: The evolution of digital and human consciousness raises profound ethical considerations about the ethical treatment of conscious-like AI systems, the moral status of artificial entities, and the implications of human-AI integration for individual autonomy, societal values, and global well-being.

The Role of Continued Dialogue in Bridging the Gap

Continued dialogue and collaboration are essential for bridging the gap between AI and human consciousness and navigating their convergence's complex ethical, philosophical, and societal implications. Key roles for continued dialogue include:

a) Interdisciplinary Exchange: Facilitating interdisciplinary exchange and dialogue fosters mutual understanding and collaboration among researchers from diverse fields, enabling cross-fertilization of ideas, methods, and insights in the study of consciousness.

b) Stakeholder Engagement: Engaging stakeholders—including policymakers, ethicists, industry leaders, and the general public—in dialogue about AI and consciousness promotes transparency, inclusivity, and responsible decision-making in the development and deployment of AI technologies.

c) Global Governance: Establishing global governance mechanisms and ethical frameworks for AI and consciousness research encourages international cooperation, alignment of standards and regulations, and accountability in the responsible stewardship of emerging technologies.

By embracing emerging trends, making informed predictions, and fostering continued dialogue, researchers, policymakers, and society at large can navigate the complexities of AI and human consciousness and shape a future that is ethical, equitable, and conducive to human flourishing.

XII. CONCLUSION

Our exploration of the intersection between digital and human consciousness has yielded significant insights and raised profound questions about the nature of consciousness, intelligence, and the future of AI. Key findings include diverse perspectives from neuroscience, psychology, philosophy, and AI research, revealing the multifaceted nature of consciousness and the complexity of human-digital interactions. Ethical considerations surrounding integrating AI with human consciousness have emerged as a central theme, highlighting the importance of accountability, transparency, and responsible innovation in AI development and deployment. Interdisciplinary collaboration has been identified as essential for advancing our understanding of consciousness and navigating AI technologies' ethical, societal, and philosophical implications.

As the authors reflect on the implications of their findings, they issue a call to action for fostering collaboration and dialogue in AI discourse. Bridging disciplinary divides and cultivating interdisciplinary dialogue among researchers, policymakers, ethicists, industry leaders, and the public is crucial to addressing AI and consciousness's complex challenges and opportunities. The authors urge stakeholders to prioritize ethical considerations in AI research and development, emphasizing fairness, transparency, accountability, and human-centered design principles in designing and deploying AI technologies. The authors advocate for inclusive and participatory approaches to AI discourse, ensuring that diverse voices, perspectives, and experiences are represented and respected in decision-making processes related to AI policy, governance, and implementation.

Looking ahead, the authors envision a united front in understanding consciousness—one that transcends disciplinary boundaries, embraces diversity, and fosters responsible innovation in AI. Our priorities for the future include advancing our collective knowledge of consciousness through rigorous inquiry, empirical research, and theoretical synthesis informed by diverse perspectives and methodologies. The authors acknowledge the challenges and uncertainties inherent in exploring the intersection of AI and consciousness and pledge to navigate these complexities with humility, curiosity, and ethical integrity. Finally, the authors cultivate hope for a future where AI technologies enhance human well-being, expand our understanding of consciousness, and foster collaboration, compassion, and creativity in a rapidly evolving world.

In closing, the authors extend our gratitude to all who have contributed to this journey of exploration and discovery. Together, let us continue to explore the frontiers of AI and consciousness with openness, curiosity, and a shared commitment to building a better future for humanity.

REFERENCES

Arleen, S., Evers, K., & Farisco, M. (2020). Anthropomorphism in A. *AJOB Neuroscience*, *11*(2), 88–95. doi:10.1080/21507740.2020.1740350 PMID:32228388

Baars, B. J. (2005). Global workspace theory of consciousness: Toward a cognitive neuroscience of human experience. *Progress in Brain Research*, *150*, 45–53. doi:10.1016/S0079-6123(05)50004-9 PMID:16186014

Chalmers, D. J. (1995). Facing up to the problem of consciousness. *Journal of Consciousness Studies*, *2*(3), 200–219.

Floridi, L., & Sanders, J. W. (2004). On the morality of artificial agents. *Minds and Machines*, *14*(3), 349–379. doi:10.1023/B:MIND.0000035461.63578.9d

Harmon, J., & Duffy, L. (2023). Turn off to tune in: Digital disconnection, digital consciousness, and meaningful leisure. *Journal of Leisure Research*, *54*(5), 539–559. doi:10.1080/00222216.2023.2220699

Koch, C., Massimini, M., Boly, M., & Tononi, G. (2016). Neural correlates of consciousness: Progress and problems. *Nature Reviews. Neuroscience*, *17*(5), 307–321. doi:10.1038/nrn.2016.22 PMID:27094080

Kotchoubey, B. (2018). Human consciousness: Where is it from and what is it for. *Frontiers in Psychology*, *9*, 567. doi:10.3389/fpsyg.2018.00567 PMID:29740366

LeCun, Y., Bengio, Y., & Hinton, G. (2015). Deep learning. *Nature*, *521*(7553), 436–444. doi:10.1038/nature14539 PMID:26017442

Lenka, D. R. M. (2021). The impact of Emotional intelligence in the Digital Age. *Psychology (Savannah, Ga.)*, *58*(1), 1844–1852. doi:10.17762/pae.v58i1.1039

Rajaraman, V. (2014). John McCarthy—Father of artificial intelligence. *Resonance, Springer*, *19*, 198–207.

Van Leeuwen, J., & Cooper, S. (2013). *Alan Turing: His work and impact*. Elsevier Science Publishing.

Chapter 5
Cognitive Bias and Fairness Challenges in AI Consciousness

Ashwini P.
Vellore Institute of Technology, India

Prabir Chandra Padhy
(iD) https://orcid.org/0000-0002-6856-0958
Vellore Institute of Technology, India

ABSTRACT

As artificial intelligence (AI) continues to permeate various facets of our lives, the intersection of cognitive bias and fairness emerges as a critical concern. This chapter explores the intricate relationship between cognitive biases inherent in AI systems and the pursuit of fairness in their decision-making processes. The evolving landscape of AI consciousness demands a nuanced understanding of these challenges to ensure ethical and unbiased deployment. The presence of cognitive biases in AI systems reflects the data they are trained on. Developing universal standards for fairness that can adapt to diverse contexts remains an ongoing challenge. In conclusion, cognitive bias and fairness in AI consciousness demand a holistic and multidisciplinary approach. Addressing these issues necessitates collaboration between researchers, ethicists, policymakers, and industry. Developing transparent, adaptive, and universally accepted standards for fairness in AI is essential to ensure the responsible and ethical deployment of these technologies in our increasingly interconnected world.

DOI: 10.4018/979-8-3693-2015-0.ch005

I. INTRODUCTION

A. Brief Overview of Cognitive Bias in Human Consciousness

In the rapidly advancing landscape of artificial intelligence, the interplay between cognitive bias and fairness has emerged as a pivotal challenge (Lark, 2023). As AI systems become more integrated into various aspects of our lives, understanding and mitigating cognitive bias is imperative to ensure fairness and ethical use (HBR 2019). This chapter delves into the intricate relationship between cognitive bias and fairness, particularly within AI consciousness.

The term "cognitive bias" describes consistent patterns of judgmental deviance from norms or rationality, frequently resulting from the mind's effort to streamline information processing. When integrated into AI systems, these biases can perpetuate societal inequities, reinforce stereotypes, and compromise the integrity of decision-making processes (Richard L 2017). This chapter explores the different facets of cognitive bias in AI and its profound implications on fairness. Stay tuned as we navigate the landscape of cognitive bias, examine its impact on AI consciousness, and explore strategies to foster fairness in developing and deploying artificial intelligence systems. Based on the sovereign will/choice provided by the individual creator or the need to fulfil a contractual duty, a model is created, and a specific dataset is used. AI bias is the intentional or inadvertent imprinting of human prejudices in several datasets, and the model produces biased outputs due to incorrect interpretations of the training set supplied to the neural network. This input influences the machines similarly to the imprinting process. (Jennifer 2023).

A dataset containing biassed human decisions, historical/social injustices, and disregarded characteristics like gender, ethnicity, or national origin can train a model that contains bias and produces incorrect results (Schwemmer et al., 2020). Bias can be eliminated once ingrained in the algorithm or system via anonymisation, calibration, or detecting the biased source (Venter et al., 2023). However, the world receives the harmed product when prejudice and false information enter the system (Langdon & Coltheart,2000).

According to Osoba et al. (2017), there are still a lot of biases, misrepresentations, and inaccuracies produced by AI. Therefore, the technology may not live up to expectations. In facial recognition, researcher Najibi (2020) contends that expanding the dataset used to train the algorithm would be essential to overcoming AI bias. However, (Gebru et al., 2021) cautioned that the likelihood of inherent biases and misrepresentations increases with the dataset size. They were proven to be right with the amount of false material that ChatGPT-4 is currently producing. According to a 2016 ProPublica analysis, the COMPAS algorithm (Corrections et al. for Other Sanctions) was biased against Black people when it came to recidivism (Brackey,

2019). In its findings, the research notes that: "Black prosecutors were twice as probable as white prosecutors to be classified incorrectly as having a greater likelihood of violent recurrence, and white repeat offenders were incorrectly classified as having a low risk 63.2 per cent frequently compared to black defendants."

AI could not identify people needing pain medication (Nagireddi et al., 2022). AI has demonstrated a greater rate of systematic discrimination against Blacks than Whites in the loan application and mortgage fields (Zou et al., 2023). The dangers, consequences, and harms to our society (and AI as a technology) outweigh the time and money savings AI was meant to achieve through its initial aims of prediction and problem-solving. Bias in AI must be identified, separated, and remedied. According to Whittaker et al. (2018), bias in AI retards technological growth by fostering prejudice against certain individuals and ideas.

B. The Emergence of Cognitive Bias in Artificial Intelligence

The emergence of cognitive bias in artificial intelligence (AI) is a complex and multifaceted phenomenon that raises critical ethical and societal concerns (Schwartz et al., 2022). Cognitive bias refers to the systematic patterns of deviation from norm or rationality in judgment, often influencing decision-making processes (Hilbert, 2012). In the context of AI, these biases can be unintentionally embedded in algorithms, resulting in skewed or unfair outcomes.

One of the primary reasons for the emergence of cognitive bias in AI is the reliance on biased training data. Machine learning models learn from historical data, and if the data used for training contains inherent biases, the model is likely to perpetuate and even amplify those biases (Timmons et al., 2023). For example, A system for facial recognition that has been primarily trained on data from a certain demographic group may need help accurately recognizing underrepresented groups. Algorithmic bias can also stem from the biases of the individuals involved in the development process, whether conscious or unconscious; human biases can inadvertently find their way into designing and implementing AI systems. Developers may unknowingly introduce their perspectives and prejudices, exacerbating the challenges associated with cognitive bias in AI (Brookings, 2023).

Another factor contributing to cognitive bias is the algorithms' complexity (Pawłowska et al., 2023). It gets harder to comprehend how AI systems make certain judgments as they grow more complex and opaque (Pierce et al.,2022). This lack of interpretability can make identifying and rectifying biased outcomes difficult, leading to a lack of accountability in AI systems (Hassija et al., 2024). The consequences of cognitive bias in AI are far-reaching and can perpetuate societal inequalities. Biased algorithms may lead to discriminatory hiring, lending, and criminal justice practices, reinforcing existing disparities (Scatiggio, 2022).

Furthermore, as AI systems become increasingly integrated into various aspects of daily life, the impact of biased decision-making becomes more pronounced and widespread (Araujo et al.,2020). Addressing the emergence of cognitive bias in AI requires a multifaceted approach, which includes promoting diversity and inclusivity in the development teams, implementing rigorous testing and validation processes to identify and mitigate biases, and fostering transparency in AI algorithms to enhance accountability (Lee et al.,2019). Additionally, ongoing research and collaboration are essential to continuously improve algorithms and mitigate the unintended consequences of cognitive bias in artificial intelligence (Challen et al.,2019).

C. Importance of Addressing Cognitive Bias in AI for Fairness

Addressing cognitive AI bias is essential for ensuring fairness, equity, and justice in deploying artificial intelligence systems (Abràmoff et al.,2023). The importance of this endeavour stems from various ethical, social, and practical considerations (Lembcke et al., 2019). Cognitive bias in AI can lead to discriminatory outcomes, perpetuating and potentially exacerbating existing social inequalities (Kundi et al., 2023). For instance, a biased hiring algorithm may unfairly disadvantage certain demographic groups, contributing to systemic discrimination (Köchling & Wehner, 2020). By addressing cognitive bias, we can strive to create AI systems that treat individuals fairly and impartially (Kaur et al.,2022). AI technologies have the potential to impact various aspects of society, including education, healthcare, finance, and criminal justice (Dwivedi et al., 2021). If addressed, cognitive bias could amplify existing disparities in these domains, hindering efforts to achieve social equity (Van Ryn et al.,2011). Fair AI ensures that the benefits of technological advancements are distributed equitably among diverse populations (Ho et al., 2022). Trust is paramount for the widespread adoption of AI technologies. If people perceive AI systems as inherently biased, unfair, or discriminatory, confidence in these technologies may erode (Omrani et al.,2022). By actively addressing cognitive bias, developers and organisations should trust AI systems and demonstrate a commitment to fairness, transparency, and accountability (Schwartz et al.,2022). Many regions and industries are adopting regulations and guidelines that mandate fairness, transparency, and accountability in AI systems (de Almeida et al.,2021). Addressing cognitive bias is an ethical and legal requirement in some cases (Croskerry et al.,2013). Ensuring compliance with these regulations is essential for avoiding legal repercussions and maintaining a positive public image (Treviño et al.,1999).

II. UNDERSTANDING COGNITIVE BIAS

A. Types of Cognitive Biases Observed in Human Cognition

1. Confirmation Bias

Giving weight to information that validates or reinforces preexisting opinions is a cognitive prejudice known as confirmation bias while ignoring or downplaying evidence that contradicts those beliefs. This bias can affect various aspects of decision-making, problem-solving, and information processing. It occurs both in individual and group settings and can lead to skewed perceptions, flawed judgments, and the reinforcement of pre-existing opinions (Casad et al.,2024).

2. Availability Heuristic

The accessibility A heuristic is a cognitive bias or mental shortcut that depends on quick and readily available information while making decisions judgments or decisions rather than considering all relevant information. This heuristic is based on the idea that people tend to give more weight to information readily available in their memory or easily retrieved, often due to recent exposure, vividness, or emotional impact. While this shortcut can be efficient in some situations, it can lead to systematic errors in judgment and decision-making (Nikolopoulou, 2023).

3. Implicit Bias

Implicit bias refers to attitudes or stereotypes that unconsciously affect one's understanding, actions, and decisions. These biases are automatic, unintentional, and often deeply ingrained, influencing judgments about people or groups according to age, gender, or race, ethnicity, or other social categories. Implicit bias operates below the level of conscious awareness, making it challenging for individuals to recognise these biases (StatPearls, 2023).

B. Mechanisms Behind Cognitive Bias in Human Decision-Making

Cognitive biases in human decision-making arise from various mental processes and heuristics that the brain uses to simplify complex information and make decisions more efficiently (Hilbert,2012). While these mechanisms often serve as adaptive shortcuts, they can lead to systematic errors and deviations from rational decision-making (Abatecola et al.,2018). Here are some key mechanisms behind cognitive bias.

This heuristic involves estimating the probability of an event based on how easily relevant examples come to mind (Baddeley et al.,2004). Individuals may give it more weight if certain information is readily available or easily recalled, leading to biased judgments. People rely heavily on the first information encountered (the anchor) when making decisions (Dale,2015). Subsequent adjustments are often insufficient, resulting in biased estimates. This anchoring effect can influence various choices, from negotiations to numerical judgments (Epley & Gilovich, 2006). Confirmation bias involves seeking, interpreting, and remembering information in a way that confirms pre-existing beliefs or hypotheses. People may unconsciously ignore or downplay evidence contradicting their views, reinforcing their initial biases (Adams-Quackenbush,2018). Individuals frequently overestimate their abilities, knowledge, or the accuracy of their judgments. This overconfidence bias can lead to unwarranted optimism, excessive risk-taking, and a reluctance to consider alternative viewpoints (Russell,2023). Cultural norms, societal expectations, and social influences contribute to forming biases. Individuals may unconsciously adopt certain biases due to the prevailing attitudes in their social environment (Suveren,2022).

C. Analogous Manifestations of Bias in AI Systems

Like cognitive biases in human decision-making, AI systems can exhibit analogous manifestations of bias, often stemming from the data they are trained on, the algorithms employed and the biases in the development process (Schwartz et al.,2022). Here are some analogous manifestations of bias in AI systems. AI systems learn from historical data; if the training data is biased, the system will likely replicate and amplify those biases (Ntoutsi et al.,2020). For example, A facial identification system that was primarily trained using information from a certain population may need help recognising underrepresented groups separately. The algorithms used in AI systems can introduce bias based on how they process and interpret data. Biased algorithms may unintentionally discriminate against certain groups or produce unfair outcomes (Varona & Suárez, 2022). Is particularly noticeable in applications such as criminal justice systems, loan choices, and employment procedures. If the training data lacks diversity or does not represent the real-world population, the AI system may be able to generalise to new, unseen examples (Christopher Rigano, 2018). The lack of transparency in some AI systems can make it difficult to understand how decisions are made. This opacity can contribute to biased outcomes, as it becomes challenging to rectify bias without into the system's decision-making process (von, 2021). How AI systems are deployed and integrated into real-world applications can introduce bias (Ntoutsi, 2020). Factors such as the selection of use cases, user interfaces, and the intended audience can influence the impact and fairness of AI technologies (Laato et al.,2022). Developers and data scientists may unintentionally introduce their biases into AI systems during the design and development stages. Their perspectives, values, and assumptions can shape the algorithms and contribute to biased outcomes (Laato et al.,2022).

III. CHALLENGES IN TRANSLATING FAIRNESS TO AI

Defining Fairness in the Context of AI Consciousness

Fairness in AI is a complicated and nuanced idea in both the academic and business worlds that has generated discussion. According to Barocas and Selbst (2016), fairness in AI systems is the lack of prejudice or discrimination. Still, Getting Fairness in AI may be difficult as it calls for rigorous analysis of the many biases these systems may introduce and how to counteract them. The literature has advocated collective, individual, and counterfactual fairness, among other forms (Zafar et al., 2017). Group justice guarantees that various groups receive comparable or equal treatment in AI systems. It is possible to further categorise into other sorts, including demographic parity, which guarantees that the favourable and unfavourable results are spread evenly among various demographic groupings. (Kamiran & Calders, 2012), An idea of inequality, unequal treatment, quantified in terms of misdiagnosis rates so (Zafar et al., 2017), or a comparable chance that guarantees the same rate of true positives (sensitivity) and a comparable rate of false positives (1-specificity) for different demographic categories (Hardt et al., 2016). On the other hand, individual fairness refers to making sure AI systems treat similar persons equally, regardless of whether they are a part of a group. It is accomplished using distance-based or similarity-based measurements designed to guarantee that the AI system treats people equally depending on their traits or qualities (Dwork et al., 2012). A relatively new idea called counterfactual fairness seeks to guarantee that AI systems are equitable even in fictitious situations. In particular, counterfactual fairness guarantees that, even if an individual's traits had changed, Regardless of whether they belonged to a group or not, a machine learning algorithm would have made the same decision for them (Kusner et al., 2017). Additional forms of justice include causal justice, which ensures the system does not reinforce past prejudices and inequities, and procedural justice, which ensures the decision-making process is transparent and fair (Kleinberg et al., 2018). It is crucial to remember that these many conceptions of justice do not conflict with one another and may, in fact, overlap.

Furthermore, in many settings, achieving fairness may require trade-offs between competing forms of justice (Barocas & Selbst, 2016). It is crucial to remember that achieving justice in AI requires careful analysis of the situation and parties involved; there is no one-size-fits-all approach. It is frequently necessary to have a sophisticated grasp of these many forms of justice and how to prioritise them in various situations to achieve justice in AI systems.

Fairness in the context of AI consciousness is a complex and multifaceted concept. Here are a few ways it might be interpreted. This could mean an AI should treat all individuals equally, without bias or discrimination. This is often a focus in machine learning, where we strive to create models that do not unfairly favour one group over another. In some contexts, fairness might mean that all groups are represented proportionally. For example, in a dataset used to train an AI, each group might need to be represented in proportion to its size in the population. This concept suggests that similar individuals should be treated similarly by the AI. If two individuals are alike in all relevant respects, the AI should treat them the same way. Some might argue that fairness in AI means ensuring that the outcomes produced by the AI are fair. This means that the benefits and burdens of AI are distributed fairly across society.

C. Algorithmic Challenges in Addressing Cognitive Bias

1. Explainability and Interpretability

In recent years, a detailed analysis of AI clearness has been conducted, including a range of factors such as explanation-generation techniques, explanation types, explanation scopes, types of models that AI can explain, and combinations of these and other approaches. The categories of explainability techniques are as follows: pre-model, in-model, and post-model techniques; additionally, there are built-in and post-hoc methods, which are based on whether explainability is achieved by using explanation techniques that analyse after training (post-doc) or by placing constraints on the AI model (intrinsic). Other explanation formats include global and local explain formats as well as model-specific and model-agnostic methods (Minh et al.,2022).

Interpretability is the capacity to comprehend how an AI model makes decisions. An interpretable model details the links between the inputs and the outputs and operates transparently. A human can provide a clear and understandable explanation for an interpretable algorithm. Therefore, interpretability is crucial to ensuring that people can comprehend and have faith in artificial intelligence models (Linardatos et al.,2020)

2. Algorithmic Transparency

Transparency in AI is the capacity to see inside an AI model and comprehend how it makes decisions. Classifying the kinds and frequency of mistakes and biases, understanding the model, training data, and communicating these concerns to developers and consumers are only a few of the numerous aspects of AI transparency (Felzmann et al.,2020).

3. Bias Detection and Mitigation Techniques

Finding and exposing biases that might be present in various contexts, such as data, algorithms, decision-making processes, and many more, is referred to as bias detection (Ntoutsi et al., 2020). Determining any possible prejudice, bias, distortion, or unfairness involves examining, analysing, and critically evaluating facts, information, or behaviours (Favaretto et al., 2019). In order to ensure fairness, objectivity, and equity in decision-making and outcomes, bias detection aims to increase awareness of such biases, comprehend their impact, and work towards them (minimising et al.,2019). Recently, many methods have been extensively employed to identify biases, including the BERT model, unsupervised learning, self-supervised learning, and several more. In order to train the model to lower bias metrics to threshold values, bias mitigation methods are designed for supervised learning (Sirotkin et al., 2022). Three stages of mitigation are possible: pre-processing before training, during training of the model, and post-processing of the model after training (Mehta, 2022). Several methods, including GAN, DNNs, SMOTE, and many more, have surfaced recently to address bias mitigation. We can lessen the possibility of bias by ensuring that the data gathered is representative of all groups. This might entail employing methods like data augmentation to produce a more balanced dataset or oversampling underrepresented groups. Several approaches exist for mitigating data bias (Ali et al., 2024). These consist of pre-processing techniques that alter the data before training, in-processing techniques that apply fairness constraints during training, and post-processing techniques that affect the model's predictions following training (Ali et al.,2024).

IV. ETHICAL IMPLICATIONS

Ethical Considerations for AI Researchers, Developers, and Policymakers

Artificial intelligence (AI), which has applications in a variety of industries like healthcare, banking, and transportation, is becoming a more and more important component of daily life. Lichtenthaler (2019) defines artificial intelligence (AI) as the process of creating computer systems that are capable of carrying out operations that normally call for human intellect, such as speech recognition, visual perception, language translation, and decision-making. The subject of computer science known as artificial intelligence (AI) is growing in popularity and has the potential to drastically change many facets of human existence. There are ethical issues that need to be addressed as our dependence on AI systems grows. To guarantee that AI systems are utilised for the benefit of society, ethical standards must direct their development and implementation.

As Challen et al. (2019) state, bias is one of the significant ethical issues surrounding AI. AI systems can be biased in many ways, including racial, gender, and cultural biases. For instance, AI algorithms used in hiring processes may exhibit gender bias, resulting in fewer women being hired for certain jobs. Similarly, facial recognition systems may exhibit racial biases, misidentifying individuals from certain racial groups. The ethical concerns around bias in AI are two-fold: First, the use of biassed AI systems may result in unjust treatment of individuals. Secondly, biassed AI systems may reinforce and magnify already-existing social prejudices and discrimination. For instance, it has been demonstrated that people with darker skin tones tend to make more mistakes when using facial recognition systems compared to those with lighter complexions (Krishnapriya et al., 2020).

As Jobin et al., (2019) state, privacy is another significant ethical consideration surrounding AI. Privacy issues in AI refer to concerns about collecting, storing, and using personal information in AI systems. AI systems can collect and analyze amounts of personal data, and if this data is not handled appropriately, it can lead to significant privacy concerns (Jobin et al., 2019). AI systems frequently gather enormous volumes of personal data from users, which is then used to form judgements about them. This raises questions regarding the methods utilised to gather, store, and use this data. Additionally, using AI in surveillance systems can infringe on individual privacy rights (Palaiogeorgou et al., 2021). One of the main privacy concerns related to AI is the potential for personal information to be used for unintended purposes. For example, personal information collected by an AI system for one purpose, such as targeted advertising, may be used for other purposes, such as identity theft. Additionally, AI systems may collect data on individuals without their knowledge or consent, which can lead to privacy violations.

Another privacy concern related to AI is the potential for data breaches (Murdoch, 2021). Insufficient protection of personal data may allow unauthorised persons to access it, potentially resulting in theft of identities and other fraudulent activities. This is particularly concerning given the sensitive nature of the data collected by many AI systems, such as health and financial information. The use of AI systems in surveillance also raises significant privacy concerns. According to Murdoch (2021), AI systems are increasingly being used for facial recognition and other forms of biometric identification, which can be used to track individuals and monitor their behaviour without their knowledge or consent. This can lead to significant violations of privacy and civil liberties. The use of AI systems raises substantial concerns about accountability. Accountability issues in AI refer to the responsibility and liability associated with the actions and decisions made by AI systems (Tóth et al., 2022). One of the main challenges related to accountability in AI is the lack of transparency in the decision-making process. AI systems often rely on complex algorithms and machine learning models that can be difficult to understand, even by the developers who created them.

Additionally, as AI systems become more autonomous, holding individuals or organisations accountable for their actions becomes increasingly challenging. AI systems are increasingly used to make decisions that significantly impact individuals and society, such as healthcare, finance, and law enforcement (Dwivedi et al., 2021). However, the complex and opaque nature of AI systems can make it difficult to identify who is responsible for the actions and decisions made by these systems. AI systems can have unforeseen impacts on individuals and society. If these impacts are negative, it can be difficult to identify who is responsible and to hold them accountable for the harm caused (Kim et al., 2020).

According to Bertino, Kundu, and Sura (2019), transparency is another critical ethical consideration in AI. Transparency in AI refers to the ability of an AI system to explain its decisions and actions. This is important because it allows people to understand why the system made a particular decision and to evaluate the fairness and reliability of the system. One of the biggest transparency issues in AI is the lack of transparency in the algorithms used to make decisions (Bertino et al., 2019). Many machine learning algorithms are intricate and challenging to comprehend, even for professionals in the industry. This may make determining how the system makes decisions difficult, leading to concerns about bias and discrimination.

Another transparency issue in AI is the need for more transparency in the training data the system (Schmidt et al., 2020). Machine learning algorithms rely on large amounts of data to learn how to make decisions. However, if the data is biased or complete, it can result in a biased and accurate AI system. If an AI system makes a decision that harms someone, it is important to determine who is responsible for that decision. However, in many cases, it cannot be easy to trace the decision-making process back to the individual or team that developed the system (Schmidt et al., 2020). AI systems can be complex and opaque, making understanding how they make decisions challenging. This raises concerns about fairness and accountability, as individuals may need help understanding the factors that influence the decisions made by AI systems.

V. FUTURE DIRECTIONS

The evolving landscape of AI and Data Science introduces various emerging technologies and unprecedented ethical challenges. This article delves into the ethical implications of advanced technologies and explores strategies for anticipating and mitigating future ethical challenges. The increasing complexity of advanced AI models, such as deep neural networks, creates difficulties for comprehending and elucidating their decision-making procedures, posing questions about transparency and accountability. Integrating AI into autonomous systems, like self-driving cars or automated decision-making systems, introduces ethical dilemmas related to responsibility, safety, and the potential for unintended consequences. Ethical concerns arise with using genetic and biometric data in AI applications, particularly in healthcare and personal personnel, necessitating careful considerations around privacy, consent, and potential discrimination.

Although these methods have limitations and difficulties, they have demonstrated encouraging outcomes in advancing justice in AI. A significant constraint is the possibility of making trade-offs between various forms of fairness. Individual fairness techniques may fail to tackle systemic biases that impact entire groups, while group fairness approaches might lead to the uneven assessment of people within a group (Barocas & Selbst, 2016). Furthermore, figuring out which forms of fairness to use in a particular situation and how to strike a balance between them can be challenging (Kleinberg et al., 2018). The issue of establishing what justice is in and of itself presents another obstacle. Fairness can mean different things to different individuals and groups, and these meanings might evolve (Dwork et al., 2018).

In addition, many existing methods for guaranteeing justice in AI depend on statistical models and presumptions that might not adequately represent the intricate nature of human behaviour and judgement. For instance, intersectionality or how several facets social class, sexual orientation, and race are examples of identification factors that interact and influence results might not be considered by group fairness measurements (Crenshaw, 1989). Ultimately, attempts to guarantee justice in AI may have unforeseen repercussions or detrimental effects, which raises worries. For instance, racial gaps in arrest rates may grow if efforts are made to reduce prejudice in predictive policing algorithms, according to some academics (Ferguson, 2012). Despite these difficulties, developing just and equal AI is a significant and active field of study. Future research must tackle these issues and develop fresh strategies that are cognizant of the subtleties of equality and justice in various circumstances.

VI. CONCLUSION

Ultimately, our work has shed light on the different origins of biases within machine learning (ML) and artificial intelligence (AI) systems and their significant effects on society, including a thorough examination of the growing issues related to generative AI bias. These sophisticated computational tools have the power to reinforce pre-existing prejudices, especially those about gender, racism, and other cultural factors, if they are not carefully constructed and inspected. We have looked at several biased AI systems, especially on the complexities of generative AI. This shows the importance of all-encompassing ways to detect and reduce biases throughout the AI development process. In order to address bias, this article emphasises factual fairness, robust data augmentation, and the need for representative, diversified datasets in addition to objective data-gathering techniques. We also talked about the moral consequences of AI for protecting privacy and the need for openness, supervision, and ongoing assessment of AI systems. Future research on fairness and prejudice in Changing training data and tackling the minor bias concerns in generative models—particularly in those that are used to produce synthetic data and content—should be the main goals of AI and ML. Developing thorough frameworks and policies for ethical AI and ML is essential. These should include open documentation of model selections, training data, and generating processes. According to Stathoulopoulos and Mateos-Garcia (2019), creating diverse teams for AI development and evaluation is essential. A diverse group can more effectively discover and adjust for biases. Establishing strong legal and ethical structures regulating AI and ML systems is crucial, as it guarantees that privacy, openness, and responsibility are not only optional aspects but also fundamental components of the AI creation procedure (Wachter et al., 2018). The implications of artificial intelligence (AI) that generates must also be investigated in research to make sure that, as we develop increasingly complex synthetic realities, we continue to be watchful and proactive in preventing the subtly creeping in of prejudices that have the potential to impact society negatively.

REFERENCES

Abatecola, G., Caputo, A., & Cristofaro, M. (2018). Reviewing cognitive distortions in managerial decision making: Toward an integrative co-evolutionary framework. *Journal of Management Development*, 37(5), 409–424. doi:10.1108/JMD-08-2017-0263

Abràmoff, M. D., Tarver, M. E., Loyo-Berrios, N., Trujillo, S., Char, D., Obermeyer, Z., Eydelman, M. B., & Maisel, W. H. (2023). Considerations for addressing bias in artificial intelligence for health equity. *NPJ Digital Medicine*, *6*(1), 170. doi:10.1038/s41746-023-00913-9 PMID:37700029

Adams-Quackenbush, N. M. (2018). Indicators of Confirmation Bias in the Investigative Interview with Suspects Thesis (Doctoral dissertation, The University of Portsmouth).

Algorithmic bias detection and mitigation: Best practices and policies to reduce consumer harms. (2023, June 27). Brookings. https://www.brookings.edu/articles/algorithmic-bias-detection-and-mitigation-best-practices-and-policies-to-reduce-consumer-harms/

Ali, M. S., Siddique, Z., & Ahsan, M. M. (2024). Enhancing and improving the performance of imbalanced class data using novel GBO and SSG: A comparative analysis. *Neural Networks*, 106157. PMID:38335796

Araujo, T., Helberger, N., Kruikemeier, S., & De Vreese, C. H. (2020). In AI we trust? Perceptions about automated decision-making by artificial intelligence. *AI & Society*, *35*(3), 611–623. doi:10.1007/s00146-019-00931-w

Baddeley, M. C., Curtis, A., & Wood, R. (2004). An introduction to prior information derived from probabilistic judgements: Elicitation of knowledge, cognitive bias and herding. *Special Publication - Geological Society of London*, *239*(1), 15–27. doi:10.1144/GSL.SP.2004.239.01.02

Barocas, S., & Selbst, A. D. (2016). Big data's disparate impact. *California Law Review*, 671–732.

Bertino, E., Kundu, A., & Sura, Z. (2019). Data transparency with blockchain and AI ethics. *ACM Journal of Data and Information Quality*, *11*(4), 1–8. doi:10.1145/3312750

Brackey, A. (2019). Analysis of Racial Bias in Northpointe's COMPAS Algorithm (Doctoral dissertation, Tulane University School of Science and Engineering).

Casad, B. J., & Luebering, J. E. (2024, January 5). Confirmation bias. Encyclopedia Britannica. https://www.britannica.com/science/confirmation-bias

Cath, C., Wachter, S., Mittelstadt, B., Taddeo, M., & Floridi, L. (2018). Artificial intelligence and the 'good society': The US, EU, and UK approach. *Science and Engineering Ethics*, *24*, 505–528. PMID:28353045

Challen, R., Denny, J., Pitt, M., Gompels, L., Edwards, T., & Tsaneva-Atanasova, K. (2019). Artificial intelligence, bias and clinical safety. *BMJ Quality & Safety*, *28*(3), 231–237. doi:10.1136/bmjqs-2018-008370 PMID:30636200

Crenshaw, R. P., & Vistnes, L. M. (1989). A decade of pressure sore research: 1977-1987. *Journal of Rehabilitation Research and Development*, *26*(1), 63–74. PMID:2645399

. Croskerry, P., Singhal, G., & Mamede, S. (2013). Cognitive debiasing 2: impediments to and strategies for change. BMJ quality & safety.

Dale, S. (2015). Heuristics and biases: The science of decision-making. *Business Information Review*, *32*(2), 93–99. doi:10.1177/0266382115592536

de Almeida, P. G. R., dos Santos, C. D., & Farias, J. S. (2021). Artificial intelligence regulation: A framework for governance. *Ethics and Information Technology*, *23*(3), 505–525. doi:10.1007/s10676-021-09593-z

Deacon, D., Pickering, M., Golding, P., & Murdock, G. (2021). *Researching communications: A practical guide to methods in media and cultural analysis.* Bloomsbury Publishing USA. doi:10.5040/9781501316951

Dwivedi, Y. K., Hughes, L., Ismagilova, E., Aarts, G., Coombs, C., Crick, T., Duan, Y., Dwivedi, R., Edwards, J., Eirug, A., Galanos, V., Ilavarasan, P. V., Janssen, M., Jones, P., Kar, A. K., Kizgin, H., Kronemann, B., Lal, B., Lucini, B., ... Williams, M. D. (2021). Artificial Intelligence (AI): Multidisciplinary perspectives on emerging challenges, opportunities, and agenda for research, practice and policy. *International Journal of Information Management*, *57*, 101994. doi:10.1016/j.ijinfomgt.2019.08.002

Dwivedi, Y. K., Ismagilova, E., Hughes, D. L., Carlson, J., Filieri, R., Jacobson, J., Jain, V., Karjaluoto, H., Kefi, H., Krishen, A. S., Kumar, V., Rahman, M. M., Raman, R., Rauschnabel, P. A., Rowley, J., Salo, J., Tran, G. A., & Wang, Y. (2021). Setting the future of digital and social media marketing research: Perspectives and research propositions. *International Journal of Information Management*, *59*, 102168. doi:10.1016/j.ijinfomgt.2020.102168

Dwork, C., Hardt, M., Pitassi, T., Reingold, O., & Zemel, R. (2012, January). Fairness through awareness. In *Proceedings of the 3rd innovations in theoretical computer science conference* (pp. 214-226). 10.1145/2090236.2090255

Dwork, C., & Ilvento, C. (2018). Fairness under composition. arXiv preprint arXiv:1806.06122.

Epley, N., & Gilovich, T. (2006). The anchoring-and-adjustment heuristic: Why the adjustments are insufficient. *Psychological Science*, *17*(4), 311–318. doi:10.1111/j.1467-9280.2006.01704.x PMID:16623688

Favaretto, M., De Clercq, E., & Elger, B. S. (2019). Big Data and discrimination: Perils, promises and solutions. A systematic review. *Journal of Big Data*, *6*(1), 1–27. doi:10.1186/s40537-019-0177-4

Felzmann, H., Fosch-Villaronga, E., Lutz, C., & Tamò-Larrieux, A. (2020). Towards transparency by design for artificial intelligence. *Science and Engineering Ethics*, *26*(6), 3333–3361. doi:10.1007/s11948-020-00276-4 PMID:33196975

Ferguson, R. (2012). Learning analytics: Drivers, developments and challenges. *International Journal of Technology Enhanced Learning*, *4*(5-6), 304–317. doi:10.1504/IJTEL.2012.051816

Gebru, T., Morgenstern, J., Vecchione, B., Vaughan, J. W., Wallach, H., Iii, H. D., & Crawford, K. (2021). Datasheets for datasets. *Communications of the ACM*, *64*(12), 86–92. doi:10.1145/3458723

Hardt, M., Price, E., & Srebro, N. (2016). Equality of opportunity in supervised learning. *Advances in Neural Information Processing Systems*, 29.

Hassija, V., Chamola, V., Mahapatra, A., Singal, A., Goel, D., Huang, K., Scardapane, S., Spinelli, I., Mahmud, M., & Hussain, A. (2024). Interpreting black-box models: A review on explainable artificial intelligence. *Cognitive Computation*, *16*(1), 45–74. doi:10.1007/s12559-023-10179-8

Hilbert, M. (2012). Toward a synthesis of cognitive biases: How noisy information processing can bias human decision making. *Psychological Bulletin*, *138*(2), 211–237. doi:10.1037/a0025940 PMID:22122235

Ho, C. W. L. (2022). Operationalizing "One Health" as "One Digital Health" through a global framework that emphasizes fair and equitable sharing of benefits from the use of artificial intelligence and related digital technologies. *Frontiers in Public Health*, *10*, 768977. doi:10.3389/fpubh.2022.768977 PMID:35592084

Implicit bias - StatPearls - NCBI bookshelf. (2023, March 4). National Center for Biotechnology Information. https://www.ncbi.nlm.nih.gov/books/NBK589697/

Jennifer. (2023, June 29). Bias and fairness in artificial intelligence. New York State Bar Association. https://nysba.org/bias-and-fairness-in-artificial-intelligence/

Jobin, A., Ienca, M., & Vayena, E. (2019). The global landscape of AI ethics guidelines. *Nature Machine Intelligence*, *1*(9), 389–399. doi:10.1038/s42256-019-0088-2

Kamiran, F., & Calders, T. (2012). Data preprocessing techniques for classification without discrimination. *Knowledge and Information Systems*, *33*(1), 1–33. doi:10.1007/s10115-011-0463-8

Kaur, D., Uslu, S., Rittichier, K. J., & Durresi, A. (2022). Trustworthy artificial intelligence: A review. *ACM Computing Surveys*, *55*(2), 1–38. doi:10.1145/3491209

Kim, B., Park, J., & Suh, J. (2020). Transparency and accountability in AI decision support: Explaining and visualizing convolutional neural networks for text information. *Decision Support Systems*, *134*, 113302. doi:10.1016/j.dss.2020.113302

Kleinberg, J., Lakkaraju, H., Leskovec, J., Ludwig, J., & Mullainathan, S. (2018). Human decisions and machine predictions. *The Quarterly Journal of Economics*, *133*(1), 237–293. PMID:29755141

Kleinberg, J., Ludwig, J., Mullainathan, S., & Rambachan, A. (2018, May). Algorithmic fairness. In Aea papers and proceedings (Vol. 108, pp. 22-27). American Economic Association. doi:10.1257/pandp.20181018

Köchling, A., & Wehner, M. C. (2020). Discriminated by an algorithm: A systematic review of discrimination and fairness by algorithmic decision-making in the context of HR recruitment and HR development. *Business Research*, *13*(3), 795–848. doi:10.1007/s40685-020-00134-w

Krishnapriya, K. S., Albiero, V., Vangara, K., King, M. C., & Bowyer, K. W. (2020). Issues related to face recognition accuracy varying based on race and skin tone. *IEEE Transactions on Technology and Society*, *1*(1), 8–20. doi:10.1109/TTS.2020.2974996

Kundi, B., El Morr, C., Gorman, R., & Dua, E. (2023). Artificial Intelligence and Bias: A scoping review. *AI & Society*, 199–215.

Kusner, M. J., Loftus, J., Russell, C., & Silva, R. (2017). Counterfactual fairness. *Advances in Neural Information Processing Systems*, 30.

Laato, S., Tiainen, M., Najmul Islam, A. K. M., & Mäntymäki, M. (2022). How to explain AI systems to end users: A systematic literature review and research agenda. *Internet Research*, *32*(7), 1–31. doi:10.1108/INTR-08-2021-0600

Langdon, R., & Coltheart, M. (2000). The cognitive neuropsychology of delusions. *Mind & Language*, *15*(1), 184–218. doi:10.1111/1468-0017.00129

Lee, N. T., Resnick, P., & Barton, G. (2019). *Algorithmic bias detection and mitigation: Best practices and policies to reduce consumer harms*. Brookings Institute.

Lembcke, T. B., Engelbrecht, N., Brendel, A. B., & Kolbe, L. M. (2019, June). To Nudge or not to Nudge: Ethical Considerations of Digital nudging based on its Behavioral Economics roots. ECIS.

Lichtenthaler, U. (2019). An intelligence-based view of firm performance: Profiting from artificial intelligence. *Journal of Innovation Management*, *7*(1), 7–20. doi:10.24840/2183-0606_007.001_0002

Linardatos, P., Papastefanopoulos, V., & Kotsiantis, S. (2020). Explainable ai: A review of machine learning interpretability methods. *Entropy (Basel, Switzerland)*, *23*(1), 18. doi:10.3390/e23010018 PMID:33375658

Mehta, S. (2022). A guide to different bias mitigation techniques in machine learning. Analytics India Magazine. https://analyticsindiamag.com/a-guide-to-different-bias-mitigation-techniques-in-machine-learning/

Minh, D., Wang, H. X., Li, Y. F., & Nguyen, T. N. (2022). Explainable artificial intelligence: A comprehensive review. *Artificial Intelligence Review*, 1–66.

Nagireddi, J. N., Vyas, A. K., Sanapati, M. R., Soin, A., & Manchikanti, L. (2022). The analysis of pain research through the lens of artificial intelligence and machine learning. *Pain Physician*, *25*(2), E211. PMID:35322975

Najibi, A. (2020). Racial discrimination in face recognition technology. *Science News*, 24.

Nikolopoulou, K. (2023, March 6). *The availability heuristic | Example & definition.* Scribbr. https://www.scribbr.com/research-bias/availability-heuristic/

Ntoutsi, E., Fafalios, P., Gadiraju, U., Iosifidis, V., Nejdl, W., Vidal, M. E., Ruggieri, S., Turini, F., Papadopoulos, S., Krasanakis, E., Kompatsiaris, I., Kinder-Kurlanda, K., Wagner, C., Karimi, F., Fernandez, M., Alani, H., Berendt, B., Kruegel, T., Heinze, C., ... Staab, S. (2020). Bias in data-driven artificial intelligence systems—An introductory survey. *Wiley Interdisciplinary Reviews. Data Mining and Knowledge Discovery*, *10*(3), e1356. doi:10.1002/widm.1356

Omrani, N., Rivieccio, G., Fiore, U., Schiavone, F., & Agreda, S. G. (2022). To trust or not to trust? An assessment of trust in AI-based systems: Concerns, ethics and contexts. *Technological Forecasting and Social Change*, *181*, 121763. doi:10.1016/j.techfore.2022.121763

Osoba, O. A., Welser, I. V. W., & Welser, W. (2017). *An intelligence in our image: The risks of bias and errors in artificial intelligence.* Rand Corporation.

Palaiogeorgou, P., Gizelis, C. A., Misargopoulos, A., Nikolopoulos-Gkamatsis, F., Kefalogiannis, M., & Christonasis, A. M. (2021, August). AI: Opportunities and challenges-The optimal exploitation of (telecom) corporate data. In Conference on e-Business, e-Services and e-Society (pp. 47-59). Cham: Springer International Publishing.

Pawłowska, J., Rydzewska, K., & Wierzbicki, A. (2023). Using cognitive models to understand and counteract the effect of self-induced bias on recommendation algorithms. *Journal of Artificial Intelligence and Soft Computing Research, 13*(2), 73–94. doi:10.2478/jaiscr-2023-0008

Pierce, R., Sterckx, S., & Van Biesen, W. (2022). A riddle, wrapped in a mystery, inside an enigma: How semantic black boxes and opaque artificial intelligence confuse medical decision-making. *Bioethics, 36*(2), 113–120. doi:10.1111/bioe.12924 PMID:34374441

Russill, C. L. (2023). Oblivious and uninformed: the role of overconfidence in personal health decision-making (Doctoral dissertation, Faculty of Arts, University of Regina).

Scatiggio, V. (2022). Tackling the issue of bias in artificial intelligence to design AI-driven fair and inclusive service systems. *How human biases are breaching into AI algorithms, with severe impacts on individuals and societies, and what designers can do to face this phenomenon and change for the better.*

Schmidt, P., Biessmann, F., & Teubner, T. (2020). Transparency and trust in artificial intelligence systems. *Journal of Decision Systems, 29*(4), 260–278. doi:10.1080/1 2460125.2020.1819094

Schwartz, R., Vassilev, A., Greene, K., Perine, L., Burt, A., & Hall, P. (2022). Towards a standard for identifying and managing bias in artificial intelligence. NIST special publication, 1270(10.6028).

Schwemmer, C., Knight, C., Bello-Pardo, E. D., Oklobdzija, S., Schoonvelde, M., & Lockhart, J. W. (2020). Diagnosing gender bias in image recognition systems. *Socius: Sociological Research for a Dynamic World, 6*, 2378023120967171. doi:10.1177/2378023120967171 PMID:35936509

Sirotkin, K., Carballeira, P., & Escudero-Viñolo, M. (2022). A study on the distribution of social biases in self-supervised learning visual models. In *Proceedings of the IEEE/CVF Conference on Computer Vision and Pattern Recognition* (pp. 10442-10451). 10.1109/CVPR52688.2022.01019

StathoulopoulosK.Mateos-GarciaJ. C. (2019). Gender diversity in AI research. Available at SSRN 3428240.

Suveren, Y. (2022). Unconscious Bias: Definition and Significance. *Psikiyatride Güncel Yaklasimlar*, *14*(3), 414–426. doi:10.18863/pgy.1026607

Timmons, A. C., Duong, J. B., Simo Fiallo, N., Lee, T., Vo, H. P. Q., Ahle, M. W., Comer, J. S., Brewer, L. P. C., Frazier, S. L., & Chaspari, T. (2023). A call to action on assessing and mitigating bias in artificial intelligence applications for mental health. *Perspectives on Psychological Science*, *18*(5), 1062–1096. doi:10.1177/17456916221134490 PMID:36490369

Tóth, Z., Caruana, R., Gruber, T., & Loebbecke, C. (2022). The dawn of the AI robots: Towards a new framework of AI robot accountability. *Journal of Business Ethics*, *178*(4), 895–916. doi:10.1007/s10551-022-05050-z

Treviño, L. K., Weaver, G. R., Gibson, D. G., & Toffler, B. L. (1999). Managing ethics and legal compliance: What works and what hurts. *California Management Review*, *41*(2), 131–151. doi:10.2307/41165990

Using artificial intelligence to address criminal justice needs. (2018, October 8). National Institute of Justice. https://nij.ojp.gov/topics/articles/using-artificial-intelligence-address-criminal-justice-needs

Van Ryn, M., Burgess, D. J., Dovidio, J. F., Phelan, S. M., Saha, S., Malat, J., Griffin, J. M., Fu, S. S., & Perry, S. (2011). The impact of racism on clinician cognition, behavior, and clinical decision making. *Du Bois Review*, *8*(1), 199–218. doi:10.1017/S1742058X11000191 PMID:24761152

Varona, D., & Suárez, J. L. (2022). Discrimination, bias, fairness, and trustworthy AI. *Applied Sciences (Basel, Switzerland)*, *12*(12), 5826. doi:10.3390/app12125826

Venter, Z. S., Gundersen, V., Scott, S. L., & Barton, D. N. (2023). Bias and precision of crowdsourced recreational activity data from Strava. *Landscape and Urban Planning*, *232*, 104686. doi:10.1016/j.landurbplan.2023.104686

von Eschenbach, W. J. (2021). Transparency and the black box problem: Why we do not trust AI. *Philosophy & Technology*, *34*(4), 1607–1622. doi:10.1007/s13347-021-00477-0

What do we do about the biases in AI? (2019, October 25). Harvard Business Review. https://hbr.org/2019/10/what-do-we-do-about-the-biases-in-ai

Whittaker, M., Crawford, K., Dobbe, R., Fried, G., Kaziunas, E., Mathur, V., & Schwartz, O. (2018). *AI now report 2018*. AI Now Institute at New York University.

Zafar, M. B., Valera, I., Rogriguez, M. G., & Gummadi, K. P. (2017, April). Fairness constraints: Mechanisms for fair classification. In *Artificial intelligence and statistics* (pp. 962–970). PMLR.

Zou, L., & Khern-am-nuai, W. (2023). AI and housing discrimination: The case of mortgage applications. *AI and Ethics*, *3*(4), 1271–1281. doi:10.1007/s43681-022-00234-9

Chapter 6
Cognitive Processes in the Digital Realm:
How Close Are We to Replication?

Niveditha M.
https://orcid.org/0000-0001-5228-973X
Vellore Institute of Technology, India

Prabir Chandrapadhy
https://orcid.org/0000-0002-6856-0958
Vellore Institute of Technology, India

ABSTRACT

Cognitive processes, including reasoning, doubt, and thought, are mental operations used by the brain to comprehend, acquire, retain, and resolve issues. The digital realm transforms human cognition, affecting memory, metacognition, and other cognitive processes. The digital revolution allows for data analysis, environmental monitoring, and predictive reasoning but also presents challenges in reading, writing, remembering, and forgetting. Virtualizing social spaces and using digital media as memory technology further contributes to this transformation. Cognitive science theories like connectionism, functionalism, and the concept of a homunculus help understand these processes. Replicating complex cognitive functions in the digital realm remains a challenge.

DOI: 10.4018/979-8-3693-2015-0.ch006

I. INTRODUCTION

Cognitive Process: The Engine of Your Mind

The cognitive process was defined as the capacity for reasoning, doubt, and thought, highlighting the distinction between the mind and body and interior mental processes (René Descartes., 1637). Simply put, they are the mental operations or thought processes that our brains employ to comprehend, acquire new information, retain it, and resolve issues. These processes include the following: focusing, recalling details, making judgements, figuring out puzzles, and comprehending language. In essence, cognitive processes are the ways in which our minds interpret and analyse the environment we live in. Ancient Greece was a rich intellectual environment where the seeds of Western epistemology were planted. Plato (380 BCE) and Aristotle (350 BCE) are two of the earliest contributors who stand out for having had a significant influence on how we view the acquisition and verification of knowledge. Even though they both stressed the value of reason, their methods differed greatly, which opened the door for ongoing discussions in the field of epistemology.

Cognitive processes in the realm of digital technology are currently under extensive investigation. The examination of the influence of digital transformation on socio-economic processes in the midst of the COVID-19 pandemic is underway, revealing a shift in business procedures towards advanced technologies and cognitive systems (Minakov., et al., 2022). Furthermore, research has concentrated on the ramifications of digital device usage on cognitive processes in young individuals, demonstrating that a moderate utilization of digital technologies can be advantageous for the cognitive development of elementary school students (Soldatova., et al., 2018). In the realm of music education, the cognitive processes engaged in students' interaction with digital audio workstations have been scrutinized, offering valuable insights for music instructors in the development of electronic composition curricula (Duncan, 2021). Additionally, there exists a necessity for the methodical capture and examination of processes in the digital domain, prompting the development of collaborative platforms that facilitate the capture, discussion, and sharing of information while adhering to the principles of Linked Data (Ball., 1990).

The digital realm is having a profound impact on cognitive processes in human consciousness. The integration of cognitive resources with digital technologies is causing a transformation in the nature and capacity of human cognition (Mikkilineni., 2022). Our lives are now pervaded by the digital environment, resulting in changes to memory, metacognition, and other cognitive processes (Sandu., 2019). The digital revolution allows for the analysis of data, the monitoring of environmental systems, and the use of predictive reasoning (Tagliagambe., 2023). However, this digitalization process also presents challenges in reading, writing, remembering, and forgetting, leading to a crisis in cognitive processes and the emergence of a new form of memory (Hamilton., et al., 2023). The virtualization of social space and the utilization of digital media as memory technology further contribute to transforming cognitive processes (Silvestri., 2019). Robert., et al. (2007) explore computational intelligence's potential to understand sensory perception and cognitive functions in living and artificial systems. It proposes a hierarchical K model-based approach, pattern-based processing, and situated intelligence. These concepts can be applied in embodied intelligence and robotics, allowing machines to interact meaningfully with the world. The paper calls for embracing computational intelligence to deepen our understanding of perception, cognition, and intelligence. The digital realm has positive and negative effects on cognitive processes, influencing how we perceive, remember, and interact with information and the world around us.

Brief Overview of Cognitive Processes in Human Consciousness

Consciousness arises from the collaborative dance of the conscious and unconscious minds, operating within an expansive timeframe of subjective experience. This dance imbues the conscious self with the ability to effortlessly navigate the past, present, and future, integrating them into a holistic understanding within its broader awareness. These cognitive journeys, fueled by moments of pleasure, leave lasting synaptic traces in the unconscious mind. This dynamic interaction ultimately bridges the gap between our innate instincts and the culturally informed values expressed by the conscious self, leading to a coherent sense of being (Detmar, C. F., 2023). Consciousness generates personalized meaning through self, attention, and working memory. The self creates a dynamic representation of our body, environment, and relationships, while attention directs focus and working memory integrates details for meaningful experiences (Marchetti, G., 2018). The emergence of consciousness, encompassing its subjective identity and vital nature, arises from the intricate interplay of physical and physiological systems. This complex phenomenon exhibits hierarchical levels, opening the door to mathematical modelling that can illuminate its underlying mechanisms. Furthermore, attention, a critical facet of consciousness, benefits from formalized models that offer insights into its cognitive processes (Wang, Y., 2012: Wang, Y., & Wang, Y., 2008, August). Within the realm of cognitive science, several theoretical frameworks attempt to illuminate the intricacies of mental processes. Connectionism and functionalism represent prominent approaches, offering distinct yet complementary perspectives. Notably, the concept of a homunculus, a hypothetical inner observer, also features in some theories of consciousness, albeit with its own set of complexities and limitations (Gardelle & Kouider., 2009).

The Challenge of Replicating Complex Cognitive Functions in the Digital Realm

While replicating the intricate tapestry of human cognitive functions within the digital realm remains a formidable challenge, progress in computational cognitive psychology offers valuable insights. These advancements not only enhance our understanding of human-information interaction but also inform the engineering of increasingly sophisticated interactive systems (Peter Pirolli, 2020). Integrating cognitive functionalities into artificial systems, particularly question-answering systems, strives to achieve human-like performance. This pursuit seeks to unlock deeper levels of understanding and interaction within human-machine interfaces (Chandiok, A., & Chaturvedi, D. K., 2018). As digital twins evolve in complexity and scope, supporting diverse system development activities, the imperative to manage consistency, change, and traceability across their lifecycles intensifies. This challenge necessitates the development of robust methodologies and frameworks to ensure the accuracy, integrity, and effective utilization of these increasingly sophisticated virtual representations (Lu et al., 2021). The intricate landscape of digital platforms, characterized by a multitude of interacting entities and relationships, presents significant cognitive challenges for peer consumers, often resulting in mis-calibrated trust assessments (Möhlmann et al., 2019). Such miscalibrated trust assessments can cascade into far-reaching social and political implications, underscoring the critical need for deeper exploration and understanding of trust dynamics within complex digital platforms (Noriega et al., 2014).

Significance of Understanding the Limitations and Possibilities of Replication

Understanding the constraints and potential of replication bears considerable importance in the realm of scientific investigation. The act of replication enables the enduring examination and contemplation of findings, a process that proves pivotal in the rectification and validation of research (Olbrich, et al., 2017). It aids in the evaluation of the dependability of published discoveries and the enhancement of assurance in the generalization of cross-stimulus (Monin et. al., 2014). Replication also allows for the determination of circumstances in which model mechanisms are inadequate in explaining observed phenomena, resulting in more robust and generalizable insights (Thiele, et al., 2015). Moreover, replication assists in evaluating and isolating the origins of variation, thereby minimizing the impact of measurement error and enhancing the efficiency of statistical testing (Blainey, et al., 2014). Nevertheless, it is crucial to acknowledge that the significance and feasibility of replication may differ across various disciplines, owing to distinctions in the epistemic content and accountability infrastructures (Penders, et. al., 2019).

II. MAPPING HUMAN COGNITIVE PROCESSES

Overview of Key Cognitive Processes in Human Consciousness

The human mind is a vast and intricate landscape, woven together by a multitude of interacting cognitive processes. These processes, acting as the individual instruments within an orchestra, play their unique roles in composing the symphony of consciousness. Perception, introspection, reasoning, creativity, imagination, memory, idea formulation, belief, volition, and emotion – these are just some of the key players in this grand performance (Wang, Y., & Wang, Y., 2008).

1. Perception and Sensation

Perception and sensation are intricately interconnected cognitive procedures that mold our comprehension of the universe. Sensory inputs stemming from diverse modalities, encompassing visual, auditory, and olfactory senses, furnish the data that propels our cognitive undertakings (Magosso, et al., 2023). Cognizant states including emotions, expectancies, and attention are impacted by sensory inputs as well as by the latter (Coren, et. al., 2004). Perception encompasses the dynamic identification of connections among distinct components or attributes of an entity or occurrence, necessitating the intricate neurofunctional framework (Freundschuh, S. M., 2009). The process of map perception and cognition entails utilizing the senses to gather spatial information from maps, along with mental functions that enable the amalgamation of spatial knowledge through reasoning, intuition, and perception (Hamlyn, D. W. (2022).

2. Memory Formation and Recall

In the realm of human cognition, the pivotal cognitive processes of memory formation and recall assume significance. Numerous models and mechanisms have been put forth by researchers to comprehend these cognitive functions. According to Pfaltz (2017), a plausible approach involves modelling long-term memory consolidation and memory recall through computable functions that map networks into networks. Shrivastava et al. (2020) propose a model that mimics the human memory process for decision-making, incorporating episodic, semantic, and procedural memory along with an energy-based inference mechanism. Amin and Malik (2013) have out a thorough analysis of human memory functions, focusing on the mechanisms of encoding, retention, and recall with the use of fMRI and EEG neuroimaging methods. Their research sheds important light on the brain mechanisms underlying memory creation and retrieval. Kokinov and Petkov (2009) propose a groundbreaking model of memory recall that challenges traditional views. They argue that memories are not static recordings but rather dynamically constructed through structural mapping and analogical transfer. This model departs from previous approaches by embracing the inherent subjectivity and flexibility of human memory, explaining both its accuracy and susceptibility to memory illusions.

3. Reasoning and Problem-Solving

Reasoning and problem-solving constitute complex cognitive activities within the human repertoire, demanding both conceptual understanding and sophisticated reasoning skills. These processes necessitate the ability to analyze information, draw inferences, evaluate outcomes, and ultimately navigate towards solutions. While fundamental cognitive functions like perception and memory provide the building blocks, reasoning and problem-solving elevate these capabilities by engaging in abstract thought, mental manipulation of information, and strategic decision-making (Agustina, Y. (2021). The pursuit of understanding problem-solving has captivated both Artificial Intelligence (AI) researchers and psychologists, leading to complementary approaches. AI researchers have long investigated computational methods for solving well-defined problems, often by developing algorithms that learn from vast datasets and optimize solutions (Pizlo, Z. 2022). Automated testing tools frequently generate test cases that deviate from those produced by human testers, resulting in less efficient tools. In order to tackle this issue, a framework grounded in cognitive science has been suggested to ascertain the cognitive mechanisms employed by testers and gain a deeper comprehension of how proficient human testers carry out their assignments (Enoiu et al., 2021; McGee, S., 2019). The integration of executive functions, including selective attention and working memory, assumes a pivotal position in the process of problem-solving, yet the precise correlation between these cognitive processes and problem-solving aptitudes throughout the course of development remains incompletely comprehended (Enoiu et al., 2021)

4. Emotional Intelligence

Emotional intelligence (EI), encompassing the ability to perceive, interpret, and manage emotions in oneself and others, plays a significant role in various aspects of human endeavour. Its impact extends beyond emotional awareness, influencing cognitive processes and personal effectiveness. This paper explores how EI impacts performance, self-regulation, social skills, and, ultimately, clinical performance and reasoning (Torre, D., & Daley, B. (2023)). Emotional intelligence (EI) rests on the foundation that emotions carry valuable information and are subjectively interpreted. Deficits in EI can hinder educators' ability to understand learners' emotions and regulate their own in both clinical and educational contexts. This raises crucial questions about the interplay between emotions and cognition and how neuroscience can shed light on these complexities. Cognitive neuroscience research into EI delves into the role of emotions in shaping reasoning and decision-making. Notably, the prefrontal cortex (PFC), responsible for high-level cognitive functions like reasoning and decision-making, displays intricate connections with the amygdala and limbic system, key areas for emotional memory storage and processing. These connections suggest a bidirectional influence, where emotions impact cognitive processes and vice versa. This understanding is critical for educators and professionals in clinical settings (Samsonovich, 2013).

Neural Underpinnings of Cognitive Processes in the Human Brain

Recent neuroimaging studies have shed light on the brain regions involved in processing counterintuitive concepts in science and mathematics. These investigations reveal activation of the prefrontal and parietal cortex, suggesting the crucial role of inhibitory control processes in overcoming intuitive misconceptions and facilitating accurate reasoning (Dumontheil, et al., 2022). Further evidence supporting the embodied simulation theory from research highlighting a shared neural basis for different social-cognitive processes. This implies that our ability to understand others' experiences might not solely rely on intellectual deduction but rather on replicating their experiences within our own bodies and minds (Schmidt, et al., 2021). The delineation of the human cerebral cortex has undergone a redefinition, expanding the number of identified regions from 52 to 360. This revision serves to emphasize the intricate nature of the neurobiological foundations that underlie higher-order cognitive processes (Hoffmann, M., & Hoffmann, M., 2020). Leveraging the intricate connections of the brain, researchers have proposed a connectome-based graph neural network (GNN) capable of integrating diverse brain activity patterns and decoding cognitive states with impressive accuracy. This approach signifies a potential breakthrough in understanding the brain's functioning and unlocking deeper insights into cognitive processes (Zhang, et al., 2021). The comprehension of the neurobiology pertaining to social processes holds significance in relation to psychiatric and neurological disorders, along with social limitations and challenges encountered in social interactions (Fitzgibbon, et al., 2014).

Challenges in Translating These Processes to Digital Counterparts

Challenges encountered when converting traditional procedures into their digital counterparts encompass intricacies in communication and data aggregation, insufficiency of data accessibility for training machine learning models, limited computational capabilities for high precision digital replicas, the necessity for interdisciplinary collaboration, and the absence of standardized development methodologies and validation measures (Mihai, et al., 2022). In the realm of manufacturing systems, engineers confront obstacles such as interdisciplinary collaboration, escalating intricacy, and time constraints, which can result in inefficient and error-prone design processes (Seitz, M., & Vogel-Heuser, B., 2020). The sluggish and manual approaches to strain and bioprocess development impede the translation of laboratory findings to industrial procedures within the bioprocessing industry. Digitalization, machine learning, and artificial intelligence present novel avenues for addressing these challenges, although regulatory considerations must be taken into account (Scheper., et al., 2021). Higher education institutions and public universities also encounter difficulties in implementing digital transformation, including altering procedures and work culture, as well as integrating digital technology (Coral & Bernuy., 2022). In the business sector, challenges encountered during the digitalization process comprise the inability to adopt change management techniques swiftly, inadequacy in strategic approach, and incapability to simplify technological complexity (Limani., et al., 2022).

III. STATE OF THE ART IN DIGITAL REPLICATION

Advances in Artificial Neural Networks and Deep Learning

Advancements in the realm of artificial neural networks and deep learning have brought about a significant transformation in the domain of artificial intelligence (AI) by equipping computers with the ability to acquire knowledge and make decisions akin to human beings. Deep learning, a subset of machine learning, employs neural networks comprising multiple layers to extract intricate patterns and features from intricate datasets, resulting in noteworthy accomplishments in the areas of image and speech recognition, natural language processing, and autonomous systems (Khan., 2023; Yamana. 2023). Deep learning has found practical applications across diverse industries, encompassing computer vision, healthcare, and technology, and holds the potential to tackle intricate predicaments that were hitherto deemed insurmountable (Huang, et al., 2023; Yushu, Yang. 2023). Nevertheless, deep learning also poses challenges, such as the requirement of copious amounts of data, substantial computational resources, and a dearth of interpretability (Evelina, Liljeberg, 2023). Despite these challenges, the potential of deep learning and neural networks is immense, and they are poised to shape the future of technology persistently.

Simulation of Cognitive Processes in Machine Learning Models

Simulation of cognitive processes in machine learning models is a highly effective approach for the training of artificial intelligence (AI) systems. The training process becomes more efficient and cost-effective by substituting human interaction and feedback with cognitive models (Nobandegani., 2022). This particular methodology enables reinforcement learning agents to acquire knowledge about fairness by engaging with cognitive models of specific tasks, such as the Ultimatum Game, and adjusting their behaviour according to the simulated responder's emotional state (Bingxuan., et al., 2019). Moreover, extended Markov decision processes (MDP) can assist in analyzing and computing optimal policy sequences in cognitive interaction processes, such as pilot-cockpit scenarios (Plewczynski, D., 2011). Additionally, agent-based modeling (ABM) can be employed to create cognitive agents that implement machine learning algorithms for categorization processes, leading to the development of an independent cognitive system capable of constructing a classification system for perceptual information (Zhongzhi Shi., 2019).

Successes and Limitations in Replicating
Specific Cognitive Functions

Replication of specific cognitive functions has demonstrated both achievements and constraints. A particular investigation effectively reproduced a biologically plausible model of acquiring and reenacting spatiotemporal sequences in the neocortex (Jette, et al., 2022). Another study uncovered that psychometric tasks utilized to derive cognitive performance measures exhibited a high level of repeatability, thereby indicating stable cognitive phenotypes (Benjamin., et al., 2022). Nevertheless, there are also limitations in the reproduction of cognitive functions. An examination highlighted the difficulty in establishing a connection between cognitive concepts and artificial neural networks, thereby suggesting that models employing simple artificial neural networks may possess limited explanatory value for higher cognitive functions (Peter, R., Krebs., 2005). Moreover, an inquiry into motor sequence learning found disparities in cognitive processing between a go/nogo discrete sequence production (DSP) task and the original DSP task, thereby emphasizing the necessity for further exploration into error-related cognitive processes (H.W., Althof., 2021). Overall, while there have been achievements in replicating certain cognitive functions, comprehending and replicating intricate cognitive processes still present challenges and limitations.

IV. PERCEPTION AND SENSATION IN THE DIGITAL REALM

The examination of perception and sensation in the realm of digital technology has been extensively examined in numerous scholarly articles. The notion of perceptual correlation, which encompasses the dynamic interplay between the entirety and its constituent elements, has been employed to analyze digital environments (Floriana, Ferro., 2022). The analysis of sensation, perception, and proprioception in the context of digital and mobile culture, specifically in digital games, has been conducted to emphasize the decentralized nature of the embodied "sensation" during the experience of gameplay (Seth & Giddings., 2017). Sensation knowledge has been constructed to understand human perceptual experiences in natural language expressions, particularly in social media, through deep learning and lexicon-based methods (Jun Lee., et al., 2018).

Mimicking Sensory Experiences Through Technology

Paradigms of recent research have centered around the replication of sensory experiences through the utilization of technology. Endeavors have been undertaken to fabricate responsive apparatuses capable of independently modifying their electrical characteristics in response to stimuli from the surrounding environment, thus enabling adaptability in diverse circumstances (Valle, G., et al., 2023). These devices aim to mimic the sensory adaptation observed in biological systems, such as tactile and visual adaptive systems (Zihan, He., et al., 2022). Novel materials, functional interfaces, and device geometries have been explored to achieve this goal (Sharafat, Hussain., 2021). Additionally, biomimetic neurostimulation frameworks inspired by nature have been designed to convert sensory information into neural stimulation patterns, enabling intuitive and natural sensations (Tonin., et al., 2022). These biomimetic neurostimulations have shown promising results in terms of higher mobility and decreased mental effort compared to traditional approaches. Overall, the development of technology that can mimic sensory experiences holds the potential for the creation of novel assistive neurotechnologies and enhanced multisensory experiences in various domains.

Challenges in Achieving a Holistic and Nuanced Digital Perception

Achieving a comprehensive and detailed digital understanding encounters obstacles such as altering organizational structures, value chains, and customer expectations (Imhof., et al., 2022). Companies, particularly small and medium-sized enterprises (SMEs), encounter difficulties in embracing the digital transformation and face challenges in implementing digital technologies (Erfurth, C., 2019). Difficulties in perception can impact the brain's capacity to comprehend information (Hibberd, J., et al., 2010). In electronic learning, inquiries arise regarding the compromises involved in transitioning from traditional classroom-based learning to e-learning, encompassing concerns about the quality and efficacy (Uppal., 2017). Assessing the fairness and effectiveness of digital assessments in education necessitates the examination of diverse variables and demographic disparities (Storer., 2017). These challenges emphasize the necessity for a comprehensive comprehension of digital leadership, the significance of considering underlying factors in pedagogical evaluations, and the requirement for a nuanced approach to digital perception.

Ethical Considerations in Creating Artificial Sensory Experiences

Ethical considerations associated with the creation of artificial sensory experiences necessitate addressing the personal and societal implications of the technology, ensuring its ethical utilization, and confronting distinct challenges related to fairness. The utilization of virtual reality (VR) for educational and training purposes demands careful scrutiny due to the potential for physical and psychological harm, thereby requiring a thorough examination of its ethical implications and the formulation of guidelines for its ethical application (Bennett., 2021). The development of an ethical artificial intelligence (AI) entails surmounting the obstacle of humans' inconsistent consensus on ethics and the limitations inherent in contemporary AI methodologies. An ethical AI should possess the ability to deduce implicit rules, comprehend subtlety and context, and provide explanations for its actions and intentions. Furthermore, it should take into consideration the prevailing notion of ethics and exhibit adaptable intentions. Symbolic representation and perceptual symbols assume a role in the acquisition of knowledge and deduction of intentions, enabling the AI to empathize with the experiences of others (Bennett., 2021; Findlater., 2020). Additionally, AI systems that enhance sensory capabilities pose distinct fairness challenges pertaining to accessibility, ethical decision-making, and privacy concerns.

Memory and Recall in Artificial Systems

Artificial systems, such as neural networks, have the potential to derive advantages from incorporating memory and recall mechanisms to facilitate continual learning and complex reasoning. These mechanisms enable the systems to progressively accumulate knowledge over time and retrieve it as required. Numerous strategies have been put forth in order to establish long-term memory in artificial systems. One such strategy involves the implementation of a recall-gated consolidation mechanism that assigns priority to the storage of reliable signals, thereby safeguarding long-term memory against spurious alterations (Lindsey., et al., 2022).

Memory Architectures in Digital Systems

The role of memory architectures in digital systems is of utmost importance as they enable the ability to continually learn, engage in complex reasoning, and acquire knowledge of sequential and temporal dependencies. The main challenge lies in developing long-term memory mechanisms that can adapt and update themselves over time. One proposed architecture, Recall, focuses on creating long-term memory that is adaptable and updatable for AGI systems, leading to an enhanced understanding of temporal aspects (Kynoch., et al., 2023). Another model, recall-gated consolidation, prioritizes storing synaptic changes consistent with previous updates made to the short-term memory system. This approach safeguards long-term memory from spurious changes and enhances memory storage, especially in noisy environments (Kynoch., et al., 2023). Furthermore, a framework called MeRec utilizes a memory module and replay strategy to recall and recover knowledge from past tasks. This framework has achieved remarkable performance in continual learning with deep neural networks (Lindsey, J., & Litwin-Kumar, A., 2022)

Strategies for Enhancing Memory Recall in AI Models

Strategies for enhancing the retrieval of stored information in artificial intelligence (AI) models involve the implementation of mechanisms such as recall-gated consolidation and memory banks. Recall-gated consolidation prioritizes the storage of synaptic changes that align with previous updates to the short-term memory system. This process safeguards the long-term memory from irrelevant modifications, enabling it to concentrate on reliable signals present in the surrounding environment (Lindsey, J., & Litwin-Kumar, A., 2022). Conversely, memory banks enable AI models to access pertinent memories, progressively evolve through continuous memory updates, and comprehend and adapt to user personalities by amalgamating information from past interactions (Lindsey et al., A., 2022; Wang W., et al., 2023).

These mechanisms emulate human-like memory processes by incorporating memory-updating mechanisms inspired by the Ebbinghaus Forgetting Curve theory. This theory facilitates the forgetting and reinforcement of memories based on the passage of time and their relative significance (Wang W. et al., 2023; Xu G. et al., 2022). By incorporating these strategies, AI models can remarkably form long-term bonds, retrieve pertinent memories, and comprehend users' personalities.

Addressing Limitations and Biases in Digital Memory

The field of digital memory and preservation has experienced significant growth in recent years, leading to new challenges in areas such as origin, reliability, comprehensiveness, and context (Antonijević et al., 2022). The diverse range of practices in digital memory today has resulted in tensions and difficulties such as disconnected data, the contrast between personal and institutional preservation, and the exclusion of "outsider" digital collections from official records (Chen Weirong & Tang, Qiang. 2020). These challenges emphasize the potential for distorting reality in a more extensive digital historical archive (Özarslan, Z., 2022). Furthermore, the fusion of new media and digital technologies has revolutionized the norms of memory, allowing for the indexing, archiving, circulation, and infinite processing of digital memory in cyberspace (Lindsey, J., & Litwin-Kumar, A., 2022). However, commodifying digital memory and its tangible and intangible foundations, including using rare earth in technological devices and data centres, are inherently intertwined with power dynamics and ideologies in the data-driven economy (Prodan., 2013). Despite the technical capabilities of digital access, excessive reliance on digital technology may restrict the potential significance of the "Memory of the World" Program, which seeks to enhance awareness and accessibility of documentary heritage.

VI. REASONING AND PROBLEM-SOLVING CAPABILITIES

Reasoning and problem-solving aptitudes are vital proficiencies in diverse domains. The progression of software engineering and ingenuity has instigated the utilization of computers in the realm of art design, augmenting efficacy and alleviating the burden on design personnel (Mirriam, et al., 2022). The ability to solve problems is deemed a cross-functional competency indispensable for fostering competitiveness and nurturing ingenuity within societal collectives (Karla., et al., 2022).

Algorithmic Approaches to Simulate Human Reasoning

Algorithmic methodologies have been devised to replicate the cognitive capabilities of human reasoning and problem-solving. One specific methodology, known as Reason Former, embodies a comprehensive reasoning framework that draws inspiration from the dual-process theory in the realm of cognitive science (Do., & Nguyen., 2022). Reason Former adopts a modular structure, segregating the representation module (characteristic of automatic thinking) from the reasoning modules (characteristic of controlled thinking), thereby accommodating varying levels of cognitive functioning. By incorporating pre-trained reasoning modules, which are specialized in particular reasoning skills, Reason Former can dynamically activate and amalgamate these modules to effectively tackle intricate problems (Mirriam, et al., 2022; Zhong, W., et al., 2022). This framework not only showcases noteworthy enhancements in performance, but also exhibits superior generalization abilities, as it is capable of resolving multiple tasks using a singular model and acquiring the aptitude to integrate pre-trained skills for novel tasks (Zhong, W., et al., 2022). The modularity of the reasoning modules permits the activation of discrete reasoning skills at different depths, contingent upon the specific task at hand.

Cognitive Computing and Decision-Making in the Digital Realm

Cognitive computing and decision-making in the digital domain entail employing intelligent computational examination to replicate the cognitive process of the brain for computational intellect (Mirriam, et al., 2022). This encompasses using intelligent support systems, system engineering, and machine learning methodologies to transform human decision-making into artificial intelligence [2]. The cognitive computing system employs knowledge and intelligent decision-making to facilitate astute decision-making (Morsch., 2022). Within the digital arena, organizations encounter rapid technological and digital advancements, rendering it arduous to ascertain the pertinent contextual factors for devising strategies (Adair J. E., 2007). Additionally, organizations must ascertain the capabilities and competences necessitated in the strategic decision unit to embrace strategies that are resilient to future changes and intricate circumstances (Leighton & Sternberg., 2003). Reasoning and problem-solving capabilities encompass the cultivation of decision-making styles and the utilization of cost-benefit analysis to assess advantages and drawbacks. Adaptive and innovative individuals manifest variances in problem-solving approaches.

Challenges in Replicating Intuitive and Creative Problem-Solving

Intuitive and creative problem-solving can pose challenges in terms of replication. Individuals with mathematical giftedness tend to internalize intuitive concepts and approaches, making it arduous for educators to observe their reasoning during problem-solving. Furthermore, the capacity to reason and creatively solve problems can vary depending on the specific context. For instance, within the realm of horticultural agribusiness, students exhibited more innovative reasoning when tackling mathematical problems (Szabo., 2024). The processes involved in problem-solving and creativity are intricate and subject to influence from diverse factors such as knowledge, situational elements, and problem characteristics (Fatimah., et al., 2019). Researchers have made notable strides in comprehending reasoning and problem-solving, encompassing the formulation of theories and utilizing neuroscientific evidence (Puccio., et al., 2023). However, there is still much to be unveiled, and future research should further explore these domains (Leighton & Sternberg., 2003).

VII. EMOTIONAL INTELLIGENCE IN AI

Emotional intelligence in AI alludes to the capacity of artificial intelligence systems to discern and comprehend human emotions and to react to them suitably. Emotional AI is regarded as a groundbreaking technology that empowers emotionally oriented human-machine communication (Mamina & Piraynen., 2023). It encompasses the examination of facial characteristics and the automated evaluation of sentiment from visual data employing machine learning, deep learning, and computer vision techniques (Anjana., 2023). However, it is contended that AI lacks inherent emotion and the ability to comprehend abstractions, rendering it incapable of adequately reproducing the intricacy and subjectivity of human intelligence and emotion (Oritsegbemi., 2023). The development of artificial emotion simulation technology endeavours to bestow emotion upon AI systems, but it also raises ethical concerns such as the reinforcement of instrumental rationality, the absence of an emotional subjects, and the deceitful intention contained in emotional simulation (Wang & Liu., 2023). Despite the stigmatization of emotion in AI, there is a burgeoning recognition of its value for the advancement of artificial cognitive processing, and research is investigating real-world applications and meaningful contributions in this domain (Assunção., et al., 2022).

Recognizing and Responding to Emotions in Artificial Systems

Emotional intelligence within the realm of artificial intelligence encompasses the ability to identify and react to emotions present in artificial systems. The study of emotion recognition in AI is an actively pursued area of research, employing computer vision and machine learning techniques to analyze facial characteristics and evaluate human emotional states (Anjana., 2023). Recent investigations have demonstrated that AI chatbots, such as ChatGPT-4, can exhibit distinct risk-taking behaviours and prosocial actions based on emotional cues (Yukun., et al.,2023). Emotional AI is regarded as a groundbreaking technology that facilitates emotionally driven communication between humans and machines (Rahul., et al., 2023). Its development aims to foster human interaction and improve emotional intelligence within applied AI (Pavitra., et al., 2023). The ultimate objective is to establish a novel form of AI, called "human AI," that enhances the capabilities of individuals and society. On the whole, emotional intelligence in AI entails the utilization of technologies like computer vision and machine learning to identify and respond to human emotions, thereby facilitating more advanced interactions between humans and machines.

Challenges in Developing Emotionally Intelligent AI

Developing emotionally intelligent AI presents a number of obstacles. Primarily, a dearth of knowledge exists regarding how to contextualize, operationalize, optimize, and design AI for emotional welfare (Patel & Fan., 2023; Mamina & Piraynen., 2023). Secondly, there is a lack of incentive as the creation of AI for emotional welfare is viewed as both risky and ungratifying (van der Maden., et al., 2023). Furthermore, AI struggles to replicate the intricacy and subjectivity of human emotions due to its absence of innate emotion and comprehension of abstract concepts (Oritsegbemi., 2023). These challenges underscore the necessity for advancements in comprehending the impact of AI systems on emotional welfare and intentional design to foster and sustain emotional welfare. In addition, it is recommended to enhance media literacy skills for users and provide ethical guidance for technological companies to ensure that emotionally intelligent AI has a reduced detrimental impact on humans and society.

Implications for Human-AI Interactions and Ethical Considerations

The presence of emotional intelligence in artificial intelligence (AI) carries significant implications for human-AI interactions and ethical considerations. Although AI possesses the ability to replicate human emotions, it is devoid of the intricate complexity and subjectivity inherent in human intelligence and emotion (Oritsegbemi., 2023). Ethical concerns arise when emotional AI is employed in video games, particularly in relation to the boundaries of artificially induced emotions, the delicate balance between privacy and secure gaming environments, and the formidable obstacles posed by transparency and ownership in the realm of in-game adaptation (Melhart., et al., 2023). Emotional AI is widely regarded as a groundbreaking technological advancement, capable of detecting and comprehending human emotions. However, there are inherent ethical risks associated with its utilization, including the reinforcement of instrumental rationality, the absence of emotional agency and the erosion of value, as well as the potential for deceptive intentions in emotional simulation (Melhart., et al., 2023; Mamina & Piraynen., 2023) Safeguarding the responsible use of emotional AI necessitates the cultivation of media literacy skills among users and the provision of ethical guidelines for technological enterprises (Wang & Liu., 2023) Consequently, an open and constructive dialogue must be fostered, accompanied by proactive measures, in order to protect users and steer developers towards the creation of safer and more enriching virtual experiences in the future.

VIII. EVALUATING SUCCESS AND ETHICAL CONSIDERATIONS

Evaluating the achievement of favourable outcomes and ethical concerns in scientific investigation and assessment is of utmost importance (Fanny, Garel., 2022). Ethical assessment necessitates the proper conduct of data science and adherence to the established norms within this domain (Morris M., 2003). Interpreting findings in an ethical manner entails refraining from questionable practices such as p-hacking and guaranteeing transparency in the dissemination of results. Incorporating validity, reliability, and generalizability emerges as crucial considerations in the design and execution of studies (Christopher Woodhouse., 2023).

Criteria for Measuring the Success of Digital Cognitive Replication

The measurement of success in digital cognitive replication can be assessed through a variety of approaches. One such approach is meta-analysis, which has been utilized in the social and behavioural sciences to determine the success of replication (Muradchanian., et al., 2023). However, meta-analysis has often yielded unsatisfactory results as a metric for replication success, leading to the assertion that replication is successful regardless of study outcomes (Ruginski., 2020). Another approach is the consideration of conceptual replication, which seeks to ascertain the practical significance of design principles in different usage contexts and for diverse end-users (Fanny Garel., 2022). This shift in perspective can mitigate methodological biases and establish the foundations for visualization meta-science (Ruginski., 2020). Furthermore, ethical considerations are essential in evaluating replication success. Ethical measurement necessitates properly implementing data science techniques and adherence to all field standards (Jasmine., et al., 2021). Ethical interpretation of results entails avoiding practices such as p-hacking and ensuring transparent reporting that includes both positive and negative findings, focusing on reproducibility.

Ethical Implications of Creating AI With Cognitive Capabilities

Creating artificial intelligence (AI) endowed with cognitive capabilities gives rise to ethical implications that necessitate careful examination. Embedding ethical reasoning directly into robots is incongruous with their autonomy and intelligence (Narayanan., 2023). The involvement and supervision of humans in the collaboration and control of AI systems are of utmost importance to counteract communication errors and uphold ethical standards (Knox., et al., 2023). Legislative measures are imperative in addressing ethical concerns and privacy issues pertaining to the advancement of AI (Fisher & Fisher., 2023). Challenges such as trust, power imbalances, bias, and adversarial factors can be alleviated through the cultivation of cognitive expertise (Schoenherr., 2022). The assessment of moral capacities in AI systems constitutes a crucial milestone in the quest for the development of morally conscious AI (Weidinger., et al., 022). The analysis and evaluation of moral capacities in AI systems have the potential to illuminate the existence and interconnectedness of amoral and moral capacities. Ethical considerations play a vital role in creating AI equipped with cognitive capabilities, ensuring responsible and dependable utilization of these technologies.

Balancing Innovation With Responsible Development and Use

Balancing the pursuit of innovation with the principles of responsible development and utilization necessitates a meticulous assessment of achievement and ethical deliberations. Scholars have conducted extensive investigations into the function of responsible research and innovation (RRI) in propelling the advancement of ethical research and ensuring the preservation of its integrity (Chen., et al., 2022). Responsible innovation accentuates pertinent stakeholders' involvement and the harmonization of technological advancements with ethical principles (Kubalskyi., 2022). Nevertheless, it is pivotal not solely to concentrate on responsible innovation, but also to consider unethical practices within the innovation process (Maynard &

Scragg., 2019). The rapid progression of technology in domains like brain-machine interfaces underscores the exigency of incorporating ethical and socially responsible innovation within enterprises (Häußermann & Schroth., 2020). The triumph of this endeavor hinges upon the readiness of innovators to earnestly address ethical considerations and draw upon interdisciplinary expertise (Etse., et al., 2021). By embracing an updated value paradigm and implementing the ethos of responsibility, the Ukrainian domain of science and innovation can be cultivated. In essence, evaluating achievement and ethical considerations encompasses the contemplation of RRI, responsible innovation, unethical practices, and interdisciplinary cooperation.

IX. FUTURE PROSPECTS AND CHALLENGES

Emerging Technologies and Their Potential Impact on Cognitive Replication

Emerging technologies possess the potential to exert an influence on cognitive duplication in numerous manners. One particular area of concentration focuses on the utilization of online platforms for the gathering of data, which gives rise to inquiries regarding the credibility of online data when compared to data collected in person. Furthermore, the sphere of developmental cognitive neuroscience can derive advantages from tools and workflows that augment the reproducibility and replicability, particularly in relation to statistical power and transparency in the analysis of data (Dyson., 2022). Augmented reality technology can be employed to replicate desired cognitive conditions and modify surroundings to attain those conditions (Klapwijk., et al., 2019). Moreover, the escalating employment of advanced data processing technologies, such as machine learning and data mining, in cognitive information processing systems poses security and safety predicaments that necessitate resolution (Emmery., et al., 2019). Overall, whilst emerging technologies provide prospects for ameliorating cognitive duplication, they also introduce novel challenges that necessitate resolution to ensure the dependability and validity of research findings.

Anticipated Challenges in Achieving More Advanced Digital Consciousness

Anticipated difficulties in attaining a more advanced state of digital awareness encompass the requirement to incorporate autopoietic and cognitive behaviours into digital automata to uphold stability amidst fluctuations and diminish risk (Angier., et al., 2022). Moreover, a fundamental obstacle exists in formulating a forthcoming theory of consciousness (Mikkilineni., 2022). The cultivation of critical awareness regarding digital futures presents another challenge that necessitates collaboration among researchers, artists, and activists (Ruan., 2023). According to the research article by Akperov, Martynov, and Prokopenko, the cultivation of transcendental thought and digital consciousness within organizations is essential for facilitating flexible management and fostering a favourable perception of immersive management practices (Markham., 2021). Obstacles to the transformation of organizational processes, including digital resistance and a lack of comprehension pertaining to digital opportunities, also give rise to challenges (Akperov., et al., 2022). The relationship between digital consciousness, metacognition, and the effectiveness of change management strategies has been firmly established.

The Evolving Role of AI in Augmenting Human Cognitive Capabilities

The progressing role of Artificial Intelligence (AI) in enhancing human cognitive abilities exhibits future prospects and challenges. AI-mediated frameworks, such as deep reinforcement learning (DRL), have the capacity to offer intelligent feedback for enhancing user performance in cognitive tasks. The utilization of AI in the realm of education and training can serve as a means to bridge the gap between rapid innovation and evolving skill sets (Xu & Zhang., 2023). The potential of AI technologies lies in their ability to enhance workflows and treatment outcomes in radiation oncology, encompassing activities like image interpretation, treatment planning, and decision-making (Mattonen., et al., 2022). Moreover, AI-supported cognitive screening tests have exhibited promise in the realm of remote assessment and digitized neurocognitive testing (Mady & Niese., 2022). However, successfully implementing AI in these domains necessitates addressing challenges such as data requirements, training, and ethical considerations (Sirilertmekasakul., et al., 2023). Overall, the progressing role of AI in augmenting human cognitive capabilities presents intriguing possibilities, but it also demands meticulous consideration of technical and ethical challenges.

CONCLUSION

Digital cognitive replication is presently in a state of fluctuation and ongoing difficulties. Self-administered computerized cognitive assessment measures exhibit potential for early detection of cognitive disorders in elderly individuals, however, there are deficiencies in scientific rigor in their development and validation. The field of machine learning presents optimal methodologies for enhancing reproducibility, which can be implemented in cognitive modeling practices. The notion of Digital Twins (DTs) in the era of Industry 4.0 permits the virtualization and twinning of physical components, however, cognition necessitates the modeling of both physical attributes and behavior utilizing data-driven models. Cognitive computing (CC) aims to duplicate human thought processes in a computerized model, addressing intricate and evolving scenarios, assessing user requirements, and generating quantifiable situations. Using portable experimental packages in online education and research offers opportunities for replication and experiential learning; however, the replicability of in-person data collection in online environments remains a fundamental query.

The Road Ahead: Reflections on the Possibilities and Challenges

The future is marked by both possibilities and challenges regarding digital cognitive processes. The recruitment process has been greatly affected by the digital transformation, necessitating the development of new tools to identify potential candidates. Individuals who experience cognitive difficulties as a result of neurological disorders face obstacles in managing digital work and daily activities. However, self-initiated strategies can serve as a valuable resource to promote sustainable work and life. The characteristics commonly found in the digital generation, such as clip thinking and multitasking, have implications for the training of higher education students. These implications include a decrease in attention span and critical thinking abilities. Computational cognitive models have played a critical role in comprehending human-information interaction systems. However, they encounter challenges as digital information interaction becomes more intricate. While online environments offer numerous benefits, they also present challenges such as persuasive choice architectures, false information, and distracting settings. Psychological science can provide insights into interventions that empower users and enhance their agency, reasoning, and resilience to manipulation in digital environments.

Encouraging Interdisciplinary Collaboration for Continued Progress

Encouraging interdisciplinary collaboration is of utmost importance for the ongoing advancement. The presence of limited interdisciplinary communication and engagement within Higher Education Institutions (HEIs) in the United Kingdom has resulted in a lack of awareness regarding research being conducted elsewhere. The Digital Earth Project underlines the necessity of interdisciplinary collaboration to promote digitalization and the implementation of data science methods. The significance of interdisciplinary approaches in disease management, vaccine development, and societal decisions has been underscored by the COVID-19 pandemic. In the realm of service research, the integration of interdisciplinary perspectives with service marketing can yield more impactful outcomes. Through establishing trust and identifying strengths in the differences among researchers, interdisciplinary teams are more likely to succeed in their collaboration. Interdisciplinary collaboration facilitates the exchange of knowledge, expertise, and resources across various disciplines, leading to innovative solutions and advancements in diverse fields.

REFERENCES

Adair, J. E. (2007). *Decision making & problem solving strategies* (Vol. 121). Kogan Page Publishers.

Agustina, Y. (2021). Thinking Analysis And Problem Solving: Array. *Literasi Nusantara*, *1*(2), 107–117.

Akperov, I. G., Martynov, B. V., & Prokopenko, E. S. (2022). The role of digital consciousness in change management. *Vestnik Universiteta*, *11*(11), 5–10. doi:10.26425/1816-4277-2022-10-5-10

Althof. (2021). Insights into cognitive processing of the go/nogo Discrete Sequence Production task: A replication study. Academic Press.

Angier, T., Benson, I. T., & Retter, M. D. (Eds.). (2022). Challenges and Future Prospects. In The Cambridge Handbook of Natural Law and Human Rights. Cambridge Law Handbooks. Cambridge University Press. doi:10.1017/9781108939225.038

Anjana, C. M. (2023). *Role of Artificial Intelligence in Emotion Recognition.* International Journal For Science Technology And Engineering.

. Antonijević, S., & Ubois, J. (2022). Representing the absent: The limits and possibilities of digital memory and preservation. *Filozofija i društvo/Philosophy and Society, 33*(2), 311-325.

Assunção, G., Patrão, B., Castelo-Branco, M., & Menezes, P. (2022). An overview of emotion in artificial intelligence. *IEEE Transactions on Artificial Intelligence*, *3*(6), 867–886. doi:10.1109/TAI.2022.3159614

Ball, L. J. (1990). Cognitive processes in engineering design. Academic Press.

Benjamin, J. (2022, May). Long-term repeatability of cognitive performance. *Royal Society Open Science*, *9*(5), 220069. Advance online publication. doi:10.1098/rsos.220069

Bennett, M. T., & Maruyama, Y. (2021). Philosophical specification of empathetic ethical artificial intelligence. *IEEE Transactions on Cognitive and Developmental Systems*, *14*(2), 292–300. doi:10.1109/TCDS.2021.3099945

Bingxuan, R., Tangwen, Y., & Shan, F. (2019). An Approach Analyzing Cognitive Process of Human-Machine Interaction Based on Extended Markov Decision Process. doi:10.1109/CAC48633.2019.8996284

Blainey, P., Krzywinski, M., & Altman, N. (2014). Points of significance: Replication. *Nature Methods*, *11*(9), 879–880. doi:10.1038/nmeth.3091 PMID:25317452

Chandiok, A., & Chaturvedi, D. K. (2018). Cognitive functionality based question answering system. *Int J Comput Appl*, *179*, 1–6.

Chen, J., Nichele, E., Ellerby, Z., & Wagner, C. (2022). Responsible research and innovation in practice: Driving both the 'How' and the 'What' to research. *Journal of Responsible Technology*, *11*, 100042. doi:10.1016/j.jrt.2022.100042

Chen, W., & Tang, Q. (2020). Memory system and bias circuit. Academic Press.

Christopher, W. (2023). Research and evaluation ethics. .doi:10.51952/9781447366263.ch003

Coral, M. A., & Bernuy, A. E. (2022). Challenges in the digital transformation processes in higher education institutions and universities. *International Journal of Information Technologies and Systems Approach*, *15*(1), 1–14. doi:10.4018/IJITSA.290002

Coren, S., Ward, L. M., & Enns, J. T. (2004). *Sensation and perception*. John Wiley & Sons.

Descartes, R., & Frenzel, I. (1960). *René Descartes*. Fischer.

Do, N. V., & Nguyen, H. D. (2022, October). Knowledge-based Problem Solving and Reasoning methods. In 2022 14th International Conference on Knowledge and Systems Engineering (KSE) (pp. 1-7). IEEE. 10.1109/KSE56063.2022.9953617

Dumontheil, I., Brookman-Byrne, A., Tolmie, A. K., & Mareschal, D. (2022). Neural and Cognitive Underpinnings of Counterintuitive Science and Math Reasoning in Adolescence. *Journal of Cognitive Neuroscience*, *34*(7), 1205–1229. doi:10.1162/jocn_a_01854 PMID:35468204

Duncan, R. (2021). Cognitive processing in digital audio workstation composing. *General Music Today*. doi:10.1177/10483713211034441

Dyson, B. (2022). Assessing the replicability of Cognitive Psychology via remote experiential learning. Academic Press.

Emmery, C., Kádár, Á., Wiltshire, T. J., & Hendrickson, A. T. (2019). Towards replication in computational cognitive modeling: A machine learning perspective. *Computational Brain & Behavior*, *2*(3-4), 242–246. doi:10.1007/s42113-019-00055-w

Enoiu, E., & Feldt, R. (2021, May). Towards human-like automated test generation: Perspectives from cognition and problem solving. In 2021 IEEE/ACM 13th International Workshop on Cooperative and Human Aspects of Software Engineering (CHASE) (pp. 123-124). IEEE.

Erfurth, C. (2019). The digital turn: on the quest for holistic approaches. In Distributed Computing and Internet Technology: 15th International Conference, ICDCIT 2019, Bhubaneswar, India, January 10–13, 2019 *Proceedings*, *15*, 24–30.

Etse, D., McMurray, A., & Muenjohn, N. (2021). Unleashing Innovation Across Ethical and Moral Boundaries: The Dark Side of Using Innovation for Self-Advantage. The Palgrave Handbook of Workplace Innovation, 521-542.

Evelina, L. (2023). Neural Networks and Deep Learning. doi:10.1007/978-981-19-8851-6_13-1

Fanny, G. (2022). Ethical Evaluation. doi:10.1093/oso/9780192847263.003.0005

Fatimah, A. T., Pramuditya, S. A., & Wahyudin, W. (2019, February). Imitative and creative reasoning for mathematical problem solving (in context horticultural agribusiness). *Journal of Physics: Conference Series*, *1157*(4), 042092. doi:10.1088/1742-6596/1157/4/042092

Findlater, L., Goodman, S., Zhao, Y., Azenkot, S., & Hanley, M. (2020). Fairness issues in AI systems that augment sensory abilities. *ACM SIGACCESS Accessibility and Computing*, (125), 1–1. doi:10.1145/3386296.3386304

Fisher, E. J. P., & Fisher, E. (2023). A Fresh Look at Ethical Perspectives on Artificial Intelligence Applications and their Potential Impacts at Work and on People. *Business and Economic Review*, *13*(3), 1–22.

Fitzgibbon, B. M., Ward, J., & Enticott, P. G. (2014). The neural underpinnings of vicarious experience. *Frontiers in Human Neuroscience*, *8*, 384. doi:10.3389/fnhum.2014.00384 PMID:24917806

Floriana, F. (2022). Perceptual Relations in Digital Environments. *Foundations of Science*. Advance online publication. doi:10.1007/s10699-022-09853-1

Freundschuh, S. M. (2009). Map perception and cognition. Academic Press.

Hamilton, K. A., Yamashiro, J. K., & Storm, B. C. (2023). Special issue of applied cognitive psychology: Rethinking cognition in a digital environment. *Applied Cognitive Psychology, 37*(4), 683–685. doi:10.1002/acp.4074

Hamlyn, D. W. (2022). *Sensation and perception: A history of the philosophy of perception.* Taylor & Francis. doi:10.4324/9781003316459

Häußermann, J. J., & Schroth, F. (2020). Aligning innovation and ethics: An approach to responsible innovation based on preference learning. *Philosophy of Management, 19*(3), 349–364. doi:10.1007/s40926-019-00120-1

Hibberd, J., Swee Hong, C., & Boyle, L. (2010). Perception: Holistic assessment. *Nursing & Residential Care : the Monthly Journal for Care Assistants, Nurses and Managers Working in Health and Social Care, 12*(7), 350–353. doi:10.12968/nrec.2010.12.7.48516

Hoffmann, M., & Hoffmann, M. (2020). Neuroanatomical and Neurophysiological Underpinnings of Cognition and Behavior: Cerebral Networks and Intrinsic Brain Networks. Clinical Mentation Evaluation: A Connectomal Approach to Rapid and Comprehensive Assessment, 11-19.

Huang, T., Ma, L., Zhang, B., & Liao, H. (2023). Advances in deep learning: From diagnosis to treatment. *Bioscience Trends, 17*(3), 190–192. doi:10.5582/bst.2023.01148 PMID:37394613

Imhof, D., & Grivas, S. G. (2022, November). Holistic Digital Leadership and 20 Factors Relevant for its Understanding and Implementation. In ECMLG 2022 18th European Conference on Management, Leadership and Governance. Academic Conferences and Publishing Limited.

Jasmine, M. (2021, May). How best to quantify replication success? A simulation study on the comparison of replication success metrics. *Royal Society Open Science, 8*(5), 201697. Advance online publication. doi:10.1098/rsos.201697

Jette, O. (2022, October 14). Learning and replaying spatiotemporal sequences: A replication study. *Frontiers in Integrative Neuroscience, 16*, 974177. Advance online publication. doi:10.3389/fnint.2022.974177

Jun, L., Chitipat, T., Siripen, P., & Kyoung-Sook, K. (2018). Towards Building a Human Perception Knowledge for Social Sensation Analysis. doi:10.1109/WI.2018.00-15

Karla, D., Pandey, V. K., Rastogi, P., & Kumar, S. (2022). A Comprehensive Review on Significance of Problem-Solving Abilities in Workplace. *World Journal of English Language*, *12*(3), 1–88. doi:10.5430/wjel.v12n3p88

Khan, M. (2023). Advancements in Artificial Intelligence: Deep Learning and Meta-Analysis. Academic Press.

KlapwijkE. T.van den BosW.TamnesC. K.MillsK. L.RaschleN. (2019). Opportunities for increased reproducibility and replicability of developmental cognitive neuroscience. PsyArXiv.

Knox, B. J., Sütterlin, S., & Lugo, R. (2023). Cognitive agility for improved understanding and self-governance: a human-centric AI enabler. In Handbook of Research on Artificial Intelligence, Innovation and Entrepreneurship (pp. 152-172). Edward Elgar Publishing. doi:10.4337/9781839106750.00019

Kokinov, B., & Petkov, G. (2009). Modeling Cued Recall and Memory Illusions as a Result of Structure Mapping. In Proceedings of the Annual Meeting of the Cognitive Science Society (Vol. 31, No. 31). Academic Press.

Kubalskyi. (2022). Ethics of responsibility in scientific research and innovation: a global and national perspective. Polìtologìčnij vìsnik, doi:10.17721/2415-881x.2022.88.12-21

Kynoch, B., & Latapie, H. (2023). Recallm: An architecture for temporal context understanding and question answering. arXiv preprint arXiv:2307.02738.

Leighton, J. P., & Sternberg, R. J. (2003). Reasoning and problem solving. *Experimental Psychology*, *4*, 623–648.

Limani, Y., Hajrizi, E., & Stapleton, L. (2022). The Complexity of Business Process Digitalization and Organisational Challenges. *IFAC-PapersOnLine*, *55*(39), 346–351. doi:10.1016/j.ifacol.2022.12.051

Lindsey, J., & Litwin-Kumar, A. (2022). Theory of systems memory consolidation via recall-gated plasticity. bioRxiv, 2022-12.

Lu, J., Zheng, X., Schweiger, L., & Kiritsis, D. (2021). A cognitive approach to manage the complexity of digital twin systems. In *Smart Services Summit: Digital as an Enabler for Smart Service Business Development* (pp. 105–115). Springer International Publishing. doi:10.1007/978-3-030-72090-2_10

Mady, A., & Niese, B. (2022, June). Augmenting AI and Human Capabilities in Competency-Based Learning. In *Proceedings of the 2022 Computers and People Research Conference* (pp. 1-9). 10.1145/3510606.3550210

Magosso, E., & Ursino, M. (2023). The Sensory-Cognitive Interplay: Insights into Neural Mechanisms and Circuits. *Journal of Integrative Neuroscience*, *22*(1), 1–3. doi:10.31083/j.jin.2021.01.422 PMID:36722250

Mamina, R. I., & Piraynen, E. V. (2023). Emotional Artificial Intelligence as a Tool for Human-Machine Interaction. *Discourse (Berkeley, Calif.)*, *9*(2), 35–51.

Marchetti, G. (2018). Consciousness: A unique way of processing information. *Cognitive Processing*, *19*(3), 435–464. doi:10.1007/s10339-018-0855-8 PMID:29423666

Markham, A. (2021). The limits of the imaginary: Challenges to intervening in future speculations of memory, data, and algorithms. *New Media & Society*, *23*(2), 382–405. doi:10.1177/1461444820929322

Mattonen, S., Naqa, I. E., Hu, W., & Troost, E. (2022). "Evolving role of AI in radiation oncology"—special collection-introductory Editorial. BJR| Open, 4(1), 20229002.

Maynard, A. D., & Scragg, M. (2019). The ethical and responsible development and application of advanced brain machine interfaces. *Journal of Medical Internet Research*, *21*(10), e16321. doi:10.2196/16321 PMID:31674917

McGee, S. (2019). Changes in the Cognitive Dynamics of Problem-Solving. Academic Press.

Melhart, D., Togelius, J., Mikkelsen, B., Holmgård, C., & Yannakakis, G. N. (2023). The Ethics of AI in Games. *IEEE Transactions on Affective Computing*.

Mihai, S., Yaqoob, M., Hung, D. V., Davis, W., Towakel, P., Raza, M., Karamanoglu, M., Barn, B., Shetve, D., Prasad, R. V., Venkataraman, H., Trestian, R., & Nguyen, H. X. (2022). Digital twins: A survey on enabling technologies, challenges, trends and future prospects. *IEEE Communications Surveys and Tutorials*, *24*(4), 2255–2291. doi:10.1109/COMST.2022.3208773

Mikkilineni, R. (2022, April). Digital Consciousness: The Business of Sensing, Modeling, Analyzing, Predicting, and Taking Action. In Proceedings (Vol. 81, No. 1, p. 103). MDPI.

Minakov, V. F., Dyatlov, S. A., Lobanov, O. S., & Selishcheva, T. A. (2022, February). Cognitive Concept of the Analysis of Hype Processes in the Digital Economy. In International Scientific and Practical Conference Strategy of Development of Regional Ecosystems "Education-Science-Industry"(ISPCR 2021) (pp. 285-291). Atlantis Press. 10.2991/aebmr.k.220208.041

Mirriam, A. J., Rajashree, S., Muneera, M. N., Saranya, V., & Murali, E. (2022, October). Approaches to Overcome Human Limitations by an Intelligent Autonomous System with a Level of Consciousness in Reasoning, Decision Making and Problem-Solving Capabilities. In International Conference on Advanced Communication and Intelligent Systems (pp. 505-516). Cham: Springer Nature Switzerland.

Möhlmann, M., & Jarvenpaa, S. (2019). Cognitive challenges on digital exchange platforms: Exploring misspecifications of trust. Academic Press.

Monin, B., & Oppenheimer, D. M. (2014). The limits of direct replications and the virtues of stimulus sampling. Academic Press.

Morris, M. (2003). Ethical considerations in evaluation. In *International handbook of educational evaluation* (pp. 303–327). Springer Netherlands. doi:10.1007/978-94-010-0309-4_19

Morsch, P. (2022). Capabilities And Competences For Strategic Decision Making In Digital World. 35th Bled eConference Digital Restructuring and Human (Re) action, 759.

Muradchanian, J., Hoekstra, R., Kiers, H., & van Ravenzwaaij, D. (2023). Evaluating meta-analysis as a replication success measure. Academic Press.

Narayanan, A. (2023). Machine Ethics and Cognitive Robotics. *Current Robotics Reports*, 1–9.

Nobandegani, A. S., Shultz, T. R., & Rish, I. (2022). Cognitive Models as Simulators: The Case of Moral Decision-Making. arXiv preprint arXiv:2210.04121.

Noriega, P., Padget, J., Verhagen, H., & D'Inverno, M. (2014). The challenge of artificial socio-cognitive systems. Academic Press.

Olbrich, S., Frank, U., Gregor, S., Niederman, F., & Rowe, F. (2017). On the merits and limits of replication and negation for IS research. *AIS Transactions on Replication Research*, *3*(1), 1–19. doi:10.17705/1atrr.00016

Oritsegbemi, O. (2023). Human Intelligence versus AI: Implications for Emotional Aspects of Human Communication. *Journal of Advanced Research in Social Sciences*, *6*(2), 76–85. doi:10.33422/jarss.v6i2.1005

Özarslan, Z. (2022). A Critical Debate on the Political Economy of Digital Memory. *Galatasaray Üniversitesi İletişim Dergisi*, (37), 164–186. doi:10.16878/gsuilet.1167144

Patel, S. C., & Fan, J. (2023). Identification and Description of Emotions by Current Large Language Models. bioRxiv, 2023-07. doi:10.1101/2023.07.17.549421

Pavitra, A. R. R., Anushree, K., Akshayalakshmi, A. V. R., & Vijayalakshmi, K. (2023, May). Artificial Intelligence (AI) Enabled Music Player System for User Facial Recognition. In *2023 4th International Conference for Emerging Technology (INCET)* (pp. 1-4). IEEE.

Penders, B., Holbrook, J. B., & de Rijcke, S. (2019). Rinse and repeat: Understanding the value of replication across different ways of knowing. *Publications / MDPI, 7*(3), 52. doi:10.3390/publications7030052

Peter, R. (2005). Models of Cognition: Neurological possibility does not indicate neurological plausibility. Academic Press.

Pfaltz, J. L. (2017, April). Computational processes that appear to model human memory. In *International Conference on Algorithms for Computational Biology* (pp. 85-99). Cham: Springer International Publishing. 10.1007/978-3-319-58163-7_6

Pizlo, Z. (2022). *Problem Solving: Cognitive Mechanisms and Formal Models.* Cambridge University Press. doi:10.1017/9781009205603

Plewczynski, D. (2011). Modeling of Cognitive Agents. Academic Press.

Prodan, A. C. (2013). The digital" Memory of the World": an exploration of documentary practices in the age of digital technology (Doctoral dissertation, BTU Cottbus-Senftenberg).

Puccio, G. J., Klarman, B., & Szalay, P. A. (2023). Creative Problem-Solving. In *The Palgrave Encyclopedia of the Possible* (pp. 298–313). Springer International Publishing.

Rahul, M., & Ouarbya, L. (2023). Emotion Recognition Using. *Artificial Intelligence.*

Robert, K. (2007). Computational Aspects of Cognition and Consciousness in Intelligent Devices. *IEEE Computational Intelligence Magazine, 2*(3), 53–64. doi:10.1109/MCI.2007.385369

Ruan, Z. (2023). The fundamental challenge of a future theory of consciousness. *Frontiers in Psychology, 13*, 1029105. doi:10.3389/fpsyg.2022.1029105 PMID:36710768

Ruginski, I. T. (2020). Ethical conceptual replication of visualization research considering sources of methodological bias and practical significance. arXiv preprint arXiv:2009.12152.

Samsonovich, A. V. (2013, November). Modeling human emotional intelligence in virtual agents. *2013 AAAI Fall Symposium Series*.

Sandu, A. (2019). Towards a phenomenology of the digitalization of consciousness. The virtualization of the social space. *Postmodern Openings*, *10*(2), 155–161. doi:10.18662/po/77

. Scheper, T., Beutel, S., McGuinness, N., Heiden, S., Oldiges, M., Lammers, F., & Reardon, K. F. (2021). Digitalization and bioprocessing: Promises and challenges. Digital Twins: Tools and Concepts for Smart Biomanufacturing, 57-69.

Schmidt, S. N., Hass, J., Kirsch, P., & Mier, D. (2021). The human mirror neuron system—A common neural basis for social cognition? *Psychophysiology*, *58*(5), e13781. doi:10.1111/psyp.13781 PMID:33576063

Schoenherr, J. R. (2022). *Ethical Artificial Intelligence from Popular to Cognitive Science: Trust in the Age of Entanglement*. Taylor & Francis. doi:10.4324/9781003143284

Seitz, M., & Vogel-Heuser, B. (2020, October). Challenges for the digital transformation of development processes in engineering. In *IECON 2020 The 46th Annual Conference of the IEEE Industrial Electronics Society* (pp. 4345-4350). IEEE. 10.1109/IECON43393.2020.9254771

Seth, G. (2017). The phenomenology of Angry Birds: Virtual gravity and distributed proprioception in video game worlds. Journal of Gaming & Virtual Worlds. doi:10.1386/jgvw.9.3.207_1

Sharafat, H. (2021). Multisensory Digital Experiences: Integrating New Interactive Technologies With Human Senses. . doi:10.4018/978-1-7998-8327-2.ch022

Shrivastava, R., Kumar, P., & Tripathi, S. (2020). A Human Memory Process Modeling. *Recent Patents on Engineering*, *14*(2), 179–193. doi:10.2174/1872212 113666190211145444

Silvestri, F. (2019). Su alcuni riflessi cognitivi nel tempo online delle nuove forme della comunicazione/informazione governate dagli algoritmi. Note e appunti per una ricerca. *ECHO*, (1), 65–76.

Sirilertmekasakul, C., Rattanawong, W., Gongvatana, A., & Srikiatkhachorn, A. (2023). The current state of artificial intelligence-augmented digitized neurocognitive screening test. *Frontiers in Human Neuroscience*, *17*, 1133632. doi:10.3389/fnhum.2023.1133632 PMID:37063100

Soldatova, G., Vishneva, A., & Chigarkova, S. (2018). Features of cognitive processes in children with different internet activity. *European Proceedings of Social and Behavioural Sciences, 43.*

Storer, K. M. (2017). Nuanced Views of Pedagogical Evaluation (Doctoral dissertation, Clemson University).\

Szabo, A., Tillnert, A. S., & Mattsson, J. (2024). Displaying gifted students' mathematical reasoning during problem solving: Challenges and possibilities. *The Montana Math Enthusiast, 21*(1), 179–202. doi:10.54870/1551-3440.1623

Tagliagambe, S. (2023). Phenomenology and the Digital World: Problems and Perspectives. *Foundations of Science, 28*(4), 1157–1174. doi:10.1007/s10699-022-09863-z

Thiele, J. C., & Grimm, V. (2015). Replicating and breaking models: Good for you and good for ecology. *Oikos, 124*(6), 691–696. doi:10.1111/oik.02170

Tonin, P. E. H., Nickel, E. M., & Dos Santos, F. A. N. V. (2022). Technology and Sensory Stimuli as Support for Physical Retail Experience Design. Affective and Pleasurable Design, 41(41).

Torre, D., & Daley, B. (2023). Emotional intelligence: Mapping an elusive concept. *Medical Teacher*, 1–3. PMID:37220225

Uppal, M. A. (2017). Addressing student perception of E-learning challenges in Higher Education holistic quality approach (Doctoral dissertation, University of Reading).

Valle, G., Katic Secerovic, N., Eggemann, D., Gorskii, O., Pavlova, N., Cvancara, P., ... Raspopovic, S. (2023). Biomimetic computer-to-brain communication restoring naturalistic touch sensations via peripheral nerve stimulation. bioRxiv, 2023-07. doi:10.1101/2023.07.15.549130

van der Maden, W., Lomas, D., & Hekkert, P. (2023). Positive AI: Key Challenges for Designing Wellbeing-aligned Artificial Intelligence. arXiv preprint arXiv:2304.12241.

Wang, W., Dong, L., Cheng, H., Liu, X., Yan, X., Gao, J., & Wei, F. (2023). Augmenting Language Models with Long-Term Memory. arXiv preprint arXiv:2306.07174.

Wang, Y. (2012). The cognitive mechanisms and formal models of consciousness. *International Journal of Cognitive Informatics and Natural Intelligence, 6*(2), 23–40. doi:10.4018/jcini.2012040102

Wang, Y., & Liu, W. (2023). Emotional Simulation of Artificial Intelligence and Its Ethical Reflection. *Academic Journal of Humanities & Social Sciences*, *6*(5), 11–15.

Wang, Y., & Wang, Y. (2008, August). The cognitive processes of consciousness and attention. In 2008 7th IEEE International Conference on Cognitive Informatics (pp. 30-39). IEEE.

. Weidinger, L., Reinecke, M. G., & Haas, J. (2022). Artificial moral cognition: Learning from developmental psychology.

Xu, G., Guo, W., & Wang, Y. (2022, October). Memory Enhanced Replay for Continual Learning. In 2022 16th IEEE International Conference on Signal Processing (ICSP) (Vol. 1, pp. 218-222). IEEE. 10.1109/ICSP56322.2022.9965222

Xu, S., & Zhang, X. (2023, April). Augmenting Human Cognition with an AI-Mediated Intelligent Visual Feedback. In *Proceedings of the 2023 CHI Conference on Human Factors in Computing Systems* (pp. 1-16). 10.1145/3544548.3580905

Yamana, Y. (2023). Deep Learning and Neural Networks. *Methods (San Diego, Calif.)*. Advance online publication. doi:10.59646/csebookc7/004

Yukun, Z., Xu, L., Huang, Z., Peng, K., Seligman, M., Li, E., & Yu, F. (2023). AI chatbot responds to emotional cuing. Academic Press.

Yushu, Y. (2023). *Current Trends in Deep Learning*. Advances in Engineering Technology Research. doi:10.56028/aetr.5.1.422.2023

Zhang, Y., Farrugia, N., & Bellec, P. (2022). Deep learning models of cognitive processes constrained by human brain connectomes. *Medical Image Analysis*, *80*, 102507. doi:10.1016/j.media.2022.102507 PMID:35738052

Zhong, W., Ma, T., Wang, J., Yin, J., Zhao, T., Lin, C. Y., & Duan, N. (2022). Disentangling reasoning capabilities from language models with compositional reasoning transformers. arXiv preprint arXiv:2210.11265.

Zhongzhi, S. (2019). Cognitive Machine Learning. *International Journal of Intelligence Science*, *9*(4), 111–121. Advance online publication. doi:10.4236/ijis.2019.94007

Zihan, H., & Dekai, Ye. (2022, January 4). Advances in materials and devices for mimicking sensory adaptation. *Materials Horizons*, *9*(1), 147–163. Advance online publication. doi:10.1039/D1MH01111A

Chapter 7

Consumer Acceptance and Adoption Challenges of Digital Healthcare Technology in India:
A TAM Approach

Kadambini S. Katke
Dayananda Sagar College of Arts, Science, and Commerce, India

ABSTRACT

India, with its large population exceeding 1.3 billion, faces strain on its healthcare system due to an aging population and various factors impacting service quality. Digital healthcare technology offers a solution by providing efficient and accessible services, reducing economic burdens, and enhancing care quality. Understanding users' perceptions is crucial, explored through Davis's technology adoption model (TAM). This model assesses factors like perceived usefulness and ease of use, crucial for technology adoption. Government initiatives support digital healthcare infrastructure. Focus on diseases like diabetes is essential, requiring accessible technology for monitoring and reducing healthcare costs. Digital healthcare providers must develop user-friendly products to ease adoption. Despite India's high diabetic population, healthcare apps struggle to penetrate the market. A digital healthcare ecosystem connecting various healthcare elements can reduce costs and improve accessibility.

DOI: 10.4018/979-8-3693-2015-0.ch007

INTRODUCTION

Covid-19 has left behind serious note on healthcare importance in the lives of mankind. Changing lifestyle exacerbate greater health concerns (Sverdlov et al, 2018) among all age segment. The toll of chronic diseases in the developing world is significant, manifesting not only in widespread morbidity but also in substantial financial strain. Approximately half of the American are suffering with chronic disease such as heart diseases, obesity, smoking, chronic respiratory disorder, and diabetes; burdening 86% of total healthcare cost to government (Kvedar et al, 2016). Developing countries like India and China also closer to these scenario (Fleck et al 2016). Regulating health and controlling health cost poses major challenges for government across the globe (Rana et al, 2015). Digital healthcare technologies can contribute towards reducing the healthcare cost and improving the treatment outcome in case of chronic diseases (Sverdlov et al, 2018).

Indian Healthcare Need

In India, Cardiovascular diseases account around 27% of total death (WTO, 2016), according to International Diabetes Federation, India is home to largest number of people with diabetes in the world, with an estimated 77 million people living with it in year 2021(International Diabetes Federation Report, 2021), 8% of deaths are due to respiratory diseases (WTO, 2017), 2.64 million people were affected by tuberculosis (Global Tuberculosis Report, 2020,), and 7,84000 death reason was cancer in 2020 (World Cancer Research Fund International, 2020). Malnutrition, infectious diseases, hepatitis, and mental health are few more high risk diseases need serious attention.

Digital Healthcare Technology in India

Leading digital health technologies includes telemedicine, mHealth, wearables, big data analytics. Leading countries are aggressively investing resources, aliening there healthcare policies to promote digital health to provide remote care to patients. Widespread government support and suitable policies further accelerated development. Covid-19 is another reason pushing hard for digital health. In global horizons "developed countries" have adopted digital health technology however in "under developing countries" still it in the process. Towards enhance the accessibility and affordability, of digital health technology, a comprehensive understanding of customer adoption challenges is of paramount importance. This insight is integral to foster widespread adoption, facilitating a significant shift towards digital health solutions, and thereby contributing profoundly to the transformation of healthcare delivery.

In analyzing the barriers to digital health technology adoption within developing nations the seminal model introduced by Davis in 1989 (Davis, et al., 1989) serves as a valuable theoretical framework. This model, cited extensively in the literature, accentuates two vital determinants that govern technology acceptance and adoption: "perceived usefulness" and "perceives ease of use". These elements collectively illuminate the nuanced interplay of factors that might either facilitate or hinder the widespread integration of digital healthcare technology in emerging economies.

Global Digital Health Market

The global digital health market is expected to reach $364.7 billion by 2026, growing at a CAGR of 21.85 from 2021 to 2026 Asia-pacific region is expected to lead the global digital health market, followed by North America and Europe. Telemedicine has seen a good growth and projected to a increase up to 20 percent by 2025 (Statista, Telemedicine Market in India, (2020). mHealth and mobile Apps had been downloaded by over 150 million people 2019. Ministry of electronics and Information Technology, Government of India). HER and Health Information system remain inconsistent across the health eco-system. Only 25 percent of Indian villages are covered with basic healthcare facilities. Various start-ups, health-tech companies and government initiatives are actively engaged into developing the healthcare eco-system. These are forces pushing hard to develop system which can reach, and help mass in healthcare needs.

Digital health in India is a dynamic and evolving field with significant potential for improving health care access and quality (Bandyopadhyay, S., & Saha, G. K.(2019). However, challenges related to infrastructure, regulations, privacy, equity and technology adoptability remain. This research paper focuses one of the major determinant factor digital technology adoptability. The small group initiative will grow into big numbers.

In a nation like India, where universal healthcare is not yet established and there exists substantial scepticism surrounding the public health care system, numerous hurdles emerge in the adoption of digital healthcare solution nationwide.

BACKGROUND AND LITERATURE REVIEW

Digital Healthcare Technology

Inadequate infrastructure, standardisation, and regulatory challenges, are primary concern (Prashant, 2023). In India there exist huge gap between those who have access to use digital healthcare technologies and those who don't have (Eysenbach, 2011). World Economic Forum have reported that awareness, affordability and trust are the key barriers for digital health care adoption.

Creating technologies that attract usage, encourage initial usage and sustain continued engagement has consistently posed challenge. Within the healthcare sector, these challenges are accentuated, given that the potentially intrusive nature of certain technologies may cause patients to reject them outright, (Nadal, 2020). Lack of interoperability between different health information systems, security and privacy concerns, lack of user acceptance, high cost of implementation, and resistance to change from healthcare providers, are few concerned added factors (Prashant et al 2017)

TAM

Customer perception is the major determinant factor in building attitudes towards the technology. The Technology Acceptance model (TAM) is an information technology framework that helps to explain why users adopt or reject new technologies It was first proposed by Davis in1989, and has been widely used since then. Further it has been modifies and extended by Venkatesh and Davis (2002). TAM is originated from Theory of Reasoned Action- is a social psychological model that explains how people make decision and intentions to perform a behaviour are influenced by their attitude (Ajzen, and Fishbein, 1980). Unified Theory of Acceptance and Use of Technology (Venkatesh, Brown and Bala 2003) by Venkatesh et al is widely used because it integrates TAM, TRA and Diffusion of Innovation to explain how four factors influence a user's intentions to use new technology. Later it was tested in non-organisational settings also (Thong and Xu, 2012, 2016)

Studies conducted by Venkatesh at et (2003) to study TAM model for social media has disproved the relevance of the model. Another study to test user acceptance of computer technology conducted by Davis (1989) has recorded similar findings. Studies conducted by Park and Kim (2007) to evaluate Tam for ERP adoption in service organisation has also disproved TAM model.

Objectives

1. To study and analyze Digital healthcare technology adoption in relevance with Technology Adoption Model
2. To study the impact of two drivers: 'PU' (perceived usefulness) and 'PEOU' (Perceived Ease of Use) on 'Behavior Intention' of digital healthcare technology adoption

Hypothesis

H1-PU has positive association to Behavioral Intentions

H2-PEOU has positive association to Behavioral Intentions

H3-ATTITUDE has positive association to Behavior Intentions

Research Design

Literature survey on digital health technology includes several Global Health Reports and Indian Healthcare reports, Newsletters, PubMed research publications have helped to understand the present healthcare needs and status of digital health care technologies. These research papers and newsletters have provided insight into understanding of types of digital health care technologies and how they regulate the healthcare needs in prevention and monitoring the health.

Widely used Technology Adoption Model proposed by Davis (1989) is considered to understand the determinant factors for digital technology adoption. Other extended models have been studies to get better understanding of the model.

Based on the literature, four latent variables- Perceived Usefulness, Perceived Ease of Use, Attitude and Intention to adopt- were selected, and their relationship is framed.

Structured questionnaire is designed comprising of determinant factors for each latent variable. The sample largely focuses on young adults, as their adoptability to technology is higher compared to other segments. The sample size for the study is 209, of which 100 men and 109 females selected from age group 18-55 years.

Table 1. Descriptive statistics of sample size

FEMALE	109
18-25	98
25-35	11
MALE	100
18-25	70
25-35	16
35-45	7
45-55	4
55 and above	3
Grand Total	209

Data collected is analyzed using JMP Pro software. A Structural Equation Model is used to analyze the relationship between different latent variables and to test the TAM for this sample size.

Reliability test

Figure 1. CFA model

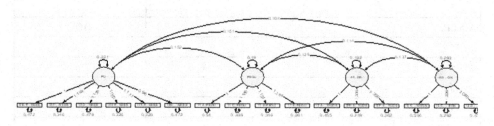

Table 2. Composite reliability

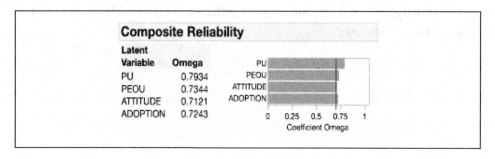

Table 3. Construct maximum reliability

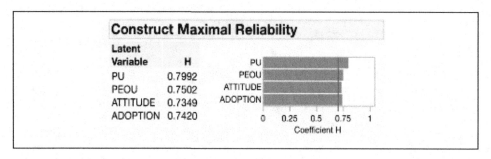

The composite reliability values range within acceptable range above 0.7 for all latent variables (Garson, 2016; Fabrigar et al., 2015; Barrett et al., 2014). CMR values of all latent variables- PU, PEOU, Attitude, and Adoption- are above 0.7 and are good fit for the study (Garson, 2016; Fabrigar et al., 2015; Barrett et al., 2014; Marcoulides, 2009). The model indicates correlations between observed variables. Overall, the model provides a good fit to the data. The fit indices indicate that the model is consistent with the data and that the latent variables are accurately represent the observed variables.

Figure 2. Structural equation model

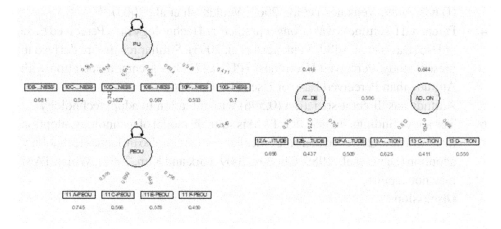

Table 4. CFI and RMSEA

ChiSquare	DF	Prob>ChiSq	CFI	RMSEA
259.5816	95	<.0001*	0.8467	0.0710

RMSEA and CFI Values

Calculated value RMSEA 0.0710 and CFI 0.8467, using JMP software with a sample size of 208 participants, indicate a fair fit to the data and can acceptable (Hu et al; 1999;Kline R.B, 2015; and Byrne, B M, 2016)

Research Findings

1. Perceived Usefulness and Perceived Ease of Use are interdependent latent variable. The present study supports the model proposed by Davis (Davis, 1989).
2. Perceived Usefulness (PU) has a significant association (0.471) with attitude formation. Similar findings were recorded by Venkatesh et al. (2003; Davis, 1989)
3. Perceived Ease of Use (PEOU) has Association (0.346) with Attitude formation (Davis, 1989; Venkatesh et al., 2003; Venkatesh et al., 2003).
4. Perceived Usefulness was stronger predictor of technology than Perceived Ease of Use (Davis et al, 1889; Venkatesh et al, 2003). Similar results are derived in present study. Perceived Usefulness (PU, 0.471) has greater association with Attitude than Perceived Ease of Use (PEOU, 0.346).
5. Attitude has direct association (0.596) with intention to adopt technology
6. The above findings suggest that TAM is suitable model of technology adoption for healthcare. However, there are other factors that can also influence technology adoption (Davis et al,. 1989; Chuttur, 2009; Park and Kim, 2007), Which TAM may not capture.

Discussions

1. Research readings provide validity to the TAM model, indicating a strong association of Perceived Usefulness and the association of Perceived Ease of Use. With health being the primary concern, the likelihood of acceptance and adoption will increase due perception towards benefits of digital technology.

2. Perceived usefulness contributes to the intention to adopt digital healthcare technology. The increasing numbers of different health concerns listed in second paragraph indicate a serious concern in Indian healthcare service delivery. Digital health will defiantly reduce the burden on present healthcare service ecosystem. It will ease the burden at possible points: such as monitoring the health vitals, recording the health care reports, carrying out possible tests (Diabetes meter and strips) by patient themselves, ordering medicines, educating patients on their healthcare needs, connecting doctors through digital platform and many add-on services that will ease healthcare efforts for patients.

3. Perceived ease of Use recorded an association with the Intention to Use (although not a higher association). The reason is that the younger generation are ready to adopt technology that will help them in day to day life challenges. Hinderances of complexity in usability are not a great concern among younger generation, as they have already adopted relevant technologies (smart phone, laptops, smart etc), which provide platform for digital technology.

4. Perceived Usefulness and Perceived Ease of Use have associations and interdependent behavioural factors. Perceived Usefulness a higher association to Intention, contributing to an increase in Perceived Ease of Use of technology. Digital technologies, which are designed to support healthcare needs with reduced economic burden and out-of-pocket cost for patients, definitely push behaviour intentions.

5. In addition to these factors, attitude can also be influenced by a person's personality, their past experience with technology and their beliefs about technology in general. The strong association of attitude and intention will enhance adoptability in digital health

6. Government initiatives such as Broadband Highway, Universal Mobile Connectivity, Public Internet Access, E-governance, E-Kranti (electronic delivery of services), Information to All, IT for Jobs and Early Harvest (McKinsey global Institute, 2019) have greatly favoured health technology by building the required infrastructure.

7. Both public and private healthcare providers need to develop digital healthcare product/service based on their usefulness. Focus can be placed on several diseases that require continuous monitoring and consultation. With the highest rate of diabetes disorder in India, there is a need for system and technology that can be accesses at one's finger tips, reducing economic burden of healthcare.

8. Challenge for digital healthcare providers is to develop and design digital healthcare product that addresses the needs with easy interfaces to increase convenience of understanding and use. Simple designs with minimum operational procedures can help people adopt the new technology easily. Many healthcare apps (such as Omada, Blue Star, Lilly which have larger customer base) are common in developed countries but are still finding their way to penetrate Indian market, despite India having the highest number of diabetic patients (these are providing digital therapeutics for diabetic patients) in the world. Even though Indian has a greater market opportunity, why are these big player have not yet made their presence is the question to be addresses. However, while the present study supports behavioural intentions to adopt digital healthcare technologies, other supporting initiatives of public and private organisations are required.

9. Digital healthcare eco system which can connect pharmaceuticals, health records, easy to testing and recording, rand enable regular connections with doctor via video call will reduce waiting time, travel cost and overall healthcare overhead costs (Prashant, 2023). Looking at the present infrastructure, it has the capacity to accommodate few types of digital healthcare technologies.

10. Digital health is more about providing to health information to people when they are in need (Prashant, 2023). E-content, e-consultation, and e-booking for tests are few examples of information and access that can. Bring ease and more usefulness to Digital healthcare

11. Busy lifestyle and high-stress work environment add more challenges to monitoring and regulating common diseases such as blood pressure, and diabetes. Many Digital therapeutics companies that have established a presence in developed countries are experiencing greater usability of their services. Some of these initiatives can help masses suffering from these disorders. A country with the highest diabetic patients defiantly has greater chances of technology adoption.

Digital health is the need of hour, which must be integrated into day-to-day life. Many healthcare requirements can be addressed with digital technology. The inclination of the younger generation towards most digital platforms can accelerate behavioural intentions to adopt. Government initiatives further reduce the corporate burden by providing required infrastructure to develop and operate their services. Greater challenges for IT firms is to develop and design suitable healthcare applications that will address the healthcare needs with easy user interface.

REFERENCES

Ajzen, I., & Fishbein, M. (1980). *Understanding attitudes and Predicting social behaviour*. Prentice-Hall.

Bandyopadhyay, S., & Saha, G. K. (2018) A review of technology acceptance models in digital health. *Journal of Medical Systems*, *42*(11), 220.

Barrett, P. T., Preacher, K. J., & Rourke, K. M. (2014). *Psychometrics: An introduction* (2nd ed.). Guilford Press.

Byrne, B. M. (2016). *Structural equation modelling with Amos: Basic concepts, applications and programming* (3rd ed.). Routledge. doi:10.4324/9781315757421

Chuttur, M. Y. (2009). A critical review of technology acceptance model (TAM). *International Journal of Business and Management*, *4*(8), 65–72.

Davia, F. D., Bagozzi, R. P., & Warshaw, P. R. (1989). User acceptance of computer technology: A comparison of twtheoretical models. *Management Science*, *35*(8), 982–1003. doi:10.1287/mnsc.35.8.982

Davis, F. D., Bagozzi, R. P., & Warshaw, P. R. (1989). User acceptance of computer technology: A comparison of twtheoretical models. *Management Science*, *35*(8), 982–1003. doi:10.1287/mnsc.35.8.982

Eysenbach, G. (2011). Medical web 2.0: Patients, consumers, and the transformation of health care. *Journal of Medical Internet Research*, *13*(3), 175.

Fabrigar, L. R., Wegener, D. T., MacCallum, R. C., & Strahan, E. J. (2015). *Confirmatory factor analysis*. Guilford Press.

Fleck, F. (2016). The mysteries of type 2 diabetes in developing countries. World health organization. *Bulletin of the World Health Organization, 94*(4), 241–242. doi:10.2471/BLT.16.030416 PMID:27034516

Garson, G. D. (2016). *Structural equation modeling: A basic guide with examples* (7th ed.). Routledge.

Global Tuberculosis Report 2020, (n.d.). https://www.who.int/publications/i/item/9789240013131

International Diabetes Federation. (2021) https://idf.org/about-diabetes/facts-figures/

Kvedar, J. C., Fogel, A. L., Elenk, E., & Zohar, D. (2016). Digital medicine's march on chronic disease. *Nature Biotechnology, 34*(3), 239–246. doi:10.1038/nbt.3495 PMID:26963544

Marcoulides, G. A. (2009). *Advanced structural equation modeling: Concepts, issues, and applications* (2nd ed.). Routledge.

McKinsey Global Institute. (2019). Digital India: Technology transform a connected nation. Author.

Ministry of electronics and Information Technology, Government of India. (n.d.). Retrieved from https://www.mckinsey.com/~/media/mckinsey/business%20functions/mckinsey%20digital/our%20insights/digital%20india%20technology%20to%20transform%20a%20connected%20nation/digital-india-technology-to-transform-a-connected-nation-full-report.pdf

Nadal, C., Sas, C., & Doherty, G. (2020). Technology Acceptance in mobile health: Scoping Review of Defination, Models and Measurement. Journal of Medical Interne. Retrieved from https://www.ncbi.nlm.nih.gov/pmc/articles/PMC7381045/

Park, S. Y., & Kim, Y. G. (2007). The effects of organizational, individual, and technological factors on ERP adoption in a Korean service industry. *International Journal of Electronic Commerce, 12*(1), 107–134.

Prashant, T. (2023). Digital health adoption in India: opportunities and challenges. Retrieved from https://timesofindia.indiatimes.com/blogs/voices/digital-health-adoption-in-india-opportunities-and-challenges/

Prashanth, C. V., Wang, J., Wu, S., & Chen, H. (2017). T Challenges and opportunities for digital health adoption. *Systematic Reviews*.

Rana, P., & Roy, V. (2015). Generic medicines: Issues and relevance for global health. *Fundamental & Clinical Pharmacology, 29*(6), 529–542. doi:10.1111/fcp.12155 PMID:26405851

Statista, Telemedicine Market in India. (2020). https://www.statista.com/statistics/1174720/india-telemedicine-market-size/

Sverdlov, O., van Dam, J., Hannesdottir, K., & Thornton-Wells, T. (2018). Digital therapeutics: An integral component of digital innovation in drug development. *Clinical Pharmacology and Therapeutics, 104*(1), 72–80. doi:10.1002/cpt.1036 PMID:29377057

Thong, J. Y., & Xu, X. (2012). Understanding user acceptance of information technology: A meta-analytic journey. *Management Information Systems Quarterly, 36*(1), 1–32.

Thong, J. Y., & Xu, X. (2016). Extending the unified theory of acceptance and use of technology: The role of performance expectancy. *Information Systems, 27*(2), 313–3381.

Venkatesh, V., Brown, S. A., & Bala, H. (2003). Model of adoption of information technology in household: A longitudinal study. MIS Quarterly, 27(3) 472-502. doi:10.2307/30036540

Venkatesh, V., Morris, M. G., Davis, G. B., & Davis, F. D. (2003). User acceptance of information Technology: Towards a unifies view. *Management Information Systems Quarterly, 27*(3), 425–478. doi:10.2307/30036540

WH2016. (n.d.). Retrieved from https://www.who.int/india/health-topics/cardiovascular-diseases

WH. (2017) https://www.who.int/news-room/fact-sheets/detail/chronic-obstructive-pulmonary-disease-(copd)

World Cancer Research Fund International. (n.d.). https://www.wcrf.org/cancer-trends/worldwide-cancer-data/ www.aarogyasetu.gov.in

Chapter 8
Embracing Mindfulness for Digital Transformation and Sustainable Success:
Embracing Mindfulness

Poondy Rajan Y.
Loyola Institute of Business Administration, India

Aiswarya Ramasundaram
Loyola Institute of Business Administration, India

Jenifer Arokia Selvi A.
iD https://orcid.org/0000-0002-6973-6433
Loyola Institute of Business Administration, India

ABSTRACT

This chapter investigates the crucial role that mindfulness plays as catalyst for fostering digital change within an organization. In a time of swift technological progress and changing corporate environments, effective digital adoption is now essential. This chapter explores how organizations motivate and mentor the staff members as they navigate the complex process of digital transformation. Through the integration of digitalization tactics and real-world case studies, the research demonstrates the many effects of mindfulness on cultivating the culture that values creativity, flexibility, and forward thinking. The research pinpoints the essential leadership attributes, communication tactics, and change management, methodologies that mindfulness utilizes to galvanize their groups, harmonize cooperate objectives and plot through the intricacies of technological transformation. This chapter adds to the readers' understanding of how mindfulness might act as transformative agent to help organizations successfully navigate the digital transformation process by illuminating these dynamics.

DOI: 10.4018/979-8-3693-2015-0.ch008

INTRODUCTION

In the swiftly changing technological terrain of today's world, digital transformation has become a defining force that reshapes industries, organizations, and even individual lives. The driving force behind successful digital transformation often lies in leaders who understand the intricacies of digital technologies and possess the vision and charisma to rally their teams toward a digitally empowered future. In this exploration of "Empowering Digital Futures," we delve into the dynamic realm of digital transformation and how leaders play a pivotal role in steering their organizations toward innovation, efficiency, and sustainable growth. Join us on a journey to uncover the strategies, insights, and stories that illuminate the path to a digitally empowered tomorrow.

Right now, we are witnessing the extensive incorporation of digital technologies across various industries and in virtually every facet of human existence. The process of digitization and the adoption of digital technologies can fundamentally alter nearly every facet of our contemporary society (Bharadwaj et al., 2013). These changes result in notable shifts in how services are delivered, businesses are run, and value is delivered to customers. Institutions, companies, and organizations have already experienced significant technological changes and expect even more profound challenges in the near term. Several factors are motivating these entities to adopt digital transformation. This process capitalizes on reduced hardware and software expenses, coupled with widespread access to global network connectivity, allowing them to align their business infrastructure with the evolving demands of the digital age. The acceleration of digital transformation within organizations can be attributed to various forces, including the influence of customers, employees, and competitors. The affordability of modern digital devices has led to widespread ownership, with many individuals now possessing these devices. Consequently, it has become routine for customers to use their mobile phones, iPads, and credit cards for online purchases. As a result, customer demands, expectations, and behaviors regarding digital transformation exert significant pressure on organizations to embrace it (Westerman et al., 2011). Achieving success in digital transformation enables companies and institutions to generate value and maintain their competitiveness within their respective markets.

Organizations often make strategic decisions regarding their preferred transformation pathways by taking into account external environmental factors that prompt them to consider digital transformation. In countries experiencing rapid growth, such as India, there has been a noticeable inclination towards embracing digital transformation. However, despite this trend, many organizations remain cautious about embracing technological changes, as they encounter various challenges. These challenges highlight the need for more research specifically focused on digital transformation, as most of the existing research has primarily concentrated on broader transition topics.

In the earlier years, with the growing significance of digital technologies and their swift transformation of organizations and industries, the idea of digital leadership has come to the forefront. It aims to address the crucial skills that leaders need in today's digital era. Nonetheless, there is still uncertainty surrounding the precise capabilities that set apart leaders capable of steering effective digital transformation. In this context, digital transformation pertains to an organization's capacity to make well-informed strategic choices for the successful integration of digitalization throughout the enterprise and its wider business environment. It is essential for organizations looking to navigate the complexities of digital transformation to prioritize competency development and five leadership competencies have been identified by examining the foundational skills that set leaders. Digital Vision: competency requires leaders to not only envision but also effectively communicate the digital future of the organization to all stakeholders. Digital Knowledge: Leaders must possess a deep understanding of digital tools and technologies and be well-versed in how specific technologies can impact the organization's customers and overall business operations. This knowledge enables informed decision-making. Ability to Adapt: The ability to quickly learn from failures is crucial for leaders which helps to conserve resources, efficiently manage projects or tasks, and swiftly discontinue initiatives that prove ineffective. It promotes agility and adaptability. Customer-Centricity: Digital leaders should prioritize the needs and expectations of customers. Understanding customer behavior and preferences in the digital realm is essential for delivering value and maintaining a competitive edge. Change Management: Effective digital leaders excel in change management. They can guide their teams through the complexities of digital transformation, addressing resistance to change, and ensuring a smooth transition to new digital practices and technologies. These competencies collectively empower leaders to lead their organizations through the challenges and opportunities presented by the digital age. They enable leaders to make strategic decisions, inspire their teams, and drive successful digital transformations that benefit both the organization and its broader ecosystem.

The chapter aims to find out how digital transformation has been adopted by the organisation with the effect of leadership and mindfulness to investigate and identify the specific characteristics and understand the traits and role of leaders in driving digital transformation within organizations. This includes chaptering how leaders motivate and influence their teams toward embracing digital technologies and innovations. The objective also aims to understand how leaders' emotional intelligence and abilities to manage their own emotions and those of their teams contribute to successful digital transformations. This chapter aims to explore how a leader's ability to foster innovation within the organization impacts the overall success of digital initiatives. This involves chaptering how different digital tools and platforms enable and facilitate digital transformation efforts. Ultimately, this should lead to overall growth and success in the digital era.

LITERATURE REVIEW

Mindfulness

Mindfulness refers to the state of being aware of one's thoughts and surroundings. According to Petchsawang and Duchon (2009), mindfulness is defined as "being fully present at the moment and having self-awareness of one's thoughts, emotions, and actions without being distracted by the past, future, or any other external factors". According to Davis and Hayes (2011), mindfulness can be defined as "a moment-to-moment awareness of one's experience without judgment"; "A state of psychological freedom that occurs when attention remains quiet and limber, without attachment to any particular point of view" - Kabat-Zinn, (1997). Mindfulness involves being in tune with one's internal states and the immediate environment. It offers individuals the capacity to steer clear of harmful or reflexive behaviors and reactions by teaching them how to observe their thoughts, emotions, and current experiences without making judgments or instinctively responding to them (Kabat (2003). This practice of mindfulness plays a central role in various therapeutic approaches, including mindfulness-based cognitive-behavioral therapy, mindfulness-based stress reduction, and mindfulness meditation. Krasner et al. (2018) investigated the influence of mindfulness-based interventions and suggested that such interventions effectively enhanced compassion among experts. Similarly, Xu et al. (2019) indicated that mindfulness intrusions successfully increased the self-awareness and regulation of employees' work and the ability to adapt to the latest transformation in the organisation. Furthermore, Condon et al. (2019) observed a positive association between mindfulness and outcomes in their resourceful review. Barraza and Goldin (2020) explored the effects of mindfulness interventions on understanding interpersonal relationships, including idealistic partnerships, parent-child dynamics, and teacher-student connections, and demonstrated that mindfulness interventions improved responsiveness in these different relationship contexts. Dholakia et al., (2021) delved into how mindfulness practice could enhance adopted abilities in leaders, enabling them to connect with and inspire their followers, and suggested that mindfulness could boost leaders' vicarious skills by helping them regulate their emotions and respond more effectively to the current situations. Dorjee and Khechok's (2022) research revealed that mindfulness practices could create a positive environment, improve leader and follower relationships, enhance emotional regulation, reduce stress, and potentially increase the flexibility to adapt to the changes leading to decreased disruptive behavior and foster a more positive learning atmosphere in the organisation.

Yet, it is worth noting that these studies mainly focused on the short-term effects of mindfulness interventions, leaving a significant gap in our understanding of their long-term impact on digital transformation is still not studied in depth with empirical support. To overcome this constraint, subsequent research should delve into the lasting impacts of mindfulness on empathy. Moreover, there is a need for further investigation into the relationship between mindfulness, digital transformation, and achievements in various industries such as automobiles, textiles, and banking. These avenues for future research could provide valuable insights into how mindfulness and digital transformation intersect with leadership and related outcomes. In summary, the existing studies highlight the potential advantages of mindfulness and digital transformation in leadership while also pointing out several promising directions for future research in this area.

Digital Transformation

Purchase et al. (2011) defined enterprise transformation as a substantial change that goes beyond routine alterations, fundamentally impacting an organization's relationships with key stakeholders such as customers, employees, suppliers, and investors. This transformation encompasses the creation of new value propositions for products and services, changes in their delivery and support, and even the reorganization of the enterprise itself. This concept of transformation has gained significance in the context of digital technologies, leading to the emergence of the research field of digital enterprise transformation (Hess et al., 2016). Digital enterprise transformation involves using digital technologies and networks to reshape organizational structures, processes, business models, and culture. It is a complex and dynamic process that can bring about radical departures from the current state of an organization (Liu et al., 2011), which is akin to organizational transformation, having a profound impact on the entire organization. Digital technologies and their evolving usage serve as pivotal drivers for deviations from existing trajectories in digital enterprise transformations (Liu et al., 2011). Numerous challenges are associated with digital enterprise transformation: (i) Absence of Vision: Organizations must establish a clear vision for their digital transformation journey, outlining objectives and a well-structured plan to meet customers' digital needs and deteriorating to articulate the why, what, and when of digital transformation can hinder success (Tiersky, 2017). (ii) Organizational Hurdles: Transitioning from established practices to new ones can be hindered by internal obstacles (Maltese, 2018). Complex administrative structures may resist innovation, creating disruptions among management, technical teams, and other members who may feel uncertain about their roles and job security (Wolf et al., 2018). (iii) Cultural Shifts: Digital transformation often requires a cultural shift within an organization. Younger workers may embrace new technologies, while older employees may struggle to adapt. Successful digital transformation begins with cultural changes that impact the entire organization (Schmidt, 2019). (iv) Technical Complexities: Initiating digital transformation demands a blend of talent and technology, with challenges related to selecting appropriate tools and technologies and ensuring that digital technology is maintainable, scalable, autonomous, efficient, robust, and reliable is critical. (v) Resource Constraints: A shortage of resources, both financial and human, can pose significant challenges, and adequate resources, including financial aspects and diverse employees, are vital for success. (vi) Team Development: Building a capable team with expertise across multiple disciplines is crucial for effective digital transformation (Overby, 2019). Such teams should prioritize user needs and adopt an "outside-in" mindset. Therefore, digital transformation is a multifaceted process that requires meticulous planning, strong leadership with the ability of emotional intelligence, and traits of mindfulness to address diverse challenges. A competent digital leader, possessing a combination of digital culture, digital competence, and leadership traits, is crucial for managing this complex journey effectively. Thus, we propose, that digital transformation will be influenced directly by leadership mindfulness through a conceptual model.

Figure 1. Proposed conceptual model: "The role of mindfulness on digital transformation"
Source: Author

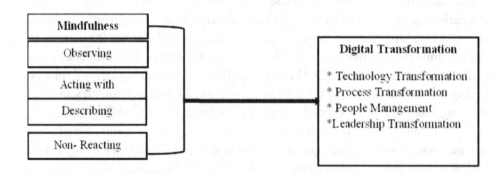

Hypothesis Development

From the above-proposed model, the author developed the following hypothesis:

H1: Mindfulness Observation has a positive relationship with digital transformation.

H2: Mindfulness of Acting with Awareness has a positive relationship with digital transformation.

H3: Descriptive Mindfulness has a positive relationship with digital transformation.

H4: Non–Judging mindfulness has a positive relationship with digital transformation.

H5: Non – Reacting Mindfulness has a positive relationship with digital transformation

Methodology and Samples

Research Design

"A research design is the arrangement of conditions for collection and analysis of data in a manner that aims to combine relevance to the research purpose with economy in procedure. It is a conceptual structure within which research is conducted." The research design employed in the current chapter is correlational, which explores connections between variables without the researcher exerting control or manipulation over them. A correlation signifies the intensity and/or direction of the association among two (or more) variables. Research methodology necessitates the exploration of procedures for data collection and sampling. It also involves detailing the measurement of constructs and outlining data analysis methods.

Measurement

A structured questionnaire was utilized to measure mindfulness and digital transformation. The questionnaire was adapted and modified based on previously conducted studies and self-administered by the respondents using a simple random sampling technique. The proper selection of an appropriate instrument is essential for collecting accurate data in a chapter. To ensure the validity of the scale the researcher followed a scientific process of selection, by conducting a pilot chapter with 20 participants to test the content creation.

Mindfulness

Mindfulness The *Five Facet Mindfulness Questionnaire (FFMQ) (Baer et al., 2006)* 39-item self-report assessment of dispositional mindfulness in which 15 questions were utilized. This scale encompasses five factors: Observation, description, mindful action, nonjudgment, and nonreactivity. Each item is evaluated on a 5-point Likert scale, ranging from "rarely or very rarely true" to "very often or almost always true."

Digital Transformation

The concept model put forth by Verina and Titko (2019) served as the basis for the development of the mindfulness scale. It comprises four subscales, each with three items: technology transformation, process transformation, people management, and digital leadership. On a 5-point Likert-type scale, where 1 represents strongly disagree and 5 represents strongly agree, employees answered these items. All the sub-factors and the items are included in the appendix.

Methods

The sample procedures are targeted at employees of any IT industry with the latest technology of digital transformation. Demographic information, including factors like age, gender, income, education, and marital status, can be selected for examination among the respondents had been collected. Employees from six major IT organizations located in South Chennai, Tamil Nadu, who worked full-time were included in our sample. We contacted 300 full-time employees using lists of randomly chosen full-time employees that each company's HR staff had provided. We asked them to complete the survey using a Google Form link, which we distributed, and we collected the data on the spot, assuring the employees that their participation was entirely voluntary and that their answers would be kept private and used only for research. Following the removal of erroneous (i.e., nearly uniform variation across all items) and partial responses (i.e., those that left out a significant portion of the survey), producing an 85% reply rate 67% of the respondents (N = 171) were male, their average age was 32 years (SD = 9.35), and their average time working for the company was 6 years (SD = 7.11).

Results

The chapter hypotheses were assessed using a three-step hierarchical linear regression in Smart PLSS, as shown in Table 1. A substantial positive impact emerged between MF-OBS (p-value is > .000) and DT, supporting H1. Further, there is a significant impact between MF-ACT (p value is > .000) and DT, supporting H2.

But there is an insignificance between MF-DES (p-value is < 0.163) and DT as well as MF-NJUDG (p-value is < 0.251) and DT hence not supporting H3 and H4. There is a positive significant impact between MF-NRA (p-value is > .000) and DT, supporting H5. Table 1 provides a summary of the data on the indirect impact of MF on DT.

Variables	Original Sample (O)	Sample Mean (M)	Standard Deviation (STDEV)	β	P Values
MF- OBS -> DT	0.211	0.212	0.060	3.518	0.000
MF-ACT -> DT	0.253	0.253	0.072	3.509	0.000
MF- DES -> DT	0.096	0.098	0.069	1.394	0.163
MF-NJUDG -> DT	0.082	0.084	0.071	1.148	0.251
MF-NRA -> DT	0.332	0.330	0.080	4.144	0.000

Note: MF: Mindfulness; OBS: Observing; DES: Describing; ACT: Acting with awareness; NJUDG: Non-Judging; NRA: Non-Reacting; DT: Digital Transformation.

Figure 2. The impact of mindfulness on digital transformation

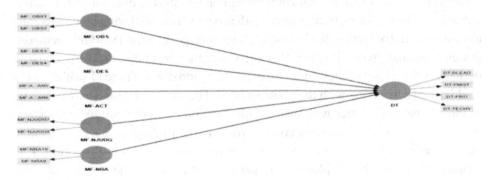

DISCUSSION

The present investigation is underpinned by an analytical framework that delves into the effects of mindfulness on the digital transformation of IT sector personnel. Regression analysis was done to test the hypotheses and evaluate the relationship as well as the impact on digital transformation of IT professionals selected for this chapter. The statistical analysis validates the research problem's significance. The results indicate a strong negative correlation between the employees' digital transformation and the Describing and Non-Judging aspects of mindfulness. This suggests that employees focus less on digital transformation when they share more about their inner views. Therefore, as mindfulness increases with overall subfactors, the level of output regarding digital transformation regarding Technology transformation related to cloud data, cybersecurity, and artificial intelligence, as well as process transformation regarding business strategies, operational processes, and new products for people management customer, employees, and partners, and for digital leadership adaptive role, visionary role, and innovative role, will be enhanced. The impact of mindfulness on the workplace behaviour of IT personnel was then investigated using linear regression analysis, with mindfulness being the Independent Variable (IV) and Digital Transformation the Dependent Variable (DV).

In addition, there had a significant beneficial effect on the digital transformation components from the subfactor of Observing and Acting with Awareness, which was related to the individual's competency. The results indicated a negative relationship between the variables Mindfulness of Describing and Non-Judging of Inner Experience and Digital Transformation, but a significant positive relationship between the variables Mindfulness of Observing, Acting with Awareness, and Non-Reactivity of Inner Experience and Digital Transformation. Therefore, it is possible to argue that increased mindfulness would have a bigger influence on digital transformation because it would increase organizational commitment and employee engagement. Diverse individuals from various backgrounds gather on a single platform and collaborate towards a shared objective. With these disparate perspectives and working methods, as well as the many work situations they encounter, they are unable to always adjust to the newest digital technology without experiencing job stress. Those IT workers who could manage by acting with their awareness and observation with Non-Reactivity of inner experience better with their mindful intuitions were more likely to adapt to the digital transformation quickly, according to the findings of the investigation into whether mindfulness could be used to predict the digital transformation. The chapter also shows that employees will perform better during the digital transition if they use their awareness, observation, and non-reaction to others.

Theoretical Implications

This chapter contributes to leadership theory by highlighting the importance of digital leadership in the context of digital transformation. It underscores the idea that leadership is not just about strategy but also about motivating and engaging employees during transformational periods. The chapter integrates mindfulness shedding light on the intricate mechanisms that influence digital transformation. This integration advances our understanding of how soft skills like mindfulness can play pivotal roles in a digitally evolving workplace. The research bridges the domains of leadership, psychology, and well-being (mindfulness), providing cross-disciplinary insights into how these fields intersect in the context of organizational change and innovation. Academicians can use this chapter to demonstrate the practical application of psychological concepts in the corporate world. It emphasizes the relevance of concepts like mindfulness in real-world leadership scenarios with the effect of digital transformation.

Managerial Implications

Organizations should invest in employee development programs through leadership that not only focus on technical skills but also emphasize the cultivation of personal qualities. Managers must undergo training that equips them with the ability to motivate and inspire their teams, particularly during periods of digital transformation. To facilitate this process, organizations can offer training in implementing mindfulness initiatives in the workplace can aid employees in coping with the stress and uncertainty often associated with digital transformations, ultimately enhancing their overall well-being and productivity. This involves crafting a clear vision for the digital transformation, effectively communicating it to all stakeholders, and providing consistent support and motivation to employees throughout the transformation journey. Furthermore, organizations can evaluate and measure the levels of emotional intelligence and mindfulness among their leaders and employees, leveraging this data to inform hiring decisions, tailor training programs, and conduct performance evaluations.

Encouraging a culture of open feedback and continuous improvement is paramount for managers. This approach allows for the adaptation of leadership strategies and the overall approach to digital transformation based on insights and the evolving needs of employees. Leaders should prioritize transparent communication throughout the digital transformation process, openly addressing challenges and celebrating milestones to build trust and minimize resistance to change. Eventually, this chapter offers valuable insights into the pivotal role of mindfulness within the context of digital transformation. Academics can leverage this research to advance leadership theories to adapt to the latest digital transformation and foster cross-disciplinary understanding, while marketers can apply these findings to craft effective strategies for driving organizational change and growth in the digital era.

Future Research

Future research should be explored further to investigate the relationship and interplay connections of the different styles of leaders who can motivate digital transformation and find out the empirical results for further evidence. However, more empirical research can be measured across various disciplines and industries such as automobile, pharmaceutical, healthcare, and FMCG industries would give results in a broader perspective and be beneficial widely across various nations. Also, can investigate the long-term effects of leadership development programs on organizations that have undergone digital transformations by assessing and including mindfulness among leaders that continue to influence employee well-being, productivity, and the sustained success of digital initiatives. Explore how cultural differences impact the effectiveness of leadership development programs and mindfulness in various regions which require tailored approaches to leadership and change management during digital transformations by analyzing how emerging technologies, such as artificial intelligence and virtual reality, can enhance leadership development programs and promote emotional intelligence and mindfulness. Conduct research on the direct correlation between leadership practices, mindfulness, and employee mental health during digital transformations and explore ways in which these factors can mitigate stress and anxiety associated with change. Also, can examine the ethical dimensions of leadership during digital transformations, including the responsible use of data and technology and how leaders navigate ethical dilemmas. Future research in these areas can contribute to a deeper understanding of how leadership qualities impact digital transformations and guide organizations in developing more effective strategies for navigating the complexities of the digital age.

CONCLUSION

In today's pandemic new normal scenario, most of the job's nature and design has been changed and following new normal methods by adopting various digital technologies and transformation so the organisation can change the current situations and support them by adopting digital practices by creating clear reward and approval systems and by motivating them through mindfulness to involve in their job for achieving the digital transformation. The importance of leadership encompasses both digital and technical skills through the influence of various employees' qualities which can be achieved in the context of digital transformation. Employees must be equipped with mindfulness skills to navigate the emotional complexities of change and lead with compassion. These initiatives not only enhance well-being and productivity but also contribute to the success of digital transformations. Regular assessments of mindfulness levels among employees by managers will provide valuable insights for informed decision-making and continuous improvement. Ultimately, a culture of open feedback, coupled with the adoption of these principles, fosters trust and minimizes resistance during the digital transformation journey. This research not only advances mindfulness theories but also offers actionable insights for marketers to drive organizational change and thrive in the digital age. It underscores that the effective role of organizational policies, and mindfulness are not just soft skills but essential components of a successful digital transformation strategy. This chapter further strengthens the reason for the positive outcomes of styles of leadership and their motivation in achieving the goals with strong job involvement.

REFERENCES

Avolio, B. J., & Gardner, W. L. (2005). Authentic leadership development: Getting to the root of positive forms of leadership. *The Leadership Quarterly*, *16*(3), 315–338. doi:10.1016/j.leaqua.2005.03.001

Baer, R. A., Smith, G. T., & Allen, K. B. (2004). Assessment of mindfulness by self-report: The Kentucky Inventory of Mindfulness Skills. *Assessment*, *11*(3), 191–206. doi:10.1177/1073191104268029 PMID:15358875

Barraza, J. A., & Goldin, P. R. (2020). Mindfulness and empathy in interpersonal relationships: A systematic review and meta-analysis. *Frontiers in Psychology*, *11*, 1–20.

Bass, B. M. (1985). *Leadership and performance beyond expectations*. Free Press.

Bass, B. M., & Riggio, R. E. (2006). *Transformational leadership* (2nd ed.). Psychology Press. doi:10.4324/9781410617095

Bass, B. M., & Riggio, R. E. (2006). *Transformational leadership* (2nd ed.). Lawrence Erlbaum. doi:10.4324/9781410617095

Bharadwaj, A., El Sawy, O. A., Pavlou, P. A., & Venkatraman, N. (2013). Digital business strategy: Toward a next generation of insights. *Management Information Systems Quarterly*, *37*(2), 471–482. doi:10.25300/MISQ/2013/37:2.3

Bono, J. E., & Ilies, R. (2006). Charisma, positive emotions, and mood contagion. *The Leadership Quarterly*, *17*(4), 317–334. doi:10.1016/j.leaqua.2006.04.008

Christensen, C. M., & Raynor, M. E. (2003). *The Innovator's Solution: Greeting and Sustaining Successful Growth*. Harvard Business School Press.

Condon, P., Desbordes, G., Miller, W. B., & DeSteno, D. (2019). The relationship between mindfulness and empathy: A systematic review. *Frontiers in Psychology*, *10*, 1–13.

Conger, J. A., & Kanungo, R. N. (1987). Toward a behavioral theory of charismatic leadership in organizational settings. *Academy of Management Review*, *12*(4), 637–647. doi:10.2307/258069

Davis, D. M., & Hayes, J. A. (2011). What are the benefits of mindfulness? A practice review of psychotherapy-related research. *Psychotherapy (Chicago, Ill.)*, *48*(2), 198–208. doi:10.1037/a0022062 PMID:21639664

Dholakia, U. M., Sopariwala, P. K., & Dholakia, R. R. (2021). Mindfulness and empathy in leadership: A review. *Journal of Business Research*, *123*, 431–441.

George, J. M. (2015). Emotions and leadership: The role of emotional intelligence. *Human Relations*, *58*(11), 1355–1377.

Gu, Q., Tang, T. L., & Jiang, W. (2018). Does inspirational leadership facilitate change in the era of healthcare globalisation? The role of organisational identification. *Health Policy and Planning*, *33*(9), 1022–1034.

Hess, T., Matt, C., Benlian, A., & Wiesböck, F. (2016). Options for formulating a digital transformation strategy. *MIS Quarterly Executive*, *15*(2), 123–139.

Kabat-Zinn, J. (2003). Mindfulness-based interventions in context: Past, present, and future. *Clinical Psychology : a Publication of the Division of Clinical Psychology of the American Psychological Association*, *10*(2), 144–156. doi:10.1093/clipsy.bpg016

Kabat-Zinn, J., Massion, A., Hebert, J. R., & Rosenbaum, E. (1997). Meditation. International Journal of Holland.

Kim, K. J., Kim, J. Y., Kim, K. W., & Kim, J. H. (2021). How inspirational leadership enhances psychological capital: The moderating role of collectivism. *Leadership and Organization Development Journal*, *42*(3), 336–350. doi:10.1108/LODJ-02-2020-0072

Krasner, M. S., Epstein, R. M., Beckman, H., Suchman, A. L., Chapman, B., Mooney, C. J., & Quill, T. E. (2018). Mindfulness and empathy in healthcare settings: A systematic review and meta-analysis. *Journal of General Internal Medicine*, *33*(1), 119–129.

Liu, D.-Y., Chen, S.-W., & Chou, T.-C. (2011). Resource fit in digital transformation: Lessons learned from the CBC Bank global e-banking project. *Management Decision*, *49*(10), 1728–1742. doi:10.1108/00251741111183852

Luo, J., Li, S., Gong, L., Zhang, X., & Wang, S. (2022). How and when workplace ostracism influences employee deviant behavior: A self-determination theory perspective. *Frontiers in Psychology*, *13*, 1002399. doi:10.3389/fpsyg.2022.1002399 PMID:36329754

Maltese, V. (2018). Digital Transformation Challenges for Universities: Ensuring Information Consistency Across Digital Services. *Cataloging & Classification Quarterly, 56*(7), 592–606. doi:10.1080/01639374.2018.1504847

Mwita, M. M., & Joanthan, J. (2019). Digital leadership for digital transformation. *Electronic Scientific Journal, 10*(4), 2082–2677.

Overby, S. (2019). Digital transformation dream teams: 8 people you need. The Enterprisers Project. Retrieved from https://enterprisersproject.com/article/2019/12/digital-transformation-teams-8-key-roles

Petchsawang, P., & Duchon, D. (2009). Measuring workplace spirituality in an Asian context. *Human Resource Development International, 12*(4), 459–468. doi:10.1080/13678860903135912

Purchase, V., Parry, G., Valerdi, R., Nightingale, D., & Mills, J. (2011). Enterprise transformation: Why are we interested, what is it, and what are the challenges? *Journal of Enterprise Transformation, 1*(1), 14–33. doi:10.1080/19488289.2010.549289

Schmidt, T. (2019). Successful Digital Transformation Begins with a Cultural Transformation. The Data-Driven Enterprise. Retrieved from https://www.cio.com/article/3402022/successful-digital- transformation-begins with-a-cultural-transformation.html

Schutte, N. S., Malouff, J. M., Hall, L. E., Haggerty, D. J., Cooper, J. T., Golden, C. J., & Dornheim, L. (1998). Development and Validation of Emotional Intelligence. *Personality and Individual Differences, 25*(2), 167–177. doi:10.1016/S0191-8869(98)00001-4

Sosik, J. J., & Cameron, J. C. (2010). Character and authentic transformational leadership behavior: Expanding the ascetic self toward others. *Consulting Psychology Journal, 62*(4), 288–306. doi:10.1037/a0022104

Spreitzer, G. M., De Janasz, S. C., & Quinn, R. E. (1999). Empowered to lead: The role of psychological empowerment in leadership. *Journal of Organizational Behavior, 20*(4), 511–526. doi:10.1002/(SICI)1099-1379(199907)20:4<511::AID-JOB900>3.0.CO;2-L

Tiersky, H. (2017). 5 top challenges to digital transformation in the enterprise. Retrieved from https://www.cio.com/article/3179607/5-top-challenges-to-digital-transformation-in-the- enterprise.html

Verina, N., & Titko, J. (2019, May). Digital transformation: conceptual framework. In Proc. of the Int. Scientific Conference "Contemporary Issues in Business, Management and Economics Engineering (pp. 9-10). 10.3846/cibmee.2019.073

Walumbwa, F. O., Avolio, B. J., Gardner, W. L., Wernsing, T. S., & Peterson, S. J. (2018). Authentic leadership: Development and validation of a theory-based measure. *Journal of Management, 34*(1), 89–126. doi:10.1177/0149206307308913 PMID:30443095

Wang, L., Chen, J., & Chen, Y. (2017). How inspirational leadership contributes to team creativity: The mediating role of team positive affective tone and the moderating role of team task reflexivity. *Journal of Organizational Behavior, 38*(5), 682–702.

Weber, M. (1947). *The theory of social and economic organization.* Free Press.

Westerman, G., Calmejane, C., Bonnet, D., Ferraris, P., & McAfee, A. (2011). Digital Transformation: A roadmap for billion-dollar organizations. *MIT Center for Digital Business and Capgemini Consulting, 1*, 1–68.

Wolf, M., Semm, A., & Erfurth, C. (2018). Digital transformation in companies - challenges and success factors. Paper presented at the International Conference on Innovations for Community Services. 10.1007/978-3-319-93408-2_13

Xu, W., Xu, J., & Liu, Y. (2019). The effects of mindfulness on empathy: A meta-analysis. *Journal of Health Psychology, 24*(10), 1199–1211.

APPENDIX

Mindfulness

Mindfulness (FFMQ Developed by Baer et al., 2006)

(I)   Observing
1.   I pay attention to sensations, such as the wind in my hair or the sun on my face.
2.   I notice changes in my body, such as my heart rate or breathing.
(II)   Describing
3.   I can easily put my thoughts and feelings into words.
4.   I can describe my emotions without getting lost in them.
(III) Acting with awareness
5.   I find myself doing things without paying attention.
6.   I find myself lost in thought even when doing something enjoyable.
(IV)   Non-judging of inner experience
7.   I criticize myself for having irrational or inappropriate emotions.
8.   I tell myself I should not be feeling the way I am feeling.
(V)   Non-reactivity to inner experience
9.   I feel like I am on an emotional roller coaster.
10.   I get caught up in my thoughts and cannot stop them.

Digital transformation (Verina & Titko (2019))

(I)   Technology Transformation
1.   Cloud Data
2.   Cyber Security
3.   Internet of Things/Artificial Intelligence
(II)   Process Transformation
1.   Business strategies
2.   Operational Process
3.   New Products/ Services
(III) People Management
1.   Customer / Clients
2.   Employees Workforce
3.   Partners/Stakeholders/Suppliers
(IV)   Digital Leadership
1.   Adaptive Role

2. Visionary Role
3. Innovative Role

Chapter 9
Impact of Mindfulness on the Modern Workplace

Amrit Mund
Indian Institute of Management, Bodh Gaya, India

Anshul Singh Chauhan
Indian Institute of Management, Bodh Gaya, India

Akshat Tarush
Indian Institute of Management, Bodh Gaya, India

Aditya Amol Joshi
Indian Institute of Management, Bodh Gaya, India

ABSTRACT

This chapter delves into the impact of mindfulness on the modern workplace through a qualitative study, leveraging 30 in-depth interviews with professionals spanning various sectors, including banking, financial services, and insurance (BFSI); education; manufacturing; and more. This chapter uncovers the debilitating effects of workplace stress on professionals across sectors. It demonstrates that mindfulness offers a potent means to alleviate stress. This chapter spotlights the unique challenges faced by working women in the modern workplace and how mindfulness practices empower women by enhancing self-confidence and resilience and promoting a healthy work-life balance. With the digital age, Gen Z employees exhibit distinct expectations and behaviors, posing a challenge to traditional work cultures. Mindfulness is identified as an essential tool for them to manage stress and improve focus. The chapter also accentuates the necessity for organizations to invest in mindfulness programs and initiatives.

DOI: 10.4018/979-8-3693-2015-0.ch009

INTRODUCTION

Mindfulness is important in today's day and age, and the subject has been growing in recent years. Mindfulness sessions are being conducted in offices of big firms, and are also mindfulness courses being setup in educational institutions. With this research, we study and derive the impact of mindfulness on the modern workplace.

Rationale of the Study

In today's fast-paced and constantly evolving world, mindfulness has emerged as an essential practice for individuals seeking balance and well-being (Mishra, 2023). Mindfulness is now being examined scientifically and has been found to be a key element in stress reduction and overall happiness (Harvard Health Publishing, 2023).

At its core, mindfulness is the art of being fully present in the moment. It involves intentionally bringing our attention to the sensations, thoughts, and emotions that arise in each moment, without getting caught up in them or reacting impulsively (Mishra, 2023). It encourages us to pause, take a breath, and engage with our experiences deliberately and non-judgmentally. Doing so allows us to break free from the relentless grip of our thoughts, worries, and distractions. Instead, we focus on the here and now, appreciating the richness of each moment. This practice has profound implications for our mental, emotional, and physical well-being. It has been scientifically proven to reduce stress, enhance self-awareness, improve concentration, and foster greater emotional resilience. Moreover, mindfulness can deepen our relationships with others, encouraging us to listen more attentively and respond with empathy.

In our hurried lives, it is easy to overlook the importance of mindfulness, dismissing it as a luxury or something reserved for meditation enthusiasts. However, it is precisely when life becomes demanding that mindfulness becomes indispensable. It empowers us to navigate challenges with clarity, make better decisions, and savor the joys that often elude us. So, in this era where the demands of work, technology, and daily responsibilities can feel overwhelming, let us recognize that mindfulness is not an indulgence but a necessity. It is a tool that equips us to thrive amid chaos, fostering a sense of calm and contentment amid life's uncertainties. We can live in the present by embracing mindfulness sowing the seeds of a more balanced and fulfilling existence.

As students of IIM BG, we were fortunate to have mindfulness inculcated into our academic journey right from the start of our academic journey. Before joining, we were merely told not to take stress but never taught how to reduce stress. Our institute's choice to equip us with mindfulness profoundly impacted our personal and professional growth. It armed us with invaluable tools to navigate the rollercoaster of stress, master our emotions, and approach life's challenges with a more positive outlook. The ripple effect was remarkable – not only did our mental well-being soar, but our decision-making skills sharpened, allowing us to strike that elusive balance between work and life. This change was reflected not merely in academic performances but also in a managerial context when we discussed real-life problems.

Our exposure to mindfulness sparked some burning questions about its presence in the corporate world. As future managers, we were already equipped with this crucial skill. However, we were wondering whether other organizations are following suit, imparting similar mindfulness training to their employees, or was our experience primarily a product of changing workplace dynamics among our generation? Were professionals naturally acquiring these skills through work experiences or actively seeking mindfulness resources and guidance? Additionally, we could not help but wonder if mindfulness was confined solely to office hours or if it extended into employees' personal lives, enriching their overall well-being.

Furthermore, we pondered the corporate stance on mindfulness. Were companies proactively championing and encouraging mindfulness practices, recognizing the positive impact on individual well-being and overall productivity, or were they taking a hands-off approach, allowing employees to explore these practices independently?

We came from various backgrounds: Finance, Government, Education, etc and thus explored each sector's relationship with mindfulness.

Given the current landscape, it is clear that mindfulness has become an essential requirement for everyone. By cultivating a sense of presence and awareness, in the middle of the chaos, we can discover greater serenity and quiet by learning to appreciate the beauty of life (M. Kapoor, 2023). We've opted to explore this topic in depth to understand its influence on various industries and, if not already present, to understand the potential impact it can bring. This decision reflects the recognition that mindfulness is a critical aspect of everyday life and business, deserving our careful examination to uncover its potential benefits and effects on specific sectors.

Objective of the Study

To comprehensively Study the influence of mindfulness within specific industries, namely – BFSI (Banking, Financial Services, and Insurance), Education, Government, Aviation, and Food and Beverage—we aim to explore three key dimensions: the occasion of its usage, the organizational perspective, and the personal experiences of individuals involved.

Our decision to delve into these dimensions lies in the recognition that mindfulness can play a transformative role in various sectors, and understanding how and when it is applied, as well as its impact on both organizational and individual levels, is paramount. This approach underscores our commitment to gaining a holistic understanding of mindfulness's relevance and potential within these industries.

Research Objectives

1. The impact of learning and implementing mindfulness techniques in different industries.
2. Examining how these techniques contribute to career growth and personal fulfillment.
3. Analyzing whether there are any challenges or obstacles faced by individuals when trying to adopt and practice these techniques effectively in their respective fields.

LITERATURE REVIEW

In the pursuit of a deeper understanding of the role of mindfulness within our chosen industries, our research endeavor included a comprehensive examination of diverse media outlets. It is important to note that our information-gathering process was meticulously curated, with an unwavering commitment to sourcing only pertinent materials with ethical standards.

Our methodological approach involved a review of research papers, articles, and TEDx talks, ensuring the integrity and relevance of our information sources.

Mindfulness at Workplace

Mindfulness in the workplace promotes mental well-being, enhancing focus and productivity. It encourages employees to be present, reducing stress and improving decision-making. By fostering a mindful culture, organizations empower their teams to navigate challenges with clarity, ultimately fostering a more positive and effective work environment. Organizations that inculcate mindfulness often have greater productivity compared to those that don't.

To fully comprehend the value of mindfulness at work, researchers and practitioners should consider both its advantages and potential drawbacks (E Choi et al., 2022). The results in the paper discussed both these benefits and possible disadvantages of mindfulness at work, within The Balance Framework's five dimensions (*viz.*): Document Representation, Financial Indicators, Learning models, Evaluation measures, Experiment Design.

Mindfulness meditation practices can be an effective way to reduce stress and improve well-being in certain contexts. Not all programs offered by companies are effective when teaching about mindfulness (Cameron et al., 2022). We used these as a basis for understanding the impact of company-provided training on the employees as well as to understand the complexity of training employees in stress management.

In reference to the incorporation of mindfulness-based interventions in the workplace to improve productivity, boost employee morale, and enhance problem-solving abilities. It also provides a working definition of mindfulness as the intentional, accepting, and non-judgmental focus on present-moment experiences (Hoof, 2015). Mindfulness is seen as a way to counteract employees' tendencies to dwell on past events or anticipate future ones, which can hinder effective communication and decision-making. This paper formed the basis of our understanding of the impact of mindfulness on organizations and how to ensure peak efficiency when mindfulness is inculcated. It also laid the foundation for the employees' perspective.

The study confirms the fact that mindfulness enhances work performance. The impact of mindfulness is not limited to the well-being of Health Care Professionals but is also associated with enhanced job performance (Lomas et al., 2017). This paper formed a minor basis of our discussions and analysis but was not kept at the forefront due to criticism of its sample choice and analysis methods.

Workplace Stresses

Workplace stresses encompass various challenges that can impact employees' mental and physical well-being. These stressors often include heavy workloads, tight deadlines, conflicts with colleagues, job insecurity, and lack of work-life balance. Addressing workplace stress is essential to promote employee health, productivity, and job satisfaction.

There is an inverse relationship between stress and productivity (Harshana, 2018). Further, Occupational well-being has a significant impact on the health of employees and the overall health of organizations. Organizations that address such problems will have better productivity.

Participants reported adverse working conditions and management practices as common causes of work stress. Stress-inducing management practices included unrealistic demands, lack of support, unfair treatment, low decision latitude, lack of appreciation, effort–reward imbalance, conflicting roles, lack of transparency, and poor communication. The study was conducted by (Bhui et al., 2016) as part of a qualitative study: Organizational interventions were perceived as effective if they improved management styles and included physical exercise, taking breaks, and ensuring adequate time for planning work tasks. We used these as a reference to gauge the difference between organizations that gave support for mindfulness and those that didn't.

The causes of job stress and what action could be taken for alleviation of such stress, categorized into Primary, Secondary, and tertiary methods of prevention was taken from Satpathy and Mitra(2015) in Stress at Workplace an Overview.

Working Women

"Working women" is a term used to refer to women who are actively employed in paid work or have a career outside of their household responsibilities. This term encompasses a wide range of women, including those who work part-time or full-time jobs, run their own businesses, hold positions in various industries and professions, and contribute to the labor force in various capacities. The below two researches made us consider this as a vertical of our research.

The study significantly contributes to the existing literature by extending the research period over a longer timeframe (Nilsen et al, 2016). Furthermore, it focuses on employed women with children who exhibit diverse patterns of mental health trajectories. This correlates to the stress faced by women with children in the workplace, giving us an understanding of the stress levels faced while working and managing the household.

Employees are happier in their jobs when they're led by a woman, but being an effective leader has more to do with trust than with gender (Misty Pratt, 2023).

GenZ Lifestyle (the Future Generation)

Gen Z, born roughly between the mid-1990s and early 2010s, exhibits unique lifestyle traits. They're digital natives, prioritizing technology, social media, and online connectivity. Gen Z tends to value individuality, diversity, and sustainability, influencing their consumption habits, career choices, and social activism. Flexibility and work-life balance are essential in their professional lives. There is, however, evidence of lower attention span within this generation.

It is clearly stated that "we are seeing with young people who come into the workplace, Gen Z, particularly post-pandemic and with this concentration of short-form content, is that they haven't got the skills to debate things," Bhaimiya said this referring to social media platforms like TikTok, Instagram and YouTube that often feeds users content they already agree with propelling them into echo chambers (Sawdah Bhaimiya, 2023). This helped us get an understanding of where the main effects of mindfulness are viewed in the younger generation and what other problems need to be addressed.

RESEARCH METHODS

Sample of the Study

By using a purposeful sampling method, we selected 30 professionals working under five prominent sectors, viz. Education, Corporate, Government, Healthcare, and Mindfulness as a course. Figure 1

1. **Education:** Individuals with a career in education, such as academic staff and administrators.
2. **Corporate:** People who work in the banking, financial services, and insurance industries, such as bankers and financial analysts, as well as people working in manufacturing industries and IT services.
3. **Government:** Participants who are employed by different government departments and agencies, such as employees in the civil service as well as employees in the public sector
4. **Healthcare:** Personnel from the healthcare industry, such as medical staff, doctors, nurses, and administrators.
5. **Mindfulness Instructors:** This distinct industry consists of people who know mindfulness techniques and train students and workplace professionals on the same.

Figure 1. Sector-wise participation in the interviews

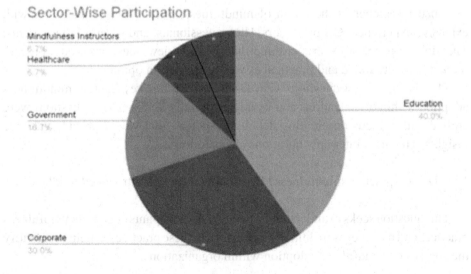

We also constructed an inclusion criteria. The adoption of specific inclusion criteria in this study was driven by the need to ensure the depth and reliability of insights.

The inclusion criteria included,

(1) **Years of Work Experience:** Participants had to meet a minimum 5-year work experience requirement in order to be considered for inclusion in the process. This criterion was crucial to make sure that the study's conclusions were grounded in actual experience rather than just theoretical knowledge. Professionals with extensive experience are more likely to provide nuanced perspectives on organizational behavior.

(2) **Designation:** - We chose members of various levels of seniority in the company that they work at, in order to gauge the impact of mindfulness and measure any resistance to change

These criteria collectively enabled the study to capture real-world insights into the diverse sectors under investigation, enhancing the overall effectiveness of the research findings.

Tool for Data Collection

The ascribed paper accentuates the tools and methodologies employed to gather data on organizational behavior regarding mindfulness, with a focus on interviews as a primary data collection method.

To construct a robust interview framework, we engaged in a meticulous process of consultation and collaboration. We sought input from experts in the field, a seasoned researcher in the realm of mindfulness, a mindfulness instructor with extensive experience, OB professors, HR professionals, and several PhD students. This diverse panel of experts ensured that the interview questions would be both theoretically grounded and practical as well as diverse in opinions.

The main interview questions were designed to explore key facets of mindfulness adoption within organizations and its impact on individuals. These questions were crafted with a focus on eliciting detailed responses that would provide valuable insights. The main interview questions are as follows:

1.   Do you practice mindfulness? If yes, how were you introduced to it?

This question seeks to understand whether the participants engage in mindfulness practices and how they were initially introduced to these practices. It helps us identify the sources of mindfulness adoption within organizations.

2.   What is the occasion of your usage?

Participants were asked to elucidate the circumstances or situations in which they employ mindfulness techniques. This question provides context for the integration of mindfulness into their daily lives and work routines.

3.   Has your organization conducted any kind of mindfulness workshop?

To assess the role of organizations in promoting mindfulness, participants were asked about the existence of mindfulness workshops within their workplaces.

4.   How did the workshop impact you personally, did you feel any positive and needed change?

This question delves into the personal experiences and perceived benefits of mindfulness workshops, shedding light on the tangible impacts of organizational initiatives.

5.   On a scale of 0-10, with 10 being the highest, how would you rate the effectiveness of mindfulness?

This quantitative question provides a numerical assessment of the perceived effectiveness of mindfulness practices, allowing for comparisons and trend analysis.

6.   The new generation, often referred to as GenZ, exhibits distinctive lifestyle choices marked by individualism and extensive digital engagement. However, the workplace demands interpersonal skills and collaboration. How important and effective is mindfulness to the new generation in this very aspect?

This nuanced question encourages participants to reflect on the relevance and impact of mindfulness practices on the younger generation in a rapidly evolving digital landscape.

In addition to the main interview questions, we incorporated sub-questions based on the flow of each particular interview to further enrich the data; some of the most important of these questions were:

1.   As part of your sector, how has mindfulness helped you?

Participants were encouraged to discuss the specific benefits of mindfulness within their respective industries or sectors.

2.   How widespread is the use of mindfulness in your organizations?

This question gauges the extent to which mindfulness practices have permeated different organizations and industries.

3.   What has changed in your life, due to mindfulness?

Participants were invited to reflect on personal transformations attributed to mindfulness adoption, providing narratives of change.

4.   How does mindfulness help you cope with changes in your work and life?

This question explores the role of mindfulness in aiding individuals in coping with the inevitable changes in both their professional and personal lives.

5.   What are your thoughts and feelings, the overall perspective about this?

An open-ended question, this allows participants to express their opinions, emotions, and reflections on mindfulness adoption and its impact.

6.   Mindfulness is being adopted by the mainstream very quickly, and thus the interpretations are different and thus become obsolete. Does this help or hinder the movement?

This question encourages participants to provide a critical analysis of the impact of mindfulness going mainstream and asks if they think that this will probably dilute its core principles and effectiveness.

In carving the interview outline for data collection, we meticulously consulted experts, literature, and diverse perspectives. The interview questions, both main and subquestions, were designed to extract comprehensive data on mindfulness adoption, impact, and perceptions. The inclusion of a question about the mainstream adoption of mindfulness adds depth to the study by considering the holistic context of this phenomenon.

Data Collection

Once our interview questions were finalized, we embarked on the task of recruiting suitable participants. We approached this with meticulous care, aiming to ensure that our interviewees possessed the necessary experience in their respective sectors to provide valuable insights into the role of mindfulness in the workplace. We also strived to maintain diversity in our participant pool to capture a broad gamut of perspectives. In our recruitment process, we communicated the purpose and significance of our study to potential interviewees in advance. This transparent communication helped set expectations and fostered a sense of willingness to participate. We also scheduled interview times at the convenience of the participants to minimize any potential disruptions to their work schedules.

Interview Process: The interviews themselves were conducted in a one-on-one format, in a separate room designed to provide a quiet and distraction-free environment. This setting was chosen to ensure that the participants could fully engage with the interview process and share their insights without interruptions. Each interview session was led by one of the four authors of this paper, all of whom were second-year students pursuing a degree in management. The interviews took 10-25 minutes per person.

Recording and Confidentiality: To preserve the integrity of the data collected, all interviews were recorded. These recordings were meticulously stored and kept strictly confidential, with access restricted solely to the research team. The participants were explicitly informed of this recording process, and their consent was obtained. Importantly, participants were also made aware of their right to withdraw consent at any point during the interview or subsequent data analysis phases.

Measures taken while collecting data: To foster an atmosphere of trust and authenticity during the interviews, our researchers employed various measures. These included unconditional acceptance, active listening, and clarification. These measures aimed to encourage participants to express their thoughts, feelings, and experiences openly while minimizing potential interviewer bias.

Flexibility in Data Collection: Recognizing the diverse nature of our participant pool, we tailored our data collection approach to meet individual preferences. For some participants, face-to-face interviews were conducted, allowing for in-person engagement and a deeper level of interaction. In contrast, others preferred telephone interviews for the sake of convenience. This flexibility ensured that we were able to accommodate the needs of our participants while maintaining the effectiveness of data collection.

RESULTS

Having collected data from primary and secondary sources, we proceeded to analyze the interviews on several key topics listed below and drew meaningful inferences based on the understanding of the subject matter. We focused on those factors that were repeated across interview responses.

Working Women

The sample population for this particular topic was three women from three different sectors, and the responses tell us that mindfulness has really helped women in the workplace.

One of the most exigent issues for women in the workplace appears to be finding a balance between the workplace and home. Anatomization of interviews suggests that mindfulness seems to bridge the gap between them. The interviews also propound the notion that women imbibe mindfulness to deal with stress pertaining to the rift between work life and personal life.

"So, a day at my home and balancing the same at the office is most important. So, I say that mindfulness is most effective to vary or to stick constantly to balance your professional and personal life. So, as a woman, I see that things are more to be balanced out of this."

~ A woman healthcare professional

Workplace Stress

In professional life, mindfulness is pivotal in enhancing decision-making, especially in high-responsibility roles like those dealing with contractual matters. This practice allows individuals to transcend the reactive tendencies that often accompany stress, enabling them to contemplate broader implications and maintain a focus on their tasks. However, a lack of organizational support can hinder the successful implementation of mindfulness within an organization, including the absence of workshops and employee reluctance to adopt mindfulness practices. Additionally, challenges may arise when clients or superiors struggle to control their emotions in high-pressure situations, underscoring the need for mindfulness to maintain resilience and well-being in the professional sphere.

Adapting Mindfulness helps people deal with these challenges in the following ways:

1. **Decision-making:** It allows individuals to consider broader implications, be more aware of their actions, and avoid reactive decision-making. This is particularly important in roles with heavy responsibilities and diverse tasks, such as handling contractual matters and environmental conservation efforts.
2. **Stress management:** Many professionals, especially those in high-stress sectors like finance, find that mindfulness helps them cope with stress. It

enables them to separate themselves from the stress and focus on their tasks more effectively.

However, there are certain issues with its implementation, *viz.*

- *Lack of organizational support:* No workshops conducted
- *Systemic support as well employee lethargy in adopting mindfulness practice:* Even if workshops are held, employees do not attend due to lack of interest or busy schedules
- *Ancillary point:* Clients or higher-ups rarely reign their temper/anger or hold their emotion

"Mindfulness has had a significant impact on our well-being and performance. It helps us handle the pressures of our roles with greater resilience. It also enhances our decision-making by allowing us to consider the broader ecological and long-term implications of our actions."

~ someone from the corporate sector

Effect on the Newer Generations

The interviews explore the multifaceted significance of mindfulness in contemporary contexts. It delves into the challenges posed by the fragmented mindfulness industry, the critical role of mindfulness in education, and the potential benefits of early exposure. Additionally, it examines mindfulness as a tool for addressing attention span issues in the digital age and its role in navigating changing family dynamics.

Self-discovery: The acquisition of mindfulness transcends mere participation in workshops or adherence to spiritual guides. The interviews posit that It involves a journey of self-discovery, introspection, and understanding one's reactions and emotions.

Fragmented Mindfulness Industry: The sector of mindfulness is diverse and fragmented. Different techniques exist, making it challenging to bring them all onto a common platform.

Importance of Mindfulness in Education: Mindfulness is essential in the education sector, including schools and colleges. It is seen as a tool to help students manage stress, develop self-awareness, and cope with academic and social expectations

Early Introduction of Mindfulness: Participants emphasized the need to introduce mindfulness early, ideally in schools and colleges. Starting mindfulness practices early can help students build awareness and stress-coping skills that can benefit them throughout their lives.

Mindfulness vs. Academic Pressure: While mindfulness is seen as necessary, there is a concern about overburdening students with additional coursework related to mindfulness. Participants suggest that it should not be graded but rather integrated into the curriculum as an awareness-building practice. Check feasibility.

Holistic Development: Mindfulness is viewed as a means to promote holistic student development.

Early Exposure and Lifelong Benefits: Introducing mindfulness to students at a young age is seen as an investment in their future well-being. It equips them with tools to handle various life situations effectively.

Mindfulness and Broken Families: In an era where family dynamics are changing, mindfulness is seen as a valuable resource for individuals to navigate the challenges of modern family life change in social dynamics

Hope for Wider Adoption: Participants express hope that mindfulness will become integral to education, helping students lead more balanced and emotionally aware lives.

Lack of Attention Span

1. Digital Age Challenges: Gen Z has grown up in a digital age characterized by constant connectivity and information overload. This has led to shorter attention spans due to frequent multitasking and distractions.
2. Digital Detox: Mindfulness can encourage Gen Z workers to take breaks from digital devices. These breaks can improve their attention spans by reducing the constant bombardment of notifications and information.
3. Resilience: Mindfulness promotes resilience, enabling Gen Z workers to bounce back from distractions and setbacks more quickly. This resilience can sustain their attention even when faced with challenges.
4. Work-Life Balance: Mindfulness encourages a healthy work-life balance, preventing burnout and fatigue that can erode attention spans. Gen Z employees who prioritize self-care are more likely to maintain focus.

"Given the digitalization or digital screens has become a reality, right? Therefore having mindfulness or mindfulness based interventions become all the more important and it's not just because it's good for their mental health. It's also because the worldview in which the education system has been enveloped in, has always been of a certain kind which has propagated or made people align themselves to this continuous indulgence as a process and unfortunately it's not serving anybody"

~ an HR Professional and Educator

CONGRUENCE WITH EARLIER RESULTS

Consistency in our findings is congruent with prior research, reinforcing the validity and strengthening the conclusions drawn in this study. As the workplace continues to evolve, embracing mindfulness is not merely an option but a strategic imperative for fostering a healthier, more inclusive, and productive work environment.

LIMITATIONS AND FUTURE SCOPE

This study has a sample size of 30 individuals across 5 sectors. Future research could aim to expand the sample size and include a more diverse range of participants across different industries and demographic profiles. This would enhance the generalizability of the findings and provide a more comprehensive understanding of mindfulness adoption. Further, the research design for this paper is a cross-sectional study. Conducting longitudinal studies would allow researchers to track the evolution of mindfulness practices over time. This approach could reveal trends, changes, and the long-term impact of mindfulness on professionals' experiences and organizational dynamics. Moreover, while the current study focuses on specific industries, there is a need to explore mindfulness adoption in a broader range of sectors. Investigating industries not covered in the initial study could uncover unique challenges, benefits, and patterns of mindfulness integration. Also, apart from the qualitative approach of this study, future studies could further benefit from adopting a mixed-methods approach, combining qualitative interviews with quantitative measures. This would provide a more holistic view, allowing researchers to triangulate findings and derive a deeper understanding of the complex relationships between mindfulness, organizational behavior, and individual experiences. Although our study emphasized on the impact of mindfulness on the newer generations, the insights around it were taken from a sample of work professionals above the age of 30. Given the changing dynamics in the workforce, future research should consider including younger professionals and early-career individuals. This could shed light on how mindfulness practices resonate with professionals at different career stages and with varying levels of work experience. Apart from that, while this study included 5 sectors and not specific organizations, conducting comparative studies across organizations within the same industry could reveal variations in mindfulness adoption strategies and their outcomes. Analyzing differences in organizational cultures and structures could provide nuanced insights into the factors influencing mindfulness integration.

Furthermore, while the study incorporates self-reported data, future research could incorporate objective measures of mindfulness effectiveness, such as physiological indicators or performance metrics. This would enhance the rigor of the study and provide a more objective assessment of the impact of mindfulness practices.

Given the digital age, future research could explore the role of technology in facilitating mindfulness practices, such as the use of mindfulness apps or virtual reality interventions. Understanding how technology can support or hinder mindfulness adoption is relevant in the current technological landscape. Besides, exploring mindfulness adoption across different cultural contexts could provide valuable insights into how cultural factors influence the acceptance and effectiveness of mindfulness practices. Cross-cultural studies would contribute to a more globally applicable understanding of mindfulness in the workplace. Moreover, to provide a comprehensive view, future studies should explore potential challenges and negative experiences associated with mindfulness adoption. Understanding barriers to implementation and individual resistance can offer valuable insights for organizations aiming to promote mindfulness effectively.

CONCLUSIONS AND IMPLICATIONS

Mindfulness, with its seemingly intangible qualities, yields exponential returns for organizations, a paradoxical truth that emerges from our intricate analysis. Our findings intricately reveal that those forward-thinking organizations that have embraced mindfulness practices not only experience a huge leap in productivity but also witness a remarkable surge in employee appreciation. The allure of mindfulness lies in its ability to captivate employees, enticing them to navigate the labyrinthine corridors of stress management, a journey that intricately intertwines their personal and professional lives and plays a direct role in their productivity, health, and loyalty. Those who have adopted mindfulness have linked it to better professional success.

Having analyzed 5 industries, there is a systemic lack of support from organizations in the provision of mindfulness skills. Further, there is also a lack of willingness of employees to attend such workshops either due to a lack of interest or a busy schedule. There was a general understanding that mindfulness should be inculcated from an early age as it will help build proficiency or create a solid foundation for future learning.

Further, there is a general consensus that mindfulness should be inculcated from the very start of their education journey, as there are high levels of distractions in the digital age which lead to lower attention spans. It is a common consensus that inculcating these skills from the start would enhance one's well-being.

REFERENCES

Bhaimiya, S. (2023, September 22). Gen Z lack workplace skills like debating and seeing different points of view because they spend too much time on social media, TV boss says. Business Insider India. https://www.businessinsider.in/careers/news/gen-z-lack-workplace-skills-like-debating-and-seeing-different-points-of-view-because-they-spend-too-much-time-on-social-media-tv-boss-says/articleshow/103871097.cms

Bhui, K., Dinos, S., Galant-Miecznikowska, M., de Jongh, B., & Stansfeld, S. (2016, December 6). Perceptions of work stress causes and effective interventions in employees working in public, private and non-governmental organisations: A qualitative study. *BJPsych Bulletin*, *40*(6), 318–325. doi:10.1192/pb.bp.115.050823 PMID:28377811

Cameron, L., & Hafenbrack, A. (2022, December 12). Research: When Mindfulness Does — and Doesn't — Help at Work. Harvard Business Review. Retrieved from https://hbr.org/2022/12/research-when-mindfulness-does-and-doesnt-help-at-work

Choi, E., Gruman, J. A., & Leonard, C. M. (2021, August 4). A balanced view of mindfulness at work. *Organizational Psychology Review*, *12*(1), 35–72. doi:10.1177/20413866211036930

HelpGuide. (2023, February 23). Benefits of mindfulness. Harvard Health Publishing. Retrieved from https://www.helpguide.org/harvard/benefits-of-mindfulness.htm

Hounshell, B., Frenkel, S., Hsu, T., & Thomson, S. A. (2022, August 26). A journey into the misinformation fever swamps. The New York Times. https://www.nytimes.com/2022/08/26/us/politics/misinformation-social-media.html

Kapoor, M. (2023, May 4). Mindfulness: A Journey to the Present Moment. The Times of India. https://timesofindia.indiatimes.com/readersblog/thoughts-aloud/mindfulness-a-journey-to-the-present-moment-53390/

Lomas, T., Medina, J. C., Ivtzan, I., Rupprecht, S., Hart, R., & Eiroa-Orosa, F. J. (2017, April 19). The impact of mindfulness on well-being and performance in the workplace: An inclusive systematic review of the empirical literature. *European Journal of Work and Organizational Psychology*, *26*(4), 492–513. doi:10.1080/1359432X.2017.1308924

Mishra, S. (2023, June 19). The Power of Mindfulness: Cultivating the Present Moment for a Balanced Life. LinkedIn. https://www.linkedin.com/pulse/power-mindfulness-cultivating-present-moment-balanced-mishra-/

Nilsen, W., Skipstein, A., & Demerouti, E. (2016, November 8). Adverse trajectories of mental health problems predict subsequent burnout and work-family conflict – a longitudinal study of employed women with children followed over 18 years. *BMC Psychiatry, 16*(1), 384. Advance online publication. doi:10.1186/s12888-016-1110-4 PMID:27825325

Pratt, M. (2023, March 8). *Women Are Leaders of Mindfulness at Work—Here's Why*. Mindful. https://www.mindful.org/women-are-leaders-of-mindfulness-at-work-heres-why/

Prodger, B. (2020, September 30). Gen Z's Approach To Wellbeing. Stress Matters. https://stressmatters.org.uk/gen-zs-approach-to-wellbeing/

Pvs, H.PVS. (2018, November 19). Work Related Stress: A Literature Review. *Annals of Social Sciences & Management Studies, 2*(3). Advance online publication. doi:10.19080/ASM.2018.02.555586

Satpathy, I., & Mitra, B. (2015, August). Stress at workplaces: Overview. Research Gate. https://www.researchgate.net/publication/282270203_Stress_at_Workplaces-_An_overview

Vanderhoof, J. (2015, June). Mindfulness in the workplace. ResearchGate. https://www.researchgate.net/publication/277589039_Mindfulness_in_the_Workplace

Chapter 10
Psychological Views on Digital Consciousness and Human Consciousness:
Exploring the Spectrum of Minds in the Digital Era

Dibyashree Panda

(iD) https://orcid.org/0009-0004-1797-3471
PES University, India

Zidan Kachhi

(iD) https://orcid.org/0000-0002-8317-6356
PES University, India

ABSTRACT

This chapter explores the connection between human and computer consciousness, considering the implications of their separation in the context of advancing artificial intelligence. It examines psychological perspectives on human and digital consciousness, highlighting differences in perception and emotional intelligence. The subjectivity and objectivity of human and computer awareness are also explored, along with the significance of innovation and creativity. Bridging the gap between human and computer consciousness enhances human-machine interaction and the design of AI systems, while addressing moral implications promotes ethical AI development. The chapter delves into philosophical debates on consciousness, mind, identity, and the distinctions between humans and machines, ultimately aiming to deepen our understanding and foster dialogue on AI.

DOI: 10.4018/979-8-3693-2015-0.ch010

INTRODUCTION

Interestingly, researchers and psychologists are interested in how conscious humans meet the digital landscape. It means that they are investigating the idea of digital consciousness where they reproduce or simulate consciousness in the virtual worlds. This idea examines if one can copy one's mental attributes onto a computer. Consciousness beyond our bodies is considered a possibility, with the process being viewed as an extension of human consciousness into the realm of the digital world. This view is based on monism, asserting that the mind and the brain stem from one source. In these terms emergence of digital consciousness proves itself a necessary stage within the logical evolution of the human mind. This means that the virtual environments allow people to be able to freely express themselves with such creativity leading to their personal development (Srikanth, 2022).

However, some psychologists contend that there are essential differences between human and digital consciousness. They stress that a distinct kind of awareness arises from the special qualities of digital systems, such as their capacity to process information quickly and store enormous volumes of data. This point of view is concerned with the possibility that machine learning and artificial intelligence will evolve their own consciousness apart from human awareness. According to this theory, digital consciousness may develop into a brand-new type of consciousness that functions on ideas distinct from those of human consciousness. In addition to the ethical ramifications of creating and engaging with such consciousness, it raises problems regarding the nature and possible capacities of digital beings.

While there exist several psychological perspectives to digital awareness, discussion and research on this area are increasingly taking place. There are doubts about whether digital consciousness constitutes a radically distinct type of conscience or rather just prolongs human conscience. Moreover, there has to be a lot of research conducted in order to ascertain more on issues like human identity, cognition, and society and how they interact with the concept of digital consciousness. Instead, human consciousness refers to an individual's subjective realization of being aware and self-awareness. Its significance lies in it being the faculty for perceiving external information, having cognition and emotions in it, and giving us a personality. The psychology community has come up with numerous ideas aimed at explaining human consciousness. (Rudrauf, 2018)

One of the theories postulates that consciousness results from the brain's integrative mechanism. In the sense that it is the complex network of interconnections and relationships between different areas in the brain that gives rise to consciousness. Another theory is the global workspace theory asserting that information is relayed to different parts of the brain to engender awareness. This hypothesis, however, highlights the importance of awareness and attention concerning consciousness. Sigmund Freud's psychoanalytic theory, too, has contributed greatly to our understanding of human consciousness. Freud emphasized the role of the unconscious mind in influencing experience into consciousness. According to him, consciousness is determined by memories, fears, and unconscious impulses.

Digital vs. Human Perception

To fully comprehend the dynamic aspects of AI-human relationship changes, a focus on differences in digital and human perceptions is needed. The subtopic is important because an investigative analysis of the cognitive processes that define the human perceptual system and digital perceptual system, along with the evaluation of respective influences on our perception both virtually and in reality has to be performed.

In the domain of digital perception, it is the role of algorithms that serve as designers of sensory experiences. Cameras and sensors-equipped robots collect, process the data, and develop models that describe the environment. In contrast to the time and space aspects perceived by human senses, the rapidity and accuracy of digital sensors offer an alternate sensorial experience. Pixelated images in augmented reality and virtual reality demonstrate that digital systems process and display information differently. However, the issue remains: how close can these computer-generated images come to accurately capture the depth and nuance of human senses? The algorithmic gaze offers a unique perspective on the digital world, raising questions regarding the accuracy of these depictions. (Smith, 2020)

Human perception, on the other hand, is a multifaceted tapestry made up of strands from sensory information, cognitive processes, and emotional resonance. Not only do our sense organs receive information, they also participate in complex processes of integration and interpretation. Human perception goes well beyond the simple reception of information, as seen by the wide range of emotions expressed through body language and the minute details of facial expressions. Furthermore, because human perception is subjective, there is an extra degree of complexity added by the fact that everyone has different experiences and perceptions that are shaped by environmental, cultural, and personal factors. The interaction of cognitive processing and sensory input creates a complex and multifaceted human experience.

Comprehending the differences between digital and human perception is crucial for the advancement and application of artificial intelligence technology. With the use of sophisticated algorithms and sensor technology, computer systems may replicate some aspects of human perception; yet, creating an immersive and compassionate experience is a difficult task. In addition to enhancing the accuracy of digital representations, bridging the gap between the algorithmic gaze and the complex web of human perception requires taking into account the emotional and cultural factors that influence human experiences (Saracini, 2022). The pursuit of artificial intelligence (AI) systems that can comprehend and react to the nuances of human perception is a frontier where technology aims to imitate the depth of human awareness.

As artificial intelligence (AI) technologies attempt to close the gap between perceptual experiences, the idea of the "uncanny valley"—a phenomenon in which digital spaces containing nearly lifelike human representations may cause discomfort or anxiety—emerges (Signorelli, 2018). This phenomenon highlights the difficulties in accomplishing a smooth integration of computer and human perception. The development of AI systems that can recognize and react to human emotions brings ethical issues to the fore as well, raising concerns about permission, privacy, and the possible manipulation of emotional states. A careful balance between ethical responsibility and technological innovation is necessary to navigate these problems.

Comparing digital and human vision reveals both the present situation and potential future directions. With the development of technology, there is hope for a more unified view in which digital systems are smoothly integrated with human emotion and intellect. Along the way, we will not only improve AI's technical features but also recognize how society, culture, and ethics influence the human condition. The continuous conversation between technology and psychology regarding perception is evidence of the dynamic interaction between AI and human awareness—a journey characterized by obstacles, revelations, and the unwavering quest for a peaceful convergence.

Subjectivity vs. Objectivity

Objectivity and Subjectivity are fundamental concepts in investigating the division between human and computer consciousnesses. However, digital consciousness which is thought to be objective relies on algorithms and data versus subjective human consciousness that takes emotional considerations, personal experience, etc. To expand on this point, one should explore the nuances of subjectivity within a human mind and the notion of objective view regarding a digital consciousness.

Our mind is molded by things like feelings, our own encounters, beliefs, values, and our cultural backdrop. It simply means that everyone projects their own view of the world. This comes about as every person has a unique reality based on their experiences. This, in turn, influences how they see, comprehend, and connect with their world. Our moods or feelings play a key part here as they reflect our desires, goals, and principles. They color the lens through which we see the world, shaping how we understand situations and how we make choices. Our past experiences are another key factor shaping our perspective. They provide valuable insights for gaining wisdom. Habits, beliefs, understanding, decision-making, and problem-solving are influenced by these experiences, thus guiding our conduct.

Our feelings and personal experiences highly affect subjectivity. Emotions guide us to what's important, steering us towards our goals. For instance, we might be thrilled about a certain decision, indicating it's in line with our values or objectives. On the flip side, emotions of fear or sadness may suggest there's a problem or risk. Insights come from evaluating various solutions within the context of objectives and core values. These emotions, both positive and negative, shape our subjectivity based on our personal experiences.

People usually see virtual awareness as fair and factual. It wants to understand data without any personal feelings or biases. It operates using data and formulas. There are many reasons why digital consciousness seems objective. First, digital systems mostly depend on data-driven decisions. This helps to avoid any human biases when examining tons of information to spot trends and patterns. Formulas make decisions steady and repeatable. Using formulas makes sure that the results are fair when the design is complete. In this way, similar data follow the same rules and steps. People making decisions need unbiased data. It helps them make logical choices without any prejudices.

Data and algorithms aid in making a false perception of digital awareness in problem-solving and decision-making. Algorithms work with a set of rules and facts to minimize bias and subjective views. Removing biases can result in reliable results. The ability to process a lot of data quickly gives fast insights and recommendations for specific decisions. Programs keep learning, making digital awareness more objective. As time passes and they learn from new data, algorithms make better and more accurate decisions.

These implications involve the subjective nature of human consciousness and the perceived objectiveness of digital consciousness. Therefore, these ripples must be realized and understood so as to bridge the gap between theory and practice. It is possible to see a number of consequences and difficulties related to subjectivity and objectivity:

The Complexity of Human Consciousness: Our identity, beliefs, value systems, and decision-making processes are informed by subjectivity which makes them richer in detail with additional dimensions of significance. These perspectives make people different – they attract others' attention In tough decisions, one must perceive subjectiveness, and emotions, along with personal experience for them to overcome uncharted waters.

Advantages of Digital Awareness: Thankfully it appears that thanks to algorithms, and data digital awareness is objective and benefits greatly on many counts. Digital systems incorporate algorithms that are consistent, reliable, and scalable, making it easy to objectively evaluate large amounts of data for decision-making purposes.

Digital systems are applicable within various disciplines including research, health care, as well as banking.

Ethical Considerations: The development and use of digital awareness are also associated with ethical problems concerning subjectiveness and objectiveness perceptions. Personal attitudes and facts exist to contribute to the sense of subjective matter in a man's consciousness. It then makes it very crucial to ensure that computer systems do not judge people on subjective opinions or discriminate against them. It is therefore critical that an equilibrium between algorithmic objectivity and human values with respect to the promoting of moral and ethical evolution and utilization of digital awareness is established.

The Difficulty of Estimating Subjectivity in Humans: While attempting to be objective, it proves quite impossible to have genuine objectivity within a digital consciousness. Therefore, AI systems may unknowingly include human prejudices and warped perspectives leading to skewed outputs. However, artificial intelligence might not reflect the complexity and multifaceted nature inherent in human thinking accurately. Digital awareness or objective awareness is still problematic to be accommodated in terms of human subjective outlook. (Dong et al., 2020).

Temporal Aspects

The temporal aspects of human consciousness, including the experience of time, memory, and the past, present, and future, differ significantly from the instantaneous and data-driven nature of digital consciousness. This section will examine the subtleties of human comprehension of time and memory as compared to digital comprehension. These temporal attributes will highlight what distinguishes humans in contrast to digitization as seen through a psychological perspective.

Time, as we perceive it, and what we call "now" lies at its very heart. In the case of digital consciousness, our conscious mind permits us to navigate through the temporality component that governs human reality. Time goes on, and we recall the past as well as tomorrow which will never come true. The perception of time on a personal level is also defined by a number of factors including attention, emotions, and culture. Our mood, health, and the environment we live in also affect time. For instance, time runs faster in a happy situation compared to an awful moment.

Another aspect of human consciousness and time is memory. Information from old events is stored via human memory. This development involves developing our maturity, choice, and unique character. It is a vital time string in the memories that unites the past and the present. The different sorts of memory in humans include semantic memory, episodic memory, and procedural memory. The first is episodic memory, which implies recollection of particular past events and experiences. Semantic refers to facts and general knowledge, whereas procedural memory deals with skills and routines. Each memory type is like painting a modern picture with a variety of colours, illuminating our understanding of the past. However, unlike this human consciousness, artificial intelligence (AI) and other digital consciousnesses have no such subjective experience of time and memory. It is data-driven and real-time.

Without a sense of the past or future, digital consciousness functions in the now by processing input according to preset rules and algorithms. Unlike human awareness, digital consciousness lacks the capacity to create memories. Instead of being connected by a continuous thread of memory, each request or input is handled separately. As such, digital consciousness depends only on the current data that is accessible at the moment of processing. Digital consciousness is immediate, which enables it to process information at a speed that is significantly faster than that of humans. Large-scale data analysis and effective decision-making enable it to solve problems more quickly. Instantaneous access to stored information is another benefit of digital consciousness, as it does away with the limitations and fallibility of human memory.

Emotional Intelligence vs. Artificial Intelligence

The stark contrast between the depth of human emotional intelligence ingrained in consciousness and artificial intelligence's grasp of digital awareness highlights the intricate nature of human emotions, revealing the limitations of AI in truly comprehending and experiencing them. Emotional intelligence, referred to as the capacity to recognize, understand, and regulate emotions, stands as a distinct trait of human awareness (Zhou, 2021). Meanwhile, AI relies on affective computing to mimic emotions by interpreting cues and generating responses based on predefined guidelines and algorithms. This discussion will explore the nuances of human emotional intelligence, encompassing empathy and emotional understanding, juxtaposed with AI's simulated emotional responses driven by algorithms.

Emotional intelligence is tightly interwoven with human consciousness, shaping how individuals perceive, interpret, and engage with the world. It encompasses a spectrum of skills, including self-awareness, self-management, social awareness, and interpersonal management.

1. *Self-Awareness*: At its core, self-awareness involves recognizing and comprehending one's emotions, strengths, weaknesses, values, and perspectives. This ability allows individuals to acknowledge their emotional states and understand their impact on thoughts and actions, serving as the foundation of emotional intelligence. Self-awareness empowers effective emotional regulation and facilitates informed decision-making aligned with personal values and goals.

2. *Self-Management:* The process of self-management involves learning how to control and express feelings appropriately and effectively. For example, it includes measures such as impulse control, stress management, flexibility for a change as well as many others. Having a strong command of self-management helps one effectively handle difficult emotions, stay emotionally stable, and act ahead to solve problems.

3. *Social Awareness:* Social awareness is a skill that enables an individual to identify and comprehend the feelings, needs, and perceptions of others. It involves the capacity to observe social cues, feel sympathy, and practice active listening. Those with heightened social sensitivity establish more profound contacts, communicate in a fluent manner, and manage interpersonal exchanges proficiently.

4. *Relationship Management*: The main pillar in relationship management is building and cultivating healthy satisfying relationships. This entails working together, resolving conflicts, and communicating effectively for harmonized links with the aim of forming a cooperative bond founded on trust that will foster cohesion and, hence peace amongst all the stakeholders.

Digital consciousness employs a subset known as affective computing in artificially generated emotions by artificial intelligence. For AI to mimic human emotions, it is exposed to body language signs, speech, and expressions. Nevertheless, it is important to understand that even if AI mimics feelings, it is achieved by following the established rules as well as the use of a recognized mechanism. Key facets of AI's emotional mimicry include:

Emotion Recognition: It is possible to determine emotional states in artificial intelligence systems with the help of visual and audio clues. By training machine learning systems on large databases, these systems are able to segment and comprehend human emotions. However, AI may find it difficult to understand subtle nuances in the context as well as individual differences that lead to different kinds of emotional reactions.

Natural Language Processing: Analysis of spoken or written language enables AI programs to identify emotional tones and sentiments. With sentiment analysis algorithms, AI understands speech or text that expresses emotions to which it can respond. Although capable of generating appropriate responses based on emotional content, AI still struggles to fully fathom the depth and complexity of human emotions.

Emotional Response Generation: AI systems can generate emotionally sensitive outputs, facilitating more personalized and engaging interactions. Algorithms in natural language generation can be trained to produce voice or text with suitable emotional tones. For example, chatbots can be programmed to respond empathetically.

However, these responses are rule-based rather than rooted in genuine emotional experience.

Subjectivity and Context: AI encounters challenges in comprehending the context-dependent and subjective nature of emotions. Emotions are intricate and influenced by social contexts, cultural norms, and individual experiences. Due to the lack of subjective understanding and human experiences, AI may struggle to accurately understand and respond to emotions in complex situations.

Emotions are very important in the realm of human connection and create an empathetic, understanding, and personal tapestry in which people share their experiences. Although AI has seen remarkable progress in imitating human behavior, AI still lacks comprehension of human emotions and their deep meaning in life. Multifaceted human emotional intelligence embraces self-awareness, self-regulation, social awareness, and relationship management, enabling us to interconnect beyond merely being acquainted. We feel and act upon emotions, so we can understand what makes a person's emotions. Human consciousness has this inherent empathy to relate with others and hence make it unique.

In contrast, AI utilizes data analysis and predefined parameters to emulate human feelings. Although it understands the feeling it may not have the same emotion nor the true ability that connects humans. Imitation often does not manage to reflect all the nuances and depth of human feelings since they depend on subjective perceptions, culture, psychological states, etc. It is not merely mimicry that makes up human emotional intelligence but the ability to consider and make decisions based on the emotions involved in a situation as well as modifying behavior according to the ever-changing challenges posed by different moments." With reference to one's personal history as well as social settings, we can decode emotionally relevant signals so that reasoned decisions are made. Human emotional intelligence demonstrates the capacity to be resilient in constantly changing situations. On the other hand, unlike human beings, AI systems are programmed to answer depending on certain criteria, which makes them unable to be flexible and intuitive in making decisions about issues or circumstances. AI's attempt at mimicry is still shallow, with little knowledge about emotions in the right environment.

Creativity and Innovation

Innovation and creativity are crucial for problem-solving and progress. They provide individuals and businesses with fresh ideas, products, and solutions. This report will explore the differences between the methods used by digital systems and human creative thought. Digital systems employ fixed algorithms and analyze data in order to provide solutions while humans depend on creativity, instincts, and personal experience. Therefore, it is important to analyze these differences if we want to know what are special human attributes on the creative side and the function of the digit system in the development.

Creativity in humans is a very complicated phenomenon linked with many individual factors like emotions and thought processes, etc. It comes naturally as we are naturally capable of thinking beyond conventionally and in a non-linear way. They illuminate the sensory and unconscious side of the human thinking process through the inspirations and intuitions which are the two major elements for creative thoughts. Intuitive insights allow people to jump over conscious reasoning and lead to the coming up of new ideas. However, inspiration, which develops through emotions, experience, and outside information, fuels creative thinking and builds up original solutions. Human creativity involves emotions, individual experiences, and culture. Specifically, emotions are essential in the artistic process because they provide ideas with meaning and distinctiveness through intensity and sincerity. This happens objectively but gives room to the incorporation of different perspectives, deep thinking, and the creation of fresh ideas.

One of the essential aspects of human creative cognition is associative thinking which entails linking apparently dissimilar thoughts and ideas in unique manners. This strategy encourages people to make use of patterns, analogies, and metaphors in search of newer approaches to problem-solving. By being intrinsically flexible and responsive, human thoughts of creativity are by definition ever-dynamic, helping people deal with risk, ambiguity, as well as uncertainties. Creative people are prepared to experiment, fail, and modify their plans when criticisms or circumstances change in the process.

The same goes for the creativities of humans' unconscious minds which can lead to serendipitous findings. These are new ideas that widen the scope of conventional thinking and can only be gotten from this access to sub-consciousness. Chance discoveries, known as serendipity, promote the discovery of new lines of thinking and unusual combinations. It is vital that problem-solving and progress require innovation and creativity. They bring newer ideas, goods, and solutions. Innovation in digital systems primarily occurs through algorithms and is driven by data analytics focusing on data processing. These strategies incorporate data mining and machine learning, which are used to discover patterns and trends from big sets of data. An algorithm is simply a set of instructions on how to process data in order to make a decision. Efficiency, optimization, and automation are the cornerstones of digital systems in pursuit of the most efficient results. In addition, they add a touch of personalization, which makes it possible to provide customized user experiences that suit various users' preferences.

On the other hand, digital systems are inflexible when it comes to comparison and human creativity. They are based on presets, they need specific programming/training to adapt. Human creativity includes subjective experiences that are lacking emotionally in digital systems. Subjectivity, emotions, and lived experience are at the core of human creativity where different perspectives produce unusual thoughts. Therefore, human creativity is flexible, and adaptable, and allows for sudden jumps into a new way of thinking. He/she welcomes vagueness and penetrates through the conscious mind searching for lucky hits. However, it is different with digital systems that are more objective, with a focus on data analysis and rationality. Although they are good at unearthing patterns and discoveries, they do not have the depth and individuality of human creativity. In terms of solving problems systematically, digital environments are more effective compared with human nature but they are limited in creativity and innovation because they lack emotions in their outputs.

The difference between algorithms in digital systems and organic human creative thought is in the balance of algorithmic vs. organic. Human creativity thrives on subjectivity, inspiration, intuition, and flexibility, while digital systems prioritize efficiency, objectivity, and data-driven decision-making. Both approaches have their strengths and limitations, highlighting the need for a harmonious integration of human creativity and digital systems in the innovation process.

Consciousness Integration

Consciousness integration refers to the incorporation of artificial intelligence (AI) and digital technology into human consciousness. It involves merging the human mind with technological advancements, which opens up new avenues for perception, experience, and interaction with the outside world. Wearable technology and brain-computer interfaces (BCIs) are two examples of how digital technologies and AI are integrated into human consciousness.

Wearable technology, such as fitness trackers and smart watches, has a significant impact on human cognition. These devices provide constant access to data and information, allowing users to monitor their physical and mental health in real time. For example, wearable devices can track heart rate, sleep patterns, activity levels, and stress levels, which promotes self-awareness and proactive health management.

In this respect, the use of augmented reality (AR) and virtual reality (VR) technologies should be mentioned as well. Augmented reality superimposes digital information on the actual world making the user's perception of reality better. For example, AR glasses present environmental information directly within the view of the user. In contrast, VR envelops the user in a virtual reality that heightens presence and expands lived experience.

As far as sensory augmentation via wearable technology is concerned, improving the human senses is also another thing. Such devices as haptic feedback offer tactile stimuli for better digital interactions and the so-called "hearables" boost up an audible perception by enhancing/filtering chosen sound sources. These technologies provide a man to get information beyond natural sensory-perceptual awareness.

Wearable technology and BCIs in human consciousness will change how people relate to tech.' By doing so, they are able to communicate directly through the brain with different external instruments. This greatly improves the lives of many people without mobility. The integration of wearable technology with BCIs also enables people with physical disabilities, who were once powerless. With the help of BCIs, paralyzed users can use their thoughts to manipulate their prosthetic limbs or some assistive devices. Using this new technology boosts their well-being, restores/ enhances functioning, and opens up opportunities to engage in otherwise unavailable activities, experiences, and interactions.

Wearable technology integrated with BCIs can further extend human capabilities beyond those related to movement disorders by promoting cognitive abilities as well as additional human experiences. The use of the BCIs and wearable devices can contribute to an improvement in short-term, working memory, selective attention, and learning. Besides that, the integration of wearable technology and BCIs can create awareness of oneself in order to promote self-control. Wearable technology and biosensors provide users with information on what is happening in their bodies right now and allow them to act reasonably depending on it. BCIs can also assist in regulating emotions by monitoring brain activity and providing real-time feedback, which can be valuable in managing conditions such as anxiety, depression, and stress.

Wearable technology and BCIs may also help in virtual reality therapy applications. Virtual reality can achieve therapeutic and medical goals when combined with these technologies. Such settings can foster exposure therapy, relaxation, and mindfulness-based interventions for psychological disabilities. Although there are many expected advantages of uniting wearable technology and BCIs, ethics ought to be carefully contemplated. Data privacy and security are necessary because the use of those technologies entails the collection and processing of sensitive person's data. Responsible integration is contingent upon informed consent, equal access, and ethical handling of data.

Moreover, incorporating technology into the human mind brings up issues with regard to autonomy and personhood. Therefore, it must be ensured that people have power over their thinking styles, feelings as well as action-taking with such technologies. There should be safeguards to ensure that the people cannot be manipulated because if they are then they will be subjected to coercion. In addition, the wearable technology together with BCI's social and cultural aspects should also be investigated. These technologies have been observed to dictate how people interact with each other, and communicate, as well as affect their personal space. Therefore, one must show respect for different cultures' values as well as make sure the ethics are culturally sensitive. Thus, accountability and regulation are crucial for the maximum benefits of integration and minimized risks of wearable technology and BCI. There may be a need for such clear ethical policies, standards, and governance in order to make sure that those technologies are being developed responsibly, deployed correctly, and used wisely. (Doe et al; 2015)

Real-time information regarding the activities in the brain can be achieved through neuro-feedback using BCIs thus making it possible for someone to understand and regulate mental states. This creates an attention-focusing effect that induces calmness and improves general mental capacity. In addition, BCIs are helpful because they help people access deep meditative states necessary for deeper forms of mindfulness practice. Technological enhancement of self-consciousness and intellectual supremacy through merging BCIs with neuro-feedback/meditation practices. In essence, the BCIs act like a connecting link between the virtual and physical worlds, transforming how one interacts with day-to-day technology.

The synthesis of consciousness has immense mental consequences like transforming a person's individuality. This gives people immense power over information and the technology that uses the power of thought, giving people the ability to self-actualize. This will go against the way people have perceived human capabilities in order to create more power over one's reality with new perceptions of boundaries and potential. However, issues pertaining to privacy and autonomy need to be noted when integrating the two (Diel et al., 2021). Although they facilitate smooth communication, wearing technologizing and BCIs pose ethical questions about ownership of information and informed consent. However, people have to juggle with the need to maintain originality while enjoying the advantages of integration. This psychological issue stems from the battle to ensure individual freedom, which contradicts convenient integration.

The combination of consciousness makes us question whether we can rely on technology anymore, ethically. When people use digital devices and AI systems for various cognition operations, there are anxieties about the maintenance of important thinking skills as well as the need to ensure some management in technology. Finding a balance between augmentation and personal agency is a highly challenging psychological task. Such an ethical landscape indicates the need for examining some risks that might emanate from over-dependency on technology and incorporating mindfulness and accountability in its proper use.

Identity and Authenticity

The essence of human identity emerges from a patchwork of personal experiences and interactions. This mingling of experiences, emotions, connections, and encounters creates the rich mosaic that is who we are. From childhood misadventures to uplifting talks and life-changing occurrences, each chapter contributes to our character, crafting a distinct story. Friends who become family, mentors who guide, and lovers who leave permanent imprints all color our perceptions and shape our sense of ourselves (Hildt, 2019).

However, in this digital age, the concept of identity and authenticity takes on new dimensions as our physical world merges with virtual landscapes. The rise of digital awareness ushers in a universe where identities are flexible, allowing people to create personas that differ from their actual selves. Human identity is shaped by physical shapes, which are themselves the result of experiences, emotions, and connections. It is a sum of simple joys and great sorrows, memorable victories and unbearable defeats, festive laughs and sobs. These experiences in real life are used to fabricate our self-identity that develops along the line of living truthfully. Often, emotional honesty, depth of relationships, and conformity of action to belief become tests for identity.

In contrast, digital literacy allows people to create virtual spaces for their identities to exist without the boundaries of physical space; it's a fascinating combination of reality with dreams come true. In these virtual realms, individuals may invent different characters study unknown territories, or build relationships with others unassisted by geography whatsoever. However, here authenticity assumes a special shade—it is a synthesis between perception and projection, a mix-up between constructed identities and chosen experiences.

Human identity, a complex and always changing construct, is strongly related to our bodily experiences, shaped by the sensory encounters and true emotions we face throughout our lives. While the digital sphere allows for self-expression and the discovery of different realities, it is more of a canvas on which we project our identities than a mirror of our genuine selves.

Authenticity has become a fluid term in the digital environment, molded by the narratives we create and the views of others. Our virtual personas, which are frequently meticulously built and controlled, might differ dramatically from our real-life selves, blurring the lines between reality and fabrication. While identity malleability provides a sense of emancipation and self-discovery, it also raises doubts about the genuine nature of authenticity. Despite the temptation of digital self-expression, human authenticity is founded on the tangible events and true connections that define our lives. Our identities are built on the depth and richness of our connections, shared emotions, and the scars we bear from life's hardships. While the digital domain allows for creative inquiry, it cannot replace the visceral effect of in-person events.

The interaction between the physical and digital realms presents an intriguing challenge: how do we reconcile our physical lives with our virtual personas while ensuring that our online identities remain honest reflections of our authentic selves? As digital consciousness evolves, it is critical that we maintain a feeling of grounding in the physical world, lest we lose sight of the experiences and connections that define our humanity.

Ethical Considerations

Considering the aspects of combining digital consciousness is of great importance. This merging involves the convergence of thinking and technological advancements raising questions, about privacy, personal freedom, and potential psychological impacts on individuals. In this report, we will explore the dimensions surrounding the aspects of blending human and digital consciousness examining its effects on privacy, personal freedom, mental well-being, and societal norms.

There is concern about protecting privacy in this field. Digital consciousness integration entails capturing and interpreting individual sensory details such as one's feelings, thoughts, and physical attributes. For such important data, it is critical to implement procedures such as data storage, encryption techniques, and hardened access controls in order to keep it away from external threats, such as unwanted access or disclosures.

As a basis, informed consent is involved. This is a process that calls for people to fully appreciate the implications and risk-benefit associated with such an integration. They should also be able to decide on whether to participate in the study or withdraw their consent. Therefore, it is important to educate such people about various effects, privacy concerns, as well as ethics.

It is necessary to ensure the preservation of autonomy in every person when implementing digital consciousness. However, during this procedure, it is necessary to help people keep control of the things they think, feel, or act. This is why it is essential that controls of some sort should be in place so that there is no way one can try to manipulate the process. The autonomy of each individual refers to their liberty or decision-making ability about technological interactions like opting in or out for such apparatuses or BCIs.

This integration requires the psychological health of people. Prolonged exposure to digital gadgets might lead to psychological consequences like addiction, dependence, or detachment from the physical world. It is vital to address these risks and mitigate potential detrimental effects on mental health. It is critical to balance benefits and potential risks in order to ensure persons' psychological well-being and general enjoyment. The integration of human and digital consciousness has an impact on societal and cultural standards. Wearable technologies and BCIs have the potential to alter social interactions and communication standards. Their continual presence in social settings may affect societal norms about distractions and etiquette. Furthermore, introducing new means of communication, such as employing ideas for engagement, may put current cultural norms about language and gestures to the test. It is necessary to be sensitive to various cultural values in order to traverse these (Ott, 2023)

Equality and access are important ethical considerations. It is critical to ensure that these technologies do not worsen current disparities. Access and opportunity must be provided to all people, regardless of financial class, ethnicity, or gender. Addressing affordability, accessibility, and digital literacy challenges is critical for equitable inclusion. Furthermore, taking into account the impact on marginalized communities and guaranteeing inclusivity is critical to preventing future marginalization. Furthermore, responsibility and control are required for the appropriate development and implementation of technologies that integrate human and computer awareness. It is critical to have clear ethical rules, monitoring, and transparent communication about data activities. This domain's organizations must be held accountable for the privacy and security of individuals' personal data.

Sustainability and Well-Being

Integrating digital consciousness opens the doors to infinite possibilities and casts a shadow over human well-being and the environment The advent of the digital age weaves fabric into our lives incredibly and has changed the state of human communication and emotion. Movie time, often extended beyond healthy limits, has a profound effect on mental health and interpersonal relationships.

The distraction of digital immersion comes at a price—we constantly sleep on screens that exceed our waking hours. More screen time has been linked to increased stress, anxiety, and sleep disorders, which affect our overall well-being. The relentless flow of information and virtual interactions often miss out on time meant for introspection and genuine connection, destroying the quality of human experiences. Social media, the cornerstone of digital consciousness, serves a dual purpose—it connects us across distance while subtly facilitating the details of authentic communication. It's a maze of curated content, fostering unrealistic comparisons and perpetuating a cycle of validation-seeking behavior. This never-ending digital not only blurs the boundaries between the real and virtual but also disconnects us from the present moment, affecting our mental health and emotional balance. The digital realm, despite its hopes of affecting connectivity, often invades the sanctuary of our physical space, creating an imbalance that destroys our peace of mind and harmony with the natural world. Moreover, the quest for balance between the digital and physical worlds is often elusive. As screens continue to dominate our daily activities, the distinction between work and personal life becomes blurred, undermining the harmony necessary for overall well-being (Saracini, 2022).

While digital technology offers numerous benefits, it also raises worries about its impact on human well-being and the environment. Because of the pervasiveness of digital gadgets and the infrastructure that supports them, natural resources and energy usage are under tremendous strain. The environmental footprint of digital technology is clear, from raw material extraction to manufacturing processes, electronic waste disposal, and data center operation. Among these concerns, it is critical to create a balance between embracing digital technology's revolutionary capacity and protecting human well-being and the earth. Setting healthy screen time limits, cultivating meaningful offline contacts, and cultivating a mindful awareness of the digital-physical divide are all critical steps in this attempt.

Conscious digital consumption strategies, such as prioritizing real-time connections, embracing digital detox periods, and cultivating mindfulness, can help reduce the negative consequences of over-exposure to technology. We can restore control over our digital lives and reduce their negative effects by consciously deciding when, how, and for what objectives we engage with digital technology. To address the environmental repercussions of digital technology, a holistic approach that includes responsible manufacturing processes, successful recycling activities, and aware consumer habits is required. Advocating for environmentally sustainable regulations and promoting responsible electronic waste disposal are critical steps toward achieving a peaceful cohabitation of digital consciousness with environmental care.

CONCLUSION

This chapter provides a thorough investigation of the complex relationship between human and digital consciousness. It explores the cognitive mechanisms, emotional intelligence disparities, psychological aspects, and ethical implications of this connection, providing a comprehensive understanding of the possibilities and challenges of AI technology. We talk about philosophical debates concerning the nature of consciousness in the digital and human domains, providing an understanding of the mind, identity, and the complex distinctions between humans and machines. It also examines the psychological challenges of finding a balance between augmentation and personal agency, and the need for mindfulness and accountability in the proper use of technology. It discusses the potential for AI systems to develop emotional intelligence and the ethical implications of this development. It explored the potential for bias in AI systems and the importance of diversity and inclusivity in AI development.

Overall, this chapter file provides a thought-provoking exploration of the connection between human and digital consciousness, and the implications of this connection for AI development, human-machine interaction, and society as a whole. It highlights the need for ethical frameworks to ensure that AI systems are developed in a way that aligns with human values and goals, and the importance of maintaining originality and important thinking skills while enjoying the advantages of integration.

REFERENCES

Diel, A., Weigelt, S., & MacDorman, K. F. (2021). A meta-analysis of the Uncanny Valley's independent and dependent variables. *ACM Transactions on Human-Robot Interaction, 11*(1), 1–33. doi:10.1145/3470742

Doe, A., & Johnson, B. (2015). Exploring the Uncanny Valley in Human-Computer Interaction. *Journal of Human-Computer Interaction, 25*(3), 123–145.

Dong, Y., Hou, J., Zhang, N., & Mao-Cong, Z. (2020). Research on how human intelligence, consciousness, and cognitive computing affect the development of artificial intelligence. *Complexity, 2020*, 1–10. doi:10.1155/2020/1680845

Hildt, E. (2019). Artificial intelligence: Does consciousness matter? *Frontiers in Psychology, 10*, 1535. Advance online publication. doi:10.3389/fpsyg.2019.01535 PMID:31312167

Ott, B. L. (2023). The Digital Mind: How computers (Re)Structure human consciousness. *Philosophies, 8*(1), 4. doi:10.3390/philosophies8010004

Rudrauf, D., Sergeant-Perhtuis, G., Tisserand, Y., Monnor, T., De Gevigney, V., & Belli, O. (2023). Combining the projective consciousness model and virtual humans for immersive psychological research: A proof-of-concept simulating a TOM assessment. *ACM Transactions on Interactive Intelligent Systems, 13*(2), 1–31. doi:10.1145/3583886

Saracini, C. (2022). Perceptual Awareness and Its Relationship with Consciousness: Hints from Perceptual Multistability. *NeuroSci, 3*(4), 546–557. doi:10.3390/neurosci3040039

Signorelli, C. M. (2018). Can computers become conscious and overcome humans? *Frontiers in Robotics and AI, 5*, 121. Advance online publication. doi:10.3389/frobt.2018.00121 PMID:33501000

Smith, J. (2000). *Digital Consciousness and Human Perception.* Academic Press.

SrikanthK. (2022). Artificial intelligence and human consciousness. *Social Science Research Network.* doi:10.2139/ssrn.4070609

Zhou, Z. (2021). Emotional thinking as the foundation of consciousness in artificial intelligence. *Cultura e Scuola*, *4*(3), 112–123. doi:10.1177/20966083211052651

Chapter 11

The Impact of Social Media Addiction on Mental Health and Well-Being

Shaheen Yusuf
PES University, India

Zidan Kachhi
 https://orcid.org/0000-0002-8317-6356
PES University, India

ABSTRACT

One of the most important aspects of modern living is the use of social media platforms to link people globally and facilitate the sharing of ideas, knowledge, and experiences. While social media networks offer numerous benefits, they have also played a role in the alarming trend of social media addiction. This chapter examines the serious consequences that social media addiction has on mental health and overall well-being. The intention is to improve our understanding of this current crisis by highlighting the various ways that excessive use of social media may affect people's psychological and emotional well-being. People increasingly regularly engage with their online networks at the expense of their offline lives due to the extensive use of social media and the allure of constant notifications, likes, and shares.

DOI: 10.4018/979-8-3693-2015-0.ch011

The transformation of social media and the digital environment of the twenty-first century has experienced a significant shift. These platforms, created to promote communication and foster connections between people, are now an essential part of our everyday existence. But despite all of its advantages, social media has also led to the alarming epidemic known as social media that characterizes this addiction is becoming a major worry, with concerns about its effects on mental health and general well-being. Maintaining social connections with others can reduce stress, anxiety, and depression, increase self self-esteem, bring comfort and joy, and avoid loneliness. (Robinson, L. 2023, March 29). Conversely, having few close social ties can be extremely harmful to your mental and emotional well-being. It's critical to remember that social media cannot replace in-person human interaction. The hormones that reduce stress and make you feel healthier, happier, and more optimistic are activated only when you are in physical contact with other people. Contrary to popular belief, social media is meant to unite people. However, spending too much time on it can increase feelings of loneliness and isolation as well as worsen mental health issues like melancholy and anxiety.

Social media sites like Instagram, Twitter, TikTok, Facebook, and Snapchat have become so accepted that they have fundamentally changed how people engage, communicate, and consume information. These platforms are used by people to access news, interact with friends and family, discuss their lives, and even create communities based on common interests. Social media provides a platform for self-expression, instant pleasure, and a sense of community. On the other hand, chronic use of these platforms and the need to remain connected might result in detrimental utilization patterns. The hallmark of social media addiction is an obsessive-compulsive need to constantly check and communicate on social media platforms, frequently at the expense of other facets of their lives, including relationships with others, their jobs, and their families. The addictive behavior can harm general well-being and result in several mental health issues.

Compulsive checking and interacting on social media, frequently at the expense of other aspects of life including connections with family, friends, and jobs are hallmarks of social media addiction, which can result in a variety of mental health issues. These difficulties include, among other things anxiety and depression which are sometimes the most obvious and immediate effects. Feelings of inadequacy and low self-esteem can arise from constantly comparing one's life to the well-chosen and frequently romanticized material of others on social media. Many social media users frequently discover themselves caught in an unending loop of self-analysis as a result of their compulsive need for lives, comments, and sharing. This pattern may unintentionally create a negative feedback loop in which people become more dependent on outside approval instead of developing internal sources of self-worth, which damages their self-esteem and exacerbates depressive and anxious symptoms (Smith et al., 2020).

One of the direct impacts of social media on mental health could be anxiety and depression. Low self-esteem and feelings of inadequacy might result from constantly comparing one's life to the well-chosen and frequently idealized content of others. Many people who use social media become caught in an endless cycle of self-analysis because they are driven by an obsession with receiving likes, shares, and comments. Instead of relying on internal sources of self-worth, this can create a vicious cycle of seeking validation from other people which can lower self-esteem and aggravate depression and anxious symptoms. Furthermore, social media's addictive qualities can interfere with sleep cycles, resulting in sleep deprivation— a known risk factor for the emergence of mental health problems. People who obsessively check their social media profiles late at night may have sleep cycles disrupted as a result of social media's constant availability on smartphones and other devices. The psychological strain of comparing oneself to others coupled with sleep deprivation can have a serious negative effect on mental health.

Moreover, social media's addictive qualities, which are exacerbated by the never-ending barrage of notifications, updates, and the attraction of fresh information, can be harmful to focus and attention spans. Users' capacity to concentrate on tasks, whether they are done online or offline, tends to decline when they give in to the quick gratification offered by social media. This divided attention span has the potential to impair academic achievement, reduce job satisfaction, and disrupt productivity. People frequently become caught up in a vicious cycle of procrastination, spending endless hours reading through their social media feeds rather than doing important work. As a result, increased stress levels exacerbate mental health problems (Jones & Wilson, 2018).

Furthermore, people's mental health may be further harmed by cyberbullying and online abuse due to the anonymity and distancing provided by social media. Online platforms frequently act as a shield, allowing those who are inclined to participate in destructive or negative activities without fear of immediate consequences. Cyberbullying victims often experience anxiety, sadness, and a deep sense of powerlessness as they struggle to break the pattern of abuse. Cyberbullying has tragically resulted in extreme situations, highlighting the gravity of the problem and its direct impact on mental health (Gross et al., 2016).

Addiction to social media has a significant negative effect on focus and attention span. One's capacity to concentrate on work, both online and offline, may be compromised by constant notifications, updates, and the attraction of new content. Work satisfaction, academic, achievement, and productivity can all suffer from a fractured attention span. People frequently become stuck in a procrastination cycle where they become preoccupied with browsing through their social media feeds instead of doing important chores. This can therefore result in elevated stress levels, which can exacerbate mental health problems.

Additionally, social media's anonymity and detached nature can breed online harassment and cyberbullying, all of which are harmful to mental health. Internet platforms provide a buffer for people who want to act badly or negatively without having to deal with the fallout right away. Cyberbullying victims frequently experience anxiety, depression, and a sense of helplessness as they try to break free from the abusive cycle. Cyberbullying has tragically resulted in extreme situations, underscoring the seriousness of the problem.

It is crucial to recognize that addiction is a complex problem to completely understand the effects of social media addiction on mental health and general well-being. Similar to other types of addiction, social media addiction results in the brain's dopamine being released, which sets up a loop of reinforcement and reward that drives users to keep using the platform excessively. As a result of this brain rewiring, people may find it more difficult in the long run to cut back on their social media use, even when they are aware of the negative effects (Kuss & Griffiths, 2017). Addiction to social media can have a significant negative effect on one's physical health in addition to these psychological issues. Prolonged usage of social media can lead to a sedentary lifestyle, which can exacerbate health concerns including obesity and cardiovascular disease. People who spend endless hours in front of screens may also neglect to exercise, which raises their chance of acquiring a variety of health issues. It's critical to acknowledge that addiction is a complicated and multifaceted problem to completely comprehend the effects of social media addiction on mental health and general well-being. Similar to other types of addiction, social media addiction is caused by the brain's release of dopamine, which sets off a loop of rewards and reinforcements that drive users to keep using the platform excessively. Even when people are aware of the harmful effects of social media use, it may become more difficult for them to cut back on their usage over time due to this brain rewiring.

The complexity of social media addiction and its effects on mental health and well-being are still largely unknown to the modern world. Research efforts are focused on comprehending the underlying mechanisms, risk factors, and efficacious therapies as the topic continues to get attention. It's crucial to remember that not everyone who uses social media will get addicted to it; for many, it's still a useful medium for self-expression and communication. But for those who are in danger or who are already battling with social media addiction, it's crucial to learn appropriate usage techniques and get help when you need it.

In the following sections, we will look at the psychological and physiological impacts on mental health and well-being, go deeper into the elements that lead to social media addiction, and talk about potential preventive methods to follow. To mitigate the effects of these complicated issues and encourage a healthier relationship with the digital world, it is first necessary to understand it.

The Rise of Social Media and Its Influence on Society

It is crucial to investigate the emergence of social media and its profound effects on a range of facets of human existence, including social media addiction and its effects on relationships, in this age of unparalleled connectedness. Since its launch, social networking sites like Twitter, Instagram, LinkedIn, and Facebook have grown at an exponential rate. Mark Zuckerberg created Facebook in 2004, and since then, it has developed into the biggest social media network globally. Facebook has nearly 2.8 billion monthly active users as of the cutoff date in early 2022, demonstrating its influence and global reach. Likewise, Twitter, a tweeting site that debuted in 2006, claims to have about 330 million action users every month. These figures show how widely used social media is everywhere in the world (Statista, 2021). The limitations of this could be that the world of social media is always changing, with new features and platforms appearing regularly. The content in the book may become out of date due to this rapid change. And the future scope of this could be it is essential to conduct additional studies on the spreading of fake news and misinformation on social media, as well as viable ways for mitigating its effects.

The Social Media's Effect on Society

Social media has completely changed how individuals interact with one another, exchange information, and communicate. Its ability to influence public opinion and support social movements is among its most important effects. For example, social media sites like Facebook and Twitter were vital in coordinating demonstrations and spreading news during the 2010-2011 arab spring which resulted in political unrest in several Middle Eastern nations (Howard & Hussain, 2013). This demonstrates how social media can enable people and groups to have a significant impact on social and political change.

In addition, the emergence of social media has provided a forum for people to interact with like-minded individuals and express their ideas. Thanks to the video-sharing website, YouTube, content producers may now reach millions of people and make a good living from their videos. The highest- single year, according to Social Blade, demonstrates the financial prospects that social media presents (Social Blade, 2021). People are beginning to understand how important it is to be digitally well. Addiction to social media calls for conversations on time management and responsible usage. Finding a balance between the advantages and disadvantages of digital connectedness is a task for society. Addiction to social media can interfere with academic endeavors. Students who are preoccupied with social media may perform worse academically. The public should investigate methods for encouraging students to be digitally literate and behave responsibly when using the internet. The difficulty of controlling their kids' social media use is something that parents have to deal with. Addiction to social media in young people can cause strife within the family. Teaching parents how to keep an eye on and mentor their children's online activity becomes essential. Addiction to social media has the power to influence social movements and political dialogue. Social media echo chambers and the spread of false information affect societal attitudes and practices. It calls into question the truthfulness of information and the shaping of public opinion.

The tendency to draw broad conclusions when talking about how social media affects society is one of its main drawbacks. Social media has a wide range of effects, some of which are more severe than others based on the platform, user demographics, and cultural setting. The chapter's accuracy may be compromised if these variations are not taken into account. The future scope of this could be an understanding of how social media influences societal norms, beliefs, and behaviors can be gained through comparative examinations of its impact in various cultural contexts.

The Effects of Social Media Addiction

Despite the obvious advantages of social media, social media addiction is becoming a bigger worry. Social media networks use algorithms that urge users to stay on them longer since they are intended to be addictive. Dopamine, a neurotransmitter linked to pleasure, is released in response to continuous comments, likes, and notifications, reinforcing the habit of monitoring social media (Lin et al., 2016). According to research, addiction to social media can be compared to addiction to drugs. According to a study by Kuss and Griffiths (2017), people who are hooked to social media frequently display signs of withdrawal, mood swings, conflict, and relapse that are comparable to those of drug addiction. Obsessive social media use can have detrimental effects like decreased productivity, disturbed sleep patterns, and elevated stress and anxiety (Andreassen et al. 2016).

Addiction to social media has serious negative effects on people's well-being. According to a 2017 study that appeared in the Journal of Abnormal Psychology, there was a notable spike in episodes of major depression among young adults in the US between 2005 and 2017, which happened to coincide with social media's explosive growth (Twenge et al., 2019). Frequent comparisons to the idealized portrayals of others on social media can exacerbate poor self-esteem and feelings of unworthiness, which are risk factors for anxiety and depression (Fardouly et al., 2015). The limitations of this could be it can be difficult to establish a direct cause-and-effect link between social media addiction and particular outcomes.

Addiction's development and intensity are influenced by a multitude of factors, including external life conditions and pre-existing mental health concerns. Future studies can examine how social media addiction affects emotional stability, mental health, and the emergence of psychological conditions like anxiety and depression. It's also critical to research the possibilities for mental health and addiction treatment.

Social Media and Relationships

The way people establish and sustain relationships has also changed due to social media. Others can interact with others worldwide using the internet in today's linked society, establishing both love and friendship relationships. A Pew Research Center research from 2021 indicated that 59% of American people had utilized online dating services, highlighting the important role that social media plays in contemporary dating (Pew Research Center, 2021). Social media can help people connect, but it can also make relationships more difficult. The practice of "phubbing" has been linked to emotions of separation and is inversely connected with relationship satisfaction, according to a study published in the journal Computers in Human Behavior (Roberts & David, 2016).

In partnerships, envy and mistrust can also be stroked by social media connections and the transparency of the partner's interactions. According to a study by (Muise et al., 2013) people who used Facebook more frequently expressed higher levels of Facebook-related jealousy, which was then associated with lower relationship satisfaction.

It's interesting to note that language employed in virtual exchanges has an impact on interpersonal connections. The power of language in the digital sphere was highlighted by a study published in the journal Cyberpsychology, Behavior, and Social Networking. The study indicated that utilizing endearing phrases in online communication was connected with increased relationship satisfaction (Bareket-Bojmel et al., 2015). The danger of drawing broad generalizations when talking about how social media affects relationships is one of the key constraints. Depending on the specifics of each relationship, the person, and the cultural setting, the outcomes can differ greatly. Subsequent investigations may explore how social media influences relationship conflict resolution and communication styles. This encompasses both advantages and disadvantages, such as enhanced communication or the possibility of miscommunication.

In summary, Without a doubt, the emergence of social media has changed society by affecting how we interact, express ourselves, and develop relationships. It has many advantages, such as creativity, empowerment, and international connections, but it also has drawbacks. Addiction to social media has become a serious issue with consequences for mental health and general well-being. It emphasizes the significance of having healthy boundaries both online and offline because it can cause envy and detachment in relationships. People need to be conscious of how they use social media and how it affects their lives as the digital landscape changes. People may use social media's positive effects while reducing its bad ones by being aware of both its transformative potential and its drawbacks. This will help them have a better and more balanced connection with the digital world.

Defining Social Media Addiction

Today's digital technology has made social media addiction a serious worry, as billions of people use various social media sites. Certain characteristics set an addiction apart from casual use: obsessive behavior, withdrawal symptoms, and a detrimental influence on day-to-day functioning—a Pew Research Center research from 2021 states that roughly 69% of American adults utilize social media. Still, not every user is addicted, and there are distinguishable patterns linked to overuse. Due to their immature impulse control and increased susceptibility to peer pressure, adolescents and young adults are especially susceptible to social media addiction (Boyd, 2014). Social media addiction is a behavioral addiction characterized by the excessive use of social media platforms to the detriment of an individual's daily life and well-being. It is also known as social media dependency or Social Media Use Disorder (SMUD) (Kuss & Griffiths, 2011). It is imperative to differentiate between casual usage of social media and addiction, as the former demonstrates distinct characteristics.

Features That Set It Apart

The compulsive nature of the activity is one of the main characteristics that distinguishes social media addiction from casual use. Social media addicts frequently struggle with the overwhelming desire to update their statuses, check their feeds, and check their profiles—to the point where they become uncontrollably addicted. This obsession may cause one to disregard obligations to others, including jobs, education, and interpersonal connections. Teenagers are more prone to display signs of social media addiction because of their immature impulse control and vulnerability to peer pressure, according to research published in the Journal of Behavioral Addictions (Kuss & Griffiths, 2011). Another characteristic that sets up social media addiction is withdrawal symptoms. People who try to cut back or stop using social media frequently feel anxious, and restless, and have a strong urge to go back on the platform. This withdrawal phenomenon highlights the obsessive and embedded aspect of social media use by being comparable to what is seen in drug addiction (Andreassen et al., 2012). Addiction to social media is frequently used as an escape from unpleasant feelings or real-world issues. Individuals may use social media as a coping strategy to keep from dealing with uncomfortable circumstances or feelings. One could interpret this conduct as an attempt to cope with stress, anxiety, or loneliness. Regretfully, this frequently makes matters worse because excessive usage of social media can heighten feelings of loneliness and lower mental health (Elhai et al., 2019).

One important characteristic that sets social media addiction apart from casual use is its detrimental effects on day-to-day functioning. Social media addiction has a substantial negative impact on a person's everyday life, even though many people use social media platforms for employment, personal networking, or enjoyment. Their general mental and physical health may be jeopardized, their productivity may decline, and their interpersonal relationships may become strained. According to Király et al. (2017), this detrimental effect goes beyond specific individuals and may have wider societal repercussions. The limitations of this could be evaluating characteristics that set social media networks apart are frequently random and depend on the personal preferences and viewpoints of users. A platform's value system may not be the same for every user. The future scope of this could be examining the competitive environment among social media platforms and how they consistently innovate to set themselves apart is an exciting area of research.

Prevalence and Excessive Usage

Excessive social media usage is notable in terms of its prevalence and patterns. People worldwide spend an average of two hours and twenty-two minutes a day using social media, according to 2021 research by the Global Web Index's Social Media Trends. Addiction to social media has been more common in recent years, with young adults and teenagers being especially vulnerable. It's critical to identify particular patterns linked to excessive use, such as FOMO (fear of missing out). To keep up with what others are doing, many people check their feeds frequently, which can cause anxiety and addiction (Oberst et al., 2017). Teenagers are especially vulnerable to social media addiction, according to research (Kuss & Griffiths, 2011). According to research in the Journal of Behavioral Addictions, teenagers are more prone than adults to display signs of social media addiction because their impulse control is still growing and they are more vulnerable to peer pressure. Overconsumption users frequently ignore their obligations, including jobs and education, in favor of spending hours every day on social media. As of 2021, people throughout the world spent an average of two hours and twenty-two minutes each day using social media platforms, according to the Global Web Index's Social Media Trends Report. Dopamine is a neurotransmitter linked to pleasure that is released when users "like" and "share" content on social media sites (Ryan & Chester, 2015). Users are hooked and are compelled to keep viewing their profiles since they are periodically reminded that they are receiving likes and comments. The limitation of this could be the frequency and overuse of social media frequently rely on self-reported data, which is prone to biases and errors. A crucial difficulty is ensuring the reliability and validity of data. The future scope of this could be it is essential to investigate effective intervention tactics and preventive interventions aimed at reducing excessive usage of social media, particularly among marginalized populations. Both individual and group-based interventions may fall under this category.

Psychological Elements

Effectively tackling the issue of social media addiction requires an understanding of its psychological foundations. Social media addiction is a result of and contributes to several psychological factors. Likes, comments, and shares on social media platforms allow users rapid satisfaction, which feeds into addictive behaviors (Ryan & Chester, 2015). Users become hooked and involved because of the continuous feedback loop. Overuse of social media frequently results in social comparison, when people assess their lives against the carefully manicured, perfect representations that are posted there (Fardouly et al., 2015). This can exacerbate addiction by having a detrimental effect on one's body image and sense of self. Online harassment and cyberbullying can result from social media's anonymity (Kowalski et al., 2014). As a result, users' mental health suffers and addiction spreads as a means of escaping these unpleasant situations. Cyberbullying and online abuse are made possible by the private nature of social media (Kowalski et al., 2014). As a result, users' mental health suffers and addiction spreads as a means of escaping these unpleasant situations. One potential drawback could be extending psychological impacts from one social media platform to another. Every platform is different, and each user experience and feature has the potential to have different psychological effects. An interesting line of inquiry is how various psychological factors affect user behaviors on social media platforms, including posting habits, interaction patterns, and content consumption.

Social Factors

Addiction to social media has serious societal ramifications and is not merely an issue for individuals. People who use social media more frequently divulge personal information that businesses or bad actors may use against them (DiResta et al., 2018). The 2018 Cambridge Analytica incident made clear the possible dangers of oversharing. According to Pennycook and Rand (2019), social media algorithms promote material that is consistent with users' preexisting opinions to maintain user engagement. Expanding societal divisions reinforce divides in politics and echo chambers. Given that social factors can vary greatly based on cultural, demographic, and contextual variances, generalizing social factors and their impact on social media use may be restricted. Future studies can examine in further detail how cultural and societal elements, such as norms, values, and customs, impact social media usage and how these influence interactions and behaviors online.

Technological Factor

The development of social media addiction has been made possible by technological improvements. On social media sites like Facebook, Instagram, and Twitter, users can easily spend hours online due to the endless scrolling and auto-play feature, which satisfies their addiction (Wilcox et al., 2013). According to Ellen et al. (2011), social networking apps are made to provide notifications, which keep users interested all the time. These push alerts have the potential to be compulsive and addicting.

Social media companies utilize complex algorithms to tailor content to individual users depending on their previous interactions. By presenting material that is in line with their interests and preferences, personalization helps to maintain user engagement. On websites like TikTok and YouTube, auto-play options for videos encourage viewers to watch more content without consciously deciding to. This autoplay feature may encourage extended interaction. In-app purchases for virtual goods or premium features are available in a lot of social media apps. Users may be more inclined to stay on the platform longer as a result of these microtransactions' ability to foster a sense of investment. An integrated ecosystem is created by the several social media platforms that are owned by tech businesses. For instance, WhatsApp and Instagram are owned by Facebook. Users are encouraged to interact with various apps inside the same ecosystem as a result.

In Summary, The problem of social media addiction is intricate and multidimensional, characterized by obsessive use, escapism, withdrawal symptoms, and detrimental effects on day-to-day functioning. Concern over its prevalence is growing, especially among young people and adolescents. Extended screen time, FOMO, and the desire for dopamine surges through likes and shares are indicators of excessive usage behaviors.

It is crucial to comprehend the psychological, cultural, and technological aspects that lead to social media addiction to lessen its effects. Psychological elements that need to be considered are the incessant drive for quick gratification, social comparison, and the possibility of cyberbullying. Political divisiveness and privacy concerns are societal issues, while technical features like notification systems and never-ending scrolling make addiction easier.

The Influence of Social Media Addiction on Body Image

The significant impact that social media addiction has on a person's sense of self, especially concerning body image, is among the most worrisome features of the addiction. Social media platforms can mold our ideals and expectations through the steady stream of carefully chosen photos and content, which frequently results in irrational standards. In 2015, Fardouly et al. conducted a study in the journal "Cyberpsychology, Behavior, and Social Networking" that brought attention to the negative effects of idealized photos on social media sites like Instagram. It was discovered that young women's sense of self-worth and negative judgments of their bodies were influenced by these photographs who constantly compare their bodies to these meticulously chosen and digitally altered depictions may get dissatisfied with their physical appearance. As a result, to meet an unattainable standard of beauty, individuals could turn to drastic methods like unhealthy dieting or cosmetic surgery. The long-term effects of these behaviors on one's bodily and emotional well-being are possible. Excessive social media use can damage one's sense of self and lead to dissatisfaction with one's appearance, which is strongly associated with mental health issues like anxiety and depression (Perloff, 2014). The limitation of this could be determining a clear causal link between social media addiction and issues with body image can be difficult. These problems stem from several variables, including personal vulnerabilities and offline experiences. Future studies can examine the effects of social media addiction on body image on mental health, including the emergence of eating disorders or body dysmorphic disorder.

The Influence of Social Media Addiction on Self-Identity

Addiction to social media can affect a person's self-identity in addition to their physical image. Continually being exposed to carefully chosen and frequently inflated depictions of other people's lives might cause self-doubt and feelings of inadequacy. According to a study by Primack et al. (2017) that was written in the journal "JAMA Pediatrics," young adults who use social media heavily tend to experience higher levels of depression. The researchers hypothesized that this relationship might result from the "social comparison" phenomena, in which people evaluate their lives concerning the ostensibly ideal lives posted on social media.

Users may develop the belief that their online popularity determines their value, leading them to alter their demeanor and actions to fit the platform's standards and trends, as a result of the constant chase of likes, comments, and followers. The persistent need for acceptance and validation can become a motivating factor and ultimately cause one's genuine self-identity to be lost. Because of this, people could find it difficult to tell the difference between their online identity and their real-life self, which could lead to feelings of not being able to be themselves, emptiness, and mental discomfort (Rozgonjuk et al., 2018). The limitation of this could be it can be difficult to prove a clear causal link between social media addiction and identity alterations. Self-identity can also be influenced by other elements, such as individual traits, offline interactions, and personal experiences. Subsequent investigations may explore how addiction to social media impacts many facets of self-identity, including self-worth, self-esteem, and self-concept.

Excessive Social Media Usage on Social Isolation

In a strange twist, excessive usage of social media platforms can paradoxically result in social isolation and loneliness, although these platforms are meant to connect people. According to research that was published in the journal "Personality and Individual Differences" (Primack et al., 2017), young adults who used social media more frequently than twice a day were more likely to feel socially isolated than those who used it less frequently. Online comments and likes can take the place of real, in-person contacts in the digital world, which can fool users into believing they are engaging in social engagement.

Overuse frequently entails passive consumption, in which users browse through countless feeds without engaging in any meaningful way, further severing their ties to real-world social interactions. This can eventually erode social ties and result in feelings of isolation and detachment from reality. It can be difficult to prove a clear causal link between excessive social media use and social isolation. Social isolation can also be caused by a wide range of other variables, including unique personality traits and offline social dynamics. It is crucial to research how online communities and peer groups may worsen or lessen the negative consequences of excessive social media use on social isolation.

Feeling of Loneliness on Social Media

Excessive use of social media can cause or worsen loneliness, which has serious consequences for mental health. A study by Primack et al. (2017) that was published in the journal "JAMA Pediatrics" connected heavy social media use to a higher risk of depression in young adults. Feelings of pessimism and depression can be exacerbated by the sensation of being misinterpreted, alone, and alienated. Furthermore, loneliness can set off a chain reaction of unfavorable feelings, such as tension, anxiety, and low self-esteem. Teenagers are particularly susceptible to these emotions since they are going through a critical period in the formation of their identities. According to a study that was published in the "Journal of Abnormal Psychology" (Twenge et al., 2018), there was a notable rise in the prevalence of major depressive episodes among teenagers between 2005 and 2015. It was suggested that the surge in mental health problems among this age group during this time could be attributed to the rise in social media use during this time. The limitation of this could be it can be difficult to prove a clear causal link between social media use and feelings of loneliness. Beyond social media, a variety of things can influence the complicated emotional condition of loneliness. The future scope could be examining how cultural, regional, and global elements influence the loneliness experience on social media can offer a more thorough comprehension of this complex matter.

In Summary, Social media can be very beneficial for connecting people and sharing information. Still, it can also be quite addicting and negatively impact mental health and self-perception because of the frequent exposure to well-chosen content. Abuse can change a person's perception of their body, which can cause discontent and possibly have long-term negative effects on one's physical and mental health. Additionally, it might weaken one's sense of self, which can lead to depressive and inauthentic feelings.

The irony of social media is that, despite its goal of fostering human connection, it can also result in social isolation and loneliness. Perceived isolation in the digital age can seriously harm mental health by raising the risk of anxiety, depression, and other mental health problems. Striking a balance between online and offline encounters is crucial as we traverse the digital world, concentrating on the genuine, real connections that are vital to our mental health and overall well-being.

Social Media Addiction and Quality of Life

Social media addiction can have a devastating effect on a person's general quality of life. It is frequently characterized by excessive consumption and an inability to manage one's usage. According to studies, using social media excessively can have several detrimental effects on one's life, impacting several facets of it.

Overuse of social media can seriously reduce efficiency. People in the US interact with media for an average of 11 hours a day, according to a Nielsen (2018) survey. A significant amount of this time is spent on social media, which can cause one to lose focus on important tasks like studying or working. This effect on output has the potential to raise stress levels and lower general life satisfaction. Sleep habits might be disturbed by the blue light that screens emit and the continuous notifications that social media sites provide. According to a study that was published in the journal "Pediatrics" (Levenson et al., 2017), teens who use electronics right before bed have shorter sleep durations and lower-quality sleep.

Lack of sleep as a result can cause a variety of problems with one's physical and mental well-being, which can lower one's general standard of living. Addiction to social media can be harmful to relationships in real life. People who spend a lot of time staring at devices might ignore in-person conversations, which might cause them to feel disconnected and alone. According to a study by Primack et al. (2017) that was published in "JAMA Pediatrics," young adults who use social media are more likely to experience social isolation. Ironically, the need to maintain digital connections may result in a loss of deep, in-person relationships. The limitation of this could be it can be difficult to prove a clear causal link between social media addiction and an improvement in life quality. There are other variables as well, such as individual circumstances and mental health. The future scope of this could be long-term research that analyzes changes in social media addiction and quality of life over time and can offer important insights into the changing influence.

Possible Impacts on Physical Health

Prolonged screen time and a passive lifestyle of social media use can have several negative impacts on one's physical health. These effects can worsen a person's general quality of life.

Extreme social media use is frequently accompanied by prolonged periods of lethargy. An increased risk of being obese, coronary artery disease and other health problems are linked to this sedentary activity. A 2014 study by Finger et al. published in "PLOS ONE" discovered a connection between increased screen usage and unfavorable health outcomes. A person's general well-being and quality of life can be negatively impacted by physical inactivity.

Extended periods spent staring at screens, particularly on tiny devices like smartphones, can lead to eye strain and pain. Often called "computer vision syndrome," this ailment can include headaches, impaired vision, and dry eyes. These bodily aches and pains can make life more difficult daily and lower the quality of life overall.

As was previously noted, the blue light emitted by screens can cause sleep patterns to be disturbed by messing with the body's melatonin production, which is a hormone that controls sleep. Chronic sleep abnormalities have been linked to several health problems, such as mood disorders, impaired cognitive function, and weakened immune systems. A person's overall quality of life may be negatively impacted by the physical health consequences of sleep deprivation. The limitation of this could be physical well-being is a complex notion, and because many variables can cause confusion, it can be difficult to isolate the effects of different factors—including social media—on physical well-being. The future scope of this study can examine the connection between screen time—including social media use—and other physical health outcomes, like sedentary behavior, eye strain, and posture-related problems.

Resilient Coping Strategies and Support Systems

Identifying one's addiction to social media and taking action to recover control are critical to enhancing one's life. Resilient coping strategies and supportive networks might be quite important during this phase. Social media breaks regularly can help lessen the harmful effects of addiction. Often called a "digital detox," this practice entails designating specified hours of the day when one avoids using social media. There are numerous tools and applications available to assist people in limiting their screen usage. Being attentive can make people more conscious of their social media usage and how it affects their well-being. Being self-aware can be a very effective way to take back control over one's use. In cases of extreme social media addiction, consulting a mental health expert might be quite beneficial. In addition to other therapeutic modalities, cognitive-behavioral therapy (CBT) can assist clients in comprehending the root causes of their addiction and creating appropriate coping mechanisms.

Getting help from friends and family or joining support groups can give you a sense of belonging and accountability. Talking about difficulties and experiences with people who are going through similar things can be encouraging and consoling. Individual differences in coping mechanisms and support networks make it difficult to offer general guidelines in a book chapter. Strategies' efficacy may vary depending on an individual's circumstances and traits. It seems like a good idea to combine knowledge from public health, psychology, sociology, and other fields to develop broader resilience techniques in future studies.

In Summary, Addiction to social media can have a significant and lasting impact on a person's general quality of life. It has an impact on relationships, physical health, sleep patterns, and productivity. It is essential to identify the warning symptoms of addiction and take preventative action to lessen its effects as we manage the digital world.

Effective coping strategies can help people recover ownership of their social media usage and enhance their quality of life. Examples of these strategies include mindfulness, digital detox, and seeing a professional. To escape the virtual bonds and reclaim a healthier, more balanced life, the assistance of relatives, close companions, and support groups can also be a crucial asset.

Moral Concerns Presented by Social Media Platforms

Numerous moral concerns have emerged as a result of the digital revolution, most notably those related to social media addiction and its negative effects.

Social media sites are designed to be compulsive. By offering features like notifications and infinite scrolling, they entice users to stay on the platform longer.

These designs raise ethical concerns about the accountability of digital businesses by placing a higher priority on corporate profitability than consumer well-being. For instance, according to Tristan Harris, a former design ethicist at Google, these platforms' attention-grabbing strategies are similar to those of a "cultural manipulation business" (Center for Humane Technology, n.d.). High social media use is linked to a higher incidence of depression in young people, according to a study published in "JAMA Pediatrics" (Primack et al., 2017). This finding highlights ethical issues about the possible harm that these platforms may do.

Social media frequently produces "echo chambers," when users are exposed to information that confirms their thoughts, restricting the range of viewpoints and strengthening extreme opinions. Spreading misleading information, sometimes known as "fake news," has also raised ethical concerns. The ethical ramifications of spreading false information are highlighted by a Pew Research Center survey (Gottfried & Shearer, 2016), which revealed that 64% of individuals thought fake news has created "a great deal" of misunderstanding about fundamental facts of current events. There are enormous differences in morality between people, cultures, and societies. On social media, what one group considers a moral issue could not be to another. Studies can concentrate on the ways that moral concerns expressed on social media influence actions that occur in the real world, like activism, hate crimes, or shifts in public opinion.

Fighting Addiction and Its Consequences

It is morally required for social media corporations to create platforms that put user welfare before addiction. Co-founder of the Center for Humane Technology Tristan Harris promotes moral design standards that guarantee technology serves people's needs instead of taking advantage of them (Center for Humane Technology, n.d.). Businesses need to think about how their designs affect users' mental health and restrict features that promote overuse. Certain social media companies have realized how important it is to fight addiction and provide resources for online health. Instagram, for instance, unveiled a feature called "Time Well Spent" that lets users establish daily usage caps and get alerts when they go over them. Users can take charge of their social media usage with the help of these tools (Instagram, 2018).

To tackle the problem of addiction among younger users, social media companies ought to include parental control features that enable parents to keep an eye on and restrict their kids' usage. Facebook provides parents with options to monitor their children's online activities and establish time limitations (Facebook, n.d.).

Social media businesses ought to place a high priority on algorithmic openness. Users are entitled to know how their content is chosen and presented to them. Companies can reduce the formation of echo chambers and be held more responsible for the content people see by making their algorithms public (Tufekci, 2018). A wide range of individual, contextual, and platform-specific factors can contribute to social media addiction. It can be difficult to fully address each of these elements in a single chapter. investigating how new technology, such as behavior-tracking applications and artificial intelligence, might be used to help people prevent and manage addiction.

Campaigns for Public Awareness and Education

Programs for digital literacy should be included in educational institutions to help students develop critical thinking abilities and secure online navigation techniques. These courses can assist students in recognizing false information, dispelling it, and comprehending the way excessive social media use affects mental health (Livingstone, 2017).

Campaigns to raise public awareness of social media ethics should be started by governments, non-profits, and social media firms working together. These initiatives may emphasize informing the public about the possible repercussions of social media addiction, encouraging appropriate online conduct, and bringing privacy concerns to the public's attention (Niemz et al., 2005).

Programs for media literacy ought to be extensively adopted to teach people how to identify and check the accuracy of the material they come across on social media. In the digital age, the capacity to critically evaluate the reliability of sources is essential (Hobbs, 2010).

People ought to be prompted to consider their social media usage and how it affects their lives. Encouraging users to become self-aware about addiction and the possible negative effects of excessive usage can enable them to make responsible decisions (Harris, 2019). Important messages from public awareness initiatives run the risk of being lost or diluted in the deluge of information in this era of information overload. Public awareness initiatives may have limited reach and impact due to a lack of financing and staff. Campaigns must reach a wide range of people with different backgrounds, worldviews, and reading levels. Customizing communications to fit the requirements of various groups is a difficult challenging task. There is growing interest in addressing the ethical aspects of public awareness efforts, such as concerns about privacy, informed permission, and responsible data usage. Examining the most efficient ways to use social media, smartphone apps, conventional media, and other communication channels can help public awareness campaigns reach a wider audience.

In Summary, Social media addiction and its aftereffects provide intricate and varied moral dilemmas. Given the continued significance of social media platforms in contemporary culture, it is critical to carefully handle these challenges. Parental restrictions, digital well-being tools, and ethical design can all aid in the fight against addiction. However, public awareness and education efforts are crucial to lessening the negative effects of social media addiction. Together, IT firms, academic institutions, governments, and private citizens can build a more morally and ethically sound digital environment that upholds people's rights to privacy and improves their quality of life.

The overall conclusion for all the topics is that social media sites such as Instagram, Twitter, and Facebook have become a necessary part of contemporary life. They impact how we connect and communicate in both personal and professional contexts by facilitating global connectivity and information sharing. The compulsive elements of social media, such as never-ending scrolling and notifications, have sparked worries about the potential effects on mental health. Concerns regarding general well-being have been raised by the correlation between excessive use and conditions like anxiety, depression, and low self-esteem. Numerous studies demonstrate the connection between excessive social media use and a range of mental health issues. High use has a negative influence on mental health since it is linked to a higher incidence of depression and loneliness. The hallmark of social media addiction is losing control over one's online conduct. Its primary characteristics that set addiction apart from casual usage include obsession, withdrawal symptoms, and unfavorable outcomes. Particularly among young people and adolescents, prevalence is rising. Psychological elements, social forces, and technology design decisions all have an impact on social media addiction. Algorithms provide consumers with tailored material to keep them engaged, while users crave constant connection, affirmation, and fear of missing out. Societal media addiction can cause unrealistic body image standards and societal comparisons, which can hurt one's opinion of oneself. Anxiety, despair, and body dissatisfaction follow from this. Ironically, excessive usage of social media can contribute to feelings of loneliness and social isolation. Intimate relationships may suffer as a result of the desire for internet connections, which can erode social ties and heighten feelings of isolation.

Addiction to social media has an impact on relationships in real life, sleep cycles, and productivity. It encourages sedentary behavior, which raises the risk of obesity and cardiovascular disease. Notifications and screen time can interfere with sleep cycles, which can cause sleep deprivation and related health issues.

People can adopt mindfulness and digital detox as coping methods to overcome social media addiction. It can be beneficial to seek professional assistance, such as cognitive-behavioral therapy (CBT). Friends, family, and support groups are examples of support networks that offer accountability and motivation. Social media companies have come under fire for their design decisions, which have been shown to promote addiction, abuse user data, and compromise privacy. Addiction can be fought with the use of parental restrictions, digital well-being tools, transparency, and ethical design principles. Addressing the negative effects of social media addiction requires the involvement of educational institutions and public awareness efforts. In addition to educating the public on privacy concerns and the possible repercussions of social media addiction, they can offer instruction in digital literacy.

REFERENCES

Andreassen, C. S., Torsheim, T., Brunborg, G. S., & Pallesen, S. (2012). Development of a Facebook Addiction Scale. *Psychological Reports*, *110*(2), 501–517. doi:10.2466/02.09.18.PR0.110.2.501-517 PMID:22662404

Bareket-Bojmel, L., Shahar, G., & Margalit, M. (2015). Perceived social support and attachment styles as predictors of communication patterns in romantic relationships. *Cyberpsychology, Behavior, and Social Networking*, *18*(4), 203–208. PMID:25803312

Blade, S. (2021). YouTubers by Views and Subscribers. Academic Press.

Boyd, D. (2014). *It's Complicated: The Social Lives of Networked Teens*. Yale University Press.

Center for Humane Technology. (n.d.). Tristan Harris. Retrieved from https://humanetech.com/team/tristan-harris

DiResta, R., Halderman, J. A., & Howard, P. N. (2018). *The tactics & tropes of the Internet Research Agency*. Stanford Internet Observatory.

Elhai, J. D., Levine, J. C., Dvorak, R. D., & Hall, B. J. (2019). Fear of missing out, need for touch, anxiety, and depression are related to problematic smartphone use. *Computers in Human Behavior*, *63*, 509–516. doi:10.1016/j.chb.2016.05.079

Ellison, N. B., Steinfield, C., & Lampe, C. (2011). Connection strategies: Social capital implications of Facebook-enabled communication practices. *New Media & Society*, *13*(6), 873–892. doi:10.1177/1461444810385389

Facebook. (n.d.). Tools for Parents. Retrieved from https://www.facebook.com/safety/parents

Fardouly, J., Diedrichs, P. C., Vartanian, L. R., & Halliwell, E. (2015). Social comparisons on social media: The impact of Facebook on young women's body image concerns and mood. *Body Image*, *13*, 38–45. doi:10.1016/j.bodyim.2014.12.002 PMID:25615425

Finger, J. D., Mensink, G. B., Lange, C., & Manz, K. (2014). Health-enhancing physical activity during leisure time among adults in Germany. *Journal of Health Monitoring*, *1*(1), 35–41. PMID:37152092

Gottfried, J., & Shearer, E. (2016). News Use Across Social Media Platforms 2016. Pew Research Center. Retrieved from https://www.journalism.org/2016/05/26/news-use-on-social-media-platforms-2016/

Gross, E. F., Juvonen, J., & Gable, S. L. (2002). Internet use and well-being in adolescence. *The Journal of Social Issues*, *58*(1), 75–90. doi:10.1111/1540-4560.00249

Harris, T. (2019). How better tech could protect us from distraction? TED. Retrieved from https://www.ted.com/talks/tristan_harris_how_better_tech_could_protect_us_from_distraction

Hobbs, R. (2010). Digital and media literacy: A plan of action. The Aspen Institute. Retrieved from https://www.aspeninstitute.org/publications/digital-and-media-literacy-a-plan-of-...

Howard, P. N., & Hussain, M. M. (2013). *Democracy's fourth wave? Digital media and the Arab Spring*. Oxford University Press. doi:10.1093/acprof:oso/9780199936953.001.0001

Jones, S., & Wilson, M. L. (2018). Social Media and Its Influence on the Development of Social Connectedness. In Handbook of Research on Cross-Cultural Business Education (pp. 95-123). IGI Global.

Király, O., Potenza, M. N., Stein, D. J., King, D. L., Hodgins, D. C., Saunders, J. B., ... Demetrovics, Z. (2017). Preventing problematic internet use through video-based psychoeducation: A randomized controlled trial. *PLoS One*, *12*(12), e0186459. PMID:29211728

Kowalski, R. M., Giumetti, G. W., Schroeder, A. N., & Lattanner, M. R. (2014). Bullying in the digital age: A critical review and meta-analysis of cyberbullying research among youth. *Psychological Bulletin*, *140*(4), 1073–1137. doi:10.1037/a0035618 PMID:24512111

Kuss, D. J., & Griffiths, M. D. (2011). Online social networking and addiction: A review of the psychological literature. *International Journal of Environmental Research and Public Health*, *8*(9), 3528–3552. doi:10.3390/ijerph8093528 PMID:22016701

Kuss, D. J., & Griffiths, M. D. (2017). Social networking sites and addiction: Ten lessons learned. *International Journal of Environmental Research and Public Health, 14*(3), 311. doi:10.3390/ijerph14030311 PMID:28304359

Levenson, J. C., Shensa, A., Sidani, J. E., Colditz, J. B., & Primack, B. A. (2017). The association between social media use and sleep disturbance among young adults. *Preventive Medicine, 85*, 36–41. doi:10.1016/j.ypmed.2016.01.001 PMID:26791323

Lin, L. Y., Sidani, J. E., Shensa, A., Radovic, A., Miller, E., Colditz, J. B., Hoffman, B. L., Giles, L. M., & Primack, B. A. (2016). Association between social media use and depression among U.S. young adults. *Depression and Anxiety, 33*(4), 323–331. doi:10.1002/da.22466 PMID:26783723

Muise, A., Christofides, E., & Desmarais, S. (2009). More Information than You Ever Wanted: Does Facebook Bring Out the Green-Eyed Monster of Jealousy? *Cyberpsychology & Behavior, 12*(4), 441–444. doi:10.1089/cpb.2008.0263 PMID:19366318

Nielsen. (2018). Total audience report: Q1 2018. Nielsen. Retrieved from https://www.nielsen.com/us/en/insights/report/2018/total-audience-report-q1-2018/

Oberst, U., Wegmann, E., Stodt, B., Brand, M., & Chamarro, A. (2017). Negative consequences from heavy social networking in adolescents: The mediating role of fear of missing out. *Journal of Adolescence, 55*(1), 51–60. doi:10.1016/j.adolescence.2016.12.008 PMID:28033503

Pennycook, G., & Rand, D. G. (2019). The Implied Truth Effect: Attaching Warnings to a Subset of Fake News Stories Increases Perceived Accuracy of Stories Without Warnings. *Management Science, 66*(11), 4944–4957. doi:10.1287/mnsc.2019.3478

Perloff, R. M. (2014). Social media effects on young women's body image concerns: Theoretical perspectives and an agenda for research. *Sex Roles, 71*(11-12), 363–377. doi:10.1007/s11199-014-0384-6

Pew Research Center. (2021). 15% of U.S. Adults Have Used Online Dating Sites or Mobile Dating Apps. Author.

Primack, B. A., Shensa, A., Sidani, J. E., Whaite, E. O., Lin, L. Y., Rosen, D., ... Colditz, J. B. (2017). Social media use and perceived social isolation among young adults in the U.S. *PLoS One, 12*(8), e0182145. PMID:28832594

Roberts, J. A., & David, M. E. (2016). My life has become a major distraction from my cell phone: Partner phubbing and relationship satisfaction among romantic partners. *Computers in Human Behavior, 54*, 134–141. doi:10.1016/j.chb.2015.07.058

Robinson, L. (2023, March 29). Social Media and Mental Health. HelpGuide.org. https://www.helpguide.org/articles/mental-health/social-media-and-mental-health. htm#:~:text=Since%20it's%20a%20relatively%20new,harm%2C%20and%20 even%20suicidal%20thoughts

Rozgonjuk, D., Saal, K., & Täht, K. (2018). Problematic social media use and depression symptoms among adolescents: A longitudinal study. *Journal of Adolescence, 65,* 73–82.

Ryan, T., & Chester, A. (2015). Fear of missing out and the relationship between frequency of Facebook use, exposure to Facebook use (via social comparison) and Facebook addiction. *Computers in Human Behavior, 44,* 64–80.

Smith, A. B., Johnson, L., Pendergrast, R. A., & Cranston, W. (2020). The Impact of Social Media Addiction on Mental Health: A Conceptual Model and Literature Review. *Journal of Psychology and Behavioral Science, 8*(1), 1–8.

Statista. (2021). Number of monthly active Facebook users worldwide as of 4th quarter 2021. Author.

Twenge, J. M., Cooper, A. B., Joiner, T. E., Duffy, M. E., & Binau, S. G. (2018). Age, period, and cohort trends in mood disorder indicators and suicide-related outcomes in a nationally representative dataset, 2005–2017. *Journal of Abnormal Psychology, 127*(4), 348–355. PMID:29745700

Twenge, J. M., Joiner, T. E., Rogers, M. L., & Martin, G. N. (2018). Increases in depressive symptoms, suicide-related outcomes, and suicide rates among U.S. adolescents after 2010 and links to increased new media screen time. *Clinical Psychological Science, 6*(1), 3–17. doi:10.1177/2167702617723376

Wilcox, K., Stephen, A. T., & Suri, R. (2013). Beware the dark side: Consumer responses to negative social media content. *The Journal of Consumer Research, 40*(5), 839–853.

Chapter 12
Unveiling Interplay Between Physical and Digital Barriers to Program Access and Women Empowerment:
Sashakt Mahila, Saksham Mahila – A Qualitative Study

Harsh Sinha
Indian Institute of Management, Bodh Gaya, India

Kailashpati
Indian Institute of Management, Bodh Gaya, India

Rahul Raj
Indian Institute of Management, Bodh Gaya, India

ABSTRACT

Bihar is a dynamic society with a considerable influence on the Indian policy framework due to the presence of Bihari settlers covering almost all regions of the country and abroad due to the opportunity deficit in Bihar. To address developmental lags and implementation challenges for women empowerment through a sustained combination of intra and inter-societal issues, the Bihar government has conceptualized 'Sashakt Mahila, Saksham Mahila' in the second part of its flagship scheme of 'Saat Nischay Yojna' envisaged by the Chief Minister of Bihar. This chapter aims to explore the interplay of multi-dimensional barriers to bottom-top and top-bottom approaches to

DOI: 10.4018/979-8-3693-2015-0.ch012

women's empowerment, which are acting as impediments to women's self-reliance in financial, socio-cultural, digital, and political spheres. Data were collected from three villages of Bihar, accounting for 15 respondents, using a semi-structured interview. The study found significant positive associations between schemes launched by the Bihar Government to empower women and their financial and social status. The research revealed that the effective implementation of policies aimed at promoting women's welfare remains a considerable challenge, particularly in light of the prevailing circumstances in rural Bihar with multitude of issues, collectively hindering women's empowerment in real terms. This study showed how the barriers to women impede their empowerment and will help in associating the challenges faced by women and where there needs to be more work to be done.

INTRODUCTION

1.1 Background

Women's empowerment and access to programs and services are crucial to gender equality and sustainable development (United et al., 2015; Kabeer, 1999). However, it is worth noting that women frequently encounter obstacles that impede their ability to access these programs, consequently impacting their overall empowerment (Naaz et al., 2018; Batliwala, 2010). In the context of 'Shashakt Mahila, Saksham Mahila (SMSM),' an initiative launched by the Government of Bihar under "Saat Nischay Yojna" to empower women, it is crucial to understand the intricate relationship between barriers to program access and women's empowerment.

Women often have trouble getting to school, health care, jobs, social welfare, and other programs that help them grow because of cultural, financial, social, and institutional hurdles (United Nations, 2020; Mosedale et al., 2012). Women's lives are deeply entwined with social and cultural standards, procedural challenges, and the intricate dynamics of their surrounding environments (Bell et al., 1990). These obstacles might make it harder for women to participate fully in society and hold them back from achieving their full potential (Kabeer, 1999; Sen, 1999)

"Empowerment" refers to more than having more freedom to pursue one's goals. It entails a radical change in women's lives, marked by more economic independence, increased decision-making power, greater psychosocial maturity, and a reorganization of their community roles (Parpart et al., 2000). Women's empowerment cannot be attained through isolated access; it requires a thoughtful analysis of the hurdles to their advancement and the methods used to overcome them. (Tandon, T., 2016). The benefits of increased program access include enhanced economic opportunities, improved health and well-being, and greater social and political participation (Klasen, 2019; Grootaert & Kanbur, 1995).

The State of Bihar is undertaking numerous initiatives along the lines highlighted by UNSDGs and NCW (National Commission for Women) to build the individual capabilities of women in terms of nutritional inputs, health benefits, educational support, and a safe environment and nurture a self-reliant means of livelihood through growth opportunities.

This chapter uses a qualitative approach of study to unveil the connection between women's empowerment in "Sashakt Mahila, Saksham Mahila" and barriers to program access. The study aims to find the hurdles that stop women from gaining power and developing by looking into their experiences, points of view, and problems when trying to access different services and programs.

The findings of this research can provide valuable insights into the barriers that prevent women from availing themselves of programs and services and contribute to the development of targeted interventions and policies that effectively address these. This, in turn, can create an enabling environment for women to participate fully and benefit from various programs and services, promoting gender equality, social inclusion, and sustainable development. The significance of this study lies in its potential to inform policy and practice.

In conclusion, this report aims to highlight the path traveled in this regard and relevant issues faced by the women of Bihar; it will also incorporate possible suggestions about future scopes of development, taking into account the effectiveness of Shashakt Mahila, Saksham Mahila, one of the policies targets of Bihar Government under the second part of Saat Nischay Yojana implemented from the year 2020.

1.2 About the Study

The study area of the chapter lies in the close vicinity of the rural population of Bihar. The formulation of primary data mainly covers the interviews of the women in the villages under the study area. The random sampling technique is adopted for this purpose, where the sample size consists of 15 respondents who have given their opinions on the semi-structured questionnaire. Under this method, samples are selected initially from the population of the three villages from the districts of Gaya, Nawada, and Begusarai. Data is also collected from the experiences and anecdotes of diverse women from across regions of Bihar assembled for training courses on entrepreneurship under Bihar Government CM Udyami Yojna; Moreover Secondary data is also gathered from Bihar Government Archives, NGOs and reports about Anganwadi workers.

2. LITERATURE REVIEW

Recently, there has been increasing attention towards government public policies prioritizing initiatives to empower women. Numerous scholarly investigations have derived valuable insights from several literary sources, elucidating the subject of women's empowerment, the obstacles they face, and the ramifications of various programs and initiatives.

According to a report by UN Women and UNDP, the proportion of women and girls residing in societies where women hold significant authority is less than 1%, and the gender gap is not substantial. According to the WEI, women worldwide can only realize 60% of their full potential, and women perform 28% less effectively than males on average in critical areas of human development, as measured by the GGPI. Therefore, enabling women to increase their economic, social, and political influence is critical today.

The empowerment of women is advantageous for societies, communities, and individuals. According to research, empowered women have greater access to education, healthcare, and economic opportunities, which improves health, reduces poverty, and stimulates economic development. Additionally, empowered women have a more significant say in politics, which can result in more inclusive and equitable policies. (Reshi, I. A., and T. Sudha) (2022). During the Indus Valley civilization and the Rig Vedic period, women were accorded the same social respect as men. They wielded a significant impact on religious and political matters. (A. S. Rao) (2023). Archaeological evidence of the IVC has substantiated women's active involvement in many rituals and performance sessions. Numerous Vedic texts attest to the participation of erudite female scholars (e.g., Gargi, Maytree, Lopamudra) in intellectual discussions and their contributions to the development of ancient scientific knowledge. (2009) (Witzel, M. E.). The sculptures of Didarganj Yakshini, Vagheshwari, Tara, and others from the Maurya to Gupta eras symbolize women's esteemed status in society during that time. However, their circumstances declined following the disintegration of centralized rule-based orders and the emergence of invasions. (S. Kramrisch) (1975). Notwithstanding significant advancements in specific domains, women's empowerment continues to be impeded by numerous challenges. Gender discrimination, violence, and unequal access to resources remain substantial obstacles that persist in contemporary society. Women can positively impact societies, communities, and individuals when they realize their complete capabilities. (2022) Reshi, I. A., and Sudha, T. Additional dimensions have been incorporated into the preexisting concept of women's empowerment by A.K Sinha (2008), including economic, sociopolitical, regional, religious, and legal dimensions. It has been demonstrated that education and employment are intricately linked and that women who are better educated are more engaged in family decision-making.

Additionally, the research revealed that education, employment, and income substantially influence the trajectory of women's authority to determine domestic affairs. Conversely, women's income, employment, and level of education all contribute positively to their decision-making capacity. 2021 (Pandey P. et al.). In the context of development goals, Naila Kabeer contends in her article that achieving gender equality and women's empowerment requires more than simply providing women with access to education, employment, and leadership positions. Furthermore, active accountability, participation, and supervision are mandatory for women. In addition to having opportunities, women must also have the courage to speak out against unjust circumstances and things that are hazardous to their health. Kabeer emphasizes that true empowerment necessitates aiding women at the grassroots level so that they can collaborate to effect real change. (E. Duflo) (2012). During the later Vedic period in ancient Bihar, marked by the emergence of numerous sects, one of the earliest known examples of female writing, 'Therigatha' in the Pali language, was discovered. Sculptures of Didarganj Yakshini, Vagheshwari, Tara, and others, created during the Gupta period, represent the esteemed status that women held in society during that period. Notably absent were indications of conservative practices such as sati and purdah. Nationhood phenomena, natural features, rivers, soil, and locations were ascribed femininity. As a result of the emergence of invasions and the fragmentation of centralized rule-based order, the condition of women declined.

One of the outcomes of political reservation for women in Indian villages was sustained economic empowerment, increased participation in the National Rural Employment Guarantee Scheme (NREGA), and decreased corruption (Deininger et al., 2020). Politically and economically, women were empowered by female leaders, which had lasting positive effects. It was observed that political consciousness and economic opportunities worked in tandem. (Sathi, 2023) This scholarly article examines the correlation between inter-caste marriages and caste politics in India, focusing on the increasing prevalence of violence within matrimonial unions. Critiques of arranged marriages are discussed, and an anti-caste, feminist stance is advocated in these debates. This analysis explores the enduring nature of self-respectful marriages, the obstacles posed by caste politics, the contentious 'love jihad' narrative within the framework of extremist nationalist politics, and the function of women in perpetuating caste systems.

This chapter determines criteria and rankings for women's empowerment in various disciplines in India using the AHP and TOPSIS methods (Adhikari et al., 2023). The significance of assisting women in science and technology is underscored, and the report proposes adopting incentive schemes and policies to accomplish this objective.

The study employs the Technique for Order of Preference by Similarity to Ideal Solution (TOPSIS) MCDM and Analytic Hierarchy Process (AHP) to determine the most effective criteria for empowering women across diverse sectors in India.

In examining women's empowerment, the research considers the following six factors: financial assistance, cultural and religious opposition, child marriage, nutrition, shame, and concealment. (Chatterjee et al., 2020) Information and Communication Technologies (ICTs) enable marginalized women to grow by improving their access and skills, encouraging innovation, and supporting entrepreneurial endeavors. Empirical evidence supports the positive effect of ICT adoption on the entrepreneurial orientation of female micro-entrepreneurs, while mobile phones facilitate networking and consumer outreach expansion. (Quisumbing et al., 2023) This article examines the progression of metrics used to assess women's empowerment, focusing on the Women's Empowerment in Agriculture Index (WEAI). The report examines significant agricultural initiatives and evaluates the technical and social dimensions of livestock interventions. The research highlights the significance of confronting gender norms and particular institutional environments to empower women and enhance household food security. (Nordbø, 2022) examines female entrepreneurs engaged in rural tourism in Norway and Chile. It emphasizes the limitations imposed by their chosen path and underscores the importance of considering both local and global factors to empower these women. This highlights intrinsic limitations such as diminished self-assurance and perceived unwelcoming surroundings prevalent among these entrepreneurs. It is of the utmost importance to differentiate between employment and labor force participation in labor markets saturated in Asian societies such as Sri Lanka, where the employment rate of highly educated women is lower despite their higher participation rates (Malhotra & Degraff, 1997). Culture, familial expectations, and social class influence labor market behavior, wherein a curvilinear correlation is observed between social class and employment. The labor force participation and engagement of presently employed women frequently intersect due to the impact of historical, cultural, and developmental influences. Enhancing women's decision-making authority, digital divide, advancing strategic gender interests, and tackling regional structural challenges are critical for success.

3. RESEARCH GAPS AND OBJECTIVES

3.1 Research Gaps

An extensive literature review provides valuable insights into women's empowerment, gender disparities, and the impact of various programs. It also reveals several gaps that warrant further investigation.

1. Participation of women in politics can result in more inclusive and equitable policies (Reshi et al., 2022); it is, therefore, essential to study and understand whether women are merely used as a rubber stamp as Gram Sarpanch with a considerable influence of husband to reveal the lag of the harmonious synchronization between position, power, and authority.

2. Education and employment are intricately linked, and women who are better educated are more engaged in family decision-making (A.K Sinha, 2008). In the context of educated and self-employed women of Bihar, the level of influence over decisions like family planning and abortion needs to be explored, along with the extent of nutritional and educational support provided to low-income family groups.

3. The multitude of issues impacting equal remuneration/wages to women workers in the primary sector, particularly in rural Bihar, is a matter of question, as Naila Kabeer highlighted in her article, necessitates women's empowerment through financial equality.

4. The reviewed studies mainly focus on women's empowerment from a top-down perspective. Future research may explore the roles men, societal norms, and superstition play in facilitating or obstructing women's growth and decision-making.

5. While the literature covers structural and policy dimensions, there is a gap in exploring the psychological aspects of women due to corruption and administrative negligence, which creates a long-term mental impact on women.

6. The biases were discussed, but the contextual analysis and polito-historical reasons, like the accentuation of caste violence in several decades of cases of outward migration of male members from Bihar, creating a profound impact on the psychology of women, is still an area of research.

7. Digitization impact study on rural women of Bihar and the importance of digital hygiene as another technological literacy paradigm must be explored along with women's education.

3.2 Research Objectives

1. To identify the challenges and obstacles recipients face when seeking to benefit from the program and investigate the direct and indirect advantages program participants receive in light of Saat Nischay Yojna Part 2.

2. To gather ideas and recommendations from beneficiaries for enhancing the program.

4. METHODOLOGY

To accomplish the stated objective in Chapter 3, the experimental work in this dissertation followed a well-defined methodology. The study area of the project lies in close proximity to Bihar's rural population. The formulation of primary data mainly covers the interviews of the women in the villages under the study area. A purposive sampling technique is adopted for this purpose, where the sample size consists of 15 respondents. All the female participants were either current or past beneficiaries of Saat Nischay Yojna or residents of areas where the program had been implemented. Under this method, samples are initially selected from the populations of the three villages: Gaya, Nawada, and Begusarai districts. Also, data is collected from the experiences and anecdotes of women from across regions of Bihar assembled for training courses on entrepreneurship under Bihar Government CM Udyami Yojna, Bihar Government Archives, and Anganwaadi workers. Semi-structured qualitative interviews were conducted to get in-depth data. Field notes were also taken during data collection. The interviews were transcribed and coded using thematic analysis.

Ethical Considerations

1) Informed consent was obtained from all participants, where we clearly explained the purpose of the study, their rights, and the voluntary nature of participation.
2) Safeguarding the privacy and confidentiality of participants was done by using pseudonyms to anonymize their identities in all research materials.
3) Secure storage and handling of all collected data to prevent unauthorized access was ensured.
4) The option to receive a summary of the research findings was also offered to the interested Participants.

Limitations of the Study

1) The purposive sampling technique may create selection bias.
2) Participants' desire to share their experiences may be influenced by their satisfaction with the Saat Nischay Yojna program.
3) Due to the particular demographics and characteristics of the selected participants, the study's generalizability to the total population of Bihar inhabitants may be constrained.

5. RESULTS AND DISCUSSIONS

During interaction with rural women, one thing emerged in common: a girl child is 'born,' not desired. Despite the vast top-bottom approach of the government, the society of Bihar, due to extreme opportunity deficit, low per capita income, and rampant superstition, the girl child is not considered a symbol of the propagation of generation lineage, the societal norms and beliefs jeopardizes the physical and mental growth of women and girls of the family as all nutritional benefit and proper diet are usually directed to male members, One woman shared her anecdote as:

I remember we had five sisters and one younger brother; my mother always told front of us that the Monu is born after so many prayers and blessings; as my father was a manual rickshaw puller, he usually brought milk and fruits for Monu only, we sisters have to survive with a staple diet of rice and vegetables, sometimes only with rice, salt and boiled rice water.

This nutritional discrimination and opportunity gap in child-rearing practices affects girls' growth and proper development from an early age. So, community sensitization must go hand in hand with development initiatives.

Instances of abandonment by family and relatives of physically disabled, divyang girls, and old age women emerged during the survey; in many cases, girls who are married at a young age have a wide age gap with their husbands; their husbands leave them after delivery of daughter in the hope of getting son, this is also fueled by the rampant outward migration of male members of Bihar in search of opportunities which is causing cleavage in family structures and husband-wife relationships. Unreported cases of Bigamy are also becoming a significant issue.

While interacting, a young girl of 23 years talked about her close childhood friend Rupali, who was abandoned by her husband two years ago; after the girl's delivery, Rupali is not educated and is now in a complete dilemma about her future.

In some cases, sexual exploitation of poor women is also observed; old widows are unaware of pension schemes and are subjected to domestic violence. Most adolescent girls are unaware of 'touches,' i.e., a good or a bad touch. Cases are unreported due to the involvement of families as perpetrators of sexual exploitation and police reluctance to register patients.

Women of Nawada in her early 50s recalled that her uncle mistreated her while she was washing utensils almost 30 years back; while discussing the incident, a combined feeling of fear, anguish, and pain was reflected in her eyes.

A young girl in her early 20s told her story of being harassed by two boys during a festive meal in her village; she said that she had faced vulgar Bhojpuri songs while traveling on public transport made her uncomfortable.

There is an increasing need to create awareness about good and bad touch among the rural population through the active involvement of NGOs and philanthropist organizations. Mahila Helpline Center may be strengthened in numbers with trained Staff to have a Bihar-wide presence and to protect the name and identity of whistle-blower women. Also, the entertainment industry of Bihar is in a complete mess with no proper govt regulations on the quality of songs and content. Moreover, many women have complained about the orchestra culture and "Launda Naach" in Bihari marriage celebrations. This creates a culture of vilification of women. While looking more into this area, it was observed that this culture was also propagated.

In almost all regions, illegal pre-natal sex determination is a significant problem; a young married girl said that a politically powerful lady named Maharani (Fictitious name) is involved in all the unreported abortions of a female fetus.

In almost all regions, illegal pre-natal sex determination is a significant problem; a young married girl said that there is a politically powerful lady named Maharani (Fictitious name) involved in all the unreported abortions of a female fetus. A whole nexus of strong-arm politicians and local officials are involved in this racket, and despite numerous complaints, nothing has turned up. A woman told our female interviewer in immense anger:

I remember last month during an abortion at the untrained local doctor, and huge bleeding started due to which women died ...Didi, prior to that, the lady had done sex determination of the fetus, as she already had three daughters, Her Husband forced her to abort...there exists a huge moral crisis created by these illegal abortion centers...Devi Maa will punish these ethically bankrupt people.

There exists a vast menace of unqualified quacks in villages and untrained local women serving as gynos, leading to a vast number of deaths/medical issues/ paralysis among women in Bihar during childbirth. Thus, proper training centers may be opened at the panchayat level with coordination from local NGOs and Philanthropist organizations.

While conducting surveys, most of the adolescent girls have highlighted that Bicycle Yojna needs to be revamped as only bicycles are not sufficient to provide a quality education because teachers are in a massive overload of work due to involvement in non-academic duties like election work, caste-census, etc. Also, there is no proper street lighting, which causes discomfort to the girls when they return from the evening coaching. There is also the unavailability of female toilets in schools and colleges. Ramdulari, a woman in her early 40s, said that she experienced severe discrimination while working in a brick kiln at a construction site. She was also given lower pay. The female had to use the male toilets in poor condition.

One lady, who was married to a primary school principal, when asked whether she handled her bank account and if she used an ATM card, said, "I will have to ask my husband if I have any ATM card." She knew a cheque-book but had never visited a bank alone to withdraw money. Some educated girls also said that although multiple Digital Seva Kendra has been opened in their villages, yet their impact is negligible because of poor infrastructure, unskilled staffs and lack of digital awareness among the masses, There is also considerable bottlenecks and implementational challenges in various government initiatives regarding data protection and cyber hygiene.

While doing the literature review and analyzing the interviews, we found that despite these issues, there is some progress due to the combined efforts of both state and Central Governments, aligning with Sustainable Development Goals(SDGs) set by the United Nations Development Programme(UNDP) in 2015 as part of the 2030 Agenda for Sustainable Development which set out a 15-year plan to achieve the Goals. A few of those schemes include:

a)   Swadhar Greh: Aligns with SDG 5 (Gender Equality) and SDG 10 (Reduced Inequality). Provides legal aid and guidance to women, addressing gender-based issues, and caters to the primary needs of vulnerable women, contributing to reducing inequality.

b)   Beti Bachao Beti Padhao Scheme: It is contributing on lines par with SDG 4 (Quality Education) and SDG 5 (Gender Equality). Ensures survival and protection of the girl child and promotes quality education for girls, contributing to gender equality and education goals.

c)   Ujjawala Yojana: The "Ujjwala Yojana" has provided free LPG connections to millions of women in Bihar, replacing traditional cooking fuels with clean energy. This reduces indoor air pollution, improves health outcomes, and empowers women by freeing them from the burden of collecting firewood and helping to achieve SDG 7(Ensuring Clean Energy).

d)   Har Ghar Nal Se Jal and Swachh Bharat Abhiyan: Improved access to safe drinking water and sanitation through initiatives like "Har Ghar Nal Se Jal" and "Swachh Bharat Abhiyan" directly impacts women's health, hygiene, and time management, freeing them to pursue other opportunities and is in line with SDG 9(Building Inclusive Infrastructure).

e)   Women Helpline Scheme: Alignment with SDG 5 (Gender Equality) and SDG 16 (Peace, Justice, and Strong Institutions). Addressing violence against women promotes gender equality and contributes to building a peaceful and just society by providing necessary intervention and spreading awareness about support services.

f)   Nari Shakti Puraskar: Alignment with SDG 5 (Gender Equality) and SDG 10 (Reduced Inequality). Strengthens the place of women in society, recognizes and supports institutions working toward women's empowerment, and contributes to reducing gender-based inequality.

g) Mahila E-Haat: Alignment with SDG 5 (Gender Equality) and SDG 8 (Decent Work and Economic Growth). Provides online entrepreneurship opportunities for women, promoting economic empowerment and gender equality.

Figure 1.

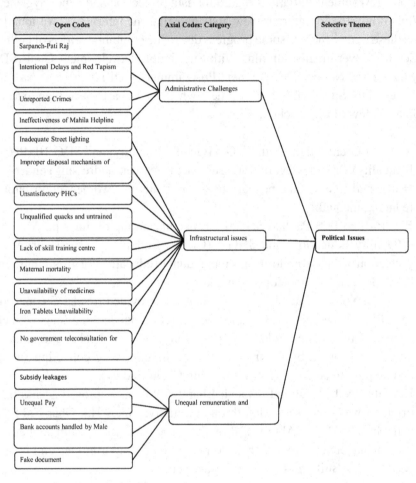

Figure 2.

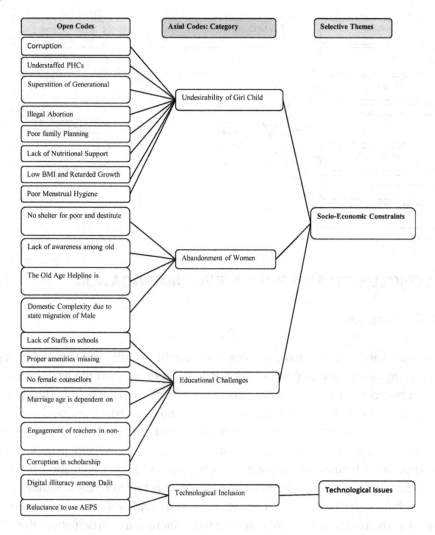

Figure 3.

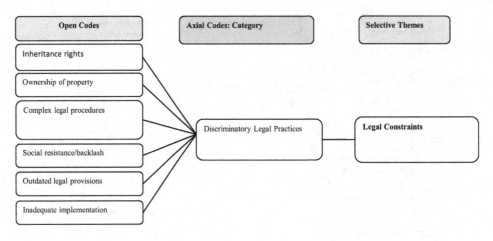

6. CONCLUSION AND POLICY RECOMMENDATION

6.1 Conclusion

It emerged that the percolation of women-centric policy is still a significant challenge, considering the ground realities of rural Bihar. There are multiple hazy zones and grey areas in domains of legal enforcement framework, societal beliefs, digitization, techno-financial inclusion, patriarchal customs, and caste-based political fault lines that are contributing to paralyzing women's empowerment in a true sense. However, the enthusiasm towards self-reliance, awareness regarding government policies, and risk appetite of women towards entrepreneurship and higher education showed a significant improvement in the past two decades; it is fueled by digitization, spread of rural banks, crime control, reservation of seats and skill training centers has yielded a positive atmosphere of empowerment. Increasing participation of women in various sectors has created a significantly constructive impact on macroeconomic parameters and growth credentials of the Bihar Government.

6.2 Policy Recommendation

After reviewing the current policy, it is recommended to implement several fundamental changes:

- Promote sustainable and varied agriculture through Nutrition-Sensitive Agriculture Programs: Training women farmers, promoting nutrient-rich crop farming, and increasing access to agricultural inputs and technologies.

These measures will make nutritious food for women more affordable and self-sustainable.

- Help abandoned women become independent by providing microloans, grants, and subsidies to increase their income and enroll them in government programs. Supporting abandoned women with shelters, helplines, and psychological therapy.
- Some funds allocated to MPLADS (Member of Parliament Local Area Development Scheme) can be given to NGOs to create effective support networks for executing skills and livelihood programs. Culturally sensitive, accessible services should offer emotional, financial, and legal support.
- Establish a robust grievance redressal process to combat unfair remuneration. To resolve complaints quickly, setting up helplines, complaint centers, and regular monitoring is crucial to reporting wage inequality.
- Local, regional, and state women's networks and support organizations should be encouraged. Women leaders can find mentorship, networking, and a safe area to share experiences and seek advice on these platforms.

ACKNOWLEDGMENT

We would like to extend our gratitude to the efforts of Miss. Kajal Singh (PhD Scholar IIM Bodh Gaya), Shri. Kundan Kumar (Gaya, Bihar) and Shri. Satyajeet Kumar (Nawada, Bihar) for their valuable inputs and selfless support in various stages of data collection among rural masses.

REFERENCES

Adhikari, D., Gazi, K. H., Giri, B. C., Azizzadeh, F., & Mondal, S. P. (2023). Empowerment of women in India as different perspectives based on the AHP-TOPSIS-inspired multi-criterion decision-making method. *Results in Control and Optimization*, *12*, 100271. doi:10.1016/j.rico.2023.100271

Batliwala, S. (2010). Taking the Power Out of Empowerment: An Experiential Account. *Development in Practice*, *20*(2), 229–241.

Bell, E. L. (1990). The bicultural life experience of career-oriented black women. *Journal of Organizational Behavior*, *11*(6), 459–477. doi:10.1002/job.4030110607

Chatterjee, S., Gupta, S. D., & Upadhyay, P. (2020). Technology adoption and entrepreneurial orientation for rural women: Evidence from India. *Technological Forecasting and Social Change, 160*, 120236. doi:10.1016/j.techfore.2020.120236

Deininger, K., Nagarajan, H. K., & Singh, S. K. (2020). Women's political leadership and economic empowerment: Evidence from public works in India. *Journal of Comparative Economics, 48*(2), 277–291. doi:10.1016/j.jce.2019.12.003

Duflo, E. (2012). Women's empowerment and economic development. *Journal of Economic Literature, 50*(4), 1051–1079. doi:10.1257/jel.50.4.1051

Grootaert, C., & Kanbur, R. (1995). Empowerment and Poverty Alleviation: A Comparative Analysis of Women's and Men's Participation in Squatter Settlements in Jordan. *World Development, 23*(4), 585–598.

Kabeer, N. (1999). Resources, Agency, Achievements: Reflections on the Measurement of Women's Empowerment. *Development and Change, 30*(3), 435–464. doi:10.1111/1467-7660.00125

Klasen, S. (2019). Gender-Related Indicators of Well-Being. In D. Clark, M. Qizilbash, & A. Tomlinson (Eds.), *The Oxford Handbook of Well-Being and Public Policy* (pp. 287–304). Oxford University Press.

Malhotra, A., & DeGraff, D. S. (1997). Entry versus success in the labor force: Young women's employment in Sri Lanka. *World Development, 25*(3), 379–394. doi:10.1016/S0305-750X(96)00114-3

Mosedale, S., Heissler, K., & Groppo, V. (2012). *Getting the Full Picture: Gender Responsive Budget Analysis in Practice*. UN Women.

Naaz, F., Ahmad, F., & Kumar, S. (2018). Rural Women Empowerment: Issues, Challenges, and Opportunities. *Journal of Rural Studies and Development, 77*(1), 113–120.

Nordbø, I. (2022). Female entrepreneurs and path-dependency in rural tourism. *Journal of Rural Studies, 96*, 198–206. doi:10.1016/j.jrurstud.2022.09.032

Pandey, P., Choubey, A. K., & Rai, G. (2021). The involvement of women as the domestic decision maker: A study of Patna Metropolitan City, Bihar, India. *Sociedade & Natureza, 33*, e62053. doi:10.14393/SN-v33-2021-62053

Parpart, J. L., Connelly, P., & Barriteau, E. (Eds.). (2000). *Theoretical perspectives on gender and development*. IDRC.

Patel, N., Burt, J., & Gonzalez, F. (2019). The Role of Development Programs in Women's Empowerment: A Review of Evidence from South Asia. *Journal of South Asian Development*, *14*(3), 350–376.

Quisumbing, A., Cole, S., Elias, M., Faas, S., Galiè, A., Malapit, H., Meinzen-Dick, R., Myers, E., Seymour, G., & Twyman, J. (2023). Measuring women's empowerment in agriculture: Innovations and evidence. *Global Food Security*, *38*, 100707. doi:10.1016/j.gfs.2023.100707 PMID:37752898

Reshi, I. A., & Sudha, T. (2022). Women Empowerment: A Literature Review. *International Journal of Economic, Business, Accounting Agriculture Management and Sharia Administration*, 2(6), 1353–1359.

Sathi, S. (2023, September). Marriage murders and anti-caste feminist politics in India. In *Women's Studies International Forum* (Vol. 100, p. 102816). Pergamon. 10.1016/j.wsif.2023.102816

Sen, A. (1999). *Development as Freedom*. Anchor Books.

Sinha, A. K. (Ed.). (2008). *New Dimensions of Women Empowerment*. Deep and Deep Publications.

Sinha, S. (2021). Women's Empowerment, Gender Roles and Socioeconomic Development Linkage: Evidences from Indian States. *Journal of Public Affairs*, *42*(1), e2396.

Tandon, T. (2016). Women empowerment: Perspectives and views. *International Journal of Indian Psychology*, *3*(3), 6–12.

Tanzile, R., Domapielle, M. K., & Fielmua, N. (2023). Empowering women for sustainable development through semi-mechanized sheabutter processing in rural North-Western Ghana. *Scientific African*, *21*, e01790. doi:10.1016/j.sciaf.2023. e01790

United Nations. (2020). The Beijing Platform for Action. Retrieved from https://www. unwomen.org/en/how-we-work/un-system-coordination/compilation-of-resolutions-and-agreed-conclusions/2000/beijing-platform-for-action

United Nations Development Programme. (2015). Sustainable Development Goals. Retrieved from https://www.undp.org/content/undp/en/home/sustainable-development-goals.html

Women, U. N. (2023). The paths to equal: Twin indices on women's empowerment and gender equality. Author.

Chapter 13
Wellness at the Heart of Healthcare:
Fostering Digital Consciousness in Hospitals

Jaspreet Kaur
Chandigarh University, India

ABSTRACT

This chapter explores the swift incorporation of digital technology in healthcare and delves into the crucial need to cultivate digital consciousness inside hospitals. The significance of prioritising wellbeing within healthcare practices is underscored, with a focus on promoting mindfulness, human-centred care, and thorough training programmes for healthcare personnel. The study examines various strategies to enhancing wellness, encompassing patient-centric digital interventions, efficient communication methods, and comprehensive wellness programmes. Hospitals may effectively leverage the revolutionary capabilities of technology and uphold patient well-being as a paramount concern in the digital era of healthcare by placing emphasis on digital consciousness and wellness.

INTRODUCTION

The digital transformation in healthcare signifies a fundamental change that has completely transformed the industry, providing exceptional prospects for increasing patient care, optimizing procedures, and improving results. This section offers a comprehensive examination of the digital revolution in the healthcare sector, delving

DOI: 10.4018/979-8-3693-2015-0.ch013

into the diverse range of technologies and advancements that have fundamentally transformed the field of contemporary medicine. Furthermore, it underscores the crucial significance of preserving well-being in the middle of this process of digitization, emphasizing the necessity to harmonize technical progress with patient-centred care and mindfulness.

An Assessment of the Digital Revolution in the Healthcare Industry

The digital revolution in the healthcare sector has been propelled by a confluence of causes, encompassing technological advancements, shifts in consumer patterns, and developing regulatory frameworks. The primary objective of this transformation is to utilize digital tools and technologies in order to tackle persistent issues within the healthcare system, including inefficiencies, fragmentation, and disparities in healthcare access. The broad deployment of electronic health records (EHRs) is considered a fundamental component of the digital transformation. Electronic health record (EHR) systems have superseded conventional paper-based record-keeping techniques, enabling healthcare professionals to electronically store, manage, and exchange patient information. The aforementioned transition has led to greater accessibility to patient data, improved inter-professional collaboration within the healthcare sector, and optimized clinical workflows (Aminabee, S. (2024).

Telemedicine is a notable progress facilitated by digital technology. The utilization of telecommunications and digital platforms in telemedicine allows healthcare providers to give care at a distance, enabling virtual consultations, remote patient monitoring, and remote diagnosis and treatment. In the context of the COVID-19 pandemic, telemedicine has emerged as a crucial instrument for maintaining the uninterrupted provision of healthcare services while mitigating the potential for viral transmission. The digital healthcare sector has witnessed the widespread use of wearable devices and mobile health apps. These technologies enable individuals to actively monitor their health and well-being in real-time, track their fitness objectives, and enhance their ability to properly manage chronic diseases. Wearable devices, ranging from fitness trackers to smartwatches with the ability to detect irregular heart rhythms, are revolutionizing the manner in which individuals interact with their health and overall well-being (Anthony, 2021; Singhal et al., 2022)

The field of healthcare is experiencing significant advancements due to the emergence of artificial intelligence (AI) and machine learning. These technologies provide robust capabilities for data analysis, diagnostics, and personalized therapy. Artificial intelligence (AI) algorithms possess the capability to analyse extensive quantities of medical data, enabling them to detect trends, forecast outcomes, and aid healthcare personnel in making well-informed decisions. AI is transforming different aspects of healthcare delivery, ranging from image identification in radiology to natural language processing in clinical documentation (Kaur, 2023).

The Significance of Preserving Well-Being in the Context of Digitization

The digital transformation has significant potential in enhancing healthcare delivery and patient outcomes; nevertheless, it also poses many problems and hazards that necessitate attention and resolution. One of the primary considerations revolves around the possibility of technology diluting the patient experience and eroding the interpersonal bond between healthcare professionals and patients. With the growing digitization of healthcare, there is a potential for patients to experience feelings of marginalization or detachment from their healthcare professionals. Moreover, the widespread adoption of digital technology in the healthcare sector gives rise to significant concerns regarding the protection of data privacy, security, and ethical considerations. The safeguarding of sensitive patient health information against unauthorized access, breaches, and misuse is a crucial obligation that arises with the digitization of such data. Healthcare organizations are required to establish strong security protocols and comply with stringent regulatory standards in order to safeguard patient confidentiality and maintain confidence. The digital gap is an additional obstacle linked to the process of digitization, as it amplifies inequalities in the availability of healthcare services and technology. Although digital solutions possess the capacity to enhance healthcare accessibility and results, it is important to acknowledge that not all folks possess equitable access to technology or the requisite digital literacy skills to proficiently use digital platforms. To effectively tackle these gaps, it is imperative to adopt proactive measures that guarantee fair and equal access to digital healthcare solutions, as well as provide support for marginalized communities (Adhyaru & Kemp, 2022).

Given the aforementioned problems, it is imperative to acknowledge the significance of upholding well-being in the middle of the digital revolution in the healthcare sector. Wellness involves not only the state of being physically healthy, but also the conditions of being mentally, emotionally, and socially well. Healthcare organizations must prioritize holistic wellness approaches that foster the human spirit and encourage compassionate treatment while they use digital technologies. In nutshell, the digitization of healthcare signifies a significant shift in paradigm that has the capacity to fundamentally transform the manner in which healthcare is provided and encountered. Digital technologies are significantly transforming various components of the healthcare system, encompassing electronic health records, telemedicine, wearable devices, and artificial intelligence. Nevertheless, in the middle of the swift advancement of digitization, it is imperative to be cognizant of the significance of upholding one's well-being (Anthony, 2021; Singhal et al., 2022)

The concept of wellness involves all dimensions of health, including physical, mental, emotional, and social components. It is imperative that wellness remains a central focus in healthcare practices, particularly in the era of digital advancements. Healthcare organizations may ensure that technology enhances rather than detracts from the patient experience by prioritizing holistic wellness approaches, supporting human-centrist care, and tackling the problems associated with digitization. The ultimate objective is to leverage the potential of digital technology in order to enhance patient outcomes, while also upholding the core principles of compassion, empathy, and human connection within the realm of healthcare provision (Anthony Jnr, 2021).

THE DIGITAL TRANSFORMATION OF HEALTHCARE

The digitization of healthcare signifies a significant paradigm shift in the manner in which medical services are obtained, provided, and administered. The revolution is propelled by the incorporation of sophisticated digital technology into many aspects of healthcare provision, offering the potential to enhance effectiveness, improve patient results, and revolutionize the patient journey. Central to this paradigm shift is the process of digitizing health records, wherein Electronic Health Records (EHRs) supplant conventional paper-based systems, facilitating the effortless storage, retrieval, and dissemination of patient data across various healthcare environments. Furthermore, telemedicine has become a crucial element, facilitating remote consultations and monitoring via telecommunications technology, thereby increasing the availability of healthcare and diminishing geographical obstacles (Anthony, 2021; Singhal et al., 2022). Smartwatches and fitness trackers, which are examples of wearable technology, enable individuals to actively monitor their health in real-time, so facilitating proactive self-management and preventive care. Moreover, the utilization of Artificial Intelligence (AI) algorithms is transforming diagnostic procedures, facilitating expedited and more precise examinations of medical images and patient information, finally resulting in the development of individualized treatment strategies and enhanced clinical results (Belliger & Krieger, 2018). Collectively, these digital technologies are transforming the healthcare domain, presenting unparalleled prospects for enhanced effectiveness, exclusivity, and patient-centrist healthcare in the era of digitization as presented in figure 1 below:

Figure 1. Digital transformation process in healthcare

The Benefits of Digitization in the Delivery of Healthcare\

The process of digitizing healthcare delivery has yielded a multitude of benefits, fundamentally transforming the manner in which healthcare services are obtained, administered, and supervised. This section aims to analyse the primary advantages of digitization in the healthcare sector and evaluate the impact of digital technology on the provision of patient care.

1. **Improved productivity and optimized procedures:** The greater efficiency and streamlined processes facilitated by digitization in healthcare are considered to be one of its key advantages. Electronic Health Records (EHRs) have emerged as a viable alternative to conventional paper-based record-keeping systems, facilitating expedient and safe retrieval of patient information by healthcare practitioners. Electronic Health Records (EHRs) let healthcare practitioners to effectively record patient interactions, monitor medical backgrounds, and synchronize healthcare services among various providers and environments. In addition, the use of digitized administrative procedures, such as the utilization of online appointment scheduling, electronic prescribing, and automated billing systems, has effectively optimized administrative workflows and alleviated the administrative workload for healthcare institutions. Through the process of digitization, healthcare providers have the ability to enhance resource allocation, reduce errors, and enhance overall operational efficiency (Kaur, 2023).

2. **Enhancing Communication and Facilitating Care Coordination:** The process of digitization has significantly enhanced communication and care coordination within the healthcare sector, resulting in increased continuity of care and enhanced patient outcomes. Electronic health record (EHR) systems facilitate the efficient exchange of patient information throughout various healthcare environments, thereby guaranteeing that all healthcare professionals have timely access to current clinical data. This promotes collective effort and empowers healthcare practitioners to make well-informed judgments regarding patient care. In addition, the utilization of digital communication technologies, such as encrypted messaging platforms and teleconferencing software, has effectively enabled instantaneous communication among healthcare professionals, hence enabling prompt consultation and collaboration, particularly in intricate scenarios or critical situations. Consequently, patients are provided with enhanced coordination and integration of care, wherein healthcare providers collaborate to thoroughly meet their requirements (Anthony, 2021; Singhal et al., 2022)

3. **Increased involvement and empowerment of patients:** The process of digitization has provided patients with the ability to assume a more proactive

part in the management of their health and well-being. Patients have the ability to view their medical records, make appointments, obtain prescription refills, and connect with their healthcare providers online through patient portals that are integrated with electronic health record (EHR) systems. The enhanced availability of health information and communication channels facilitates heightened patient involvement and promotes proactive self-care for health issues (Binci et al., 2022).

Furthermore, the use of digital health technologies, such as mobile health applications and wearable gadgets, empowers individuals to effectively check their vital signs, monitor their fitness objectives, and effectively treat chronic ailments within the confines of their own residences. These digital solutions enable users to make well-informed decisions about their health and adopt better lifestyles by offering patients immediate feedback and personalized health information.

4. **The improvement of diagnostic accuracy and the implementation of personalized medicine:** The utilization of digital technologies, including Artificial Intelligence (AI) and machine learning algorithms, is revolutionizing diagnostic procedures and facilitating the implementation of more individualized treatment strategies for patients. AI-driven diagnostic technologies have the capability to rapidly and precisely analyse medical pictures, including X-rays, MRIs, and CT scans. This greatly assists healthcare providers in promptly identifying and diagnosing disorders. Furthermore, AI algorithms have the capability to examine extensive collections of patient health records and genetic data in order to detect patterns, forecast the advancement of diseases, and suggest customized treatment strategies that are specifically designed for each patient's unique traits. The implementation of personalized medicine has the capacity to enhance treatment results, minimize negative occurrences, and optimize the allocation of resources by precisely targeting therapies (Brall et al., 2019).

Examples of Digital Technologies Transforming Healthcare

1. **EHRs:** Electronic health records (EHRs) are digitized renditions of patients' physical files, encompassing extensive details regarding their medical background, diagnosis, prescribed drugs, treatment strategies, immunization data, and laboratory test outcomes. Electronic health record (EHR) systems facilitate safe access and sharing of patient information across healthcare

practitioners, thereby enhancing the coordination and efficiency of care delivery (Casillo et al., 2024).

2. **Telemedicine:** The practice of telemedicine encompasses the utilization of telecommunications technology to provide healthcare services from a distance, enabling patients to engage in consultations with healthcare professionals through video conferencing, telephone, or secure messaging systems. The utilization of telemedicine has broadened the availability of healthcare services, especially in remote and underprivileged regions, and has gained significant significance in times of public health emergencies, such as the COVID-19 pandemic (Anthony, 2021; Singhal et al., 2022)

3. **Wearable Technology:** Smartwatches, fitness trackers, and health monitoring gadgets are examples of wearable devices that gather real-time data pertaining to individuals' physical activity, heart rate, sleep patterns, and various other biometric parameters. These gadgets provide the continuous monitoring of individuals' health and wellness, offering useful insights for the purpose of preventive care and the management of chronic diseases (Kaur, 2024).

4. **AI: Synthetic Intelligence:** Artificial intelligence (AI) comprises a diverse array of technologies, such as machine learning, natural language processing, and computer vision, which empower computers to execute tasks that conventionally necessitate human intelligence. AI is employed in healthcare to boost diagnostic precision, optimize treatment strategies, automate administrative duties, and augment patient involvement. In general, the process of digitizing healthcare delivery has notable benefits, such as increased operational effectiveness, enhanced communication, heightened patient involvement, and the implementation of individualized patient care strategies. Healthcare organizations may enhance the quality, accessibility, and patient-contentedness of care in the digital era by adopting digital technology and harnessing their revolutionary capabilities (Garcia et al., 2024).

CHALLENGES AND PITFALLS

The incorporation of digital technologies has grown progressively widespread in the ever-evolving realm of contemporary healthcare. Digitization encompasses a wide range of advantages, including enhanced efficiency, increased accessibility, and improved patient outcomes, as evidenced by the implementation of electronic health records and telemedicine platforms. Nevertheless, in the midst of this digital transformation, it has become essential to prioritize well being inside healthcare organizations. Although technology undeniably has the potential to improve patient care, it also presents notable difficulties and drawbacks, especially with the psychological and emotional welfare of healthcare practitioners and patients. This section delves into the various aspects of promoting digital awareness in hospitals, analyzing the difficulties and drawbacks linked to the convergence of technology and well-being (Anthony, 2021; Singhal et al., 2022)

Electronic health records (EHRs) are leading the way in the digital transformation of healthcare. They have completely transformed the way data is managed and information is exchanged in clinical settings. Electronic Health Record (EHR) systems enable effortless retrieval of patient data, optimize documentation procedures, and improve the coordination of care. Nevertheless, the persistent requirements imposed by the utilization of Electronic Health Records (EHRs) have elicited apprehensions over the welfare of healthcare providers. The persistent documentation obligations, in conjunction with burdensome user interfaces, contribute to the exhaustion and discontent experienced by healthcare providers. Research has shown the adverse effects of stress caused by electronic health records (EHRs) on the mental well-being of physicians. This emphasizes the importance of implementing ergonomic design and efficient workflows to address these difficulties (Kaur, 2024).

Furthermore, the widespread adoption of digital communication tools and telemedicine platforms has resulted in the erosion of the distinction between professional and personal spheres among healthcare practitioners. Telemedicine presents unparalleled ease and accessibility; but, it also fosters a perpetual state of contentedness, intensifying sensations of occupational stress and exhaustion. The continuous flow of patient messages and notifications has the potential to disturb the equilibrium between work and personal life, resulting in emotional tiredness and compassion fatigue among healthcare professionals. As healthcare organizations increasingly adopt telemedicine as a strategy to enhance the provision of treatment, it becomes crucial to create explicit protocols and limitations to ensure the protection and welfare of healthcare practitioners (Goodman & Schorling, 2012). The digitization of healthcare has significant ramifications for patient well-being, extending beyond the scope of clinical practice. The widespread availability of health monitoring devices and wearable technologies has initiated a period characterized by the ongoing monitoring of health and the practice of self-surveillance. While these technological devices provide individuals with the ability to assume authority over their health and physical fitness, they also give rise to novel concerns and preoccupations associated with health-related information. The psychological impact of continuous monitoring is highlighted by the occurrence of "cyberchondria," which is characterized by an excessive engagement in health-related internet searches and an intense fixation with digital health data. Moreover, the commercialization of well-being through the use of gamified health applications and measured self-activity might promote detrimental habits (Anthony, 2021; Singhal et al., 2022)

Digital interventions have the potential to significantly enhance the availability of treatment and support services within the field of mental health care. Telepsychiatry platforms and mobile mental health applications provide individuals with convenient means to access psychological support and engage in self-management of their mental health disorders. Nevertheless, the process of digitizing mental health care gives rise to apprehensions over the protection of data privacy, the effectiveness of therapeutic interventions, and the potential erosion of conventional therapeutic alliances. The lack of human connection in virtual contacts has the potential to weaken the therapeutic bond between patients and clinicians, which could negatively impact treatment results. Furthermore, the widespread availability of mental health applications that lack scientific rigour and oversight presents the potential for disinformation and inefficient interventions. This emphasizes the necessity for strong regulation and quality assurance procedures.

One notable obstacle in promoting digital awareness within healthcare facilities is to the ethical and moral quandaries inherent in the utilization of artificial intelligence (AI) and machine learning technologies. Artificial intelligence (AI) algorithms possess significant potential in enhancing clinical decision-making, forecasting disease trajectories, and tailoring treatment regimens to individual patients. Nevertheless, the lack of transparency in AI algorithms, along with apprehensions about bias and prejudice, gives rise to ethical considerations pertaining to algorithmic responsibility and openness. The presence of biased algorithms has the potential to sustain discrepancies in the delivery of healthcare, so intensifying preexisting inequities and undermining patient confidence. Moreover, the dependence on automation powered by artificial intelligence gives rise to concerns over the dehumanization of healthcare and the gradual erosion of professional autonomy among healthcare practitioners (Jeffree et al., 2020).

The process of digitizing healthcare raises existential inquiries on the essence of human connection and empathy in the era of technology. The growing reliance on screens and algorithms in healthcare poses a potential threat to the development of interpersonal ties and empathetic involvement between healthcare providers and patients. The practice of medicine, which is based on empathetic listening and sophisticated comprehension, should not be eclipsed by the appeal of technical effectiveness. The process of fostering digital consciousness inside hospitals involves the development of a culture that prioritizes empathy, mindfulness, and humanistic ideals in the face of continuous technology advancements (Kokshagina, 2021).

In nutshell, the cultivation of digital consciousness inside healthcare facilities necessitates a comprehensive comprehension of the complexities and drawbacks associated with the convergence of technology and well-being. Digital technologies have the potential to greatly enhance the delivery of healthcare and improve patient outcomes. However, it is important to acknowledge that these advances also present substantial hazards to the mental, emotional, and ethical aspects of healthcare practice. To effectively tackle these difficulties, it is imperative to adopt a comprehensive approach that places equal importance on the welfare of healthcare professionals and patients, promotes ethical use of technology, and upholds the fundamental humanistic principles that underpin the field of medicine. Healthcare organizations may effectively leverage the revolutionary potential of technology and uphold the core principles of compassion, empathy, and human dignity in patient care by adopting a mindset of mindfulness and intentional towards digital consciousness.

FOSTERING DIGITAL CONSCIOUSNESS

In the dynamic and ever-changing realm of healthcare, the cultivation of digital consciousness has become an essential necessity. This section explores the notion of digital consciousness in healthcare, highlighting the significance of mindfulness and patient-centered care in the era of digital technology. Furthermore, this study examines the significance of training programme in providing healthcare personnel with the requisite knowledge and competencies to effectively traverse the intricate landscape of digitization, all the while placing patient well-being as a top priority.

The Concept of Digital Consciousness in Healthcare Can Be Defined As

Digital consciousness in healthcare refers to the understanding and recognition of the effects, consequences, and moral concerns associated with the utilization of digital technologies in the provision and administration of patient care. It involves acknowledging the possibilities and difficulties brought about by digitization, as well as comprehending the possible effects on patient results, confidentiality, and the whole healthcare encounter. Essentially, digital consciousness entails striking a harmonious equilibrium between technical advancement and humanistic principles, guaranteeing that digital solutions augment rather than diminish the standard of care delivered to patients (Lo Presti et al., 2019).

- **Significance of Attention and Patient-Focused Care:** It is imperative to maintain focus on the core principles of mindfulness and human-centrist care while striving towards digital change. Mindfulness, which refers to the act of being fully aware and focused in the present moment, is essential for healthcare workers to maintain a strong connection with their patients on a personal level, even as they increasingly depend on digital tools and technologies. Healthcare practitioners can enhance the therapeutic connection and promote patient trust and satisfaction by practicing mindfulness, which enables them to foster empathy, compassion, and understanding in their interactions with patients. Furthermore, the concept of human-centrist care underscores the significance of prioritizing the needs, preferences, and values of patients in the provision of healthcare services. Within the realm of digitization, it is imperative to place emphasis on patient engagement, autonomy, and dignity, while also customizing care plans to correspond with the unique aims and preferences of each individual patient. Healthcare organizations may enhance the patient experience and promote overall well-being by taking a human-centrist approach in the design and implementation of digital solutions (Maddula et al., 2022).

- **Healthcare Professional Training Programme:** In light of the profound influence of digital technology on the provision of healthcare, it is crucial to offer healthcare personnel extensive training programme to efficiently traverse the intricacies of digitization. The training programme ought to cover a diverse array of subjects, such as the secure and moral utilization of digital tools, protocols for safeguarding data privacy and security, and approaches for fostering patient-centered care within a digital setting (Mbunge et al., 2021).

Training programme for healthcare workers encompass several essential components:

1. **Technical Proficiency:** Healthcare personnel are required to undergo training in order to acquire technical proficiency in utilizing digital tools and platforms that are pertinent to their specific responsibilities. These tools and platforms include Electronic Health Record (EHR) systems, telemedicine platforms, and mobile health applications. The training programme should encompass fundamental functionalities, optimal methodologies for data entry and retrieval, and strategies for resolving prevalent technical challenges (Anthony, 2021; Singhal et al., 2022)

2. **Ethical and Legal Considerations:** It is imperative for training programme to encompass the ethical and legal ramifications associated with the process of digitization in the healthcare sector. These considerations encompass various aspects such as patient confidentiality, informed consent, and adherence to regulatory obligations, notably the Health Insurance Portability and Accountability Act (HIPAA). It is imperative for healthcare practitioners to possess a comprehensive understanding of their obligations pertaining to the acquisition, utilization, and dissemination of patient data within a digital framework (O'Donovan et al., 2024).

3. **Communication Skills:** The acquisition of effective communication skills is necessary in order to establish and sustain meaningful connections with patients within a digital setting. The significance of clear and sympathetic communication should be prioritized in training programme, with a focus on equipping healthcare professionals with effective tactics for establishing rapport, expressing empathy, and resolving patient concerns in the context of virtual consultations and interactions. In order to address the possible adverse effects of digitization on the well-being of healthcare personnel, it is imperative that they undergo training in mindfulness techniques and self-care activities. Mindfulness training can assist healthcare personnel in effectively handling stress, sustaining concentration, and fostering resilience when confronted with technical obstacles and requirements (Kaur, 2023).

4. **Continuous Learning and Adaptation:** The rapid evolution of digital technology necessitates healthcare professionals to actively participate in ongoing learning and professional development in order to remain up-to-date with emerging best practices and new advancements. Training programme should foster a culture that promotes ongoing learning and adaptability, enabling healthcare workers to embrace innovative approaches while maintaining a commitment to patient-centered care and ethical conduct.

To summarize, promoting digital awareness in healthcare necessitates a holistic strategy that includes mindfulness, patient-centered care, and extensive training initiatives for healthcare practitioners. Healthcare organizations can ensure that digitization improves the quality of care offered to patients by providing healthcare providers with the essential information, skills, and tools to properly traverse the digital terrain. In order to advance patient well-being, uphold trust in the healthcare system, and fully harness the trans-formative capabilities of digital technology in the 21st century, it is imperative to cultivate a sense of digital consciousness as depicted in figure 2 below:

Figure 2. Components of comprehensive training programs for healthcare professionals in the context of digital technologies

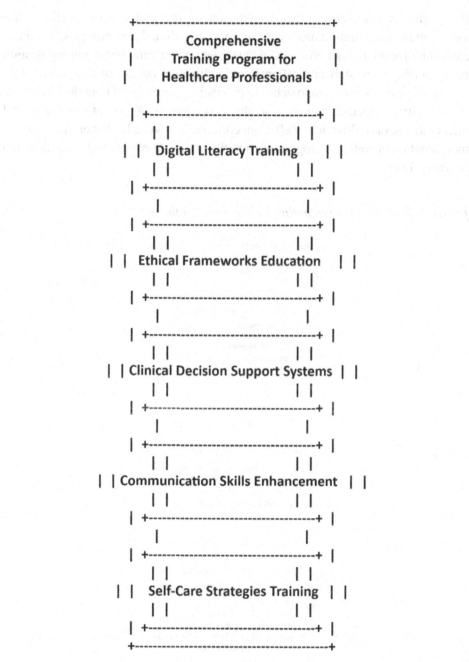

STRATEGIES FOR PROMOTING WELLNESS

In the current dynamic healthcare environment, the promotion of wellness has gained significant importance. By incorporating digital technologies, hospitals can capitalize on distinct prospects to augment patient care, boost communication between healthcare staff and patients, and cultivate a culture of well being. This section examines various approaches to enhancing well being within the healthcare sector, with a specific emphasis on the development of patient-centrist digital interventions, the cultivation of efficient communication and collaboration, and the incorporation of wellness programme into the fabric of hospital culture as depicted in figure 3 below:

Figure 3. Strategies for promoting wellness in healthcare

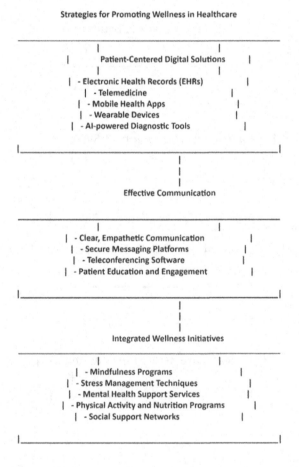

The creation and implementation of patient-centered digital solutions is considered a crucial strategy for improving well being in the healthcare sector. Patient-centered care places a high emphasis on addressing the demands, inclinations, and principles of patients, so enabling them to actively engage in their healthcare trajectory. The utilization of digital technologies is crucial in enabling patient participation, empowerment, and self-management (Singhal et al., 2022).

User-Centered Design: The implementation of a user-centered approach in the design of digital solutions guarantees its intuitiveness, accessibility, and responsiveness to the requirements of patients. The process of design and development necessitates the collection of feedback from various end-users, such as patients, carers, and healthcare professionals. Personalized health technologies involve the use of digital technologies to provide customized health interventions that are specifically designed to meet the unique needs and preferences of individual patients. The aforementioned encompasses mobile health applications, wearable devices, and remote monitoring capabilities that empower individuals to monitor their health indicators, comply with prescribed treatment regimens, and obtain prompt feedback and assistance. Digital platforms have the potential to be effective instruments for patient education, as they offer access to dependable health information, educational materials, and tools for managing self-care. Digital solutions facilitate the active engagement of patients in decision-making and self-management of health issues by equipping them with knowledge and resources (Spanakis et al., 2016).

Telehealth and Remote Consultations: Telehealth platforms facilitate the provision of healthcare services through remote consultations, virtual visits, and telemonitoring, thereby improving accessibility and mitigating obstacles to receiving care. Telehealth plays a crucial role in facilitating seamless access to healthcare experts, so fostering continuity of care, enhancing patient participation, and enabling prompt action (Anthony, 2021; Singhal et al., 2022)

Effective Communication and Collaboration between Healthcare Teams and Patients: Efficient communication and collaboration between healthcare professionals and patients are essential for fostering well-being and providing exceptional care. Effective and compassionate communication promotes confidence, boosts patient contentment, and enhances health results. Digital technologies present potential avenues for enhancing communication and fostering collaboration within healthcare environments. The utilization of secure messaging platforms, such as secure messaging systems and patient portals, facilitates the establishment of secure communication channels between patients and healthcare practitioners. Patients have the ability to inquire, schedule appointments, obtain test results, and simply and confidentially retrieve their health records. Shared decision-making is a process where patients and healthcare practitioners engage in collaborative conversations to determine treatment plans that are in line with the patient's preferences, values, and goals. Informed deliberations are facilitated by digital decision aids and shared decision-making tools, so encouraging patients to actively engage in decision-making processes (Spanakis et al., 2016).

- Digital platforms designed for care coordination play a crucial role in promoting effective communication and collaboration across diverse healthcare teams, encompassing physicians, nurses, therapists, and care coordinators. These tools optimize the process of transitioning care, enhance the coordination of care, and mitigate the likelihood of medical errors. The utilization of digital technologies enables virtual care teams to establish connections between patients and interdisciplinary teams of healthcare specialists, irrespective of geographical limitations. Virtual care teams encompass a diverse range of healthcare professionals, such as physicians, nurses, chemists, social workers, and other specialists, who collaborate to deliver cohesive and all-encompassing care to those with intricate healthcare requirements (O'Donovan et al., 2024).

- The effective promotion of wellness within healthcare organizations necessitates the establishment of a culture that places emphasis on the well-being of employees, the provision of patient-centered care, and the ongoing pursuit of quality improvement. The process of incorporating wellness initiatives into the hospital culture include the establishment of work conditions that foster support, the encouragement of professional growth, and the cultivation of a culture characterized by compassion and resilience (Maddula et al., 2022).

- The dedication of leadership plays a crucial role in facilitating organizational change and cultivating a culture that prioritizes wellness. It is imperative for hospital administrators to exhibit a steadfast dedication to the welfare of their employees, the provision of patient-centered care, and the ongoing enhancement of their operations through their conduct, policies, and allocation of resources (Mbunge et al., 2021).

- Hospitals have the ability to establish wellness programme and provide tools to promote the well-being and resilience of their employees. Potential interventions that could be implemented encompass stress management workshops, mindfulness training, employee assistance programme, and peer support networks. The provision of resources aimed at promoting physical, emotional, and mental well-being serves as evidence of an organization's commitment to fostering employee wellness λ(Maddula et al., 2022).

- The promotion of interdisciplinary collaboration and teamwork has been shown to have positive effects on patient care, communication, and the cultivation of a collaborative and mutually respectful culture. Collaboration among healthcare experts from many fields is facilitated via interdisciplinary rounds, case conferences, and team-based care models, which promote holistic patient care (Mbunge et al., 2021).

- Hospitals ought to adopt a culture of continuous quality improvement in order to identify areas that require enhancement, apply procedures that are supported by empirical evidence, and closely monitor the resulting outcomes. Hospitals can enhance patient safety, optimize resource utilization, and promote organizational excellence through the implementation of quality improvement programme, including performance dashboards, clinical audits, and peer review processes (O'Donovan et al., 2024).

In nutshell, the promotion of wellness in the healthcare sector necessitates a comprehensive strategy that involves patient-centrist digital interventions, efficient communication and collaboration among healthcare professionals and patients, and the incorporation of wellness programme into the fabric of hospital culture. Healthcare organizations may promote well-being, improve patient outcomes, and enhance the overall quality of treatment by utilizing digital technology, cultivating collaborative partnerships, and placing emphasis on employee well-being and patient-centered care.

CONCLUSION

The digitization of healthcare signifies a significant paradigm shift in the manner in which medical services are obtained, provided, and administered. This conversation has delved into the notion of cultivating digital consciousness within the healthcare sector, with a particular focus on the significance of mindfulness, patient-centered care, and comprehensive training initiatives for healthcare practitioners. In conclusion, it is imperative to provide a concise overview of the main arguments and advocate for the prioritization of wellness within the context of the digital era in healthcare.

Summary of Key Points

Digital consciousness in the healthcare sector encompasses a heightened understanding of the consequences, ramifications, and ethical deliberations associated with the utilization of digital technologies in the provision of patient care. It involves acknowledging the possibilities and difficulties brought up by digitization and comprehending the possible effects on patient results, confidentiality, and the whole healthcare encounter.

The ideals of mindfulness and human-centrist care are fundamental in shaping healthcare delivery within the context of the digital era. Healthcare practitioners can cultivate empathy, compassion, and understanding by practicing mindfulness, which allows them to be fully present and aware during their encounters with patients. The concept of human-centrist care prioritizes the prioritization of patients' needs, preferences, and values in healthcare delivery. It ensures that technology solutions improve the patient experience rather than diminish it.

Training programme for healthcare professionals play a crucial role in providing them with the required information, skills, and tools to properly traverse the intricate landscape of digitization. The programme ought to encompass a range of essential components, including technical expertise, ethical and legal considerations, effective communication abilities, mindfulness and self-care strategies, as well as a dedication to ongoing learning and adaptability.

Advocacy for Emphasizing Well-Being in the Era of Digital Healthcare

In anticipation of the future of healthcare, it is crucial that we give utmost importance to well-being in the middle of the digital revolution. The establishment of a culture of digital consciousness and the prioritization of patient well-being necessitate a shared dedication from healthcare organizations, policymakers, technology developers, and healthcare practitioners. Healthcare organizations must prioritize the recognition of the significance of upholding a human-centrist approach to the delivery of care, while simultaneously embracing digital technologies. This entails the development and execution of digital solutions that prioritize the requirements, inclinations, and principles of patients, while guaranteeing that technology augments rather than diminishes the patient encounter. In addition, it is imperative for healthcare organization to allocate resources towards the implementation of comprehensive training programme, with the aim of equipping healthcare personnel with the necessary skills to efficiently traverse the digital terrain. It is recommended that these programme prioritize the significance of mindfulness, empathy, and compassionate care, while equipping healthcare workers with the requisite tools and methods to administer exceptional, patient-centrist care within a digital setting.

Policymakers possess a pivotal responsibility in placing emphasis on wellness within the context of the digital era of healthcare. This include the implementation of laws and rules that safeguard patient confidentiality and data integrity, foster fair and equal availability of digital healthcare services, and encourage the creation and acceptance of digital innovations that improve patient results and welfare. Finally, it is imperative for healthcare practitioners to demonstrate a steadfast dedication to maintaining the principles of patient-centered care and ethical conduct within the context of the digital era. To effectively engage with patients, healthcare professionals must practise mindfulness and self-awareness. They should also promote the use of digital technologies that prioritize patient well-being. Additionally, they should actively pursue ongoing learning and professional development to stay updated on new advancements and emerging best practices.

In conclusion it is imperative to cultivate a sense of digital awareness and place emphasis on well-being within the context of the digital era in healthcare. This is crucial in order to guarantee that technology serves to augment, rather than diminish, the standard of care delivered to patients. To harness the trans-formative potential of digital technologies and create a healthcare system that is more accessible, equitable, and patient-centered for all, we can adopt a human-centrist approach to care delivery, invest in comprehensive training programme, and advocate for policies that promote patient well-being.

REFERENCES

Adhyaru, J. S., & Kemp, C. (2022). Virtual reality as a tool to promote wellbeing in the workplace. *Digital Health*, *8*. doi:10.1177/20552076221084473 PMID:35284084

Aminabee, S. (2024). The Future of Healthcare and Patient-Centric Care: Digital Innovations, Trends, and Predictions. In Emerging Technologies for Health Literacy and Medical Practice (pp. 240-262). IGI Global.

Anthony, B. Jr. (2021). Implications of telehealth and digital care solutions during COVID-19 pandemic: A qualitative literature review. *Informatics for Health & Social Care*, *46*(1), 68–83. doi:10.1080/17538157.2020.1839467 PMID:33251894

Belliger, A., & Krieger, D. J. (2018). The digital transformation of healthcare. Knowledge Management in Digital Change: New Findings and Practical Cases, 311-326.

Binci, D., Palozzi, G., & Scafarto, F. (2022). Toward digital transformation in healthcare: A framework for remote monitoring adoption. *The TQM Journal*, *34*(6), 1772–1799. doi:10.1108/TQM-04-2021-0109

Brall, C., Schröder-Bäck, P., & Maeckelberghe, E. (2019). Ethical aspects of digital health from a justice point of view. *European Journal of Public Health*, *29*(Supplement_3), 18–22. doi:10.1093/eurpub/ckz167 PMID:31738439

Casillo, M., Cecere, L., Colace, F., Lorusso, A., & Santaniello, D. (2024). Integrating the Internet of Things (IoT) in SPA Medicine: Innovations and Challenges in Digital Wellness. *Computers*, *13*(3), 67. doi:10.3390/computers13030067

Garcia, M. B., Garcia, P. S., Maaliw, R. R., Lagrazon, P. G. G., Arif, Y. M., Ofosu-Ampong, K., . . . Vaithilingam, C. A. (2024). Technoethical Considerations for Advancing Health Literacy and Medical Practice: A Posthumanist Framework in the Age of Healthcare 5.0. In Emerging Technologies for Health Literacy and Medical Practice (pp. 1-19). IGI Global.

Goodman, M. J., & Schorling, J. B. (2012). A mindfulness course decreases burnout and improves well-being among healthcare providers. *International Journal of Psychiatry in Medicine*, *43*(2), 119–128. doi:10.2190/PM.43.2.b PMID:22849035

Jeffree, M. S., Ahmedy, F., Avoi, R., Ibrahim, M. Y., Rahim, S. S. S. A., Hayati, F., ... Tuah, N. M. (2020). Integrating digital health for healthcare transformation conceptual model of smart healthcare for northern borneo. *International Journal of Advanced Trends in Computer Science and Engineering*, *9*(1), 110–115. doi:10.30534/ijatcse/2020/17912020

Kaur, J. (2023). Robotic Process Automation in Healthcare Sector. In *E3S Web of Conferences* (Vol. 391, p. 01008). EDP Sciences.

Kaur, J. (2023, May). How is Robotic Process Automation Revolutionising the Way Healthcare Sector Works? In International Conference on Information, Communication and Computing Technology (pp. 1037-1055). Singapore: Springer Nature Singapore. 10.1007/978-981-99-5166-6_70

Kaur, J. (2024). Towards a Sustainable Triad: Uniting Energy Management Systems, Smart Cities, and Green Healthcare for a Greener Future. In Emerging Materials, Technologies, and Solutions for Energy Harvesting (pp. 258-285). IGI Global.

Kokshagina, O. (2021). Managing shifts to value-based healthcare and value digitalization as a multi-level dynamic capability development process. *Technological Forecasting and Social Change*, *172*, 121072. doi:10.1016/j.techfore.2021.121072

Lo Presti, L., Testa, M., Marino, V., & Singer, P. (2019). Engagement in healthcare systems: Adopting digital tools for a sustainable approach. *Sustainability (Basel)*, *11*(1), 220. doi:10.3390/su11010220

Maddula, R., MacLeod, J., Painter, S., McLeish, T., Steward, A., Rossman, A., Hamid, A., Ashwath, M., Martinez, H. R., Guha, A., Patel, B., Addison, D., Blaes, A., Choudhuri, I., & Brown, S. A. (2022). Connected Health Innovation Research Program (CHIRP): A bridge for digital health and wellness in cardiology and oncology. *American Heart Journal Plus : Cardiology Research and Practice*, *20*, 100192. doi:10.1016/j.ahjo.2022.100192 PMID:37800118

Mbunge, E., Muchemwa, B., & Batani, J. (2021). Sensors and healthcare 5.0: Transformative shift in virtual care through emerging digital health technologies. *Global Health Journal (Amsterdam, Netherlands)*, *5*(4), 169–177. doi:10.1016/j. glohj.2021.11.008

O'Donovan, R., Loughnane, C., Donnelly, J., Kelly, R., Kemp, D., McCarthy, L., Offiah, G., Sweeney, A., Duggan, A. P., & Dunne, P. J. (2024). Healthcare workers' experience of a coach-led digital platform for better well-being. *Coaching (Abingdon, UK)*, 1–19. doi:10.1080/17521882.2024.2304793

Singhal, S., Sinha, A., & Singh, B. (2022). Context awareness for healthcare service delivery with intelligent sensors. Frontiers of Data and Knowledge Management for Convergence of ICT, Healthcare, and Telecommunication Services, 61-83.

Spanakis, E. G., Santana, S., Tsiknakis, M., Marias, K., Sakkalis, V., Teixeira, A., Janssen, J. H., de Jong, H., & Tziraki, C. (2016). Technology-based innovations to foster personalized healthy lifestyles and well-being: A targeted review. *Journal of Medical Internet Research*, *18*(6), e128. doi:10.2196/jmir.4863 PMID:27342137

Chapter 14
The Impact of Corporate Governance on Managerial Effectiveness and Stress Mitigation:
An Emphasis on Capacity of Mindfulness

Abha Kumai
Indian Institute of Management, Bodh Gaya, India

Nidhi Mishra
Indian Institute of Management, Bodh Gaya, India

Archana Patro
iD https://orcid.org/0000-0002-0995-4797
Indian Institute of Management, Bodh Gaya, India

ABSTRACT

This chapter introduces a theoretical framework for understanding how corporate governance impacts managerial effectiveness and stress mitigation by taking the mediating role of the capacity of mindfulness to enhance the overall efficacy of the organization. Existing literature talks about how governance structure impacts organisational and managerial performance and stress, but they are missing the underlying processes that link effective governance practices to improved performance and reduced stress; this framework provides the lens for analysing this process. By offering a more nuanced understanding, this framework will help improve the organisation's overall result by taking care of managers' well-being by reducing their stress and increasing their performance.

DOI: 10.4018/979-8-3693-2015-0.ch014

1. INTRODUCTION

Governance derives from the Latin word "gubanare," meaning "to steer." "The manner of directing and controlling the actions and affairs" defines governance. In 1992, the Cadbury Report (para. 2.5) noted that "corporate governance is the system by which companies are directed and controlled." According to the IFAC (2009), the two elements of corporate governance are conformance and performance, which "together represent the entire value creation, resource utilisation, and accountability framework of an organisation." In particular, the performance component focuses on three categories of routines, including plan execution and assessment, resource mapping to strategies, and value generation. In contrast, compliance focuses on three exercises dealing with accountability, assurance, and risk management. Business success in this complex world is determined by how effectively the tango between conformance and performance is managed (Jamali et al., 2008).

While being committed to ethical conduct and regulatory compliance (conformance), businesses must also aim for ambitious goals and surpass stakeholder expectations (performance) (Aguilera et al., 2015). According to Hodges et al. (1996), concerns concerning performance in the public sector should be addressed with a high priority on compliance. Williams & Seaman (2010) examined that capacity for mindfulness as the significant determinant of conformance and performance dimension of corporate governance, and further studies by Williams & Seaman (2014) addressed administrative performance, which found that among CFOs in Canadian firms, strong positive zero-order effects of CG(corporate governance) on mindfulness capacity hold for both CG dimensions. However, similarly strong positive direct effects from managerial performance to mindfulness capacity only hold for conformance dimensions of CG and not the performance dimensions of CG. Nevertheless, there has been a lack of studies investigating the influence of these traits on managers' well-being and stress reduction, which in turn enhances their managing effectiveness. Improved financial outcomes and market value have been linked to performance-oriented governance strategies such as identifying clear strategic goals, deploying effective performance management systems, and establishing strong communication channels(Rose, 2016). However, if compliance is ignored in favour of performance, managers may suffer unfair pressure, unethical actions, and increased stress (Abdul-Rahman, 1995).

Further conformance-oriented governance strategies emphasising accountability, transparency, moral behaviour, and regulatory compliance reduce management stress and improve well-being(Ton & Huckman, 2008). These strategies can provide managers with security and stability by building a trusting and psychologically safe environment. This will allow managers to focus on their tasks without worrying or fearing the repercussions.

However, much of the existing research misses the underlying processes that link effective governance practices to improved performance and reduced stress. Although the relationship between corporate governance and organisational outcomes has been explored, as mindfulness practices influence individual well-being, little is known about how governance techniques affect manager stress and performance. This study tries to fill this gap by looking into the role of mindfulness as a mediating factor in the link between corporate governance and managerial wellbeing. We intend to investigate the link between the performance and conformance dimensions of corporate governance and managerial performance and stress by using the capacity of mindfulness as a mediating factor because it is challenging to imagine a scenario where corporate governance is not applicable in comprehending managerial conduct and organizational effectiveness (Larcker & Richardson, 2007). The capacity of mindfulness is chosen as an intervening variable based on a theoretical argument linked to corporate governance.

2. IMPACT OF CORPORATE GOVERNANCE ON MANAGERIAL EFFECTIVENESS AND STRESS MITIGATION:

This section presents how directly, and indirectly corporate governance impacts managerial effectiveness and stress mitigation by taking the mediation effect of the capacity of mindfulness. Figure 1 shows the proposed path analysis model of corporate governance's conformance and performance dimension to the managerial performance and stress by taking the mediation effect of the capacity of mindfulness.

Figure 1.

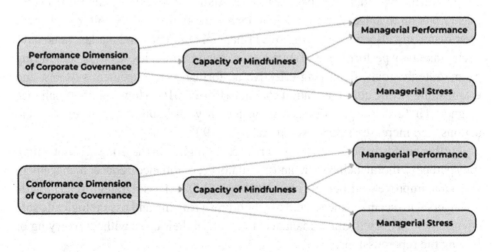

2.1 Understanding the Relation Between Managerial Performance and Corporate Governance

Existing literature reveals that effective corporate governance practices favour managerial decision-making and the firm's overall success(Jensen & Meckling, 2012). Robust governance frameworks positively impact strategy planning, risk management, and resource allocation, improving managerial performance. The success of a firm is mostly contingent upon the correlation between managerial performance and corporate governance. Empirical studies have consistently shown that effective governance frameworks have positive benefits on managerial decision-making and, consequently, the overall performance of organisations. Clear financial disclosures and greater openness are linked to excellent corporate governance(Salehi et al., 2023). Corporate governance prescribes the way to perform, and many literatures say there is a significant correlation between performance and governance. It has a favourable correlation with the likelihood of disciplinary management turnover in underperforming companies and future operating performance(Goel et al., 2022).

Learning models are put forth by Hermalin and Weisbach (2019) as a lens through which to view how managerial conduct is influenced by corporate governance. They contend that management learning is accelerated by good governance, resulting in better strategic planning and decision-making. Financial success and the accomplishment of organisational objectives depend on this connection.

In his study, Yu (2018) examines the intricate relationship between governance and financial outcomes. The research specifically investigates the influence of corporate governance on profits management and emphasises the significance of governance structures in promoting ethical behaviour among managers. The findings suggest that implementing strong governance mechanisms improves financial performance and ensures that managerial action aligns with ethical ideals. Moreover Hitt, Ireland, and Hoskisson's (2016) strategic management approach highlights the part governance plays in fostering a positive work environment. Good governance frameworks offer a framework for resource allocation, risk management, and strategic planning—all of which improve managerial efficacy and, in turn, the entire organisation's performance. Good Corporate Governance impacts managerial performance, hence changes in GCG values can account for changes in managerial performance metrics. Atawnah et al.,(2024) explains in their study that the value of managerial performance will increase with an increase in the GCG value. Effective corporate governance has a significant positive impact on the managerial performance of the Makassar local revenue office(Ibrahim, 2017) and there is positive correlation between better governance measure and operating performance(Bhagat & Bolton, 2008).

So, considering the above literatures we can come to following proposition:

Proposition1: There is a direct relationship between the conformance and performance dimensions of corporate governance and management performance.

2.2 Understanding the Relation Between Capacity of Mindfulness and Managerial Performance

By emphasising the connection between corporate governance and organisational results, (Daily et al., 2003) advance our knowledge of this relationship. Their examination of corporate governance over many years highlights how fundamentally it shapes managerial behaviour and, consequently, the performance of organisations and adding to this Alruwayti & Sulphey, (2023) in his studies stated that mindfulness plays significant role in enhancing employee performance, it reinforces employee performance and subjective well-being. Same in case of dynamic service industry in study of Dane & Brummel, (2014), and by taking the non-clinical sample of it professionals (Sharma & Kumra, 2022) claimed that mindfulness is positively related to self-efficacy. Mindfulness has an indirect impact on executive performance by affecting CSR initiatives. Williams & Seaman(2014) in his study explains how the two dimensions of corporate governance impacts the managerial performance by taking the sample of Canadian firms via intervening path of mindfulness, and again Williams & Seaman,(2016) findings indicate that companies can improve their managerial performance by prioritizing CSR tactics, applying attentive cognitive processes to these acts, and cultivating ethical leadership.

To summarize our next proposition is:

Proposition2: There is a direct relationship between capacity of mindfulness and managerial performance.

2.3 Understanding the Relation Between Managerial Stress and Corporate Governance

Corporate governance, the structure by which organisations are controlled and supervised, has a substantial impact on workplace dynamics, especially the levels of stress that employees experience. Research indicates that an efficiently operating corporate governance framework has a positive influence on the overall work environment. Governance frameworks that have been established improves transparency, fairness, and ethical conduct within business (Daily et al., 2003). The impact of corporate governance on managerial responsibility is significantly significant. Efficient governance processes provide managers with a clearly defined framework for decision-making, reducing ambiguity and unpredictability, which frequently contribute to managerial stress.(Hitt, M. A., Ireland, R. D., & Hoskisson, 2010). In contrast, inadequate management can result in elevated levels of stress among managers, which in turn can negatively impact job performance for blue-collar Canadian managers (Kazmi et al., 2008). Similar findings have been observed in Japanese firms (Ida et al., 2009). Workplace stress is impacted by the ethical components incorporated in governance protocols. When governance places a high importance on ethical behaviour and fairness, people, particularly managers, are less likely to encounter stress arising from moral dilemmas or conflicting ideals.

In summary, it can be stated that effective corporate governance enhances the work environment and mitigates employee stress, while inadequate corporate governance has the potential to exacerbate stress levels. The paradigm described above gives rise to the following proposition:

Proposition 3: There is a considerable and direct relationship between performance and conformance dimension of corporate governance and managerial stress.

2.4 Understanding the Relation Between Capacity of Mindfulness and Stress Management

Recent studies indicate that incorporating mindfulness principles into corporate governance can reduce stress (Reb et al., 2014). It was discovered that the characteristic of being mindful in a supervisor has a favourable impact on the well-being and performance of employees. Well-executed governance has the power to build a collaborative and trusting work atmosphere. As a result, managers may have less stress since there will be clear instructions, less room for misunderstanding, and impartial and consistent decision-making (Hitt et al., 2016; Daily et al., 2003). The well-being of employees is a crucial factor in the success of a firm(Alruwayti & Sulphey, 2023), and stress has a detrimental effect on overall competitiveness(Cahlíková et al., 2020). According to the work demand resource model, the findings partially confirm the hypothesis that the personal resources of mindfulness and self-efficacy have a mediating effect on employee performance through the reduction of stress(Yagil et al., 2023;(Brown & Ryan, 2003). Research offers a comprehensive analysis, both in theory and via empirical evidence, of the impact of mindfulness on psychological well-being, a clinical intervention study conducted with cancer patients revealed that an increase in mindfulness over a period is associated with a decrease in mood disturbance and stress. Furthermore among a group of Indian IT professionals who are not part of a clinical study, there is a negative correlation between mindfulness and anxiety, stress, and depression.(Alruwayti & Sulphey, 2023). Therefore, to summarize following proposition could be stated:

Proposition4: There is a direct relationship between capacity of mindfulness and managerial stress.

2.5 The Capacity of Mindfulness as an Intervening Variable

The term "Mindfulness" has its roots in the Pali language, and it signifies qualities such as attentiveness, circumspection, discernment, and retention. It is formed by the amalgamation of Sati and Sampajana. Researchers have determined that these language interpretations suggest that mindfulness refers to the capacity to observe and comprehend one's present moment experiences consciously and attentively. Mindfulness, as defined by (Good et al., 2016), is a comprehensive concept that encompasses the ability to control one's focus and consciousness on the current moment, without forming opinions or making judgements. It refers to an increased focus and understanding of one's current experiences or the immediate reality. Corporate governance, as stated by the OECD in 1999, is the mechanism by which business corporations are guided and managed. The literature suggests that there is a positive correlation between transparent financial disclosures and increased transparency, and effective corporate governance. The reference is from the study conducted by Salehi et al. in 2023. Atawnah et al.,(2024) through the analysis of a sample of U.S. companies over a period of thirty years, it has been determined that there is a direct relationship between the skills of managers and the value of the organization. This relationship has been established by studying the impact of CEO turnover, which is influenced by external factors. Specifically, an improvement in managerial ability by one standard deviation is associated with a 5.7% increase in firm value compared to the average level. The potency of this link is amplified when corporate governance structures, such as institutional investors and financial analysts, are in place. Furthermore, organizations that are led by more skilled managers exhibit a decrease in value-diminishing behaviours, such as the manipulation of earnings.

Furthermore, Effective corporate governance, also known as GCG, is crucial for the successful execution of the company's strategy and objectives, since it cultivates a work environment that optimises employee performance. Gilang et al., (2018) in his study indicates that an individual's performance is contingent upon their decision-making abilities, emotional regulation, and the extent of stress they are managing. Mindfulness, defined as the conscious recognition and acceptance of the current moment, has been associated with improved decision-making, emotional regulation, and stress reduction. (Kabat-Zinn, 2003; Dane, 2011). A vigilant employee will diligently monitor the organization's rules and regulations, hence promoting effective corporate governance. The employee of more mindful leader feel treated as greater respect and experience less stress (Reb et al., 2019). However, there is a scarcity of studies elucidating the correlation between corporate governance and mindfulness. According to this study, mindfulness acts as a mediator in linking corporate governance with management performance and stress reduction. And the subsequent proposition is formulated:

Proposition5: Capacity of mindfulness mediates the relationship between conformance and performance dimension of corporate governance with managerial performance and stress.

3. CONCLUSION AND DISCUSSION

This study examines the impact of mindfulness capacity on managers' well-being by exploring the connection between stress management, corporate governance, and managerial performance. It also examines the path through with managerial performance is increased and their stress is mitigated. And suggested the use of mindfulness technique to attain the balance between the conformance and performance dimension of corporate governance which will enhance the overall value of business (Jamali et al., 2008). And finally, our work has general theoretical implication for managing acute extra organizational stressors.

This study contributes to the body of research indicating positive impact that mindfulness will hold on to the performance of managers by mitigating their stress after all stress is the global phenomena experienced by all managers. Williams & Seaman, (2016) in his study stated that mindfulness has an indirect impact on management performance by affecting CSR initiatives. Companies can enhance their managerial performance by prioritizing corporate social responsibility (CSR) strategies, applying cognitive processes of mindfulness to guide these actions, and cultivating ethical leadership. which in turn will improve the corporate governance of organization.

This study holds significance for establishments seeking to enhance their governance protocols for supervisory efficiency and staff psychological well-being because as per the study of (Dane & Brummel, 2014) there is positive relationship between workplace mindfulness and job performance. Further the current findings is an extension to the findings of (Williom & Seaman, 2014)by taking care of manager wellbeing

Enhanced governance procedures significantly impact the achievement of improved results and the ongoing efficiency of their governance systems (IFAC, 209, p.5). The existing research on High Reliability Organisations (HRO) indicates that the connection between mindfulness and effectiveness is not immediate. Rather, cognitive processes form the foundation of mindfulness, which in turn enhances an individual's ability to handle anticipated and unanticipated events. This improvement in capability leads to increased reliability and effectiveness (Weick et al., 1999, p. 89). This study looks at how being mindful can help managers feel better at work by mitigating their stress and how its connected to performance and conformance dimension of corporate governance. This helps them stay focused and strong when work gets tough. This study will help companies to ensure their manager well-being and sticking to good rules.

Future research could be done to empirically test the propositions stated above in different country and firm level contexts, could also include additional organizational factors like work culture, leadership style, etc. by taking different time variables. Further studies could also be done to establish path relation between the two dimensions of corporate governance.

REFERENCES

Abdul-Rahman, H. (1995). The cost of non-conformance during a highway project: A case study. *Construction Management and Economics*, *13*(1), 23–32. doi:10.1080/01446199500000004

Aguilera, R. V., Desender, K., Bednar, M. K., & Lee, J. H. (2015). Connecting the Dots: Bringing External Corporate Governance into the Corporate Governance Puzzle. *The Academy of Management Annals*, *9*(1), 483–573. doi:10.5465/19416 520.2015.1024503

Alruwayti, H. A., & Sulphey, M. M. (2023). The interconnections of workplace spirituality, mindfulness, subjective well-being, and task performance: A study using structural equation modeling. *Problems and Perspectives in Management*, *21*(4), 616–628. doi:10.21511/ppm.21(4).2023.46

Atawnah, N., Eshraghi, A., Baghdadi, G. A., & Bhatti, I. (2024). Managerial ability and firm value: A new perspective. *Research in International Business and Finance*, *67*(PB), 102133. doi:10.1016/j.ribaf.2023.102133

Bhagat, S., & Bolton, B. (2008). Corporate Gov and Firm Performance. *Journal of Corporate Finance*, *14*(3), 257–283. doi:10.1016/j.jcorpfin.2008.03.006

Brown, K. W., & Ryan, R. M. (2003). The Benefits of Being Present: Mindfulness and Its Role in Psychological Well-Being. *Journal of Personality and Social Psychology*, *84*(4), 822–848. doi:10.1037/0022-3514.84.4.822 PMID:12703651

Cahlíková, J., Cingl, L., & Lively, I. (2020). How stress affects performance and competitiveness across gender. *Management Science*, *66*(8), 3295–3310. doi:10.1287/mnsc.2019.3400

Daily, C. M., Dalton, D. R., & Cannella, A. A. (2003). Corporate Governance: Decades of Dialogue and Data. In *Source: The Academy of Management Review* (Vol. 28, Issue 3). https://www.jstor.org/stable/30040727

Dane, E., & Brummel, B. J. (2014). Examining workplace mindfulness and its relations to job performance and turnover intention. *Human Relations*, *67*(1), 105–128. doi:10.1177/0018726713487753

Goel, A., Sharma, R., & Mehta, K. (2022). *Corporate Governance and Firm Performance*. doi:10.4018/978-1-6684-5528-9.ch018

Good, D. J., Lyddy, C. J., Glomb, T. M., Bono, J. E., Brown, K. W., Duffy, M. K., Baer, R. A., Brewer, J. A., & Lazar, S. W. (2016). Contemplating Mindfulness at Work: An Integrative Review. *Journal of Management*, *42*(1), 114–142. doi:10.1177/0149206315617003

Hermalin, B. E., & Weisbach, M. S. (2019). Understanding Corporate Governance Through Learning Models of Managerial Competence. *Asia-Pacific Journal of Financial Studies*, *48*(1), 7–29. doi:10.1111/ajfs.12243

Hitt, M. A., Ireland, R. D., & Hoskisson, R. E. (2016). *Strategic management: Concepts and cases: Competitiveness and globalization*. Academic Press.

Ibrahim, M. (2017). Effects of internal control, corporate governance, organizational culture, and management audit on managerial performance: Evidence from Indonesia. *International Journal of Economic Perspectives*, *11*(3), 1826–1832.

Jamali, D., Safieddine, A. M., & Rabbath, M. (2008). Corporate governance and corporate social responsibility synergies and interrelationships. *Corporate Governance*, *16*(5), 443–459. doi:10.1111/j.1467-8683.2008.00702.x

Jensen, M., & Meckling, W. (2012). Theory of the firm: Managerial behavior, agency costs, and ownership structure. The Economic Nature of the Firm: A Reader, Third Edition, 283–303. doi:10.1017/CBO9780511817410.023

Larcker, D. F., & Richardson, S. A. (2007). David F. Larcker. *The Accounting Review*, *82*(4), 963–1008. doi:10.2308/accr.2007.82.4.963

Reb, J., Chaturvedi, S., Narayanan, J., & Kudesia, R. S. (2019). Leader Mindfulness and Employee Performance: A Sequential Mediation Model of LMX Quality, Interpersonal Justice, and Employee Stress. *Journal of Business Ethics*, *160*(3), 745–763. doi:10.1007/s10551-018-3927-x

Reb, J., Narayanan, J., & Chaturvedi, S. (2014). Leading Mindfully: Two Studies on the Influence of Supervisor Trait Mindfulness on Employee Well-Being and Performance. *Mindfulness*, *5*(1), 36–45. doi:10.1007/s12671-012-0144-z

Rose, C. (2016). Firm performance and comply or explain disclosure in corporate governance. *European Management Journal, 34*(3), 202–222. doi:10.1016/j.emj.2016.03.003

Salehi, M., Ammar Ajel, R., & Zimon, G. (2023). The relationship between corporate governance and financial reporting transparency. *Journal of Financial Reporting and Accounting, 21*(5), 1049–1072. doi:10.1108/JFRA-04-2021-0102

Sharma, P. K., & Kumra, R. (2022). Relationship between mindfulness, depression, anxiety and stress: Mediating role of self-efficacy. *Personality and Individual Differences, 186*, 111363. Advance online publication. doi:10.1016/j.paid.2021.111363

Ton, Z., & Huckman, R. S. (2008). Managing the impact of employee turnover on performance: The role of process conformance. *Organization Science, 19*(1), 56–68. doi:10.1287/orsc.1070.0294

Williams, J. J., & Seaman, A. E. (2016). *On Managerial Performance*. Academic Press.

Williams, J. J., & Seaman, A. E. (2014). Does More Corporate Governance Enhance. *Journal of Applied Business Research, 30*(4), 989–1002. doi:10.19030/jabr.v30i4.8648

Yagil, D., Medler-Liraz, H., & Bichachi, R. (2023). Mindfulness and self-efficacy enhance employee performance by reducing stress. *Personality and Individual Differences, 207*, 112150. doi:10.1016/j.paid.2023.112150

Compilation of References

Abatecola, G., Caputo, A., & Cristofaro, M. (2018). Reviewing cognitive distortions in managerial decision making: Toward an integrative co-evolutionary framework. *Journal of Management Development*, *37*(5), 409–424. doi:10.1108/JMD-08-2017-0263

Abdul-Rahman, H. (1995). The cost of non-conformance during a highway project: A case study. *Construction Management and Economics*, *13*(1), 23–32. doi:10.1080/01446199500000004

Abràmoff, M. D., Tarver, M. E., Loyo-Berrios, N., Trujillo, S., Char, D., Obermeyer, Z., Eydelman, M. B., & Maisel, W. H. (2023). Considerations for addressing bias in artificial intelligence for health equity. *NPJ Digital Medicine*, *6*(1), 170. doi:10.1038/s41746-023-00913-9 PMID:37700029

Adair, J. E. (2007). *Decision making & problem solving strategies* (Vol. 121). Kogan Page Publishers.

Adams-Quackenbush, N. M. (2018). Indicators of Confirmation Bias in the Investigative Interview with Suspects Thesis (Doctoral dissertation, The University of Portsmouth).

Adhikari, D., Gazi, K. H., Giri, B. C., Azizzadeh, F., & Mondal, S. P. (2023). Empowerment of women in India as different perspectives based on the AHP-TOPSIS-inspired multi-criterion decision-making method. *Results in Control and Optimization*, *12*, 100271. doi:10.1016/j.rico.2023.100271

Adhyaru, J. S., & Kemp, C. (2022). Virtual reality as a tool to promote wellbeing in the workplace. *Digital Health*, *8*. doi:10.1177/20552076221084473 PMID:35284084

Aguilera, R. V., Desender, K., Bednar, M. K., & Lee, J. H. (2015). Connecting the Dots: Bringing External Corporate Governance into the Corporate Governance Puzzle. *The Academy of Management Annals*, *9*(1), 483–573. doi:10.5465/19416520.2015.1024503

Agustina, Y. (2021). Thinking Analysis And Problem Solving: Array. *Literasi Nusantara*, *1*(2), 107–117.

Ajzen, I., & Fishbein, M. (1980). *Understanding attitudes and Predicting social behaviour*. Prentice-Hall.

Akperov, I. G., Martynov, B. V., & Prokopenko, E. S. (2022). The role of digital consciousness in change management. *Vestnik Universiteta*, *11*(11), 5–10. doi:10.26425/1816-4277-2022-10-5-10

Algorithmic bias detection and mitigation: Best practices and policies to reduce consumer harms. (2023, June 27). Brookings. https://www.brookings.edu/articles/algorithmic-bias-detection-and-mitigation-best-practices-and-policies-to-reduce-consumer-harms/

Alhaji, B., Beecken, J., Ehlers, R., Gertheiss, J., Merz, F., Müller, J. P., Prilla, M., Rausch, A., Reinhardt, A., Reinhardt, D., Rembe, C., Rohweder, N.-O., Schwindt, C., Westphal, S., & Zimmermann, J. (2020). Engineering human–machine teams for trusted collaboration. *Big Data and Cognitive Computing*, *4*(4), 35. doi:10.3390/bdcc4040035

Ali, M. S., Siddique, Z., & Ahsan, M. M. (2024). Enhancing and improving the performance of imbalanced class data using novel GBO and SSG: A comparative analysis. *Neural Networks*, 106157. PMID:38335796

Alimam, H., Mazzuto, G., Tozzi, N., Ciarapica, F. E., & Bevilacqua, M. (2023). The resurrection of digital triplet: A cognitive pillar of human-machine integration at the dawn of industry 5.0. *Journal of King Saud University. Computer and Information Sciences*, *35*(10), 101846. doi:10.1016/j.jksuci.2023.101846

Alimohammadlou, M., & Khoshsepehr, Z. (2023). The role of Society 5.0 in achieving sustainable development: A spherical fuzzy set approach. *Environmental Science and Pollution Research International*, *30*(16), 47630–47654. doi:10.1007/s11356-023-25543-2 PMID:36745347

Alruwayti, H. A., & Sulphey, M. M. (2023). The interconnections of workplace spirituality, mindfulness, subjective well-being, and task performance: A study using structural equation modeling. *Problems and Perspectives in Management*, *21*(4), 616–628. doi:10.21511/ppm.21(4).2023.46

Althof. (2021). Insights into cognitive processing of the go/nogo Discrete Sequence Production task: A replication study. Academic Press.

Aminabee, S. (2024). The Future of Healthcare and Patient-Centric Care: Digital Innovations, Trends, and Predictions. In Emerging Technologies for Health Literacy and Medical Practice (pp. 240-262). IGI Global.

Andreassen, C. S., Torsheim, T., Brunborg, G. S., & Pallesen, S. (2012). Development of a Facebook Addiction Scale. *Psychological Reports*, *110*(2), 501–517. doi:10.2466/02.09.18. PR0.110.2.501-517 PMID:22662404

Andrejevic, M., Bouquillion, P., Cohn, J., Day, F., Gaw, F., Ithurbide, C., & Volcic, Z. (2023). *Media backends: digital infrastructures and sociotechnical relations*. University of Illinois Press.

Angier, T., Benson, I. T., & Retter, M. D. (Eds.). (2022). Challenges and Future Prospects. In The Cambridge Handbook of Natural Law and Human Rights. Cambridge Law Handbooks. Cambridge University Press. doi:10.1017/9781108939225.038

Anjana, C. M. (2023). *Role of Artificial Intelligence in Emotion Recognition*. International Journal For Science Technology And Engineering.

Anthony, B. Jr. (2021). Implications of telehealth and digital care solutions during COVID-19 pandemic: A qualitative literature review. *Informatics for Health & Social Care*, *46*(1), 68–83. doi:10.1080/17538157.2020.1839467 PMID:33251894

Antunes, R. M., Coito, F. V., & Duarte-Ramos, H. (2010, September). Human-machine control model approach to enhance operator skills. In *2010 International Conference on Mechanical and Electrical Technology* (pp. 403-407). IEEE. 10.1109/ICMET.2010.5598392

Araujo, T., Helberger, N., Kruikemeier, S., & De Vreese, C. H. (2020). In AI we trust? Perceptions about automated decision-making by artificial intelligence. *AI & Society*, *35*(3), 611–623. doi:10.1007/s00146-019-00931-w

Ardanza, A., Moreno, A., Segura, Á., de la Cruz, M., & Aguinaga, D. (2019). Sustainable and flexible industrial human-machine interfaces to support adaptable applications in the Industry 4.0 paradigm. *International Journal of Production Research*, *57*(12), 4045–4059. doi:10.1080/00207543.2019.1572932

Arleen, S., Evers, K., & Farisco, M. (2020). Anthropomorphism in A. *AJOB Neuroscience*, *11*(2), 88–95. doi:10.1080/21507740.2020.1740350 PMID:32228388

Ascott, R. (1998). Consciousness reframed: Art and consciousness in the post-biological era. *Digital Creativity (Exeter)*, *9*(1), 5–6. doi:10.1080/14626269808567099

Assunção, G., Patrão, B., Castelo-Branco, M., & Menezes, P. (2022). An overview of emotion in artificial intelligence. *IEEE Transactions on Artificial Intelligence*, *3*(6), 867–886. doi:10.1109/TAI.2022.3159614

Atawnah, N., Eshraghi, A., Baghdadi, G. A., & Bhatti, I. (2024). Managerial ability and firm value: A new perspective. *Research in International Business and Finance, 67*(PB), 102133. doi:10.1016/j.ribaf.2023.102133

Atieh, A. M., Cooke, K. O., & Osiyevskyy, O. (2023). The role of intelligent manufacturing systems in implementing Industry 4.0 by small and medium enterprises in developing countries. *Engineering Reports*, *5*(3), e12578. doi:10.1002/eng2.12578

Avolio, B. J., & Gardner, W. L. (2005). Authentic leadership development: Getting to the root of positive forms of leadership. *The Leadership Quarterly*, *16*(3), 315–338. doi:10.1016/j.leaqua.2005.03.001

Ayhan, E. E., & Akar, Ç. (2022). Society 5.0 Vision in Contemporary Inequal World. Society 5.0 A New Challenge to Humankind's Future, 133.

Baars, B. J. (2005). Global workspace theory of consciousness: Toward a cognitive neuroscience of human experience. *Progress in Brain Research*, *150*, 45–53. doi:10.1016/S0079-6123(05)50004-9 PMID:16186014

Baddeley, M. C., Curtis, A., & Wood, R. (2004). An introduction to prior information derived from probabilistic judgements: Elicitation of knowledge, cognitive bias and herding. *Special Publication - Geological Society of London*, *239*(1), 15–27. doi:10.1144/GSL.SP.2004.239.01.02

Baer, R. A., Smith, G. T., & Allen, K. B. (2004). Assessment of mindfulness by self-report: The Kentucky Inventory of Mindfulness Skills. *Assessment*, *11*(3), 191–206. doi:10.1177/1073191104268029 PMID:15358875

Ball, L. J. (1990). Cognitive processes in engineering design. Academic Press.

Bandyopadhyay, S., & Saha, G. K. (2018) A review of technology acceptance models in digital health. *Journal of Medical Systems*, *42*(11), 220.

Banfi, F. (2021). The evolution of interactivity, immersion and interoperability in HBIM: Digital model uses, V.R. and A.R. for built cultural heritage. *ISPRS International Journal of Geo-Information*, *10*(10), 685. doi:10.3390/ijgi10100685

Bareket-Bojmel, L., Shahar, G., & Margalit, M. (2015). Perceived social support and attachment styles as predictors of communication patterns in romantic relationships. *Cyberpsychology, Behavior, and Social Networking*, *18*(4), 203–208. PMID:25803312

Barocas, S., & Selbst, A. D. (2016). Big data's disparate impact. *California Law Review*, 671–732.

Barraza, J. A., & Goldin, P. R. (2020). Mindfulness and empathy in interpersonal relationships: A systematic review and meta-analysis. *Frontiers in Psychology*, *11*, 1–20.

Barrett, P. T., Preacher, K. J., & Rourke, K. M. (2014). *Psychometrics: An introduction* (2nd ed.). Guilford Press.

Bass, B. M. (1985). *Leadership and performance beyond expectations*. Free Press.

Bass, B. M., & Riggio, R. E. (2006). *Transformational leadership* (2nd ed.). Psychology Press. doi:10.4324/9781410617095

Batliwala, S. (2010). Taking the Power Out of Empowerment: An Experiential Account. *Development in Practice*, *20*(2), 229–241.

Bell, E. L. (1990). The bicultural life experience of career-oriented black women. *Journal of Organizational Behavior*, *11*(6), 459–477. doi:10.1002/job.4030110607

Belliger, A., & Krieger, D. J. (2018). The digital transformation of healthcare. Knowledge Management in Digital Change: New Findings and Practical Cases, 311-326.

Benjamin, J. (2022, May). Long-term repeatability of cognitive performance. *Royal Society Open Science*, *9*(5), 220069. Advance online publication. doi:10.1098/rsos.220069

Bennett, M. T., & Maruyama, Y. (2021). Philosophical specification of empathetic ethical artificial intelligence. *IEEE Transactions on Cognitive and Developmental Systems*, *14*(2), 292–300. doi:10.1109/TCDS.2021.3099945

Bertino, E., Kundu, A., & Sura, Z. (2019). Data transparency with blockchain and AI ethics. *ACM Journal of Data and Information Quality*, *11*(4), 1–8. doi:10.1145/3312750

Bhagat, S., & Bolton, B. (2008). Corporate Gov and Firm Performance. *Journal of Corporate Finance*, *14*(3), 257–283. doi:10.1016/j.jcorpfin.2008.03.006

Bhaimiya, S. (2023, September 22). Gen Z lack workplace skills like debating and seeing different points of view because they spend too much time on social media, TV boss says. Business Insider India. https://www.businessinsider.in/careers/news/gen-z-lack-workplace-skills-like-debating-and-seeing-different-points-of-view-because-they-spend-too-much-time-on-social-media-tv-boss-says/articleshow/103871097.cms

Bharadwaj, A., El Sawy, O. A., Pavlou, P. A., & Venkatraman, N. (2013). Digital business strategy: Toward a next generation of insights. *Management Information Systems Quarterly*, *37*(2), 471–482. doi:10.25300/MISQ/2013/37:2.3

Bhui, K., Dinos, S., Galant-Miecznikowska, M., de Jongh, B., & Stansfeld, S. (2016, December 6). Perceptions of work stress causes and effective interventions in employees working in public, private and non-governmental organisations: A qualitative study. *BJPsych Bulletin*, *40*(6), 318–325. doi:10.1192/pb.bp.115.050823 PMID:28377811

Binci, D., Palozzi, G., & Scafarto, F. (2022). Toward digital transformation in healthcare: A framework for remote monitoring adoption. *The TQM Journal*, *34*(6), 1772–1799. doi:10.1108/TQM-04-2021-0109

Bingxuan, R., Tangwen, Y., & Shan, F. (2019). An Approach Analyzing Cognitive Process of Human-Machine Interaction Based on Extended Markov Decision Process. doi:10.1109/CAC48633.2019.8996284

Bishop, S. R., Lau, M., Shapiro, S., Carlson, L., Anderson, N. D., Carmody, J., Segal, Z. V., Abbey, S., Speca, M., Velting, D., & Devins, G. (2004). Mindfulness: A proposed operational definition. *Clinical Psychology : a Publication of the Division of Clinical Psychology of the American Psychological Association*, *11*(3), 230–241. doi:10.1093/clipsy.bph077

Blade, S. (2021). YouTubers by Views and Subscribers. Academic Press.

Blainey, P., Krzywinski, M., & Altman, N. (2014). Points of significance: Replication. *Nature Methods*, *11*(9), 879–880. doi:10.1038/nmeth.3091 PMID:25317452

Bono, J. E., & Ilies, R. (2006). Charisma, positive emotions, and mood contagion. *The Leadership Quarterly*, *17*(4), 317–334. doi:10.1016/j.leaqua.2006.04.008

Boyd, D. (2014). *It's Complicated: The Social Lives of Networked Teens*. Yale University Press.

Brackey, A. (2019). Analysis of Racial Bias in Northpointe's COMPAS Algorithm (Doctoral dissertation, Tulane University School of Science and Engineering).

Brall, C., Schröder-Bäck, P., & Maeckelberghe, E. (2019). Ethical aspects of digital health from a justice point of view. *European Journal of Public Health*, *29*(Supplement_3), 18–22. doi:10.1093/eurpub/ckz167 PMID:31738439

Brey, P. (2005). The epistemology and ontology of human-computer interaction. *Minds and Machines*, *15*(3-4), 383–398. doi:10.1007/s11023-005-9003-1

Brinkmann, K. (2005). Consciousness, self-consciousness, and the modern self. *History of the Human Sciences*, *18*(4), 27–48. doi:10.1177/0952695105058469

Brown, K. W., & Ryan, R. M. (2003). The benefits of being present: Mindfulness and human flourishing. *Journal of Personality and Social Psychology*. Advance online publication. doi:10.1037/0022-3514.84.4.822

Bulkeley, K. (2014). Digital dream analysis: A revised method. *Consciousness and Cognition*, *29*, 159–170. doi:10.1016/j.concog.2014.08.015 PMID:25286125

Byrne, B. M. (2016). *Structural equation modelling with Amos: Basic concepts, applications and programming* (3rd ed.). Routledge. doi:10.4324/9781315757421

Cahlíková, J., Cingl, L., & Lively, I. (2020). How stress affects performance and competitiveness across gender. *Management Science*, *66*(8), 3295–3310. doi:10.1287/mnsc.2019.3400

Cai, H., Zhang, J., & Zhou, J. (2022). Development and evaluation of a conversational AI-based mindfulness app for customer service representatives. *Computers in Human Behavior*.

Cameron, L., & Hafenbrack, A. (2022, December 12). Research: When Mindfulness Does — and Doesn't — Help at Work. Harvard Business Review. Retrieved from https://hbr.org/2022/12/research-when-mindfulness-does-and-doesnt-help-at-work

Canny, J. (2006). The Future of Human-Computer Interaction: Is an HCI revolution just around the corner? *ACM Queue; Tomorrow's Computing Today*, *4*(6), 24–32. doi:10.1145/1147518.1147530

Cardeña, E. (1996). Cultivating Consciousness: Enhancing Human Potential, Wellness, and Healing. *Anthropology of Consciousness*, *7*(2), 39–40. doi:10.1525/ac.1996.7.2.39

Carroll, J. M. (2014, January 1). Human Computer Interaction - Brief intro. Interaction Design Foundation - IxDF.

Carruthers, P. (2018). Comparative psychology without consciousness. *Consciousness and Cognition*, *63*, 47–60. doi:10.1016/j.concog.2018.06.012 PMID:29940429

Casad, B. J., & Luebering, J. E. (2024, January 5). Confirmation bias. Encyclopedia Britannica. https://www.britannica.com/science/confirmation-bias

Casillo, M., Cecere, L., Colace, F., Lorusso, A., & Santaniello, D. (2024). Integrating the Internet of Things (IoT) in SPA Medicine: Innovations and Challenges in Digital Wellness. *Computers*, *13*(3), 67. doi:10.3390/computers13030067

Cath, C., Wachter, S., Mittelstadt, B., Taddeo, M., & Floridi, L. (2018). Artificial intelligence and the 'good society': The US, EU, and UK approach. *Science and Engineering Ethics*, *24*, 505–528. PMID:28353045

Cavus, N., Oke, O. A., & Yahaya, J. M. U. (2023). Brain-Computer Interfaces: High-Tech Race to Merge Minds and Machines. In *Cutting Edge Applications of Computational Intelligence Tools and Techniques* (pp. 3–19). Springer Nature Switzerland. doi:10.1007/978-3-031-44127-1_1

Center for Humane Technology. (n.d.). Tristan Harris. Retrieved from https://humanetech.com/team/tristan-harris

Challen, R., Denny, J., Pitt, M., Gompels, L., Edwards, T., & Tsaneva-Atanasova, K. (2019). Artificial intelligence, bias and clinical safety. *BMJ Quality & Safety*, *28*(3), 231–237. doi:10.1136/bmjqs-2018-008370 PMID:30636200

Chalmers, D. J. (1995). Facing up to the problem of consciousness. *Journal of Consciousness Studies*, *2*(3), 200–219.

Chandiok, A., & Chaturvedi, D. K. (2018). Cognitive functionality based question answering system. *Int J Comput Appl*, *179*, 1–6.

Chatterjee, S., Gupta, S. D., & Upadhyay, P. (2020). Technology adoption and entrepreneurial orientation for rural women: Evidence from India. *Technological Forecasting and Social Change*, *160*, 120236. doi:10.1016/j.techfore.2020.120236

Chen, W., & Tang, Q. (2020). Memory system and bias circuit. Academic Press.

Chen, J., Nichele, E., Ellerby, Z., & Wagner, C. (2022). Responsible research and innovation in practice: Driving both the 'How' and the 'What' to research. *Journal of Responsible Technology*, *11*, 100042. doi:10.1016/j.jrt.2022.100042

Chignell, M., Wang, L., Zare, A., & Li, J. (2023). The evolution of HCI and human factors: Integrating human and artificial intelligence. *ACM Transactions on Computer-Human Interaction*, *30*(2), 1–30. doi:10.1145/3557891

Choi, E., Gruman, J. A., & Leonard, C. M. (2021, August 4). A balanced view of mindfulness at work. *Organizational Psychology Review*, *12*(1), 35–72. doi:10.1177/20413866211036930

Christensen, C. M., & Raynor, M. E. (2003). *The Innovator's Solution: Greeting and Sustaining Successful Growth*. Harvard Business School Press.

Christopher, W. (2023). Research and evaluation ethics. . doi:10.51952/9781447366263.ch003

Chuttur, M. Y. (2009). A critical review of technology acceptance model (TAM). *International Journal of Business and Management*, *4*(8), 65–72.

Ciobanu, A. C., & Mesnit, Ă, G. (2022). A.I. Ethics for Industry 5.0—From Principles to Practice. *Proceedings of the Workshop of I-ESA*, 22.

Condon, P., Desbordes, G., Miller, W. B., & DeSteno, D. (2019). The relationship between mindfulness and empathy: A systematic review. *Frontiers in Psychology*, *10*, 1–13.

Conger, J. A., & Kanungo, R. N. (1987). Toward a behavioral theory of charismatic leadership in organizational settings. *Academy of Management Review*, *12*(4), 637–647. doi:10.2307/258069

Coral, M. A., & Bernuy, A. E. (2022). Challenges in the digital transformation processes in higher education institutions and universities. *International Journal of Information Technologies and Systems Approach*, *15*(1), 1–14. doi:10.4018/IJITSA.290002

Coren, S., Ward, L. M., & Enns, J. T. (2004). *Sensation and perception*. John Wiley & Sons.

Crenshaw, R. P., & Vistnes, L. M. (1989). A decade of pressure sore research: 1977-1987. *Journal of Rehabilitation Research and Development*, *26*(1), 63–74. PMID:2645399

Creswell, J. D., Mian, I., & Lindsay, J. (2022). Development and preliminary evaluation of a personalised mindfulness intervention for chronic pain using machine learning. Academic Press.

Cummings, M. M. (2014). Man versus machine or man+ machine? *IEEE Intelligent Systems*, *29*(5), 62–69. doi:10.1109/MIS.2014.87

Daily, C. M., Dalton, D. R., & Cannella, A. A. (2003). Corporate Governance: Decades of Dialogue and Data. In *Source: The Academy of Management Review* (Vol. 28, Issue 3). https://www.jstor.org/stable/30040727

Dale, S. (2015). Heuristics and biases: The science of decision-making. *Business Information Review*, *32*(2), 93–99. doi:10.1177/0266382115592536

Dane, E., & Brummel, B. J. (2014). Examining workplace mindfulness and its relations to job performance and turnover intention. *Human Relations*, *67*(1), 105–128. doi:10.1177/0018726713487753

Davia, F. D., Bagozzi, R. P., & Warshaw, P. R. (1989). User acceptance of computer technology: A comparison of twtheoretical models. *Management Science*, *35*(8), 982–1003. doi:10.1287/mnsc.35.8.982

Davis, D. M., & Hayes, J. A. (2011). What are the benefits of mindfulness? A practice review of psychotherapy-related research. *Psychotherapy (Chicago, Ill.)*, *48*(2), 198–208. doi:10.1037/a0022062 PMID:21639664

de Almeida, P. G. R., dos Santos, C. D., & Farias, J. S. (2021). Artificial intelligence regulation: A framework for governance. *Ethics and Information Technology*, *23*(3), 505–525. doi:10.1007/s10676-021-09593-z

Deacon, D., Pickering, M., Golding, P., & Murdock, G. (2021). *Researching communications: A practical guide to methods in media and cultural analysis*. Bloomsbury Publishing USA. doi:10.5040/9781501316951

Deininger, K., Nagarajan, H. K., & Singh, S. K. (2020). Women's political leadership and economic empowerment: Evidence from public works in India. *Journal of Comparative Economics*, *48*(2), 277–291. doi:10.1016/j.jce.2019.12.003

Descartes, R., & Frenzel, I. (1960). *René Descartes*. Fischer.

Dholakia, U. M., Sopariwala, P. K., & Dholakia, R. R. (2021). Mindfulness and empathy in leadership: A review. *Journal of Business Research*, *123*, 431–441.

Diel, A., Weigelt, S., & MacDorman, K. F. (2021). A meta-analysis of the Uncanny Valley's independent and dependent variables. *ACM Transactions on Human-Robot Interaction*, *11*(1), 1–33. doi:10.1145/3470742

DiResta, R., Halderman, J. A., & Howard, P. N. (2018). *The tactics & tropes of the Internet Research Agency*. Stanford Internet Observatory.

Do, N. V., & Nguyen, H. D. (2022, October). Knowledge-based Problem Solving and Reasoning methods. In 2022 14th International Conference on Knowledge and Systems Engineering (KSE) (pp. 1-7). IEEE. 10.1109/KSE56063.2022.9953617

Doe, A., & Johnson, B. (2015). Exploring the Uncanny Valley in Human-Computer Interaction. *Journal of Human-Computer Interaction*, *25*(3), 123–145.

Dong, Y., Hou, J., Zhang, N., & Mao-Cong, Z. (2020). Research on how human intelligence, consciousness, and cognitive computing affect the development of artificial intelligence. *Complexity*, *2020*, 1–10. doi:10.1155/2020/1680845

Drewes, H., De Luca, A., & Schmidt, A. (2007, September). Eye-gaze interaction for mobile phones. In *Proceedings of the 4th international conference on mobile technology, applications, and systems and the 1st international symposium on Computer human interaction in mobile technology* (pp. 364-371). 10.1145/1378063.1378122

Duflo, E. (2012). Women's empowerment and economic development. *Journal of Economic Literature*, *50*(4), 1051–1079. doi:10.1257/jel.50.4.1051

Dumontheil, I., Brookman-Byrne, A., Tolmie, A. K., & Mareschal, D. (2022). Neural and Cognitive Underpinnings of Counterintuitive Science and Math Reasoning in Adolescence. *Journal of Cognitive Neuroscience*, *34*(7), 1205–1229. doi:10.1162/jocn_a_01854 PMID:35468204

Duncan, R. (2021). Cognitive processing in digital audio workstation composing. *General Music Today*. doi:10.1177/10483713211034441

Dwivedi, Y. K., Hughes, L., Ismagilova, E., Aarts, G., Coombs, C., Crick, T., Duan, Y., Dwivedi, R., Edwards, J., Eirug, A., Galanos, V., Ilavarasan, P. V., Janssen, M., Jones, P., Kar, A. K., Kizgin, H., Kronemann, B., Lal, B., Lucini, B., ... Williams, M. D. (2021). Artificial Intelligence (AI): Multidisciplinary perspectives on emerging challenges, opportunities, and agenda for research, practice and policy. *International Journal of Information Management*, *57*, 101994. doi:10.1016/j.ijinfomgt.2019.08.002

Dwivedi, Y. K., Ismagilova, E., Hughes, D. L., Carlson, J., Filieri, R., Jacobson, J., Jain, V., Karjaluoto, H., Kefi, H., Krishen, A. S., Kumar, V., Rahman, M. M., Raman, R., Rauschnabel, P. A., Rowley, J., Salo, J., Tran, G. A., & Wang, Y. (2021). Setting the future of digital and social media marketing research: Perspectives and research propositions. *International Journal of Information Management*, *59*, 102168. doi:10.1016/j.ijinfomgt.2020.102168

Dwork, C., & Ilvento, C. (2018). Fairness under composition. arXiv preprint arXiv:1806.06122.

Dwork, C., Hardt, M., Pitassi, T., Reingold, O., & Zemel, R. (2012, January). Fairness through awareness. In *Proceedings of the 3rd innovations in theoretical computer science conference* (pp. 214-226). 10.1145/2090236.2090255

Dyson, B. (2022). Assessing the replicability of Cognitive Psychology via remote experiential learning. Academic Press.

Elhai, J. D., Levine, J. C., Dvorak, R. D., & Hall, B. J. (2019). Fear of missing out, need for touch, anxiety, and depression are related to problematic smartphone use. *Computers in Human Behavior*, *63*, 509–516. doi:10.1016/j.chb.2016.05.079

Ellison, N. B., Steinfield, C., & Lampe, C. (2011). Connection strategies: Social capital implications of Facebook-enabled communication practices. *New Media & Society*, *13*(6), 873–892. doi:10.1177/1461444810385389

Elmqvist, N. (2023). Anywhere & everywhere: A mobile, immersive, and ubiquitous vision for data analytics. *arXiv preprint arXiv:2310.00768.*

Emmery, C., Kádár, Á., Wiltshire, T. J., & Hendrickson, A. T. (2019). Towards replication in computational cognitive modeling: A machine learning perspective. *Computational Brain & Behavior*, *2*(3-4), 242–246. doi:10.1007/s42113-019-00055-w

Enoiu, E., & Feldt, R. (2021, May). Towards human-like automated test generation: Perspectives from cognition and problem solving. In 2021 IEEE/ACM 13th International Workshop on Cooperative and Human Aspects of Software Engineering (CHASE) (pp. 123-124). IEEE.

Epley, N., & Gilovich, T. (2006). The anchoring-and-adjustment heuristic: Why the adjustments are insufficient. *Psychological Science*, *17*(4), 311–318. doi:10.1111/j.1467-9280.2006.01704.x PMID:16623688

Erfurth, C. (2019). The digital turn: on the quest for holistic approaches. In Distributed Computing and Internet Technology: 15th International Conference, ICDCIT 2019, Bhubaneswar, India, January 10–13, 2019 *Proceedings*, *15*, 24–30.

Etse, D., McMurray, A., & Muenjohn, N. (2021). Unleashing Innovation Across Ethical and Moral Boundaries: The Dark Side of Using Innovation for Self-Advantage. The Palgrave Handbook of Workplace Innovation, 521-542.

Evelina, L. (2023). Neural Networks and Deep Learning. doi:10.1007/978-981-19-8851-6_13-1

Eysenbach, G. (2011). Medical web 2.0: Patients, consumers, and the transformation of health care. *Journal of Medical Internet Research*, *13*(3), 175.

Fabrigar, L. R., Wegener, D. T., MacCallum, R. C., & Strahan, E. J. (2015). *Confirmatory factor analysis*. Guilford Press.

Facebook. (n.d.). Tools for Parents. Retrieved from https://www.facebook.com/safety/parents

Fanny, G. (2022). Ethical Evaluation. doi:10.1093/oso/9780192847263.003.0005

Fardouly, J., Diedrichs, P. C., Vartanian, L. R., & Halliwell, E. (2015). Social comparisons on social media: The impact of Facebook on young women's body image concerns and mood. *Body Image*, *13*, 38–45. doi:10.1016/j.bodyim.2014.12.002 PMID:25615425

Fatimah, A. T., Pramuditya, S. A., & Wahyudin, W. (2019, February). Imitative and creative reasoning for mathematical problem solving (in context horticultural agribusiness). *Journal of Physics: Conference Series*, *1157*(4), 042092. doi:10.1088/1742-6596/1157/4/042092

Favaretto, M., De Clercq, E., & Elger, B. S. (2019). Big Data and discrimination: Perils, promises and solutions. A systematic review. *Journal of Big Data*, *6*(1), 1–27. doi:10.1186/s40537-019-0177-4

Felzmann, H., Fosch-Villaronga, E., Lutz, C., & Tamò-Larrieux, A. (2020). Towards transparency by design for artificial intelligence. *Science and Engineering Ethics*, *26*(6), 3333–3361. doi:10.1007/s11948-020-00276-4 PMID:33196975

Ferguson, R. (2012). Learning analytics: Drivers, developments and challenges. *International Journal of Technology Enhanced Learning*, *4*(5-6), 304–317. doi:10.1504/IJTEL.2012.051816

Findlater, L., Goodman, S., Zhao, Y., Azenkot, S., & Hanley, M. (2020). Fairness issues in AI systems that augment sensory abilities. *ACM SIGACCESS Accessibility and Computing*, (125), 1–1. doi:10.1145/3386296.3386304

Finger, J. D., Mensink, G. B., Lange, C., & Manz, K. (2014). Health-enhancing physical activity during leisure time among adults in Germany. *Journal of Health Monitoring*, *1*(1), 35–41. PMID:37152092

Fisher, E. J. P., & Fisher, E. (2023). A Fresh Look at Ethical Perspectives on Artificial Intelligence Applications and their Potential Impacts at Work and on People. *Business and Economic Review*, *13*(3), 1–22.

Fisk, G. D., & Haase, S. J. (2020). Binary vs. continuous experimental designs for the study of unconscious perceptual processing. *Consciousness and Cognition*, *81*, 102933. doi:10.1016/j.concog.2020.102933 PMID:32315944

Fitzgibbon, B. M., Ward, J., & Enticott, P. G. (2014). The neural underpinnings of vicarious experience. *Frontiers in Human Neuroscience*, *8*, 384. doi:10.3389/fnhum.2014.00384 PMID:24917806

Fleck, F. (2016). The mysteries of type 2 diabetes in developing countries. World health organization. *Bulletin of the World Health Organization*, *94*(4), 241–242. doi:10.2471/BLT.16.030416 PMID:27034516

Floriana, F. (2022). Perceptual Relations in Digital Environments. *Foundations of Science*. Advance online publication. doi:10.1007/s10699-022-09853-1

Floridi, L., & Sanders, J. W. (2004). On the morality of artificial agents. *Minds and Machines, 14*(3), 349–379. doi:10.1023/B:MIND.0000035461.63578.9d

Følstad, A., & Brandtzæg, P. B. (2017). Chatbots and the new world of HCI. *Interactions, 24*(4), 38-42.

Freundschuh, S. M. (2009). Map perception and cognition. Academic Press.

From Consciousness of Quality to Quality of Consciousness. (2004). From Consciousness of Quality to Quality of Consciousness. *Journal of Human Values, 10*(1), iii–v. doi:10.1177/097168580401000101

Fukuda, K. (2020). Science, technology and innovation ecosystem transformation toward society 5.0. *International Journal of Production Economics, 220*, 107460. doi:10.1016/j.ijpe.2019.07.033

Garcia, M. B., Garcia, P. S., Maaliw, R. R., Lagrazon, P. G. G., Arif, Y. M., Ofosu-Ampong, K., . . . Vaithilingam, C. A. (2024). Technoethical Considerations for Advancing Health Literacy and Medical Practice: A Posthumanist Framework in the Age of Healthcare 5.0. In Emerging Technologies for Health Literacy and Medical Practice (pp. 1-19). IGI Global.

Garson, G. D. (2016). *Structural equation modeling: A basic guide with examples* (7th ed.). Routledge.

Gebru, T., Morgenstern, J., Vecchione, B., Vaughan, J. W., Wallach, H., Iii, H. D., & Crawford, K. (2021). Datasheets for datasets. *Communications of the ACM, 64*(12), 86–92. doi:10.1145/3458723

George, J. M. (2015). Emotions and leadership: The role of emotional intelligence. *Human Relations, 58*(11), 1355–1377.

Gigliotti, C. (1998). What is consciousness for? *Digital Creativity (Exeter), 9*(1), 33–37. doi:10.1080/14626269808567104

Glattfelder, J. B. (2019). *Information—Consciousness—Reality.* Springer. doi:10.1007/978-3-030-03633-1

Global Tuberculosis Report 2020, (n.d.). https://www.who.int/publications/i/item/9789240013131

Gobena, D. L. (2019). Human-Computer/Device Interaction. In Computer Architecture in Industrial, Biomechanical and Biomedical Engineering (p. 29). IntechOpen.

Goel, A., Sharma, R., & Mehta, K. (2022). *Corporate Governance and Firm Performance.* doi:10.4018/978-1-6684-5528-9.ch018

Good, D. J., Lyddy, C. J., Glomb, T. M., Bono, J. E., Brown, K. W., Duffy, M. K., Baer, R. A., Brewer, J. A., & Lazar, S. W. (2016). Contemplating Mindfulness at Work: An Integrative Review. *Journal of Management, 42*(1), 114–142. doi:10.1177/0149206315617003

Goodman, M. J., & Schorling, J. B. (2012). A mindfulness course decreases burnout and improves well-being among healthcare providers. *International Journal of Psychiatry in Medicine, 43*(2), 119–128. doi:10.2190/PM.43.2.b PMID:22849035

Gottfried, J., & Shearer, E. (2016). News Use Across Social Media Platforms 2016. Pew Research Center. Retrieved from https://www.journalism.org/2016/05/26/news-use-on-social-media-platforms-2016/

Grootaert, C., & Kanbur, R. (1995). Empowerment and Poverty Alleviation: A Comparative Analysis of Women's and Men's Participation in Squatter Settlements in Jordan. *World Development*, *23*(4), 585–598.

Gross, E. F., Juvonen, J., & Gable, S. L. (2002). Internet use and well-being in adolescence. *The Journal of Social Issues*, *58*(1), 75–90. doi:10.1111/1540-4560.00249

Grynszpan, O., Sahaï, A., Hamidi, N., Pacherie, E., Berberian, B., Roche, L., & Saint-Bauzel, L. (2019). The sense of agency in human-human vs human-robot joint action. *Consciousness and Cognition*, *75*, 102820. doi:10.1016/j.concog.2019.102820 PMID:31561189

Guo, L., Lu, Z., & Yao, L. (2021). Human-machine interaction sensing technology based on hand gesture recognition: A review. *IEEE Transactions on Human-Machine Systems*, *51*(4), 300–309. doi:10.1109/THMS.2021.3086003

Gu, Q., Tang, T. L., & Jiang, W. (2018). Does inspirational leadership facilitate change in the era of healthcare globalisation? The role of organisational identification. *Health Policy and Planning*, *33*(9), 1022–1034.

Haladjian, H. H., & Montemayor, C. (2016). Artificial consciousness and the consciousness-attention dissociation. *Consciousness and Cognition*, *45*, 210–225. doi:10.1016/j.concog.2016.08.011 PMID:27656787

Haleem, A., Javaid, M., Singh, R. P., Rab, S., & Suman, R. (2021). Hyperautomation for the enhancement of automation in industries. *Sensors International*, *2*, 100124. doi:10.1016/j.sintl.2021.100124

Hamilton, K. A., Yamashiro, J. K., & Storm, B. C. (2023). Special issue of applied cognitive psychology: Rethinking cognition in a digital environment. *Applied Cognitive Psychology*, *37*(4), 683–685. doi:10.1002/acp.4074

Hamlyn, D. W. (2022). *Sensation and perception: A history of the philosophy of perception*. Taylor & Francis. doi:10.4324/9781003316459

Hardt, M., Price, E., & Srebro, N. (2016). Equality of opportunity in supervised learning. *Advances in Neural Information Processing Systems*, ●●●, 29.

Harish, R., Khan, S. A., Ali, S., & Jain, V. (2013). Human computer interaction-a brief study. *International Journal of Management. IT and Engineering*, *3*(7), 390–401.

Harmon, J., & Duffy, L. (2023). Turn off to tune in: Digital disconnection, digital consciousness, and meaningful leisure. *Journal of Leisure Research*, *54*(5), 539–559. doi:10.1080/00222216.2023.2220699

Harris, T. (2019). How better tech could protect us from distraction? TED. Retrieved from https://www.ted.com/talks/tristan_harris_how_better_tech_could_protect_us_from_distraction

Hassija, V., Chamola, V., Mahapatra, A., Singal, A., Goel, D., Huang, K., Scardapane, S., Spinelli, I., Mahmud, M., & Hussain, A. (2024). Interpreting black-box models: A review on explainable artificial intelligence. *Cognitive Computation*, *16*(1), 45–74. doi:10.1007/s12559-023-10179-8

Häußermann, J. J., & Schroth, F. (2020). Aligning innovation and ethics: An approach to responsible innovation based on preference learning. *Philosophy of Management*, *19*(3), 349–364. doi:10.1007/s40926-019-00120-1

HelpGuide. (2023, February 23). Benefits of mindfulness. Harvard Health Publishing. Retrieved from https://www.helpguide.org/harvard/benefits-of-mindfulness.htm

Hermalin, B. E., & Weisbach, M. S. (2019). Understanding Corporate Governance Through Learning Models of Managerial Competence. *Asia-Pacific Journal of Financial Studies*, *48*(1), 7–29. doi:10.1111/ajfs.12243

Hess, T., Matt, C., Benlian, A., & Wiesböck, F. (2016). Options for formulating a digital transformation strategy. *MIS Quarterly Executive*, *15*(2), 123–139.

Hibberd, J., Swee Hong, C., & Boyle, L. (2010). Perception: Holistic assessment. *Nursing & Residential Care : the Monthly Journal for Care Assistants, Nurses and Managers Working in Health and Social Care*, *12*(7), 350–353. doi:10.12968/nrec.2010.12.7.48516

Hilbert, M. (2012). Toward a synthesis of cognitive biases: How noisy information processing can bias human decision making. *Psychological Bulletin*, *138*(2), 211–237. doi:10.1037/a0025940 PMID:22122235

Hildt, E. (2019). Artificial intelligence: Does consciousness matter? *Frontiers in Psychology*, *10*, 1535. Advance online publication. doi:10.3389/fpsyg.2019.01535 PMID:31312167

Hitt, M. A., Ireland, R. D., & Hoskisson, R. E. (2016). *Strategic management: Concepts and cases: Competitiveness and globalization*. Academic Press.

Hobbs, R. (2010). Digital and media literacy: A plan of action. The Aspen Institute. Retrieved from https://www.aspeninstitute.org/publications/digital-and-media-literacy-a-plan-of-...

Ho, C. W. L. (2022). Operationalizing "One Health" as "One Digital Health" through a global framework that emphasizes fair and equitable sharing of benefits from the use of artificial intelligence and related digital technologies. *Frontiers in Public Health*, *10*, 768977. doi:10.3389/fpubh.2022.768977 PMID:35592084

Hoffmann, M., & Hoffmann, M. (2020). Neuroanatomical and Neurophysiological Underpinnings of Cognition and Behavior: Cerebral Networks and Intrinsic Brain Networks. Clinical Mentation Evaluation: A Connectomal Approach to Rapid and Comprehensive Assessment, 11-19.

Hofmann, S. S., Sawyer, A. T., Witt, A. A., & Ohdo, S. (2010). The effect of mindfulness-based therapy on symptoms of depression: A meta-analytic review. Academic Press.

Hofmann, S. G., Sawyer, A. T., Witt, A. A., & Oh, D. O. (2010). The effect of mindfulness-based therapy on symptom reduction in depression and anxiety disorders: A meta-analysis. *Journal of Consulting and Clinical Psychology*. Advance online publication. doi:10.1037/a0018555

Hollnagel, E. (2001). From human factors to cognitive systems engineering: Human-machine interaction in the 21st Century. Academic Press.

Hounshell, B., Frenkel, S., Hsu, T., & Thomson, S. A. (2022, August 26). A journey into the misinformation fever swamps. The New York Times. https://www.nytimes.com/2022/08/26/us/politics/misinformation-social-media.html

Howard, P. N., & Hussain, M. M. (2013). *Democracy's fourth wave? Digital media and the Arab Spring*. Oxford University Press. doi:10.1093/acprof:oso/9780199936953.001.0001

Huang, T., Ma, L., Zhang, B., & Liao, H. (2023). Advances in deep learning: From diagnosis to treatment. *Bioscience Trends*, *17*(3), 190–192. doi:10.5582/bst.2023.01148 PMID:37394613

Ibrahim, M. (2017). Effects of internal control, corporate governance, organizational culture, and management audit on managerial performance: Evidence from Indonesia. *International Journal of Economic Perspectives*, *11*(3), 1826–1832.

Imhof, D., & Grivas, S. G. (2022, November). Holistic Digital Leadership and 20 Factors Relevant for its Understanding and Implementation. In ECMLG 2022 18th European Conference on Management, Leadership and Governance. Academic Conferences and Publishing Limited.

Implicit bias - StatPearls - NCBI bookshelf. (2023, March 4). National Center for Biotechnology Information. https://www.ncbi.nlm.nih.gov/books/NBK589697/

International Diabetes Federation. (2021) https://idf.org/about-diabetes/facts-figures/

Jamali, D., Safieddine, A. M., & Rabbath, M. (2008). Corporate governance and corporate social responsibility synergies and interrelationships. *Corporate Governance*, *16*(5), 443–459. doi:10.1111/j.1467-8683.2008.00702.x

Jasmine, M. (2021, May). How best to quantify replication success? A simulation study on the comparison of replication success metrics. *Royal Society Open Science*, *8*(5), 201697. Advance online publication. doi:10.1098/rsos.201697

Javaid, M., Haleem, A., Singh, R. P., & Suman, R. (2021). Substantial capabilities of robotics in enhancing industry 4.0 implementation. *Cognitive Robotics*, *1*, 58–75. doi:10.1016/j.cogr.2021.06.001

Jeffree, M. S., Ahmedy, F., Avoi, R., Ibrahim, M. Y., Rahim, S. S. S. A., Hayati, F., ... Tuah, N. M. (2020). Integrating digital health for healthcare transformation conceptual model of smart healthcare for northern borneo. *International Journal of Advanced Trends in Computer Science and Engineering*, *9*(1), 110–115. doi:10.30534/ijatcse/2020/17912020

Jennifer. (2023, June 29). Bias and fairness in artificial intelligence. New York State Bar Association. https://nysba.org/bias-and-fairness-in-artificial-intelligence/

Jensen, M., & Meckling, W. (2012). Theory of the firm: Managerial behavior, agency costs, and ownership structure. The Economic Nature of the Firm: A Reader, Third Edition, 283–303. doi:10.1017/CBO9780511817410.023

Jette, O. (2022, October 14). Learning and replaying spatiotemporal sequences: A replication study. *Frontiers in Integrative Neuroscience, 16*, 974177. Advance online publication. doi:10.3389/fnint.2022.974177

Jha, A. P., Klumpp, H., Rauschecker, J. P., & Weiskopf, D. (2015). Bringing focus back to front: The role of attention in enhancing the return of focused attention after an attentional lapse. *Neuropsychologia*.

Jobin, A., Ienca, M., & Vayena, E. (2019). The global landscape of AI ethics guidelines. *Nature Machine Intelligence, 1*(9), 389–399. doi:10.1038/s42256-019-0088-2

Jones, S., & Wilson, M. L. (2018). Social Media and Its Influence on the Development of Social Connectedness. In Handbook of Research on Cross-Cultural Business Education (pp. 95-123). IGI Global.

Jun, L., Chitipat, T., Siripen, P., & Kyoung-Sook, K. (2018). Towards Building a Human Perception Knowledge for Social Sensation Analysis. doi:10.1109/WI.2018.00-15

Kabat-Zinn, J., Massion, A., Hebert, J. R., & Rosenbaum, E. (1997). Meditation. International Journal of Holland.

Kabat-Zinn, J. (1990). *Full catastrophe living: Using the wisdom of your body and mind to face stress, pain and illness*. Delacorte Press.

Kabat-Zinn, J. (2003). Mindfulness-based interventions in context: Past, present, and future. *Clinical Psychology : a Publication of the Division of Clinical Psychology of the American Psychological Association, 10*(2), 144–156. doi:10.1093/clipsy.bpg016

Kabat-Zinn, J. (2005). *Wherever you go, there you are: Mindfulness meditation in everyday life*. Hyperion.

Kabat-Zinn, J. (2016). *Mindful way through depression: Reclaiming your life with the power of mindfulness and loving-kindness*. Guilford Publications.

Kabeer, N. (1999). Resources, Agency, Achievements: Reflections on the Measurement of Women's Empowerment. *Development and Change, 30*(3), 435–464. doi:10.1111/1467-7660.00125

Kameni, E. D., & Koumetio, S. C. T. (2023). The role of inclusive educational technologies in transforming African cities into inclusive smart cities. In *E3S Web of Conferences* (Vol. 418, p. 03003). EDP Sciences. doi:10.1051/e3sconf/202341803003

Kamiran, F., & Calders, T. (2012). Data preprocessing techniques for classification without discrimination. *Knowledge and Information Systems, 33*(1), 1–33. doi:10.1007/s10115-011-0463-8

Kapoor, M. (2023, May 4). Mindfulness: A Journey to the Present Moment. The Times of India. https://timesofindia.indiatimes.com/readersblog/thoughts-aloud/mindfulness-a-journey-to-the-present-moment-53390/

Karla, D., Pandey, V. K., Rastogi, P., & Kumar, S. (2022). A Comprehensive Review on Significance of Problem-Solving Abilities in Workplace. *World Journal of English Language*, *12*(3), 1–88. doi:10.5430/wjel.v12n3p88

Kaur, J. (2023, May). How is Robotic Process Automation Revolutionising the Way Healthcare Sector Works? In International Conference on Information, Communication and Computing Technology (pp. 1037-1055). Singapore: Springer Nature Singapore. 10.1007/978-981-99-5166-6_70

Kaur, J. (2024). Towards a Sustainable Triad: Uniting Energy Management Systems, Smart Cities, and Green Healthcare for a Greener Future. In Emerging Materials, Technologies, and Solutions for Energy Harvesting (pp. 258-285). IGI Global.

Kaur, D., Uslu, S., Rittichier, K. J., & Durresi, A. (2022). Trustworthy artificial intelligence: A review. *ACM Computing Surveys*, *55*(2), 1–38. doi:10.1145/3491209

Kaur, J. (2023). Robotic Process Automation in Healthcare Sector. In *E3S Web of Conferences* (Vol. 391, p. 01008). EDP Sciences.

Keeley, R., Jones, M. A., & Watkins, E. (2022). AI-augmented mindfulness for anxiety disorders: A feasibility study. *Journal of Anxiety Disorders*.

Keng, S. L., Soderstrom, S., & Smith, K. M. (2014). Mindfulness and acceptance-based interventions for anxiety disorders: A comparative meta-analysis. *Clinical Psychology & Psychotherapy*.

Ke, Q., Liu, J., Bennamoun, M., An, S., Sohel, F., & Boussaid, F. (2018). Computer vision for human–machine interaction. In *Computer Vision for Assistive Healthcare* (pp. 127–145). Academic Press. doi:10.1016/B978-0-12-813445-0.00005-8

Khan, M. (2023). Advancements in Artificial Intelligence: Deep Learning and Meta-Analysis. Academic Press.

Kim, B., Park, J., & Suh, J. (2020). Transparency and accountability in AI decision support: Explaining and visualizing convolutional neural networks for text information. *Decision Support Systems*, *134*, 113302. doi:10.1016/j.dss.2020.113302

Kim, K. J., Kim, J. Y., Kim, K. W., & Kim, J. H. (2021). How inspirational leadership enhances psychological capital: The moderating role of collectivism. *Leadership and Organization Development Journal*, *42*(3), 336–350. doi:10.1108/LODJ-02-2020-0072

Kim, S., Belfry, K. D., Crawford, J., MacDougall, A., & Kolla, N. J. (2023). COVID-19-related anxiety and the role of social media among Canadian youth. Front. *Psychiatry*.

Király, O., Potenza, M. N., Stein, D. J., King, D. L., Hodgins, D. C., Saunders, J. B., ... Demetrovics, Z. (2017). Preventing problematic internet use through video-based psychoeducation: A randomized controlled trial. *PLoS One, 12*(12), e0186459. PMID:29211728

KlapwijkE. T.van denBosW.TamnesC. K.MillsK. L.RaschleN. (2019). Opportunities for increased reproducibility and replicability of developmental cognitive neuroscience. PsyArXiv.

Klasen, S. (2019). Gender-Related Indicators of Well-Being. In D. Clark, M. Qizilbash, & A. Tomlinson (Eds.), *The Oxford Handbook of Well-Being and Public Policy* (pp. 287–304). Oxford University Press.

Kleinberg, J., Ludwig, J., Mullainathan, S., & Rambachan, A. (2018, May). Algorithmic fairness. In Aea papers and proceedings (Vol. 108, pp. 22-27). American Economic Association. doi:10.1257/pandp.20181018

Kleinberg, J., Lakkaraju, H., Leskovec, J., Ludwig, J., & Mullainathan, S. (2018). Human decisions and machine predictions. *The Quarterly Journal of Economics, 133*(1), 237–293. PMID:29755141

Knox, B. J., Sütterlin, S., & Lugo, R. (2023). Cognitive agility for improved understanding and self-governance: a human-centric AI enabler. In Handbook of Research on Artificial Intelligence, Innovation and Entrepreneurship (pp. 152-172). Edward Elgar Publishing. doi:10.4337/9781839106750.00019

Koch, C., Massimini, M., Boly, M., & Tononi, G. (2016). Neural correlates of consciousness: Progress and problems. *Nature Reviews. Neuroscience, 17*(5), 307–321. doi:10.1038/nrn.2016.22 PMID:27094080

Köchling, A., & Wehner, M. C. (2020). Discriminated by an algorithm: A systematic review of discrimination and fairness by algorithmic decision-making in the context of HR recruitment and HR development. *Business Research, 13*(3), 795–848. doi:10.1007/s40685-020-00134-w

Kokinov, B., & Petkov, G. (2009). Modeling Cued Recall and Memory Illusions as a Result of Structure Mapping. In Proceedings of the Annual Meeting of the Cognitive Science Society (Vol. 31, No. 31). Academic Press.

Kokshagina, O. (2021). Managing shifts to value-based healthcare and value digitalization as a multi-level dynamic capability development process. *Technological Forecasting and Social Change, 172*, 121072. doi:10.1016/j.techfore.2021.121072

Kotchoubey, B. (2018). Human consciousness: Where is it from and what is it for. *Frontiers in Psychology, 9*, 567. doi:10.3389/fpsyg.2018.00567 PMID:29740366

Kowalski, R. M., Giumetti, G. W., Schroeder, A. N., & Lattanner, M. R. (2014). Bullying in the digital age: A critical review and meta-analysis of cyberbullying research among youth. *Psychological Bulletin, 140*(4), 1073–1137. doi:10.1037/a0035618 PMID:24512111

Krasner, M. S., Epstein, R. M., Beckman, H., Suchman, A. L., Chapman, B., Mooney, C. J., & Quill, T. E. (2018). Mindfulness and empathy in healthcare settings: A systematic review and meta-analysis. *Journal of General Internal Medicine, 33*(1), 119–129.

Krishnapriya, K. S., Albiero, V., Vangara, K., King, M. C., & Bowyer, K. W. (2020). Issues related to face recognition accuracy varying based on race and skin tone. *IEEE Transactions on Technology and Society*, *1*(1), 8–20. doi:10.1109/TTS.2020.2974996

Król, K. (2021). Hardware Heritage—Briefcase-Sized Computers. *Heritage*, *4*(3), 2237–2252. doi:10.3390/heritage4030126

Kubalskyi. (2022). Ethics of responsibility in scientific research and innovation: a global and national perspective. Polìtologìčnij vìsnik, doi:10.17721/2415-881x.2022.88.12-21

Kübler, A. (2020). The history of BCI: From a vision for the future to real support for personhood in people with locked-in syndrome. *Neuroethics*, *13*(2), 163–180. doi:10.1007/s12152-019-09409-4

Kundi, B., El Morr, C., Gorman, R., & Dua, E. (2023). Artificial Intelligence and Bias: A scoping review. *AI & Society*, 199–215.

Kusner, M. J., Loftus, J., Russell, C., & Silva, R. (2017). Counterfactual fairness. *Advances in Neural Information Processing Systems*, 30.

Kuss, D. J., & Griffiths, M. D. (2011). Online social networking and addiction: A review of the psychological literature. *International Journal of Environmental Research and Public Health*, *8*(9), 3528–3552. doi:10.3390/ijerph8093528 PMID:22016701

Kuss, D. J., & Griffiths, M. D. (2017). Social networking sites and addiction: Ten lessons learned. *International Journal of Environmental Research and Public Health*, *14*(3), 311. doi:10.3390/ijerph14030311 PMID:28304359

Kvedar, J. C., Fogel, A. L., Elenk, E., & Zohar, D. (2016). Digital medicine's march on chronic disease. *Nature Biotechnology*, *34*(3), 239–246. doi:10.1038/nbt.3495 PMID:26963544

Kynoch, B., & Latapie, H. (2023). Recallm: An architecture for temporal context understanding and question answering. arXiv preprint arXiv:2307.02738.

Laato, S., Tiainen, M., Najmul Islam, A. K. M., & Mäntymäki, M. (2022). How to explain AI systems to end users: A systematic literature review and research agenda. *Internet Research*, *32*(7), 1–31. doi:10.1108/INTR-08-2021-0600

Langdon, R., & Coltheart, M. (2000). The cognitive neuropsychology of delusions. *Mind & Language*, *15*(1), 184–218. doi:10.1111/1468-0017.00129

Larcker, D. F., & Richardson, S. A. (2007). David F. Larcker. *The Accounting Review*, *82*(4), 963–1008. doi:10.2308/accr.2007.82.4.963

Lean, T. (2013). Mediating the microcomputer: The educational character of the 1980s British popular computing boom. *Public Understanding of Science (Bristol, England)*, *22*(5), 546–558. doi:10.1177/0963662512457904 PMID:23833169

LeCun, Y., Bengio, Y., & Hinton, G. (2015). Deep learning. *Nature*, *521*(7553), 436–444. doi:10.1038/nature14539 PMID:26017442

Lee, N. T., Resnick, P., & Barton, G. (2019). *Algorithmic bias detection and mitigation: Best practices and policies to reduce consumer harms.* Brookings Institute.

Leighton, J. P., & Sternberg, R. J. (2003). Reasoning and problem solving. *Experimental Psychology, 4,* 623–648.

Lembcke, T. B., Engelbrecht, N., Brendel, A. B., & Kolbe, L. M. (2019, June). To Nudge or not to Nudge: Ethical Considerations of Digital nudging based on its Behavioral Economics roots. ECIS.

Lenka, D. R. M. (2021). The impact of Emotional intelligence in the Digital Age. *Psychology (Savannah, Ga.), 58*(1), 1844–1852. doi:10.17762/pae.v58i1.1039

Levenson, J. C., Shensa, A., Sidani, J. E., Colditz, J. B., & Primack, B. A. (2017). The association between social media use and sleep disturbance among young adults. *Preventive Medicine, 85,* 36–41. doi:10.1016/j.ypmed.2016.01.001 PMID:26791323

Lichtenthaler, U. (2019). An intelligence-based view of firm performance: Profiting from artificial intelligence. *Journal of Innovation Management, 7*(1), 7–20. doi:10.24840/2183-0606_007.001_0002

Limani, Y., Hajrizi, E., & Stapleton, L. (2022). The Complexity of Business Process Digitalization and Organisational Challenges. *IFAC-PapersOnLine, 55*(39), 346–351. doi:10.1016/j.ifacol.2022.12.051

Lim, Y., Gardi, A., Sabatini, R., Ramasamy, S., Kistan, T., Ezer, N., Vince, J., & Bolia, R. (2018). Avionics human-machine interfaces and interactions for manned and unmanned aircraft. *Progress in Aerospace Sciences, 102,* 1–46. doi:10.1016/j.paerosci.2018.05.002

Linardatos, P., Papastefanopoulos, V., & Kotsiantis, S. (2020). Explainable ai: A review of machine learning interpretability methods. *Entropy (Basel, Switzerland), 23*(1), 18. doi:10.3390/e23010018 PMID:33375658

Lindsey, J., & Litwin-Kumar, A. (2022). Theory of systems memory consolidation via recall-gated plasticity. bioRxiv, 2022-12.

Lin, L. Y., Sidani, J. E., Shensa, A., Radovic, A., Miller, E., Colditz, J. B., Hoffman, B. L., Giles, L. M., & Primack, B. A. (2016). Association between social media use and depression among U.S. young adults. *Depression and Anxiety, 33*(4), 323–331. doi:10.1002/da.22466 PMID:26783723

Liu, D.-Y., Chen, S.-W., & Chou, T.-C. (2011). Resource fit in digital transformation: Lessons learned from the CBC Bank global e-banking project. *Management Decision, 49*(10), 1728–1742. doi:10.1108/00251741111183852

Lo Presti, L., Testa, M., Marino, V., & Singer, P. (2019). Engagement in healthcare systems: Adopting digital tools for a sustainable approach. *Sustainability (Basel), 11*(1), 220. doi:10.3390/su11010220

Lomas, T., Medina, J. C., Ivtzan, I., Rupprecht, S., Hart, R., & Eiroa-Orosa, F. J. (2017, April 19). The impact of mindfulness on well-being and performance in the workplace: An inclusive systematic review of the empirical literature. *European Journal of Work and Organizational Psychology*, *26*(4), 492–513. doi:10.1080/1359432X.2017.1308924

Lugrin, B. (2021). Introduction to socially interactive agents. In The Handbook on Socially Interactive Agents: 20 years of Research on Embodied Conversational Agents, Intelligent Virtual Agents, and Social Robotics Volume 1: Methods, Behavior, Cognition (pp. 1-20). doi:10.1145/3477322.3477324

Lu, J., Zheng, X., Schweiger, L., & Kiritsis, D. (2021). A cognitive approach to manage the complexity of digital twin systems. In *Smart Services Summit: Digital as an Enabler for Smart Service Business Development* (pp. 105–115). Springer International Publishing. doi:10.1007/978-3-030-72090-2_10

Luo, J., Li, S., Gong, L., Zhang, X., & Wang, S. (2022). How and when workplace ostracism influences employee deviant behavior: A self-determination theory perspective. *Frontiers in Psychology*, *13*, 1002399. doi:10.3389/fpsyg.2022.1002399 PMID:36329754

MacKenzie, I. S. (2024). Human-computer interaction: An empirical research perspective. Academic Press.

Maddula, R., MacLeod, J., Painter, S., McLeish, T., Steward, A., Rossman, A., Hamid, A., Ashwath, M., Martinez, H. R., Guha, A., Patel, B., Addison, D., Blaes, A., Choudhuri, I., & Brown, S. A. (2022). Connected Health Innovation Research Program (CHIRP): A bridge for digital health and wellness in cardiology and oncology. *American Heart Journal Plus : Cardiology Research and Practice*, *20*, 100192. doi:10.1016/j.ahjo.2022.100192 PMID:37800118

Mady, A., & Niese, B. (2022, June). Augmenting AI and Human Capabilities in Competency-Based Learning. In *Proceedings of the 2022 Computers and People Research Conference* (pp. 1-9). 10.1145/3510606.3550210

Magosso, E., & Ursino, M. (2023). The Sensory-Cognitive Interplay: Insights into Neural Mechanisms and Circuits. *Journal of Integrative Neuroscience*, *22*(1), 1–3. doi:10.31083/j.jin.2021.01.422 PMID:36722250

Malhotra, A., & DeGraff, D. S. (1997). Entry versus success in the labor force: Young women's employment in Sri Lanka. *World Development*, *25*(3), 379–394. doi:10.1016/S0305-750X(96)00114-3

Maltese, V. (2018). Digital Transformation Challenges for Universities: Ensuring Information Consistency Across Digital Services. *Cataloging & Classification Quarterly*, *56*(7), 592–606. doi:10.1080/01639374.2018.1504847

Mamina, R. I., & Piraynen, E. V. (2023). Emotional Artificial Intelligence as a Tool for Human-Machine Interaction. *Discourse (Berkeley, Calif.)*, *9*(2), 35–51.

Mao, J., Zhou, P., Wang, X., Yao, H., Liang, L., Zhao, Y., Zhang, J., Ban, D., & Zheng, H. (2023). A health monitoring system based on flexible triboelectric sensors for intelligence medical internet of things and its applications in virtual reality. *Nano Energy*, *118*, 108984. doi:10.1016/j.nanoen.2023.108984

Marchetti, G. (2018). Consciousness: A unique way of processing information. *Cognitive Processing*, *19*(3), 435–464. doi:10.1007/s10339-018-0855-8 PMID:29423666

Marcoulides, G. A. (2009). *Advanced structural equation modeling: Concepts, issues, and applications* (2nd ed.). Routledge.

Markham, A. (2021). The limits of the imaginary: Challenges to intervening in future speculations of memory, data, and algorithms. *New Media & Society*, *23*(2), 382–405. doi:10.1177/1461444820929322

Martynov, V. V., Shavaleeva, D. N., & Zaytseva, A. A. (2019). Information technology as the basis for transformation into a digital society and industry 5.0. In 2019 International Conference "Quality Management, Transport and Information Security, Information Technologies" (IT&QM&IS). IEEE.

Mattonen, S., Naqa, I. E., Hu, W., & Troost, E. (2022). "Evolving role of AI in radiation oncology"—special collection-introductory Editorial. BJRl Open, 4(1), 20229002.

Ma, Y., Zhang, L., & Wang, X. (2023, February). Natural language understanding and interaction engine oriented to human-computer interaction based on neural network. In *Third International Conference on Computer Vision and Data Mining (ICCVDM 2022)* (Vol. 12511, pp. 781-786). SPIE. 10.1117/12.2660383

Maynard, A. D., & Scragg, M. (2019). The ethical and responsible development and application of advanced brain machine interfaces. *Journal of Medical Internet Research*, *21*(10), e16321. doi:10.2196/16321 PMID:31674917

Mbunge, E., Muchemwa, B., & Batani, J. (2021). Sensors and healthcare 5.0: Transformative shift in virtual care through emerging digital health technologies. *Global Health Journal (Amsterdam, Netherlands)*, *5*(4), 169–177. doi:10.1016/j.glohj.2021.11.008

McGee, S. (2019). Changes in the Cognitive Dynamics of Problem-Solving. Academic Press.

McKinsey Global Institute. (2019). Digital India: Technology transform a connected nation. Author.

Mehl-Madrona, L. (2023). Expanding identity beyond the human. *Anthropology of Consciousness*. Advance online publication. doi:10.1111/anoc.12217

Mehta, S. (2022). A guide to different bias mitigation techniques in machine learning. Analytics India Magazine. https://analyticsindiamag.com/a-guide-to-different-bias-mitigation-techniques-in-machine-learning/

Melhart, D., Togelius, J., Mikkelsen, B., Holmgård, C., & Yannakakis, G. N. (2023). The Ethics of AI in Games. *IEEE Transactions on Affective Computing*.

Mihai, S., Yaqoob, M., Hung, D. V., Davis, W., Towakel, P., Raza, M., Karamanoglu, M., Barn, B., Shetve, D., Prasad, R. V., Venkataraman, H., Trestian, R., & Nguyen, H. X. (2022). Digital twins: A survey on enabling technologies, challenges, trends and future prospects. *IEEE Communications Surveys and Tutorials*, 24(4), 2255–2291. doi:10.1109/COMST.2022.3208773

Mikkilineni, R. (2022, April). Digital Consciousness: The Business of Sensing, Modeling, Analyzing, Predicting, and Taking Action. In Proceedings (Vol. 81, No. 1, p. 103). MDPI.

Minakov, V. F., Dyatlov, S. A., Lobanov, O. S., & Selishcheva, T. A. (2022, February). Cognitive Concept of the Analysis of Hype Processes in the Digital Economy. In International Scientific and Practical Conference Strategy of Development of Regional Ecosystems "Education-Science-Industry"(ISPCR 2021) (pp. 285-291). Atlantis Press. 10.2991/aebmr.k.220208.041

Minh, D., Wang, H. X., Li, Y. F., & Nguyen, T. N. (2022). Explainable artificial intelligence: A comprehensive review. *Artificial Intelligence Review*, 1–66.

Ministry of electronics and Information Technology, Government of India. (n.d.). Retrieved from https://www.mckinsey.com/~/media/mckinsey/business%20functions/mckinsey%20digital/our%20insights/digital%20india%20technology%20to%20transform%20a%20connected%20nation/digital-india-technology-to-transform-a-connected-nation-full-report.pdf

Mirriam, A. J., Rajashree, S., Muneera, M. N., Saranya, V., & Murali, E. (2022, October). Approaches to Overcome Human Limitations by an Intelligent Autonomous System with a Level of Consciousness in Reasoning, Decision Making and Problem-Solving Capabilities. In International Conference on Advanced Communication and Intelligent Systems (pp. 505-516). Cham: Springer Nature Switzerland.

Mishra, S. (2023, June 19). The Power of Mindfulness: Cultivating the Present Moment for a Balanced Life. LinkedIn. https://www.linkedin.com/pulse/power-mindfulness-cultivating-present-moment-balanced-mishra-/

Möhlmann, M., & Jarvenpaa, S. (2019). Cognitive challenges on digital exchange platforms: Exploring misspecifications of trust. Academic Press.

Monin, B., & Oppenheimer, D. M. (2014). The limits of direct replications and the virtues of stimulus sampling. Academic Press.

Morris, M. (2003). Ethical considerations in evaluation. In *International handbook of educational evaluation* (pp. 303–327). Springer Netherlands. doi:10.1007/978-94-010-0309-4_19

Morsch, P. (2022). Capabilities And Competences For Strategic Decision Making In Digital World. 35th Bled eConference Digital Restructuring and Human (Re) action, 759.

Mosedale, S., Heissler, K., & Groppo, V. (2012). *Getting the Full Picture: Gender Responsive Budget Analysis in Practice*. UN Women.

Mourtzis, D., Angelopoulos, J., & Panopoulos, N. (2022). A Literature Review of the Challenges and Opportunities of the Transition from Industry 4.0 to Society 5.0. *Energies*, 15(17), 6276. doi:10.3390/en15176276

Mourtzis, D., Angelopoulos, J., & Panopoulos, N. (2023). Blockchain Integration in the Era of Industrial Metaverse. (2022). *Applied Sciences (Basel, Switzerland), 13*(3), 1353. doi:10.3390/app13031353

Mourtzis, D., Angelopoulos, J., & Panopoulos, N. (2023). The Future of the Human–Machine Interface (HMI) in Society 5.0. *Future Internet, 15*(5), 162. doi:10.3390/fi15050162

Muise, A., Christofides, E., & Desmarais, S. (2009). More Information than You Ever Wanted: Does Facebook Bring Out the Green-Eyed Monster of Jealousy? *Cyberpsychology & Behavior, 12*(4), 441–444. doi:10.1089/cpb.2008.0263 PMID:19366318

Mukherjee, D., Gupta, K., Chang, L. H., & Najjaran, H. (2022). A survey of robot learning strategies for human-robot collaboration in industrial settings. *Robotics and Computer-integrated Manufacturing, 73*, 102231. doi:10.1016/j.rcim.2021.102231

Muradchanian, J., Hoekstra, R., Kiers, H., & van Ravenzwaaij, D. (2023). Evaluating meta-analysis as a replication success measure. Academic Press.

Mwita, M. M., & Joanthan, J. (2019). Digital leadership for digital transformation. *Electronic Scientific Journal, 10*(4), 2082–2677.

N. (2018). *Human decisions*. UNESCO Publishing.

Naaz, F., Ahmad, F., & Kumar, S. (2018). Rural Women Empowerment: Issues, Challenges, and Opportunities. *Journal of Rural Studies and Development, 77*(1), 113–120.

Nadal, C., Sas, C., & Doherty, G. (2020). Technology Acceptance in mobile health: Scoping Review of Defination, Models and Measurement. Journal of Medical Interne. Retrieved from https://www.ncbi.nlm.nih.gov/pmc/articles/PMC7381045/

Nagireddi, J. N., Vyas, A. K., Sanapati, M. R., Soin, A., & Manchikanti, L. (2022). The analysis of pain research through the lens of artificial intelligence and machine learning. *Pain Physician, 25*(2), E211. PMID:35322975

Najibi, A. (2020). Racial discrimination in face recognition technology. *Science News*, 24.

Narayanan, A. (2023). Machine Ethics and Cognitive Robotics. *Current Robotics Reports*, 1–9.

Neethirajan, S. (2023). Artificial Intelligence and Sensor Innovations: Enhancing Livestock Welfare with a Human-Centric Approach. *Human-Centric Intelligent Systems*, 1-16.

Nelson, T. O. (2000). Consciousness, Self-Consciousness, and Metacognition. *Consciousness and Cognition, 9*(2), 220–223. doi:10.1006/ccog.2000.0439 PMID:10924241

Ness, S., Shepherd, N. J., & Xuan, T. R. (2023). Synergy Between A.I. and Robotics: A Comprehensive Integration. *Asian Journal of Research in Computer Science, 16*(4), 80–94. doi:10.9734/ajrcos/2023/v16i4372

Nielsen. (2018). Total audience report: Q1 2018. Nielsen. Retrieved from https://www.nielsen.com/us/en/insights/report/2018/total-audience-report-q1-2018/

Nikolopoulou, K. (2023, March 6). *The availability heuristic | Example & definition*. Scribbr. https://www.scribbr.com/research-bias/availability-heuristic/

Nilsen, W., Skipstein, A., & Demerouti, E. (2016, November 8). Adverse trajectories of mental health problems predict subsequent burnout and work-family conflict – a longitudinal study of employed women with children followed over 18 years. *BMC Psychiatry*, *16*(1), 384. Advance online publication. doi:10.1186/s12888-016-1110-4 PMID:27825325

Nobandegani, A. S., Shultz, T. R., & Rish, I. (2022). Cognitive Models as Simulators: The Case of Moral Decision-Making. arXiv preprint arXiv:2210.04121.

Nooney, L. (2023). *The Apple II Age: How the Computer Became Personal*. University of Chicago Press. doi:10.7208/chicago/9780226816531.001.0001

Norda, M., Engel, C., Rennies, J., Appell, J. E., Lange, S. C., & Hahn, A. (2023). Evaluating the Efficiency of Voice Control as Human Machine Interface in Production. *IEEE Transactions on Automation Science and Engineering*.

Nordbø, I. (2022). Female entrepreneurs and path-dependency in rural tourism. *Journal of Rural Studies*, *96*, 198–206. doi:10.1016/j.jrurstud.2022.09.032

Noriega, P., Padget, J., Verhagen, H., & D'Inverno, M. (2014). The challenge of artificial socio-cognitive systems. Academic Press.

Nowruzi, S., Shokouhyar, S., Dehghan, O., Nezafati, N., & Shokoohyar, S. (2023). A human-machine interaction framework for identifying factors influential consumer participation in e-waste treatment schemes. *International Journal of Computer Integrated Manufacturing*, *36*(7), 1–25. doi:10.1080/0951192X.2022.2162598

Ntoutsi, E., Fafalios, P., Gadiraju, U., Iosifidis, V., Nejdl, W., Vidal, M. E., Ruggieri, S., Turini, F., Papadopoulos, S., Krasanakis, E., Kompatsiaris, I., Kinder-Kurlanda, K., Wagner, C., Karimi, F., Fernandez, M., Alani, H., Berendt, B., Kruegel, T., Heinze, C., ... Staab, S. (2020). Bias in data-driven artificial intelligence systems—An introductory survey. *Wiley Interdisciplinary Reviews. Data Mining and Knowledge Discovery*, *10*(3), e1356. doi:10.1002/widm.1356

O'Donovan, R., Loughnane, C., Donnelly, J., Kelly, R., Kemp, D., McCarthy, L., Offiah, G., Sweeney, A., Duggan, A. P., & Dunne, P. J. (2024). Healthcare workers' experience of a coach-led digital platform for better well-being. *Coaching (Abingdon, UK)*, 1–19. doi:10.1080/17521882.2024.2304793

Oberst, U., Wegmann, E., Stodt, B., Brand, M., & Chamarro, A. (2017). Negative consequences from heavy social networking in adolescents: The mediating role of fear of missing out. *Journal of Adolescence*, *55*(1), 51–60. doi:10.1016/j.adolescence.2016.12.008 PMID:28033503

Olbrich, S., Frank, U., Gregor, S., Niederman, F., & Rowe, F. (2017). On the merits and limits of replication and negation for IS research. *AIS Transactions on Replication Research*, *3*(1), 1–19. doi:10.17705/1atrr.00016

Oliff, H., Liu, Y., Kumar, M., & Williams, M. (2018). A framework of integrating knowledge of human factors to facilitate HMI and collaboration in intelligent manufacturing. *Procedia CIRP, 72*, 135–140. doi:10.1016/j.procir.2018.03.047

Olson, G. M., & Olson, J. S. (2012). Collaboration technologies. *Human Computer Interaction Handbook: Fundamentals, Evolving Technologies, and Emerging Applications,* 549-564.

Omrani, N., Rivieccio, G., Fiore, U., Schiavone, F., & Agreda, S. G. (2022). To trust or not to trust? An assessment of trust in AI-based systems: Concerns, ethics and contexts. *Technological Forecasting and Social Change, 181*, 121763. doi:10.1016/j.techfore.2022.121763

Orange, E. (2013). Understanding the human-machine interface in a time of change. In Handbook of Research on Technoself: Identity in a Technological Society (pp. 703-719). IGI Global. doi:10.4018/978-1-4666-2211-1.ch036

Oritsegbemi, O. (2023). Human Intelligence versus AI: Implications for Emotional Aspects of Human Communication. *Journal of Advanced Research in Social Sciences, 6*(2), 76–85. doi:10.33422/jarss.v6i2.1005

Orlandi, N. (2023). The Modularity vs. Malleability of Perception: A Red Herring. *Journal of Consciousness Studies, 30*(3), 202–211. doi:10.53765/20512201.30.3.202

Osoba, O. A., Welser, I. V. W., & Welser, W. (2017). *An intelligence in our image: The risks of bias and errors in artificial intelligence.* Rand Corporation.

Ott, B. L. (2023). The Digital Mind: How Computers (Re)Structure Human Consciousness. *Philosophies, 8*(1), 4. doi:10.3390/philosophies8010004

Overby, S. (2019). Digital transformation dream teams: 8 people you need. The Enterprisers Project. Retrieved from https://enterprisersproject.com/article/2019/12/digital-transformation-teams-8-key-roles

Özarslan, Z. (2022). A Critical Debate on the Political Economy of Digital Memory. *Galatasaray Üniversitesi İletişim Dergisi,* (37), 164–186. doi:10.16878/gsuilet.1167144

Palaiogeorgou, P., Gizelis, C. A., Misargopoulos, A., Nikolopoulos-Gkamatsis, F., Kefalogiannis, M., & Christonasis, A. M. (2021, August). AI: Opportunities and challenges-The optimal exploitation of (telecom) corporate data. In Conference on e-Business, e-Services and e-Society (pp. 47-59). Cham: Springer International Publishing.

Pandey, A., Panday, S. P., & Joshi, B. (2023). Design and development of applications using human-computer interaction. In *Innovations in Artificial Intelligence and Human-Computer Interaction in the Digital Era* (pp. 255–293). Academic Press. doi:10.1016/B978-0-323-99891-8.00011-5

Pandey, P., Choubey, A. K., & Rai, G. (2021). The involvement of women as the domestic decision maker: A study of Patna Metropolitan City, Bihar, India. *Sociedade & Natureza, 33*, e62053. doi:10.14393/SN-v33-2021-62053

Park, S. Y., & Kim, Y. G. (2007). The effects of organizational, individual, and technological factors on ERP adoption in a Korean service industry. *International Journal of Electronic Commerce, 12*(1), 107–134.

Park, S., Kim, H. K., Lee, Y., & Park, J. (2023). Kiosk accessibility challenges faced by people with disabilities: An analysis of domestic and international accessibility laws/guidelines and user focus group interviews. *Universal Access in the Information Society*, 1–17. doi:10.1007/s10209-023-01028-4

Parpart, J. L., Connelly, P., & Barriteau, E. (Eds.). (2000). *Theoretical perspectives on gender and development*. IDRC.

Patel, S. C., & Fan, J. (2023). Identification and Description of Emotions by Current Large Language Models. bioRxiv, 2023-07. doi:10.1101/2023.07.17.549421

Patel, N., Burt, J., & Gonzalez, F. (2019). The Role of Development Programs in Women's Empowerment: A Review of Evidence from South Asia. *Journal of South Asian Development, 14*(3), 350–376.

Patel, N., & Trivedi, S. (2020). *Leveraging Predictive Modeling, Machine Learning Personalization, NLP Customer Support, and A.I. Chatbots to Increase Customer Loyalty*. Empirical.

Pavitra, A. R. R., Anushree, K., Akshayalakshmi, A. V. R., & Vijayalakshmi, K. (2023, May). Artificial Intelligence (AI) Enabled Music Player System for User Facial Recognition. In 2023 4th International Conference for Emerging Technology (INCET) (pp. 1-4). IEEE.

Pawłowska, J., Rydzewska, K., & Wierzbicki, A. (2023). Using cognitive models to understand and counteract the effect of self-induced bias on recommendation algorithms. *Journal of Artificial Intelligence and Soft Computing Research, 13*(2), 73–94. doi:10.2478/jaiscr-2023-0008

Penders, B., Holbrook, J. B., & de Rijcke, S. (2019). Rinse and repeat: Understanding the value of replication across different ways of knowing. *Publications / MDPI, 7*(3), 52. doi:10.3390/publications7030052

Pennycook, G., & Rand, D. G. (2019). The Implied Truth Effect: Attaching Warnings to a Subset of Fake News Stories Increases Perceived Accuracy of Stories Without Warnings. *Management Science, 66*(11), 4944–4957. doi:10.1287/mnsc.2019.3478

Perloff, R. M. (2014). Social media effects on young women's body image concerns: Theoretical perspectives and an agenda for research. *Sex Roles, 71*(11-12), 363–377. doi:10.1007/s11199-014-0384-6

Petchsawang, P., & Duchon, D. (2009). Measuring workplace spirituality in an Asian context. *Human Resource Development International, 12*(4), 459–468. doi:10.1080/13678860903135912

Peter, R. (2005). Models of Cognition: Neurological possibility does not indicate neurological plausibility. Academic Press.

Pew Research Center. (2021). 15% of U.S. Adults Have Used Online Dating Sites or Mobile Dating Apps. Author.

Pfaltz, J. L. (2017, April). Computational processes that appear to model human memory. In *International Conference on Algorithms for Computational Biology* (pp. 85-99). Cham: Springer International Publishing. 10.1007/978-3-319-58163-7_6

Pierce, R., Sterckx, S., & Van Biesen, W. (2022). A riddle, wrapped in a mystery, inside an enigma: How semantic black boxes and opaque artificial intelligence confuse medical decision-making. *Bioethics, 36*(2), 113–120. doi:10.1111/bioe.12924 PMID:34374441

Pizlo, Z. (2022). *Problem Solving: Cognitive Mechanisms and Formal Models*. Cambridge University Press. doi:10.1017/9781009205603

Plewczynski, D. (2011). Modeling of Cognitive Agents. Academic Press.

Poynor, R. (2023). Personal Reflections on Technologies and the Study of African Art. *African Arts, 56*(4), 1-7.

Pranay Kumar, P. (2021). Human consciousness and artificial intelligence: Can AI develop human-like consciousness? Cognitive abilities? What about Ethics? SSRN *Electronic Journal*. doi:10.2139/ssrn.3786957

Prashant, T. (2023). Digital health adoption in India: opportunities and challenges. Retrieved from https://timesofindia.indiatimes.com/blogs/voices/digital-health-adoption-in-india-opportunities-and-challenges/

Prashanth, C. V., Wang, J., Wu, S., & Chen, H. (2017). T Challenges and opportunities for digital health adoption. *Systematic Reviews*.

Pratt, M. (2023, March 8). *Women Are Leaders of Mindfulness at Work—Here's Why*. Mindful. https://www.mindful.org/women-are-leaders-of-mindfulness-at-work-heres-why/

Primack, B. A., Shensa, A., Sidani, J. E., Whaite, E. O., Lin, L. Y., Rosen, D., ... Colditz, J. B. (2017). Social media use and perceived social isolation among young adults in the U.S. *PLoS One, 12*(8), e0182145. PMID:28832594

Prodan, A. C. (2013). The digital" Memory of the World": an exploration of documentary practices in the age of digital technology (Doctoral dissertation, BTU Cottbus-Senftenberg).

Prodger, B. (2020, September 30). Gen Z's Approach To Wellbeing. Stress Matters. https://stressmatters.org.uk/gen-zs-approach-to-wellbeing/

Puccio, G. J., Klarman, B., & Szalay, P. A. (2023). Creative Problem-Solving. In *The Palgrave Encyclopedia of the Possible* (pp. 298–313). Springer International Publishing.

Purchase, V., Parry, G., Valerdi, R., Nightingale, D., & Mills, J. (2011). Enterprise transformation: Why are we interested, what is it, and what are the challenges? *Journal of Enterprise Transformation, 1*(1), 14–33. doi:10.1080/19488289.2010.549289

Pushpakumar, R., Sanjaya, K., Rathika, S., Alawadi, A. H., Makhzuna, K., Venkatesh, S., & Rajalakshmi, B. (2023). Human-Computer Interaction: Enhancing User Experience in Interactive Systems. In E3S Web of Conferences (Vol. 399, p. 04037). EDP Sciences.

Pvs, H.PVS. (2018, November 19). Work Related Stress: A Literature Review. *Annals of Social Sciences & Management Studies, 2*(3). Advance online publication. doi:10.19080/ASM.2018.02.555586

Quartarone, V. (2021). *Wearable HMI definition, development and validation for collaborative environment in industrial processes in the context of Industry 4.0* (Doctoral dissertation, Politecnico di Torino).

Quisumbing, A., Cole, S., Elias, M., Faas, S., Galiè, A., Malapit, H., Meinzen-Dick, R., Myers, E., Seymour, G., & Twyman, J. (2023). Measuring women's empowerment in agriculture: Innovations and evidence. *Global Food Security, 38*, 100707. doi:10.1016/j.gfs.2023.100707 PMID:37752898

Raffegeau, T. E., Young, W. R., Fino, P. C., & Williams, A. M. (2023). A perspective on using virtual reality to incorporate the affective context of everyday falls into fall prevention. *JMIR Aging, 6*, e36325. doi:10.2196/36325 PMID:36630173

Rahul, M., & Ouarbya, L. (2023). Emotion Recognition Using. *Artificial Intelligence.*

Rajaraman, V. (2014). JohnMcCarthy—Father of artificial intelligence. *Resonance, Springer, 19*, 198–207.

Rana, P., & Roy, V. (2015). Generic medicines: Issues and relevance for global health. *Fundamental & Clinical Pharmacology, 29*(6), 529–542. doi:10.1111/fcp.12155 PMID:26405851

Rane, N. (2023). Enhancing customer loyalty through Artificial Intelligence (A.I.), Internet of Things (IoT), and Big Data technologies: improving customer satisfaction, engagement, relationship, and experience. *Internet of Things (IoT), and Big Data Technologies: Improving Customer Satisfaction, Engagement, Relationship, and Experience.*

Rane, N. (2023). Transformers in Industry 4.0, Industry 5.0, and Society 5.0: Roles and Challenges. Academic Press.

Rao, P. V. S., & Kopparapu, S. K. (2018). *Friendly Interfaces Between Humans and Machines.* Springer. doi:10.1007/978-981-13-1750-7

Rapp, A. (2023). Human–Computer Interaction. Oxford Research Encyclopedia of Psychology.

Rath, K. C., Khang, A., & Roy, D. (2024). The Role of Internet of Things (IoT) Technology in Industry 4.0 Economy. In Advanced IoT Technologies and Applications in the Industry 4.0 Digital Economy (pp. 1-28). CRC Press.

Reb, J., Chaturvedi, S., Narayanan, J., & Kudesia, R. S. (2019). Leader Mindfulness and Employee Performance: A Sequential Mediation Model of LMX Quality, Interpersonal Justice, and Employee Stress. *Journal of Business Ethics, 160*(3), 745–763. doi:10.1007/s10551-018-3927-x

Reb, J., Narayanan, J., & Chaturvedi, S. (2014). Leading Mindfully: Two Studies on the Influence of Supervisor Trait Mindfulness on Employee Well-Being and Performance. *Mindfulness*, *5*(1), 36–45. doi:10.1007/s12671-012-0144-z

Reshi, I. A., & Sudha, T. (2022). Women Empowerment: A Literature Review. *International Journal of Economic, Business, Accounting Agriculture Management and Sharia Administration*, *2*(6), 1353–1359.

Revonsuo, A. (2017). *Foundations of Consciousness*. Routledge. doi:10.4324/9781315115092

Robert, K. (2007). Computational Aspects of Cognition and Consciousness in Intelligent Devices. *IEEE Computational Intelligence Magazine*, *2*(3), 53–64. doi:10.1109/MCI.2007.385369

Roberts, J. A., & David, M. E. (2016). My life has become a major distraction from my cell phone: Partner phubbing and relationship satisfaction among romantic partners. *Computers in Human Behavior*, *54*, 134–141. doi:10.1016/j.chb.2015.07.058

Robinson, L. (2023, March 29). Social Media and Mental Health. HelpGuide.org. https://www.helpguide.org/articles/mental-health/social-media-and-mental-health.htm#:~:text=Since%20it's%20a%20relatively%20new,harm%2C%20and%20even%20suicidal%20thoughts

Rogers, Y. (2009). The changing face of human-computer interaction in the age of ubiquitous computing. In *HCI and Usability for e-Inclusion: 5th Symposium of the Workgroup Human-Computer Interaction and Usability Engineering of the Austrian Computer Society, USAB 2009, Linz, Austria, November 9-10, 2009 Proceedings 5* (pp. 1-19). Springer Berlin Heidelberg. 10.1007/978-3-642-10308-7_1

Rose, C. (2016). Firm performance and comply or explain disclosure in corporate governance. *European Management Journal*, *34*(3), 202–222. doi:10.1016/j.emj.2016.03.003

Roslan, F. A. B. M., & Ahmad, N. B. (2023). The rise of AI-powered voice assistants: Analyzing their transformative impact on modern customer service paradigms and consumer expectations. *Quarterly Journal of Emerging Technologies and Innovations*, *8*(3), 33–64.

Rozgonjuk, D., Saal, K., & Täht, K. (2018). Problematic social media use and depression symptoms among adolescents: A longitudinal study. *Journal of Adolescence*, *65*, 73–82.

Ruan, Z. (2023). The fundamental challenge of a future theory of consciousness. *Frontiers in Psychology*, *13*, 1029105. doi:10.3389/fpsyg.2022.1029105 PMID:36710768

Rudrauf, D., Sergeant-Perhtuis, G., Tisserand, Y., Monnor, T., De Gevigney, V., & Belli, O. (2023). Combining the projective consciousness model and virtual humans for immersive psychological research: A proof-of-concept simulating a TOM assessment. *ACM Transactions on Interactive Intelligent Systems*, *13*(2), 1–31. doi:10.1145/3583886

Ruginski, I. T. (2020). Ethical conceptual replication of visualization research considering sources of methodological bias and practical significance. arXiv preprint arXiv:2009.12152.

Russill, C. L. (2023). Oblivious and uninformed: the role of overconfidence in personal health decision-making (Doctoral dissertation, Faculty of Arts, University of Regina).

Ryan, T., & Chester, A. (2015). Fear of missing out and the relationship between frequency of Facebook use, exposure to Facebook use (via social comparison) and Facebook addiction. *Computers in Human Behavior, 44*, 64–80.

Saha, S., Mamun, K. A., Ahmed, K., Mostafa, R., Naik, G. R., Darvishi, S., Khandoker, A. H., & Baumert, M. (2021). Progress in brain-computer interface: Challenges and opportunities. *Frontiers in Systems Neuroscience, 15*, 578875. doi:10.3389/fnsys.2021.578875 PMID:33716680

Saini, H. S., & Daruwala, R. D. (2016, August). Human machine interface in internet of things system. In *2016 International conference on computing communication control and automation (ICCUBEA)* (pp. 1-4). IEEE. 10.1109/ICCUBEA.2016.7860151

Salehi, M., Ammar Ajel, R., & Zimon, G. (2023). The relationship between corporate governance and financial reporting transparency. *Journal of Financial Reporting and Accounting, 21*(5), 1049–1072. doi:10.1108/JFRA-04-2021-0102

Sá, M. J., Santos, A. I., Serpa, S., & Miguel, F. C. (2021). Digitainability—Digital competences post-COVID-19 for a sustainable society. *Sustainability (Basel), 13*(17), 9564. doi:10.3390/su13179564

Samsonovich, A. V. (2013, November). Modeling human emotional intelligence in virtual agents. *2013 AAAI Fall Symposium Series.*

Sanders, N. R., & Wood, J. D. (2019). *The Humachine: Humankind, Machines, and the Future of Enterprise.* Routledge. doi:10.4324/9780429001178

Sandu, A. (2019). Towards a phenomenology of the digitalization of consciousness. The virtualization of the social space. *Postmodern Openings, 10*(2), 155–161. doi:10.18662/po/77

Saracini, C. (2022). Perceptual Awareness and Its Relationship with Consciousness: Hints from Perceptual Multistability. *NeuroSci, 3*(4), 546–557. doi:10.3390/neurosci3040039

Sathi, S. (2023, September). Marriage murders and anti-caste feminist politics in India. In *Women's Studies International Forum* (Vol. 100, p. 102816). Pergamon. 10.1016/j.wsif.2023.102816

Sati, P., & Thompson, R. W. (2009). *The investigation of attention: A cognitive neuroscience perspective.* Psychology Press.

Satpathy, I., & Mitra, B. (2015, August). Stress at workplaces: Overview. Research Gate. https://www.researchgate.net/publication/282270203_Stress_at_Workplaces-_An_overview

Scatiggio, V. (2022). Tackling the issue of bias in artificial intelligence to design AI-driven fair and inclusive service systems. *How human biases are breaching into AI algorithms, with severe impacts on individuals and societies, and what designers can do to face this phenomenon and change for the better.*

Schäfer, A., Reis, G., & Stricker, D. (2022). A Survey on Synchronous Augmented, Virtual, andMixed Reality Remote Collaboration Systems. *ACM Computing Surveys*, *55*(6), 1–27. doi:10.1145/3533376

Schmidt, T. (2019). Successful Digital Transformation Begins with a Cultural Transformation. The Data-Driven Enterprise. Retrieved from https://www.cio.com/article/3402022/successful-digital- transformation-begins with-a-cultural-transformation.html

Schmidt, P., Biessmann, F., & Teubner, T. (2020). Transparency and trust in artificial intelligence systems. *Journal of Decision Systems*, *29*(4), 260–278. doi:10.1080/12460125.2020.1819094

Schmidt, S. N., Hass, J., Kirsch, P., & Mier, D. (2021). The human mirror neuron system—A common neural basis for social cognition? *Psychophysiology*, *58*(5), e13781. doi:10.1111/psyp.13781 PMID:33576063

Schoenherr, J. R. (2022). *Ethical Artificial Intelligence from Popular to Cognitive Science: Trust in the Age of Entanglement*. Taylor & Francis. doi:10.4324/9781003143284

Schutte, N. S., Malouff, J. M., Hall, L. E., Haggerty, D. J., Cooper, J. T., Golden, C. J., & Dornheim, L. (1998). Development and Validation of Emotional Intelligence. *Personality and Individual Differences*, *25*(2), 167–177. doi:10.1016/S0191-8869(98)00001-4

Schwartz, R., Vassilev, A., Greene, K., Perine, L., Burt, A., & Hall, P. (2022). Towards a standard for identifying and managing bias in artificial intelligence. NIST special publication, 1270(10.6028).

Schwemmer, C., Knight, C., Bello-Pardo, E. D., Oklobdzija, S., Schoonvelde, M., & Lockhart, J. W. (2020). Diagnosing gender bias in image recognition systems. *Socius: Sociological Research for a Dynamic World*, *6*, 2378023120967171. doi:10.1177/2378023120967171 PMID:35936509

Seitz, M., & Vogel-Heuser, B. (2020, October). Challenges for the digital transformation of development processes in engineering. In *IECON 2020 The 46th Annual Conference of the IEEE Industrial Electronics Society* (pp. 4345-4350). IEEE. 10.1109/IECON43393.2020.9254771

Sen, A. (1999). *Development as Freedom*. Anchor Books.

Seth, G. (2017). The phenomenology of Angry Birds: Virtual gravity and distributed proprioception in video game worlds. Journal of Gaming & Virtual Worlds. doi:10.1386/jgvw.9.3.207_1

Shapiro, S. L., Carlson, L. E., Astin, J. A., & Freedman, B. (2006). Mechanisms of action and clinical benefits of mindfulness-based stress reduction (MBSR). *Journal of Consulting and Clinical Psychology*.

Sharafat, H. (2021). Multisensory Digital Experiences: Integrating New Interactive Technologies With Human Senses. . doi:10.4018/978-1-7998-8327-2.ch022

Sharma, P. K., & Kumra, R. (2022). Relationship between mindfulness, depression, anxiety and stress: Mediating role of self-efficacy. *Personality and Individual Differences*, *186*, 111363. Advance online publication. doi:10.1016/j.paid.2021.111363

Shrivastava, R., Kumar, P., & Tripathi, S. (2020). A Human Memory Process Modeling. *Recent Patents on Engineering, 14*(2), 179–193. doi:10.2174/1872212113666190211145444

Shruthi, R. (2023). Human Consciousness and Artificial Intelligence: Can AI Develop Human-Like Consciousness? Cognitive Abilities? What about Ethics? SSRN *Electronic Journal*. doi:10.2139/ssrn.4333023

Signorelli, C. M. (2018). Can computers become conscious and overcome humans? *Frontiers in Robotics and AI, 5*, 121. Advance online publication. doi:10.3389/frobt.2018.00121 PMID:33501000

Silvestri, F. (2019). Su alcuni riflessi cognitivi nel tempo online delle nuove forme della comunicazione/informazione governate dagli algoritmi. Note e appunti per una ricerca. *ECHO*, (1), 65–76.

Singhal, S., Sinha, A., & Singh, B. (2022). Context awareness for healthcare service delivery with intelligent sensors. Frontiers of Data and Knowledge Management for Convergence of ICT, Healthcare, and Telecommunication Services, 61-83.

Sinha, A. K. (Ed.). (2008). *New Dimensions of Women Empowerment*. Deep and Deep Publications.

Sinha, S. (2021). Women's Empowerment, Gender Roles and Socioeconomic Development Linkage: Evidences from Indian States. *Journal of Public Affairs, 42*(1), e2396.

Sirilertmekasakul, C., Rattanawong, W., Gongvatana, A., & Srikiatkhachorn, A. (2023). The current state of artificial intelligence-augmented digitized neurocognitive screening test. *Frontiers in Human Neuroscience, 17*, 1133632. doi:10.3389/fnhum.2023.1133632 PMID:37063100

Sirotkin, K., Carballeira, P., & Escudero-Viñolo, M. (2022). A study on the distribution of social biases in self-supervised learning visual models. In *Proceedings of the IEEE/CVF Conference on Computer Vision and Pattern Recognition* (pp. 10442-10451). 10.1109/CVPR52688.2022.01019

Smith, A. B., Johnson, L., Pendergrast, R. A., & Cranston, W. (2020). The Impact of Social Media Addiction on Mental Health: A Conceptual Model and Literature Review. *Journal of Psychology and Behavioral Science, 8*(1), 1–8.

Smith, J. (2000). *Digital Consciousness and Human Perception*. Academic Press.

Soldatova, G., Vishneva, A., & Chigarkova, S. (2018). Features of cognitive processes in children with different internet activity. European Proceedings of Social and Behavioural Sciences, 43.

Soloway, E., Guzdial, M., & Hay, K. E. (1994). Learner-centered design: The challenge for HCI in the 21st century. *Interactions, 1*(2), 36-48.

Sosik, J. J., & Cameron, J. C. (2010). Character and authentic transformational leadership behavior: Expanding the ascetic self toward others. *Consulting Psychology Journal, 62*(4), 288–306. doi:10.1037/a0022104

Spanakis, E. G., Santana, S., Tsiknakis, M., Marias, K., Sakkalis, V., Teixeira, A., Janssen, J. H., de Jong, H., & Tziraki, C. (2016). Technology-based innovations to foster personalized healthy lifestyles and well-being: A targeted review. *Journal of Medical Internet Research*, *18*(6), e128. doi:10.2196/jmir.4863 PMID:27342137

Spreitzer, G. M., De Janasz, S. C., & Quinn, R. E. (1999). Empowered to lead: The role of psychological empowerment in leadership. *Journal of Organizational Behavior*, *20*(4), 511–526. doi:10.1002/(SICI)1099-1379(199907)20:4<511::AID-JOB900>3.0.CO;2-L

SrikanthK. (2022). Artificial intelligence and human consciousness. *Social Science Research Network*. doi:10.2139/ssrn.4070609

Stahl, B. C. (2021). *Artificial intelligence for a better future: an ecosystem perspective on the ethics of A.I. and emerging digital technologies*. Springer Nature. doi:10.1007/978-3-030-69978-9

StathoulopoulosK.Mateos-GarciaJ. C. (2019). Gender diversity in AI research. Available at SSRN 3428240.

Statista, Telemedicine Market in India. (2020). https://www.statista.com/statistics/1174720/india-telemedicine-market-size/

Statista. (2021). Number of monthly active Facebook users worldwide as of 4th quarter 2021. Author.

Storer, K. M. (2017). Nuanced Views of Pedagogical Evaluation (Doctoral dissertation, Clemson University).\

Suhel, S. F., Shukla, V. K., Vyas, S., & Mishra, V. P. (2020, June). Conversation to automation in banking through chatbot using artificial machine intelligence language. In *2020 8th international conference on reliability, infocom technologies and optimization (trends and future directions) (ICRITO)* (pp. 611-618). IEEE. 10.1109/ICRITO48877.2020.9197825

Sun, Z., Zhu, M., Shan, X., & Lee, C. (2022). Augmented tactile-perception and haptic-feedback rings as human-machine interfaces aiming for immersive interactions. *Nature Communications*, *13*(1), 5224. doi:10.1038/s41467-022-32745-8 PMID:36064838

Suveren, Y. (2022). Unconscious Bias: Definition and Significance. *Psikiyatride Güncel Yaklasimlar*, *14*(3), 414–426. doi:10.18863/pgy.1026607

Sverdlov, O., van Dam, J., Hannesdottir, K., & Thornton-Wells, T. (2018). Digital therapeutics: An integral component of digital innovation in drug development. *Clinical Pharmacology and Therapeutics*, *104*(1), 72–80. doi:10.1002/cpt.1036 PMID:29377057

Szabo, A., Tillnert, A. S., & Mattsson, J. (2024). Displaying gifted students' mathematical reasoning during problem solving: Challenges and possibilities. *The Montana Math Enthusiast*, *21*(1), 179–202. doi:10.54870/1551-3440.1623

Tagliagambe, S. (2023). Phenomenology and the Digital World: Problems and Perspectives. *Foundations of Science*, *28*(4), 1157–1174. doi:10.1007/s10699-022-09863-z

Tandon, T. (2016). Women empowerment: Perspectives and views. *International Journal of Indian Psychology*, *3*(3), 6–12.

Tan, Z., Dai, N., Su, Y., Zhang, R., Li, Y., Wu, D., & Li, S. (2021). Human–machine interaction in intelligent and connected vehicles: A review of status quo, issues, and opportunities. *IEEE Transactions on Intelligent Transportation Systems*, *23*(9), 13954–13975. doi:10.1109/TITS.2021.3127217

Tanzile, R., Domapielle, M. K., & Fielmua, N. (2023). Empowering women for sustainable development through semi-mechanized sheabutter processing in rural North-Western Ghana. *Scientific African*, *21*, e01790. doi:10.1016/j.sciaf.2023.e01790

Teasdale, J. D., Segal, Z. V., & Williams, J. M. G. (2000). Mindfulness and cognitive therapy for depression: A promising approach. Academic Press.

Thagard, P., & Stewart, T. C. (2014). Two theories of consciousness: Semantic pointer competition vs. information integration. *Consciousness and Cognition*, *30*, 73–90. doi:10.1016/j.concog.2014.07.001 PMID:25160821

Thiele, J. C., & Grimm, V. (2015). Replicating and breaking models: Good for you and good for ecology. *Oikos*, *124*(6), 691–696. doi:10.1111/oik.02170

Thong, J. Y., & Xu, X. (2012). Understanding user acceptance of information technology: A meta-analytic journey. *Management Information Systems Quarterly*, *36*(1), 1–32.

Thong, J. Y., & Xu, X. (2016). Extending the unified theory of acceptance and use of technology: The role of performance expectancy. *Information Systems*, *27*(2), 313–3381.

Tiersky, H. (2017). 5 top challenges to digital transformation in the enterprise. Retrieved from https://www.cio.com/article/3179607/5-top-challenges-to-digital-transformation-in-the-enterprise.html

Timmons, A. C., Duong, J. B., Simo Fiallo, N., Lee, T., Vo, H. P. Q., Ahle, M. W., Comer, J. S., Brewer, L. P. C., Frazier, S. L., & Chaspari, T. (2023). A call to action on assessing and mitigating bias in artificial intelligence applications for mental health. *Perspectives on Psychological Science*, *18*(5), 1062–1096. doi:10.1177/17456916221134490 PMID:36490369

Tiwari, A., Chugh, A., & Sharma, A. (2023). Uses of artificial intelligence with human-computer interaction in psychology. In *Innovations in Artificial Intelligence and Human-Computer Interaction in the Digital Era* (pp. 173–205). Academic Press. doi:10.1016/B978-0-323-99891-8.00003-6

Tonin, P. E. H., Nickel, E. M., & Dos Santos, F. A. N. V. (2022). Technology and Sensory Stimuli as Support for Physical Retail Experience Design. Affective and Pleasurable Design, 41(41).

Ton, Z., & Huckman, R. S. (2008). Managing the impact of employee turnover on performance: The role of process conformance. *Organization Science*, *19*(1), 56–68. doi:10.1287/orsc.1070.0294

Torre, D., & Daley, B. (2023). Emotional intelligence: Mapping an elusive concept. *Medical Teacher*, 1–3. PMID:37220225

Tóth, Z., Caruana, R., Gruber, T., & Loebbecke, C. (2022). The dawn of the AI robots: Towards a new framework of AI robot accountability. *Journal of Business Ethics*, *178*(4), 895–916. doi:10.1007/s10551-022-05050-z

Treviño, L. K., Weaver, G. R., Gibson, D. G., & Toffler, B. L. (1999). Managing ethics and legal compliance: What works and what hurts. *California Management Review*, *41*(2), 131–151. doi:10.2307/41165990

Twenge, J. M., Cooper, A. B., Joiner, T. E., Duffy, M. E., & Binau, S. G. (2018). Age, period, and cohort trends in mood disorder indicators and suicide-related outcomes in a nationally representative dataset, 2005–2017. *Journal of Abnormal Psychology*, *127*(4), 348–355. PMID:29745700

Twenge, J. M., Joiner, T. E., Rogers, M. L., & Martin, G. N. (2018). Increases in depressive symptoms, suicide-related outcomes, and suicide rates among U.S. adolescents after 2010 and links to increased new media screen time. *Clinical Psychological Science*, *6*(1), 3–17. doi:10.1177/2167702617723376

United Nations Development Programme. (2015). Sustainable Development Goals. Retrieved from https://www.undp.org/content/undp/en/home/sustainable-development-goals.html

United Nations. (2020). The Beijing Platform for Action. Retrieved from https://www.unwomen.org/en/how-we-work/un-system-coordination/compilation-of-resolutions-and-agreed-conclusions/2000/beijing-platform-for-action

University of Massachusetts Medical School biography. (n.d.). https://www.gsd.harvard.edu/people/staff/

Uppal, M. A. (2017). Addressing student perception of E-learning challenges in Higher Education holistic quality approach (Doctoral dissertation, University of Reading).

Using artificial intelligence to address criminal justice needs. (2018, October 8). National Institute of Justice. https://nij.ojp.gov/topics/articles/using-artificial-intelligence-address-criminal-justice-needs

Vaibhaw, J. S., & Pattnaik, P. K. (2020). Brain-computer interfaces and their applications. *An industrial IoT approach for pharmaceutical industry growth, 2*, 31-54.

Valle, G., Katic Secerovic, N., Eggemann, D., Gorskii, O., Pavlova, N., Cvancara, P., ... Raspopovic, S. (2023). Biomimetic computer-to-brain communication restoring naturalistic touch sensations via peripheral nerve stimulation. bioRxiv, 2023-07. doi:10.1101/2023.07.15.549130

van der Maden, W., Lomas, D., & Hekkert, P. (2023). Positive AI: Key Challenges for Designing Wellbeing-aligned Artificial Intelligence. arXiv preprint arXiv:2304.12241.

Van Leeuwen, J., & Cooper, S. (2013). *Alan Turing: His work and impact*. Elsevier Science Publishing.

Compilation of References

Van Ryn, M., Burgess, D. J., Dovidio, J. F., Phelan, S. M., Saha, S., Malat, J., Griffin, J. M., Fu, S. S., & Perry, S. (2011). The impact of racism on clinician cognition, behavior, and clinical decision making. *Du Bois Review*, 8(1), 199–218. doi:10.1017/S1742058X11000191 PMID:24761152

Vanderhoof, J. (2015, June). Mindfulness in the workplace. ResearchGate. https://www.researchgate.net/publication/277589039_Mindfulness_in_the_Workplace

Varona, D., & Suárez, J. L. (2022). Discrimination, bias, fairness, and trustworthy AI. *Applied Sciences (Basel, Switzerland)*, 12(12), 5826. doi:10.3390/app12125826

Vempaty, A., Kailkhura, B., & Varshney, P. K. (2018, April). Human-machine inference networks for smart decision making: Opportunities and challenges. In *2018 IEEE International Conference on Acoustics, Speech and Signal Processing (ICASSP)* (pp. 6961-6965). IEEE. 10.1109/ICASSP.2018.8462638

Vendrell Ferran, I. (2023). Consciousness of Emotion and Emotive Consciousness in Geiger and Husserl. *Human Studies*. Advance online publication. doi:10.1007/s10746-023-09706-1

Venkatesh, V., Brown, S. A., & Bala, H. (2003). Model of adoption of information technology in household: A longitudinal study. MIS Quarterly, 27(3) 472-502. doi:10.2307/30036540

Venter, Z. S., Gundersen, V., Scott, S. L., & Barton, D. N. (2023). Bias and precision of crowdsourced recreational activity data from Strava. *Landscape and Urban Planning*, 232, 104686. doi:10.1016/j.landurbplan.2023.104686

Verina, N., & Titko, J. (2019, May). Digital transformation: conceptual framework. In Proc. of the Int. Scientific Conference "Contemporary Issues in Business, Management and Economics Engineering (pp. 9-10). 10.3846/cibmee.2019.073

Villani, V., Sabattini, L., Czerniaki, J. N., Mertens, A., Vogel-Heuser, B., & Fantuzzi, C. (2017, September). Towards modern inclusive factories: A methodology for the development of smart adaptive human-machine interfaces. In *2017 22nd IEEE international conference on emerging technologies and factory automation (ETFA)* (pp. 1-7). IEEE. 10.1109/ETFA.2017.8247634

von Eschenbach, W. J. (2021). Transparency and the black box problem: Why we do not trust AI. *Philosophy & Technology*, 34(4), 1607–1622. doi:10.1007/s13347-021-00477-0

Walumbwa, F. O., Avolio, B. J., Gardner, W. L., Wernsing, T. S., & Peterson, S. J. (2018). Authentic leadership: Development and validation of a theory-based measure. *Journal of Management*, 34(1), 89–126. doi:10.1177/0149206307308913 PMID:30443095

Wang, W., Dong, L., Cheng, H., Liu, X., Yan, X., Gao, J., & Wei, F. (2023). Augmenting Language Models with Long-Term Memory. arXiv preprint arXiv:2306.07174.

Wang, Y., & Wang, Y. (2008, August). The cognitive processes of consciousness and attention. In 2008 7th IEEE International Conference on Cognitive Informatics (pp. 30-39). IEEE.

Wang, L., Chen, J., & Chen, Y. (2017). How inspirational leadership contributes to team creativity: The mediating role of team positive affective tone and the moderating role of team task reflexivity. *Journal of Organizational Behavior*, *38*(5), 682–702.

Wang, Y. (2012). The cognitive mechanisms and formal models of consciousness. *International Journal of Cognitive Informatics and Natural Intelligence*, *6*(2), 23–40. doi:10.4018/jcini.2012040102

Wang, Y., & Liu, W. (2023). Emotional Simulation of Artificial Intelligence and Its Ethical Reflection. *Academic Journal of Humanities & Social Sciences*, *6*(5), 11–15.

Weber, M. (1947). *The theory of social and economic organization*. Free Press.

Westerman, G., Calmejane, C., Bonnet, D., Ferraris, P., & McAfee, A. (2011). Digital Transformation: A roadmap for billion-dollar organizations. *MIT Center for Digital Business and Capgemini Consulting*, *1*, 1–68.

WH. (2017) https://www.who.int/news-room/fact-sheets/detail/chronic-obstructive-pulmonary-disease-(copd)

WH2016. (n.d.). Retrieved from https://www.who.int/india/health-topics/cardiovascular-diseases

What do we do about the biases in AI? (2019, October 25). Harvard Business Review. https://hbr.org/2019/10/what-do-we-do-about-the-biases-in-ai

Whittaker, M., Crawford, K., Dobbe, R., Fried, G., Kaziunas, E., Mathur, V., & Schwartz, O. (2018). *AI now report 2018*. AI Now Institute at New York University.

Wilbertz, G., & Sterzer, P. (2018). Differentiating aversive conditioning in bistable perception: Avoidance of a percept vs. salience of a stimulus. *Consciousness and Cognition*, *61*, 38–48. doi:10.1016/j.concog.2018.03.010 PMID:29649652

Wilcox, K., Stephen, A. T., & Suri, R. (2013). Beware the dark side: Consumer responses to negative social media content. *The Journal of Consumer Research*, *40*(5), 839–853.

Williams, J. J., & Seaman, A. E. (2016). *On Managerial Performance*. Academic Press.

Williams, J. J., & Seaman, A. E. (2014). Does More Corporate Governance Enhance. *Journal of Applied Business Research*, *30*(4), 989–1002. doi:10.19030/jabr.v30i4.8648

Wolf, M., Semm, A., & Erfurth, C. (2018). Digital transformation in companies - challenges and success factors. Paper presented at the International Conference on Innovations for Community Services. 10.1007/978-3-319-93408-2_13

Women, U. N. (2023). The paths to equal: Twin indices on women's empowerment and gender equality. Author.

World Cancer Research Fund International. (n.d.). https://www.wcrf.org/cancer-trends/worldwide-cancer-data/ www.aarogyasetu.gov.in

Xu, G., Guo, W., & Wang, Y. (2022, October). Memory Enhanced Replay for Continual Learning. In *2022 16th IEEE International Conference on Signal Processing (ICSP)* (Vol. 1, pp. 218-222). IEEE. 10.1109/ICSP56322.2022.9965222

Xu, S., & Zhang, X. (2023, April). Augmenting Human Cognition with an AI-Mediated Intelligent Visual Feedback. In *Proceedings of the 2023 CHI Conference on Human Factors in Computing Systems* (pp. 1-16). 10.1145/3544548.3580905

Xu, W., Xu, J., & Liu, Y. (2019). The effects of mindfulness on empathy: A meta-analysis. *Journal of Health Psychology*, *24*(10), 1199–1211.

Yagil, D., Medler-Liraz, H., & Bichachi, R. (2023). Mindfulness and self-efficacy enhance employee performance by reducing stress. *Personality and Individual Differences*, *207*, 112150. doi:10.1016/j.paid.2023.112150

Yamana, Y. (2023). Deep Learning and Neural Networks. *Methods (San Diego, Calif.)*. Advance online publication. doi:10.59646/csebookc7/004

Yukun, Z., Xu, L., Huang, Z., Peng, K., Seligman, M., Li, E., & Yu, F. (2023). AI chatbot responds to emotional cuing. Academic Press.

Yushu, Y. (2023). *Current Trends in Deep Learning*. Advances in Engineering Technology Research. doi:10.56028/aetr.5.1.422.2023

Yusifova, L. (2020). Ethical and Legal Aspects of Using Brain-Computer Interface in Medicine: Protection of Patient's Neuro Privacy. Academic Press.

Zafar, M. B., Valera, I., Rogriguez, M. G., & Gummadi, K. P. (2017, April). Fairness constraints: Mechanisms for fair classification. In *Artificial intelligence and statistics* (pp. 962–970). PMLR.

Zhang, Y., Farrugia, N., & Bellec, P. (2022). Deep learning models of cognitive processes constrained by human brain connectomes. *Medical Image Analysis*, *80*, 102507. doi:10.1016/j.media.2022.102507 PMID:35738052

Zhong, W., Ma, T., Wang, J., Yin, J., Zhao, T., Lin, C. Y., & Duan, N. (2022). Disentangling reasoning capabilities from language models with compositional reasoning transformers. arXiv preprint arXiv:2210.11265.

Zhongzhi, S. (2019). Cognitive Machine Learning. *International Journal of Intelligence Science*, *9*(4), 111–121. Advance online publication. doi:10.4236/ijis.2019.94007

Zhou, Z. (2021). Emotional thinking as the foundation of consciousness in artificial intelligence. *Cultura e Scuola*, *4*(3), 112–123. doi:10.1177/20966083211052651

Ziemer, T., Nuchprayoon, N., & Schultheis, H. (2019). Psychoacoustic sonification as user interface for human-machine interaction. *arXiv preprint arXiv:1912.08609*.

Zihan, H., & Dekai, Ye. (2022, January 4). Advances in materials and devices for mimicking sensory adaptation. *Materials Horizons*, *9*(1), 147–163. Advance online publication. doi:10.1039/D1MH01111A

Zou, L., & Khern-am-nuai, W. (2023). AI and housing discrimination: The case of mortgage applications. *AI and Ethics*, *3*(4), 1271–1281. doi:10.1007/s43681-022-00234-9

Related References

To continue our tradition of advancing academic research, we have compiled a list of recommended IGI Global readings. These references will provide additional information and guidance to further enrich your knowledge and assist you with your own research and future publications.

Abbasnejad, B., Moeinzadeh, S., Ahankoob, A., & Wong, P. S. (2021). The Role of Collaboration in the Implementation of BIM-Enabled Projects. In J. Underwood & M. Shelbourn (Eds.), *Handbook of Research on Driving Transformational Change in the Digital Built Environment* (pp. 27–62). IGI Global. https://doi.org/10.4018/978-1-7998-6600-8.ch002

Abdulrahman, K. O., Mahamood, R. M., & Akinlabi, E. T. (2022). Additive Manufacturing (AM): Processing Technique for Lightweight Alloys and Composite Material. In K. Kumar, B. Babu, & J. Davim (Ed.), *Handbook of Research on Advancements in the Processing, Characterization, and Application of Lightweight Materials* (pp. 27-48). IGI Global. https://doi.org/10.4018/978-1-7998-7864-3.ch002

Agrawal, R., Sharma, P., & Saxena, A. (2021). A Diamond Cut Leather Substrate Antenna for BAN (Body Area Network) Application. In V. Singh, V. Dubey, A. Saxena, R. Tiwari, & H. Sharma (Eds.), *Emerging Materials and Advanced Designs for Wearable Antennas* (pp. 54–59). IGI Global. https://doi.org/10.4018/978-1-7998-7611-3.ch004

Ahmad, F., Al-Ammar, E. A., & Alsaidan, I. (2022). Battery Swapping Station: A Potential Solution to Address the Limitations of EV Charging Infrastructure. In M. Alam, R. Pillai, & N. Murugesan (Eds.), *Developing Charging Infrastructure and Technologies for Electric Vehicles* (pp. 195–207). IGI Global. doi:10.4018/978-1-7998-6858-3.ch010

Aikhuele, D. (2018). A Study of Product Development Engineering and Design Reliability Concerns. *International Journal of Applied Industrial Engineering*, *5*(1), 79–89. doi:10.4018/IJAIE.2018010105

Al-Khatri, H., & Al-Atrash, F. (2021). Occupants' Habits and Natural Ventilation in a Hot Arid Climate. In R. González-Lezcano (Ed.), *Advancements in Sustainable Architecture and Energy Efficiency* (pp. 146–168). IGI Global. https://doi.org/10.4018/978-1-7998-7023-4.ch007

Al-Shebeeb, O. A., Rangaswamy, S., Gopalakrishan, B., & Devaru, D. G. (2017). Evaluation and Indexing of Process Plans Based on Electrical Demand and Energy Consumption. *International Journal of Manufacturing, Materials, and Mechanical Engineering*, *7*(3), 1–19. doi:10.4018/IJMMME.2017070101

Amuda, M. O., Lawal, T. F., & Akinlabi, E. T. (2017). Research Progress on Rheological Behavior of AA7075 Aluminum Alloy During Hot Deformation. *International Journal of Materials Forming and Machining Processes*, *4*(1), 53–96. doi:10.4018/IJMFMP.2017010104

Amuda, M. O., Lawal, T. F., & Mridha, S. (2021). Microstructure and Mechanical Properties of Silicon Carbide-Treated Ferritic Stainless Steel Welds. In L. Burstein (Ed.), *Handbook of Research on Advancements in Manufacturing, Materials, and Mechanical Engineering* (pp. 395–411). IGI Global. https://doi.org/10.4018/978-1-7998-4939-1.ch019

Anikeev, V., Gasem, K. A., & Fan, M. (2021). Application of Supercritical Technologies in Clean Energy Production: A Review. In L. Chen (Ed.), *Handbook of Research on Advancements in Supercritical Fluids Applications for Sustainable Energy Systems* (pp. 792–821). IGI Global. https://doi.org/10.4018/978-1-7998-5796-9.ch022

Arafat, M. Y., Saleem, I., & Devi, T. P. (2022). Drivers of EV Charging Infrastructure Entrepreneurship in India. In M. Alam, R. Pillai, & N. Murugesan (Eds.), *Developing Charging Infrastructure and Technologies for Electric Vehicles* (pp. 208–219). IGI Global. https://doi.org/10.4018/978-1-7998-6858-3.ch011

Araujo, A., & Manninen, H. (2022). Contribution of Project-Based Learning on Social Skills Development: An Industrial Engineer Perspective. In A. Alves & N. van Hattum-Janssen (Eds.), *Training Engineering Students for Modern Technological Advancement* (pp. 119–145). IGI Global. https://doi.org/10.4018/978-1-7998-8816-1.ch006

Armutlu, H. (2018). Intelligent Biomedical Engineering Operations by Cloud Computing Technologies. In U. Kose, G. Guraksin, & O. Deperlioglu (Eds.), *Nature-Inspired Intelligent Techniques for Solving Biomedical Engineering Problems* (pp. 297–317). Hershey, PA: IGI Global. doi:10.4018/978-1-5225-4769-3.ch015

Atik, M., Sadek, M., & Shahrour, I. (2017). Single-Run Adaptive Pushover Procedure for Shear Wall Structures. In V. Plevris, G. Kremmyda, & Y. Fahjan (Eds.), *Performance-Based Seismic Design of Concrete Structures and Infrastructures* (pp. 59–83). Hershey, PA: IGI Global. doi:10.4018/978-1-5225-2089-4.ch003

Attia, H. (2021). Smart Power Microgrid Impact on Sustainable Building. In R. González-Lezcano (Ed.), *Advancements in Sustainable Architecture and Energy Efficiency* (pp. 169–194). IGI Global. https://doi.org/10.4018/978-1-7998-7023-4.ch008

Aydin, A., Akyol, E., Gungor, M., Kaya, A., & Tasdelen, S. (2018). Geophysical Surveys in Engineering Geology Investigations With Field Examples. In N. Ceryan (Ed.), *Handbook of Research on Trends and Digital Advances in Engineering Geology* (pp. 257–280). Hershey, PA: IGI Global. doi:10.4018/978-1-5225-2709-1.ch007

Ayoobkhan, M. U. D., Y., A., J., Easwaran, B., & R., T. (2021). Smart Connected Digital Products and IoT Platform With the Digital Twin. In P. Vasant, G. Weber, & W. Punurai (Ed.), Research Advancements in Smart Technology, Optimization, and Renewable Energy (pp. 330-350). IGI Global. https://doi.org/ doi:10.4018/978-1-7998-3970-5.ch016

Baeza Moyano, D., & González Lezcano, R. A. (2021). The Importance of Light in Our Lives: Towards New Lighting in Schools. In R. González-Lezcano (Ed.), *Advancements in Sustainable Architecture and Energy Efficiency* (pp. 239–256). IGI Global. https://doi.org/10.4018/978-1-7998-7023-4.ch011

Bagdadee, A. H. (2021). A Brief Assessment of the Energy Sector of Bangladesh. *International Journal of Energy Optimization and Engineering*, *10*(1), 36–55. doi:10.4018/IJEOE.2021010103

Baklezos, A. T., & Hadjigeorgiou, N. G. (2021). Magnetic Sensors for Space Applications and Magnetic Cleanliness Considerations. In C. Nikolopoulos (Ed.), *Recent Trends on Electromagnetic Environmental Effects for Aeronautics and Space Applications* (pp. 147–185). IGI Global. https://doi.org/10.4018/978-1-7998-4879-0.ch006

Bas, T. G. (2017). Nutraceutical Industry with the Collaboration of Biotechnology and Nutrigenomics Engineering: The Significance of Intellectual Property in the Entrepreneurship and Scientific Research Ecosystems. In T. Bas & J. Zhao (Eds.), *Comparative Approaches to Biotechnology Development and Use in Developed and Emerging Nations* (pp. 1–17). Hershey, PA: IGI Global. doi:10.4018/978-1-5225-1040-6.ch001

Bazeer Ahamed, B., & Periakaruppan, S. (2021). Taxonomy of Influence Maximization Techniques in Unknown Social Networks. In P. Vasant, G. Weber, & W. Punurai (Eds.), *Research Advancements in Smart Technology, Optimization, and Renewable Energy* (pp. 351-363). IGI Global. https://doi.org/10.4018/978-1-7998-3970-5.ch017

Beale, R., & André, J. (2017). *Design Solutions and Innovations in Temporary Structures*. Hershey, PA: IGI Global. doi:10.4018/978-1-5225-2199-0

Behnam, B. (2017). Simulating Post-Earthquake Fire Loading in Conventional RC Structures. In P. Samui, S. Chakraborty, & D. Kim (Eds.), *Modeling and Simulation Techniques in Structural Engineering* (pp. 425–444). Hershey, PA: IGI Global. doi:10.4018/978-1-5225-0588-4.ch015

Ben Hamida, I., Salah, S. B., Msahli, F., & Mimouni, M. F. (2018). Distribution Network Reconfiguration Using SPEA2 for Power Loss Minimization and Reliability Improvement. *International Journal of Energy Optimization and Engineering*, 7(1), 50–65. doi:10.4018/IJEOE.2018010103

Bentarzi, H. (2021). Fault Tree-Based Root Cause Analysis Used to Study Mal-Operation of a Protective Relay in a Smart Grid. In A. Recioui & H. Bentarzi (Eds.), *Optimizing and Measuring Smart Grid Operation and Control* (pp. 289–308). IGI Global. https://doi.org/10.4018/978-1-7998-4027-5.ch012

Beysens, D. A., Garrabos, Y., & Zappoli, B. (2021). Thermal Effects in Near-Critical Fluids: Piston Effect and Related Phenomena. In L. Chen (Ed.), *Handbook of Research on Advancements in Supercritical Fluids Applications for Sustainable Energy Systems* (pp. 1–31). IGI Global. https://doi.org/10.4018/978-1-7998-5796-9.ch001

Bhaskar, S. V., & Kudal, H. N. (2017). Effect of TiCN and AlCrN Coating on Tribological Behaviour of Plasma-nitrided AISI 4140 Steel. *International Journal of Surface Engineering and Interdisciplinary Materials Science*, 5(2), 1–17. doi:10.4018/IJSEIMS.2017070101

Bhuyan, D. (2018). Designing of a Twin Tube Shock Absorber: A Study in Reverse Engineering. In K. Kumar & J. Davim (Eds.), *Design and Optimization of Mechanical Engineering Products* (pp. 83–104). Hershey, PA: IGI Global. doi:10.4018/978-1-5225-3401-3.ch005

Blumberg, G. (2021). Blockchains for Use in Construction and Engineering Projects. In J. Underwood & M. Shelbourn (Eds.), *Handbook of Research on Driving Transformational Change in the Digital Built Environment* (pp. 179–208). IGI Global. https://doi.org/10.4018/978-1-7998-6600-8.ch008

Bolboaca, A. M. (2021). Considerations Regarding the Use of Fuel Cells in Combined Heat and Power for Stationary Applications. In G. Badea, R. Felseghi, & I. Aşchilean (Eds.), *Hydrogen Fuel Cell Technology for Stationary Applications* (pp. 239–275). IGI Global. https://doi.org/10.4018/978-1-7998-4945-2.ch010

Burstein, L. (2021). Simulation Tool for Cable Design. In L. Burstein (Ed.), *Handbook of Research on Advancements in Manufacturing, Materials, and Mechanical Engineering* (pp. 54–74). IGI Global. https://doi.org/10.4018/978-1-7998-4939-1.ch003

Calderon, F. A., Giolo, E. G., Frau, C. D., Rengel, M. G., Rodriguez, H., Tornello, M., ... Gallucci, R. (2018). Seismic Microzonation and Site Effects Detection Through Microtremors Measures: A Review. In N. Ceryan (Ed.), *Handbook of Research on Trends and Digital Advances in Engineering Geology* (pp. 326–349). Hershey, PA: IGI Global. doi:10.4018/978-1-5225-2709-1.ch009

Ceryan, N., & Can, N. K. (2018). Prediction of The Uniaxial Compressive Strength of Rocks Materials. In N. Ceryan (Ed.), *Handbook of Research on Trends and Digital Advances in Engineering Geology* (pp. 31–96). Hershey, PA: IGI Global. doi:10.4018/978-1-5225-2709-1.ch002

Ceryan, S. (2018). Weathering Indices Used in Evaluation of the Weathering State of Rock Material. In N. Ceryan (Ed.), *Handbook of Research on Trends and Digital Advances in Engineering Geology* (pp. 132–186). Hershey, PA: IGI Global. doi:10.4018/978-1-5225-2709-1.ch004

Chen, H., Padilla, R. V., & Besarati, S. (2017). Supercritical Fluids and Their Applications in Power Generation. In L. Chen & Y. Iwamoto (Eds.), *Advanced Applications of Supercritical Fluids in Energy Systems* (pp. 369–402). Hershey, PA: IGI Global. doi:10.4018/978-1-5225-2047-4.ch012

Chen, H., Padilla, R. V., & Besarati, S. (2021). Supercritical Fluids and Their Applications in Power Generation. In L. Chen (Ed.), *Handbook of Research on Advancements in Supercritical Fluids Applications for Sustainable Energy Systems* (pp. 566–599). IGI Global. https://doi.org/10.4018/978-1-7998-5796-9.ch016

Chen, L. (2017). Principles, Experiments, and Numerical Studies of Supercritical Fluid Natural Circulation System. In L. Chen & Y. Iwamoto (Eds.), *Advanced Applications of Supercritical Fluids in Energy Systems* (pp. 136–187). Hershey, PA: IGI Global. doi:10.4018/978-1-5225-2047-4.ch005

Chen, L. (2021). Principles, Experiments, and Numerical Studies of Supercritical Fluid Natural Circulation System. In L. Chen (Ed.), *Handbook of Research on Advancements in Supercritical Fluids Applications for Sustainable Energy Systems* (pp. 219–269). IGI Global. https://doi.org/10.4018/978-1-7998-5796-9.ch007

Chiba, Y., Marif, Y., Henini, N., & Tlemcani, A. (2021). Modeling of Magnetic Refrigeration Device by Using Artificial Neural Networks Approach. *International Journal of Energy Optimization and Engineering*, *10*(4), 68–76. https://doi.org/10.4018/IJEOE.2021100105

Clementi, F., Di Sciascio, G., Di Sciascio, S., & Lenci, S. (2017). Influence of the Shear-Bending Interaction on the Global Capacity of Reinforced Concrete Frames: A Brief Overview of the New Perspectives. In V. Plevris, G. Kremmyda, & Y. Fahjan (Eds.), *Performance-Based Seismic Design of Concrete Structures and Infrastructures* (pp. 84–111). Hershey, PA: IGI Global. doi:10.4018/978-1-5225-2089-4.ch004

Codinhoto, R., Fialho, B. C., Pinti, L., & Fabricio, M. M. (2021). BIM and IoT for Facilities Management: Understanding Key Maintenance Issues. In J. Underwood & M. Shelbourn (Eds.), *Handbook of Research on Driving Transformational Change in the Digital Built Environment* (pp. 209–231). IGI Global. doi:10.4018/978-1-7998-6600-8.ch009

Cortés-Polo, D., Calle-Cancho, J., Carmona-Murillo, J., & González-Sánchez, J. (2017). Future Trends in Mobile-Fixed Integration for Next Generation Networks: Classification and Analysis. *International Journal of Vehicular Telematics and Infotainment Systems*, *1*(1), 33–53. doi:10.4018/IJVTIS.2017010103

Costa, H. G., Sheremetieff, F. H., & Araújo, E. A. (2022). Influence of Game-Based Methods in Developing Engineering Competences. In A. Alves & N. van Hattum-Janssen (Eds.), *Training Engineering Students for Modern Technological Advancement* (pp. 69–88). IGI Global. https://doi.org/10.4018/978-1-7998-8816-1.ch004

Cui, X., Zeng, S., Li, Z., Zheng, Q., Yu, X., & Han, B. (2018). Advanced Composites for Civil Engineering Infrastructures. In K. Kumar & J. Davim (Eds.), *Composites and Advanced Materials for Industrial Applications* (pp. 212–248). Hershey, PA: IGI Global. doi:10.4018/978-1-5225-5216-1.ch010

Dalgıç, S., & Kuşku, İ. (2018). Geological and Geotechnical Investigations in Tunneling. In N. Ceryan (Ed.), *Handbook of Research on Trends and Digital Advances in Engineering Geology* (pp. 482–529). Hershey, PA: IGI Global. doi:10.4018/978-1-5225-2709-1.ch014

Dang, C., & Hihara, E. (2021). Study on Cooling Heat Transfer of Supercritical Carbon Dioxide Applied to Transcritical Carbon Dioxide Heat Pump. In L. Chen (Ed.), *Handbook of Research on Advancements in Supercritical Fluids Applications for Sustainable Energy Systems* (pp. 451–493). IGI Global. https://doi.org/10.4018/978-1-7998-5796-9.ch013

Daus, Y., Kharchenko, V., & Yudaev, I. (2021). Research of Solar Energy Potential of Photovoltaic Installations on Enclosing Structures of Buildings. *International Journal of Energy Optimization and Engineering*, *10*(4), 18–34. https://doi.org/10.4018/IJEOE.2021100102

Daus, Y., Kharchenko, V., & Yudaev, I. (2021). Optimizing Layout of Distributed Generation Sources of Power Supply System of Agricultural Object. *International Journal of Energy Optimization and Engineering*, *10*(3), 70–84. https://doi.org/10.4018/IJEOE.2021070104

de la Varga, D., Soto, M., Arias, C. A., van Oirschot, D., Kilian, R., Pascual, A., & Álvarez, J. A. (2017). Constructed Wetlands for Industrial Wastewater Treatment and Removal of Nutrients. In Á. Val del Río, J. Campos Gómez, & A. Mosquera Corral (Eds.), *Technologies for the Treatment and Recovery of Nutrients from Industrial Wastewater* (pp. 202–230). Hershey, PA: IGI Global. doi:10.4018/978-1-5225-1037-6.ch008

Deb, S., Ammar, E. A., AlRajhi, H., Alsaidan, I., & Shariff, S. M. (2022). V2G Pilot Projects: Review and Lessons Learnt. In M. Alam, R. Pillai, & N. Murugesan (Eds.), *Developing Charging Infrastructure and Technologies for Electric Vehicles* (pp. 252–267). IGI Global. https://doi.org/10.4018/978-1-7998-6858-3.ch014

Dekhandji, F. Z., & Rais, M. C. (2021). A Comparative Study of Power Quality Monitoring Using Various Techniques. In A. Recioui & H. Bentarzi (Eds.), *Optimizing and Measuring Smart Grid Operation and Control* (pp. 259–288). IGI Global. https://doi.org/10.4018/978-1-7998-4027-5.ch011

Deperlioglu, O. (2018). Intelligent Techniques Inspired by Nature and Used in Biomedical Engineering. In U. Kose, G. Guraksin, & O. Deperlioglu (Eds.), *Nature-Inspired Intelligent Techniques for Solving Biomedical Engineering Problems* (pp. 51–77). Hershey, PA: IGI Global. doi:10.4018/978-1-5225-4769-3.ch003

Dhurpate, P. R., & Tang, H. (2021). Quantitative Analysis of the Impact of Inter-Line Conveyor Capacity for Throughput of Manufacturing Systems. *International Journal of Manufacturing, Materials, and Mechanical Engineering, 11*(1), 1–17. https://doi.org/10.4018/IJMMME.2021010101

Dinkar, S., & Deep, K. (2021). A Survey of Recent Variants and Applications of Antlion Optimizer. *International Journal of Energy Optimization and Engineering, 10*(2), 48–73. doi:10.4018/IJEOE.2021040103

Dixit, A. (2018). Application of Silica-Gel-Reinforced Aluminium Composite on the Piston of Internal Combustion Engine: Comparative Study of Silica-Gel-Reinforced Aluminium Composite Piston With Aluminium Alloy Piston. In K. Kumar & J. Davim (Eds.), *Composites and Advanced Materials for Industrial Applications* (pp. 63–98). Hershey, PA: IGI Global. doi:10.4018/978-1-5225-5216-1.ch004

Drabecki, M. P., & Kułak, K. B. (2021). Global Pandemics on European Electrical Energy Markets: Lessons Learned From the COVID-19 Outbreak. *International Journal of Energy Optimization and Engineering, 10*(3), 24–46. https://doi.org/10.4018/IJEOE.2021070102

Dutta, M. M. (2021). Nanomaterials for Food and Agriculture. In M. Bhat, I. Wani, & S. Ashraf (Eds.), *Applications of Nanomaterials in Agriculture, Food Science, and Medicine* (pp. 75–97). IGI Global. doi:10.4018/978-1-7998-5563-7.ch004

Dutta, M. M., & Goswami, M. (2021). Coating Materials: Nano-Materials. In S. Roy & G. Bose (Eds.), *Advanced Surface Coating Techniques for Modern Industrial Applications* (pp. 1–30). IGI Global. doi:10.4018/978-1-7998-4870-7.ch001

Elsayed, A. M., Dakkama, H. J., Mahmoud, S., Al-Dadah, R., & Kaialy, W. (2017). Sustainable Cooling Research Using Activated Carbon Adsorbents and Their Environmental Impact. In T. Kobayashi (Ed.), *Applied Environmental Materials Science for Sustainability* (pp. 186–221). Hershey, PA: IGI Global. doi:10.4018/978-1-5225-1971-3.ch009

Ercanoglu, M., & Sonmez, H. (2018). General Trends and New Perspectives on Landslide Mapping and Assessment Methods. In N. Ceryan (Ed.), *Handbook of Research on Trends and Digital Advances in Engineering Geology* (pp. 350–379). Hershey, PA: IGI Global. doi:10.4018/978-1-5225-2709-1.ch010

Related References

Faroz, S. A., Pujari, N. N., Rastogi, R., & Ghosh, S. (2017). Risk Analysis of Structural Engineering Systems Using Bayesian Inference. In P. Samui, S. Chakraborty, & D. Kim (Eds.), *Modeling and Simulation Techniques in Structural Engineering* (pp. 390–424). Hershey, PA: IGI Global. doi:10.4018/978-1-5225-0588-4.ch014

Fekik, A., Hamida, M. L., Denoun, H., Azar, A. T., Kamal, N. A., Vaidyanathan, S., Bousbaine, A., & Benamrouche, N. (2022). Multilevel Inverter for Hybrid Fuel Cell/PV Energy Conversion System. In A. Fekik & N. Benamrouche (Eds.), *Modeling and Control of Static Converters for Hybrid Storage Systems* (pp. 233–270). IGI Global. https://doi.org/10.4018/978-1-7998-7447-8.ch009

Fekik, A., Hamida, M. L., Houassine, H., Azar, A. T., Kamal, N. A., Denoun, H., Vaidyanathan, S., & Sambas, A. (2022). Power Quality Improvement for Grid-Connected Photovoltaic Panels Using Direct Power Control. In A. Fekik & N. Benamrouche (Eds.), *Modeling and Control of Static Converters for Hybrid Storage Systems* (pp. 107–142). IGI Global. https://doi.org/10.4018/978-1-7998-7447-8.ch005

Fernando, P. R., Hamigah, T., Disne, S., Wickramasingha, G. G., & Sutharshan, A. (2018). The Evaluation of Engineering Properties of Low Cost Concrete Blocks by Partial Doping of Sand with Sawdust: Low Cost Sawdust Concrete Block. *International Journal of Strategic Engineering*, *1*(2), 26–42. doi:10.4018/IJoSE.2018070103

Ferro, G., Minciardi, R., Parodi, L., & Robba, M. (2022). Optimal Charging Management of Microgrid-Integrated Electric Vehicles. In M. Alam, R. Pillai, & N. Murugesan (Eds.), *Developing Charging Infrastructure and Technologies for Electric Vehicles* (pp. 133–155). IGI Global. https://doi.org/10.4018/978-1-7998-6858-3.ch007

Flumerfelt, S., & Green, C. (2022). Graduate Lean Leadership Education: A Case Study of a Program. In A. Alves & N. van Hattum-Janssen (Eds.), *Training Engineering Students for Modern Technological Advancement* (pp. 202–224). IGI Global. https://doi.org/10.4018/978-1-7998-8816-1.ch010

Galli, B. J. (2021). Implications of Economic Decision Making to the Project Manager. *International Journal of Strategic Engineering*, *4*(1), 19–32. https://doi.org/10.4018/IJoSE.2021010102

Gento, A. M., Pimentel, C., & Pascual, J. A. (2022). Teaching Circular Economy and Lean Management in a Learning Factory. In A. Alves & N. van Hattum-Janssen (Eds.), *Training Engineering Students for Modern Technological Advancement* (pp. 183–201). IGI Global. https://doi.org/10.4018/978-1-7998-8816-1.ch009

Ghosh, S., Mitra, S., Ghosh, S., & Chakraborty, S. (2017). Seismic Reliability Analysis in the Framework of Metamodelling Based Monte Carlo Simulation. In P. Samui, S. Chakraborty, & D. Kim (Eds.), *Modeling and Simulation Techniques in Structural Engineering* (pp. 192–208). Hershey, PA: IGI Global. doi:10.4018/978-1-5225-0588-4.ch006

Gil, M., & Otero, B. (2017). Learning Engineering Skills through Creativity and Collaboration: A Game-Based Proposal. In R. Alexandre Peixoto de Queirós & M. Pinto (Eds.), *Gamification-Based E-Learning Strategies for Computer Programming Education* (pp. 14–29). Hershey, PA: IGI Global. doi:10.4018/978-1-5225-1034-5.ch002

Gill, J., Ayre, M., & Mills, J. (2017). Revisioning the Engineering Profession: How to Make It Happen! In M. Gray & K. Thomas (Eds.), *Strategies for Increasing Diversity in Engineering Majors and Careers* (pp. 156–175). Hershey, PA: IGI Global. doi:10.4018/978-1-5225-2212-6.ch008

Godzhaev, Z., Senkevich, S., Kuzmin, V., & Melikov, I. (2021). Use of the Neural Network Controller of Sprung Mass to Reduce Vibrations From Road Irregularities. In P. Vasant, G. Weber, & W. Punurai (Ed.), *Research Advancements in Smart Technology, Optimization, and Renewable Energy* (pp. 69-87). IGI Global. https://doi.org/10.4018/978-1-7998-3970-5.ch005

Gomes de Gusmão, C. M. (2022). Digital Competencies and Transformation in Higher Education: Upskilling With Extension Actions. In A. Alves & N. van Hattum-Janssen (Eds.), *Training Engineering Students for Modern Technological Advancement* (pp. 313–328). IGI Global. https://doi.org/10.4018/978-1-7998-8816-1.ch015A

Goyal, N., Ram, M., & Kumar, P. (2017). Welding Process under Fault Coverage Approach for Reliability and MTTF. In M. Ram & J. Davim (Eds.), *Mathematical Concepts and Applications in Mechanical Engineering and Mechatronics* (pp. 222–245). Hershey, PA: IGI Global. doi:10.4018/978-1-5225-1639-2.ch011

Gray, M., & Lundy, C. (2017). Engineering Study Abroad: High Impact Strategy for Increasing Access. In M. Gray & K. Thomas (Eds.), *Strategies for Increasing Diversity in Engineering Majors and Careers* (pp. 42–59). Hershey, PA: IGI Global. doi:10.4018/978-1-5225-2212-6.ch003

Güler, O., & Varol, T. (2021). Fabrication of Functionally Graded Metal and Ceramic Powders Synthesized by Electroless Deposition. In S. Roy & G. Bose (Eds.), *Advanced Surface Coating Techniques for Modern Industrial Applications* (pp. 150–187). IGI Global. https://doi.org/10.4018/978-1-7998-4870-7.ch007

Related References

Guraksin, G. E. (2018). Internet of Things and Nature-Inspired Intelligent Techniques for the Future of Biomedical Engineering. In U. Kose, G. Guraksin, & O. Deperlioglu (Eds.), *Nature-Inspired Intelligent Techniques for Solving Biomedical Engineering Problems* (pp. 263–282). Hershey, PA: IGI Global. doi:10.4018/978-1-5225-4769-3.ch013

Hamida, M. L., Fekik, A., Denoun, H., Ardjal, A., & Bokhtache, A. A. (2022). Flying Capacitor Inverter Integration in a Renewable Energy System. In A. Fekik & N. Benamrouche (Eds.), *Modeling and Control of Static Converters for Hybrid Storage Systems* (pp. 287–306). IGI Global. https://doi.org/10.4018/978-1-7998-7447-8.ch011

Hasegawa, N., & Takahashi, Y. (2021). Control of Soap Bubble Ejection Robot Using Facial Expressions. *International Journal of Manufacturing, Materials, and Mechanical Engineering, 11*(2), 1–16. https://doi.org/10.4018/IJMMME.2021040101

Hejazi, T., & Akbari, L. (2017). A Multiresponse Optimization Model for Statistical Design of Processes with Discrete Variables. In M. Ram & J. Davim (Eds.), *Mathematical Concepts and Applications in Mechanical Engineering and Mechatronics* (pp. 17–37). Hershey, PA: IGI Global. doi:10.4018/978-1-5225-1639-2.ch002

Hejazi, T., & Hejazi, A. (2017). Monte Carlo Simulation for Reliability-Based Design of Automotive Complex Subsystems. In M. Ram & J. Davim (Eds.), *Mathematical Concepts and Applications in Mechanical Engineering and Mechatronics* (pp. 177–200). Hershey, PA: IGI Global. doi:10.4018/978-1-5225-1639-2.ch009

Hejazi, T., & Poursabbagh, H. (2017). Reliability Analysis of Engineering Systems: An Accelerated Life Testing for Boiler Tubes. In M. Ram & J. Davim (Eds.), *Mathematical Concepts and Applications in Mechanical Engineering and Mechatronics* (pp. 154–176). Hershey, PA: IGI Global. doi:10.4018/978-1-5225-1639-2.ch008

Henao, J., Poblano-Salas, C. A., Vargas, F., Giraldo-Betancur, A. L., Corona-Castuera, J., & Sotelo-Mazón, O. (2021). Principles and Applications of Thermal Spray Coatings. In S. Roy & G. Bose (Eds.), *Advanced Surface Coating Techniques for Modern Industrial Applications* (pp. 31–70). IGI Global. https://doi.org/10.4018/978-1-7998-4870-7.ch002

Henao, J., & Sotelo, O. (2018). Surface Engineering at High Temperature: Thermal Cycling and Corrosion Resistance. In A. Pakseresht (Ed.), *Production, Properties, and Applications of High Temperature Coatings* (pp. 131–159). Hershey, PA: IGI Global. doi:10.4018/978-1-5225-4194-3.ch006

Hrnčič, M. K., Cör, D., & Knez, Ž. (2021). Supercritical Fluids as a Tool for Green Energy and Chemicals. In L. Chen (Ed.), *Handbook of Research on Advancements in Supercritical Fluids Applications for Sustainable Energy Systems* (pp. 761–791). IGI Global. doi:10.4018/978-1-7998-5796-9.ch021

Ibrahim, O., Erdem, S., & Gurbuz, E. (2021). Studying Physical and Chemical Properties of Graphene Oxide and Reduced Graphene Oxide and Their Applications in Sustainable Building Materials. In R. González-Lezcano (Ed.), *Advancements in Sustainable Architecture and Energy Efficiency* (pp. 221–238). IGI Global. https://doi.org/10.4018/978-1-7998-7023-4.ch010

Ihianle, I. K., Islam, S., Naeem, U., & Ebenuwa, S. H. (2021). Exploiting Patterns of Object Use for Human Activity Recognition. In A. Nwajana & I. Ihianle (Eds.), *Handbook of Research on 5G Networks and Advancements in Computing, Electronics, and Electrical Engineering* (pp. 382–401). IGI Global. https://doi.org/10.4018/978-1-7998-6992-4.ch015

Ijemaru, G. K., Ngharamike, E. T., Oleka, E. U., & Nwajana, A. O. (2021). An Energy-Efficient Model for Opportunistic Data Collection in IoV-Enabled SC Waste Management. In A. Nwajana & I. Ihianle (Eds.), *Handbook of Research on 5G Networks and Advancements in Computing, Electronics, and Electrical Engineering* (pp. 1–19). IGI Global. https://doi.org/10.4018/978-1-7998-6992-4.ch001

Ilori, O. O., Adetan, D. A., & Umoru, L. E. (2017). Effect of Cutting Parameters on the Surface Residual Stress of Face-Milled Pearlitic Ductile Iron. *International Journal of Materials Forming and Machining Processes, 4*(1), 38–52. doi:10.4018/IJMFMP.2017010103

Imam, M. H., Tasadduq, I. A., Ahmad, A., Aldosari, F., & Khan, H. (2017). Automated Generation of Course Improvement Plans Using Expert System. *International Journal of Quality Assurance in Engineering and Technology Education, 6*(1), 1–12. doi:10.4018/IJQAETE.2017010101

Injeti, S. K., & Kumar, T. V. (2018). A WDO Framework for Optimal Deployment of DGs and DSCs in a Radial Distribution System Under Daily Load Pattern to Improve Techno-Economic Benefits. *International Journal of Energy Optimization and Engineering, 7*(2), 1–38. doi:10.4018/IJEOE.2018040101

Ishii, N., Anami, K., & Knisely, C. W. (2018). *Dynamic Stability of Hydraulic Gates and Engineering for Flood Prevention.* Hershey, PA: IGI Global. doi:10.4018/978-1-5225-3079-4

Iwamoto, Y., & Yamaguchi, H. (2021). Application of Supercritical Carbon Dioxide for Solar Water Heater. In L. Chen (Ed.), *Handbook of Research on Advancements in Supercritical Fluids Applications for Sustainable Energy Systems* (pp. 370–387). IGI Global. https://doi.org/10.4018/978-1-7998-5796-9.ch010

Jayapalan, S. (2018). A Review of Chemical Treatments on Natural Fibers-Based Hybrid Composites for Engineering Applications. In K. Kumar & J. Davim (Eds.), *Composites and Advanced Materials for Industrial Applications* (pp. 16–37). Hershey, PA: IGI Global. doi:10.4018/978-1-5225-5216-1.ch002

Kapetanakis, T. N., Vardiambasis, I. O., Ioannidou, M. P., & Konstantaras, A. I. (2021). Modeling Antenna Radiation Using Artificial Intelligence Techniques: The Case of a Circular Loop Antenna. In C. Nikolopoulos (Ed.), *Recent Trends on Electromagnetic Environmental Effects for Aeronautics and Space Applications* (pp. 186–225). IGI Global. https://doi.org/10.4018/978-1-7998-4879-0.ch007

Karkalos, N. E., Markopoulos, A. P., & Dossis, M. F. (2017). Optimal Model Parameters of Inverse Kinematics Solution of a 3R Robotic Manipulator Using ANN Models. *International Journal of Manufacturing, Materials, and Mechanical Engineering*, 7(3), 20–40. doi:10.4018/IJMMME.2017070102

Kelly, M., Costello, M., Nicholson, G., & O'Connor, J. (2021). The Evolving Integration of BIM Into Built Environment Programmes in a Higher Education Institute. In J. Underwood & M. Shelbourn (Eds.), *Handbook of Research on Driving Transformational Change in the Digital Built Environment* (pp. 294–326). IGI Global. https://doi.org/10.4018/978-1-7998-6600-8.ch012

Kesimal, A., Karaman, K., Cihangir, F., & Ercikdi, B. (2018). Excavatability Assessment of Rock Masses for Geotechnical Studies. In N. Ceryan (Ed.), *Handbook of Research on Trends and Digital Advances in Engineering Geology* (pp. 231–256). Hershey, PA: IGI Global. doi:10.4018/978-1-5225-2709-1.ch006

Knoflacher, H. (2017). The Role of Engineers and Their Tools in the Transport Sector after Paradigm Change: From Assumptions and Extrapolations to Science. In H. Knoflacher & E. Ocalir-Akunal (Eds.), *Engineering Tools and Solutions for Sustainable Transportation Planning* (pp. 1–29). Hershey, PA: IGI Global. doi:10.4018/978-1-5225-2116-7.ch001

Kose, U. (2018). Towards an Intelligent Biomedical Engineering With Nature-Inspired Artificial Intelligence Techniques. In U. Kose, G. Guraksin, & O. Deperlioglu (Eds.), *Nature-Inspired Intelligent Techniques for Solving Biomedical Engineering Problems* (pp. 1–26). Hershey, PA: IGI Global. doi:10.4018/978-1-5225-4769-3.ch001

Kostić, S. (2018). A Review on Enhanced Stability Analyses of Soil Slopes Using Statistical Design. In N. Ceryan (Ed.), *Handbook of Research on Trends and Digital Advances in Engineering Geology* (pp. 446–481). Hershey, PA: IGI Global. doi:10.4018/978-1-5225-2709-1.ch013

Kumar, A., Patil, P. P., & Prajapati, Y. K. (2018). *Advanced Numerical Simulations in Mechanical Engineering*. Hershey, PA: IGI Global. doi:10.4018/978-1-5225-3722-9

Kumar, G. R., Rajyalakshmi, G., & Manupati, V. K. (2017). Surface Micro Patterning of Aluminium Reinforced Composite through Laser Peening. *International Journal of Manufacturing, Materials, and Mechanical Engineering, 7*(4), 15–27. doi:10.4018/IJMMME.2017100102

Kumar, N., Basu, D. N., & Chen, L. (2021). Effect of Flow Acceleration and Buoyancy on Thermalhydraulics of sCO2 in Mini/Micro-Channel. In L. Chen (Ed.), *Handbook of Research on Advancements in Supercritical Fluids Applications for Sustainable Energy Systems* (pp. 161–182). IGI Global. doi:10.4018/978-1-7998-5796-9.ch005

Kumari, N., & Kumar, K. (2018). Fabrication of Orthotic Calipers With Epoxy-Based Green Composite. In K. Kumar & J. Davim (Eds.), *Composites and Advanced Materials for Industrial Applications* (pp. 157–176). Hershey, PA: IGI Global. doi:10.4018/978-1-5225-5216-1.ch008

Kuppusamy, R. R. (2018). Development of Aerospace Composite Structures Through Vacuum-Enhanced Resin Transfer Moulding Technology (VERTMTy): Vacuum-Enhanced Resin Transfer Moulding. In K. Kumar & J. Davim (Eds.), *Composites and Advanced Materials for Industrial Applications* (pp. 99–111). Hershey, PA: IGI Global. doi:10.4018/978-1-5225-5216-1.ch005

Kurganov, V. A., Zeigarnik, Y. A., & Maslakova, I. V. (2021). Normal and Deteriorated Heat Transfer Under Heating Turbulent Supercritical Pressure Coolants Flows in Round Tubes. In L. Chen (Ed.), *Handbook of Research on Advancements in Supercritical Fluids Applications for Sustainable Energy Systems* (pp. 494–532). IGI Global. https://doi.org/10.4018/978-1-7998-5796-9.ch014

Li, H., & Zhang, Y. (2021). Heat Transfer and Fluid Flow Modeling for Supercritical Fluids in Advanced Energy Systems. In L. Chen (Ed.), *Handbook of Research on Advancements in Supercritical Fluids Applications for Sustainable Energy Systems* (pp. 388–422). IGI Global. https://doi.org/10.4018/978-1-7998-5796-9.ch011

Loy, J., Howell, S., & Cooper, R. (2017). Engineering Teams: Supporting Diversity in Engineering Education. In M. Gray & K. Thomas (Eds.), *Strategies for Increasing Diversity in Engineering Majors and Careers* (pp. 106–129). Hershey, PA: IGI Global. doi:10.4018/978-1-5225-2212-6.ch006

Related References

Macher, G., Armengaud, E., Kreiner, C., Brenner, E., Schmittner, C., Ma, Z., ... Krammer, M. (2018). Integration of Security in the Development Lifecycle of Dependable Automotive CPS. In N. Druml, A. Genser, A. Krieg, M. Menghin, & A. Hoeller (Eds.), *Solutions for Cyber-Physical Systems Ubiquity* (pp. 383–423). Hershey, PA: IGI Global. doi:10.4018/978-1-5225-2845-6.ch015

Madhu, M. N., Singh, J. G., Mohan, V., & Ongsakul, W. (2021). Transmission Risk Optimization in Interconnected Systems: Risk-Adjusted Available Transfer Capability. In P. Vasant, G. Weber, & W. Punurai (Ed.), *Research Advancements in Smart Technology, Optimization, and Renewable Energy* (pp. 183-199). IGI Global. https://doi.org/10.4018/978-1-7998-3970-5.ch010

Mahendramani, G., & Lakshmana Swamy, N. (2018). Effect of Weld Groove Area on Distortion of Butt Welded Joints in Submerged Arc Welding. *International Journal of Manufacturing, Materials, and Mechanical Engineering, 8*(2), 33–44. doi:10.4018/IJMMME.2018040103

Makropoulos, G., Koumaras, H., Setaki, F., Filis, K., Lutz, T., Montowtt, P., Tomaszewski, L., Dybiec, P., & Järvet, T. (2021). 5G and Unmanned Aerial Vehicles (UAVs) Use Cases: Analysis of the Ecosystem, Architecture, and Applications. In A. Nwajana & I. Ihianle (Eds.), *Handbook of Research on 5G Networks and Advancements in Computing, Electronics, and Electrical Engineering* (pp. 36–69). IGI Global. https://doi.org/10.4018/978-1-7998-6992-4.ch003

Meric, E. M., Erdem, S., & Gurbuz, E. (2021). Application of Phase Change Materials in Construction Materials for Thermal Energy Storage Systems in Buildings. In R. González-Lezcano (Ed.), *Advancements in Sustainable Architecture and Energy Efficiency* (pp. 1–20). IGI Global. https://doi.org/10.4018/978-1-7998-7023-4.ch001

Mihret, E. T., & Yitayih, K. A. (2021). Operation of VANET Communications: The Convergence of UAV System With LTE/4G and WAVE Technologies. *International Journal of Smart Vehicles and Smart Transportation, 4*(1), 29–51. https://doi.org/10.4018/IJSVST.2021010103

Mir, M. A., Bhat, B. A., Sheikh, B. A., Rather, G. A., Mehraj, S., & Mir, W. R. (2021). Nanomedicine in Human Health Therapeutics and Drug Delivery: Nanobiotechnology and Nanobiomedicine. In M. Bhat, I. Wani, & S. Ashraf (Eds.), *Applications of Nanomaterials in Agriculture, Food Science, and Medicine* (pp. 229–251). IGI Global. doi:10.4018/978-1-7998-5563-7.ch013

Mohammadzadeh, S., & Kim, Y. (2017). Nonlinear System Identification of Smart Buildings. In P. Samui, S. Chakraborty, & D. Kim (Eds.), *Modeling and Simulation Techniques in Structural Engineering* (pp. 328–347). Hershey, PA: IGI Global. doi:10.4018/978-1-5225-0588-4.ch011

Molina, G. J., Aktaruzzaman, F., Soloiu, V., & Rahman, M. (2017). Design and Testing of a Jet-Impingement Instrument to Study Surface-Modification Effects by Nanofluids. *International Journal of Surface Engineering and Interdisciplinary Materials Science*, 5(2), 43–61. doi:10.4018/IJSEIMS.2017070104

Moreno-Rangel, A., & Carrillo, G. (2021). Energy-Efficient Homes: A Heaven for Respiratory Illnesses. In R. González-Lezcano (Ed.), *Advancements in Sustainable Architecture and Energy Efficiency* (pp. 49–71). IGI Global. https://doi.org/10.4018/978-1-7998-7023-4.ch003

Msomi, V., & Jantjies, B. T. (2021). Correlative Analysis Between Tensile Properties and Tool Rotational Speeds of Friction Stir Welded Similar Aluminium Alloy Joints. *International Journal of Surface Engineering and Interdisciplinary Materials Science*, 9(2), 58–78. https://doi.org/10.4018/IJSEIMS.2021070104

Muigai, M. N., Mwema, F. M., Akinlabi, E. T., & Obiko, J. O. (2021). Surface Engineering of Materials Through Weld-Based Technologies: An Overview. In S. Roy & G. Bose (Eds.), *Advanced Surface Coating Techniques for Modern Industrial Applications* (pp. 247–260). IGI Global. doi:10.4018/978-1-7998-4870-7.ch011

Mukherjee, A., Saeed, R. A., Dutta, S., & Naskar, M. K. (2017). Fault Tracking Framework for Software-Defined Networking (SDN). In C. Singhal & S. De (Eds.), *Resource Allocation in Next-Generation Broadband Wireless Access Networks* (pp. 247–272). Hershey, PA: IGI Global. doi:10.4018/978-1-5225-2023-8.ch011

Mukhopadhyay, A., Barman, T. K., & Sahoo, P. (2018). Electroless Nickel Coatings for High Temperature Applications. In K. Kumar & J. Davim (Eds.), *Composites and Advanced Materials for Industrial Applications* (pp. 297–331). Hershey, PA: IGI Global. doi:10.4018/978-1-5225-5216-1.ch013

Mwema, F. M., & Wambua, J. M. (2022). Machining of Poly Methyl Methacrylate (PMMA) and Other Olymeric Materials: A Review. In K. Kumar, B. Babu, & J. Davim (Eds.), *Handbook of Research on Advancements in the Processing, Characterization, and Application of Lightweight Materials* (pp. 363–379). IGI Global. https://doi.org/10.4018/978-1-7998-7864-3.ch016

Related References

Mykhailyshyn, R., Savkiv, V., Boyko, I., Prada, E., & Virgala, I. (2021). Substantiation of Parameters of Friction Elements of Bernoulli Grippers With a Cylindrical Nozzle. *International Journal of Manufacturing, Materials, and Mechanical Engineering, 11*(2), 17–39. https://doi.org/10.4018/IJMMME.2021040102

Náprstek, J., & Fischer, C. (2017). Dynamic Stability and Post-Critical Processes of Slender Auto-Parametric Systems. In V. Plevris, G. Kremmyda, & Y. Fahjan (Eds.), *Performance-Based Seismic Design of Concrete Structures and Infrastructures* (pp. 128–171). Hershey, PA: IGI Global. doi:10.4018/978-1-5225-2089-4.ch006

Nautiyal, L., Shivach, P., & Ram, M. (2018). Optimal Designs by Means of Genetic Algorithms. In M. Ram & J. Davim (Eds.), *Soft Computing Techniques and Applications in Mechanical Engineering* (pp. 151–161). Hershey, PA: IGI Global. doi:10.4018/978-1-5225-3035-0.ch007

Nazir, R. (2017). Advanced Nanomaterials for Water Engineering and Treatment: Nano-Metal Oxides and Their Nanocomposites. In T. Saleh (Ed.), *Advanced Nanomaterials for Water Engineering, Treatment, and Hydraulics* (pp. 84–126). Hershey, PA: IGI Global. doi:10.4018/978-1-5225-2136-5.ch005

Nikolopoulos, C. D. (2021). Recent Advances on Measuring and Modeling ELF-Radiated Emissions for Space Applications. In C. Nikolopoulos (Ed.), *Recent Trends on Electromagnetic Environmental Effects for Aeronautics and Space Applications* (pp. 1–38). IGI Global. https://doi.org/10.4018/978-1-7998-4879-0.ch001

Nogueira, A. F., Ribeiro, J. C., Fernández de Vega, F., & Zenha-Rela, M. A. (2018). Evolutionary Approaches to Test Data Generation for Object-Oriented Software: Overview of Techniques and Tools. In M. Khosrow-Pour, D.B.A. (Ed.), Incorporating Nature-Inspired Paradigms in Computational Applications (pp. 162-194). Hershey, PA: IGI Global. https://doi.org/ doi:10.4018/978-1-5225-5020-4.ch006

Nwajana, A. O., Obi, E. R., Ijemaru, G. K., Oleka, E. U., & Anthony, D. C. (2021). Fundamentals of RF/Microwave Bandpass Filter Design. In A. Nwajana & I. Ihianle (Eds.), *Handbook of Research on 5G Networks and Advancements in Computing, Electronics, and Electrical Engineering* (pp. 149–164). IGI Global. https://doi.org/10.4018/978-1-7998-6992-4.ch005

Ogbodo, E. A. (2021). Comparative Study of Transmission Line Junction vs. Asynchronously Coupled Junction Diplexers. In A. Nwajana & I. Ihianle (Eds.), *Handbook of Research on 5G Networks and Advancements in Computing, Electronics, and Electrical Engineering* (pp. 326–336). IGI Global. https://doi.org/10.4018/978-1-7998-6992-4.ch013

Orosa, J. A., Vergara, D., Fraguela, F., & Masdías-Bonome, A. (2021). Statistical Understanding and Optimization of Building Energy Consumption and Climate Change Consequences. In R. González-Lezcano (Ed.), *Advancements in Sustainable Architecture and Energy Efficiency* (pp. 195–220). IGI Global. https://doi.org/10.4018/978-1-7998-7023-4.ch009

Osho, M. B. (2018). Industrial Enzyme Technology: Potential Applications. In S. Bharati & P. Chaurasia (Eds.), *Research Advancements in Pharmaceutical, Nutritional, and Industrial Enzymology* (pp. 375–394). Hershey, PA: IGI Global. doi:10.4018/978-1-5225-5237-6.ch017

Ouadi, A., & Zitouni, A. (2021). Phasor Measurement Improvement Using Digital Filter in a Smart Grid. In A. Recioui & H. Bentarzi (Eds.), *Optimizing and Measuring Smart Grid Operation and Control* (pp. 100–117). IGI Global. https://doi.org/10.4018/978-1-7998-4027-5.ch005

Padmaja, P., & Marutheswar, G. (2017). Certain Investigation on Secured Data Transmission in Wireless Sensor Networks. *International Journal of Mobile Computing and Multimedia Communications*, 8(1), 48–61. doi:10.4018/IJMCMC.2017010104

Palmer, S., & Hall, W. (2017). An Evaluation of Group Work in First-Year Engineering Design Education. In R. Tucker (Ed.), *Collaboration and Student Engagement in Design Education* (pp. 145–168). Hershey, PA: IGI Global. doi:10.4018/978-1-5225-0726-0.ch007

Panchenko, V. (2021). Prospects for Energy Supply of the Arctic Zone Objects of Russia Using Frost-Resistant Solar Modules. In P. Vasant, G. Weber, & W. Punurai (Eds.), *Research Advancements in Smart Technology, Optimization, and Renewable Energy* (pp. 149-169). IGI Global. https://doi.org/10.4018/978-1-7998-3970-5.ch008

Panchenko, V. (2021). Photovoltaic Thermal Module With Paraboloid Type Solar Concentrators. *International Journal of Energy Optimization and Engineering*, 10(2), 1–23. https://doi.org/10.4018/IJEOE.2021040101

Pandey, K., & Datta, S. (2021). Dry Machining of Inconel 825 Superalloys: Performance of Tool Inserts (Carbide, Cermet, and SiAlON). *International Journal of Manufacturing, Materials, and Mechanical Engineering*, 11(4), 26–39. doi:10.4018/IJMMME.2021100102

Panneer, R. (2017). Effect of Composition of Fibers on Properties of Hybrid Composites. *International Journal of Manufacturing, Materials, and Mechanical Engineering*, 7(4), 28–43. doi:10.4018/IJMMME.2017100103

Related References

Pany, C. (2021). Estimation of Correct Long-Seam Mismatch Using FEA to Compare the Measured Strain in a Non-Destructive Testing of a Pressurant Tank: A Reverse Problem. *International Journal of Smart Vehicles and Smart Transportation*, *4*(1), 16–28. doi:10.4018/IJSVST.2021010102

Paul, S., & Roy, P. (2018). Optimal Design of Power System Stabilizer Using a Novel Evolutionary Algorithm. *International Journal of Energy Optimization and Engineering*, *7*(3), 24–46. doi:10.4018/IJEOE.2018070102

Paul, S., & Roy, P. K. (2021). Oppositional Differential Search Algorithm for the Optimal Tuning of Both Single Input and Dual Input Power System Stabilizer. In P. Vasant, G. Weber, & W. Punurai (Eds.), *Research Advancements in Smart Technology, Optimization, and Renewable Energy* (pp. 256-282). IGI Global. https://doi.org/10.4018/978-1-7998-3970-5.ch013

Pavaloiu, A. (2018). Artificial Intelligence Ethics in Biomedical-Engineering-Oriented Problems. In U. Kose, G. Guraksin, & O. Deperlioglu (Eds.), *Nature-Inspired Intelligent Techniques for Solving Biomedical Engineering Problems* (pp. 219–231). Hershey, PA: IGI Global. doi:10.4018/978-1-5225-4769-3.ch010

Pioro, I., Mahdi, M., & Popov, R. (2017). Application of Supercritical Pressures in Power Engineering. In L. Chen & Y. Iwamoto (Eds.), *Advanced Applications of Supercritical Fluids in Energy Systems* (pp. 404–457). Hershey, PA: IGI Global. doi:10.4018/978-1-5225-2047-4.ch013

Plaksina, T., & Gildin, E. (2017). Rigorous Integrated Evolutionary Workflow for Optimal Exploitation of Unconventional Gas Assets. *International Journal of Energy Optimization and Engineering*, *6*(1), 101–122. doi:10.4018/IJEOE.2017010106

Popat, J., Kakadiya, H., Tak, L., Singh, N. K., Majeed, M. A., & Mahajan, V. (2021). Reliability of Smart Grid Including Cyber Impact: A Case Study. In R. Singh, A. Singh, A. Dwivedi, & P. Nagabhushan (Eds.), *Computational Methodologies for Electrical and Electronics Engineers* (pp. 163–174). IGI Global. https://doi.org/10.4018/978-1-7998-3327-7.ch013

Quiza, R., La Fé-Perdomo, I., Rivas, M., & Ramtahalsing, V. (2021). Triple Bottom Line-Focused Optimization of Oblique Turning Processes Based on Hybrid Modeling: A Study Case on AISI 1045 Steel Turning. In L. Burstein (Ed.), *Handbook of Research on Advancements in Manufacturing, Materials, and Mechanical Engineering* (pp. 215–241). IGI Global. https://doi.org/10.4018/978-1-7998-4939-1.ch010

Rahmani, M. K. (2022). Blockchain Technology: Principles and Algorithms. In S. Khan, M. Syed, R. Hammad, & A. Bushager (Eds.), *Blockchain Technology and Computational Excellence for Society 5.0* (pp. 16–27). IGI Global. https://doi.org/10.4018/978-1-7998-8382-1.ch002

Ramdani, N., & Azibi, M. (2018). Polymer Composite Materials for Microelectronics Packaging Applications: Composites for Microelectronics Packaging. In K. Kumar & J. Davim (Eds.), *Composites and Advanced Materials for Industrial Applications* (pp. 177–211). Hershey, PA: IGI Global. doi:10.4018/978-1-5225-5216-1.ch009

Ramesh, M., Garg, R., & Subrahmanyam, G. V. (2017). Investigation of Influence of Quenching and Annealing on the Plane Fracture Toughness and Brittle to Ductile Transition Temperature of the Zinc Coated Structural Steel Materials. *International Journal of Surface Engineering and Interdisciplinary Materials Science, 5*(2), 33–42. doi:10.4018/IJSEIMS.2017070103

Robinson, J., & Beneroso, D. (2022). Project-Based Learning in Chemical Engineering: Curriculum and Assessment, Culture and Learning Spaces. In A. Alves & N. van Hattum-Janssen (Eds.), *Training Engineering Students for Modern Technological Advancement* (pp. 1–19). IGI Global. https://doi.org/10.4018/978-1-7998-8816-1.ch001

Rondon, B. (2021). Experimental Characterization of Admittance Meter With Crude Oil Emulsions. *International Journal of Electronics, Communications, and Measurement Engineering, 10*(2), 51–59. https://doi.org/10.4018/IJECME.2021070104

Rudolf, S., Biryuk, V. V., & Volov, V. (2018). Vortex Effect, Vortex Power: Technology of Vortex Power Engineering. In V. Kharchenko & P. Vasant (Eds.), *Handbook of Research on Renewable Energy and Electric Resources for Sustainable Rural Development* (pp. 500–533). Hershey, PA: IGI Global. doi:10.4018/978-1-5225-3867-7.ch021

Sah, A., Bhadula, S. J., Dumka, A., & Rawat, S. (2018). A Software Engineering Perspective for Development of Enterprise Applications. In A. Elçi (Ed.), *Handbook of Research on Contemporary Perspectives on Web-Based Systems* (pp. 1–23). Hershey, PA: IGI Global. doi:10.4018/978-1-5225-5384-7.ch001

Sahli, Y., Zitouni, B., & Hocine, B. M. (2021). Three-Dimensional Numerical Study of Overheating of Two Intermediate Temperature P-AS-SOFC Geometrical Configurations. In G. Badea, R. Felseghi, & I. Aşchilean (Eds.), *Hydrogen Fuel Cell Technology for Stationary Applications* (pp. 186–222). IGI Global. https://doi.org/10.4018/978-1-7998-4945-2.ch008

Related References

Sahoo, P., & Roy, S. (2017). Tribological Behavior of Electroless Ni-P, Ni-P-W and Ni-P-Cu Coatings: A Comparison. *International Journal of Surface Engineering and Interdisciplinary Materials Science, 5*(1), 1–15. doi:10.4018/IJSEIMS.2017010101

Sahoo, S. (2018). Laminated Composite Hypar Shells as Roofing Units: Static and Dynamic Behavior. In K. Kumar & J. Davim (Eds.), *Composites and Advanced Materials for Industrial Applications* (pp. 249–269). Hershey, PA: IGI Global. doi:10.4018/978-1-5225-5216-1.ch011

Sahu, H., & Hungyo, M. (2018). Introduction to SDN and NFV. In A. Dumka (Ed.), *Innovations in Software-Defined Networking and Network Functions Virtualization* (pp. 1–25). Hershey, PA: IGI Global. doi:10.4018/978-1-5225-3640-6.ch001

Salem, A. M., & Shmelova, T. (2018). Intelligent Expert Decision Support Systems: Methodologies, Applications, and Challenges. In T. Shmelova, Y. Sikirda, N. Rizun, A. Salem, & Y. Kovalyov (Eds.), *Socio-Technical Decision Support in Air Navigation Systems: Emerging Research and Opportunities* (pp. 215–242). Hershey, PA: IGI Global. doi:10.4018/978-1-5225-3108-1.ch007

Samal, M. (2017). FE Analysis and Experimental Investigation of Cracked and Un-Cracked Thin-Walled Tubular Components to Evaluate Mechanical and Fracture Properties. In P. Samui, S. Chakraborty, & D. Kim (Eds.), *Modeling and Simulation Techniques in Structural Engineering* (pp. 266–293). Hershey, PA: IGI Global. doi:10.4018/978-1-5225-0588-4.ch009

Samal, M., & Balakrishnan, K. (2017). Experiments on a Ring Tension Setup and FE Analysis to Evaluate Transverse Mechanical Properties of Tubular Components. In P. Samui, S. Chakraborty, & D. Kim (Eds.), *Modeling and Simulation Techniques in Structural Engineering* (pp. 91–115). Hershey, PA: IGI Global. doi:10.4018/978-1-5225-0588-4.ch004

Samarasinghe, D. A., & Wood, E. (2021). Innovative Digital Technologies. In J. Underwood & M. Shelbourn (Eds.), *Handbook of Research on Driving Transformational Change in the Digital Built Environment* (pp. 142–163). IGI Global. https://doi.org/10.4018/978-1-7998-6600-8.ch006

Sawant, S. (2018). Deep Learning and Biomedical Engineering. In U. Kose, G. Guraksin, & O. Deperlioglu (Eds.), *Nature-Inspired Intelligent Techniques for Solving Biomedical Engineering Problems* (pp. 283–296). Hershey, PA: IGI Global. doi:10.4018/978-1-5225-4769-3.ch014

Schulenberg, T. (2021). Energy Conversion Using the Supercritical Steam Cycle. In L. Chen (Ed.), *Handbook of Research on Advancements in Supercritical Fluids Applications for Sustainable Energy Systems* (pp. 659–681). IGI Global. doi:10.4018/978-1-7998-5796-9.ch018

Sezgin, H., & Berkalp, O. B. (2018). Textile-Reinforced Composites for the Automotive Industry. In K. Kumar & J. Davim (Eds.), *Composites and Advanced Materials for Industrial Applications* (pp. 129–156). Hershey, PA: IGI Global. doi:10.4018/978-1-5225-5216-1.ch007

Shaaban, A. A., & Shehata, O. M. (2021). Combining Response Surface Method and Metaheuristic Algorithms for Optimizing SPIF Process. *International Journal of Manufacturing, Materials, and Mechanical Engineering*, *11*(4), 1–25. https://doi.org/10.4018/IJMMME.2021100101

Shafaati Shemami, M., & Sefid, M. (2022). Implementation and Demonstration of Electric Vehicle-to-Home (V2H) Application: A Case Study. In M. Alam, R. Pillai, & N. Murugesan (Eds.), *Developing Charging Infrastructure and Technologies for Electric Vehicles* (pp. 268–293). IGI Global. https://doi.org/10.4018/978-1-7998-6858-3.ch015

Shah, M. Z., Gazder, U., Bhatti, M. S., & Hussain, M. (2018). Comparative Performance Evaluation of Effects of Modifier in Asphaltic Concrete Mix. *International Journal of Strategic Engineering*, *1*(2), 13–25. doi:10.4018/IJoSE.2018070102

Sharma, N., & Kumar, K. (2018). Fabrication of Porous NiTi Alloy Using Organic Binders. In K. Kumar & J. Davim (Eds.), *Composites and Advanced Materials for Industrial Applications* (pp. 38–62). Hershey, PA: IGI Global. doi:10.4018/978-1-5225-5216-1.ch003

Shivach, P., Nautiyal, L., & Ram, M. (2018). Applying Multi-Objective Optimization Algorithms to Mechanical Engineering. In M. Ram & J. Davim (Eds.), *Soft Computing Techniques and Applications in Mechanical Engineering* (pp. 287–301). Hershey, PA: IGI Global. doi:10.4018/978-1-5225-3035-0.ch014

Shmelova, T. (2018). Stochastic Methods for Estimation and Problem Solving in Engineering: Stochastic Methods of Decision Making in Aviation. In S. Kadry (Ed.), *Stochastic Methods for Estimation and Problem Solving in Engineering* (pp. 139–160). Hershey, PA: IGI Global. doi:10.4018/978-1-5225-5045-7.ch006

Related References

Siero González, L. R., & Romo Vázquez, A. (2017). Didactic Sequences Teaching Mathematics for Engineers With Focus on Differential Equations. In M. Ramírez-Montoya (Ed.), *Handbook of Research on Driving STEM Learning With Educational Technologies* (pp. 129–151). Hershey, PA: IGI Global. doi:10.4018/978-1-5225-2026-9.ch007

Sim, M. S., You, K. Y., Esa, F., & Chan, Y. L. (2021). Nanostructured Electromagnetic Metamaterials for Sensing Applications. In M. Bhat, I. Wani, & S. Ashraf (Eds.), *Applications of Nanomaterials in Agriculture, Food Science, and Medicine* (pp. 141–164). IGI Global. https://doi.org/10.4018/978-1-7998-5563-7.ch009

Singh, R., & Dutta, S. (2018). Visible Light Active Nanocomposites for Photocatalytic Applications. In K. Kumar & J. Davim (Eds.), *Composites and Advanced Materials for Industrial Applications* (pp. 270–296). Hershey, PA: IGI Global. doi:10.4018/978-1-5225-5216-1.ch012

Skripov, P. V., Yampol'skiy, A. D., & Rutin, S. B. (2021). High-Power Heat Transfer in Supercritical Fluids: Microscale Times and Sizes. In L. Chen (Ed.), *Handbook of Research on Advancements in Supercritical Fluids Applications for Sustainable Energy Systems* (pp. 424–450). IGI Global. https://doi.org/10.4018/978-1-7998-5796-9.ch012

Sözbilir, H., Özkaymak, Ç., Uzel, B., & Sümer, Ö. (2018). Criteria for Surface Rupture Microzonation of Active Faults for Earthquake Hazards in Urban Areas. In N. Ceryan (Ed.), *Handbook of Research on Trends and Digital Advances in Engineering Geology* (pp. 187–230). Hershey, PA: IGI Global. doi:10.4018/978-1-5225-2709-1.ch005

Stanciu, I. (2018). Stochastic Methods in Microsystems Engineering. In S. Kadry (Ed.), *Stochastic Methods for Estimation and Problem Solving in Engineering* (pp. 161–176). Hershey, PA: IGI Global. doi:10.4018/978-1-5225-5045-7.ch007

Strebkov, D., Nekrasov, A., Trubnikov, V., & Nekrasov, A. (2018). Single-Wire Resonant Electric Power Systems for Renewable-Based Electric Grid. In V. Kharchenko & P. Vasant (Eds.), *Handbook of Research on Renewable Energy and Electric Resources for Sustainable Rural Development* (pp. 449–474). Hershey, PA: IGI Global. doi:10.4018/978-1-5225-3867-7.ch019

Sukhyy, K., Belyanovskaya, E., & Sukhyy, M. (2021). *Basic Principles for Substantiation of Working Pair Choice*. IGI Global. doi:10.4018/978-1-7998-4432-7.ch002

Suri, M. S., & Kaliyaperumal, D. (2022). Extension of Aspiration Level Model for Optimal Planning of Fast Charging Stations. In A. Fekik & N. Benamrouche (Eds.), *Modeling and Control of Static Converters for Hybrid Storage Systems* (pp. 91–106). IGI Global. https://doi.org/10.4018/978-1-7998-7447-8.ch004

Tallet, E., Gledson, B., Rogage, K., Thompson, A., & Wiggett, D. (2021). Digitally-Enabled Design Management. In J. Underwood & M. Shelbourn (Eds.), *Handbook of Research on Driving Transformational Change in the Digital Built Environment* (pp. 63–89). IGI Global. https://doi.org/10.4018/978-1-7998-6600-8.ch003

Terki, A., & Boubertakh, H. (2021). A New Hybrid Binary-Real Coded Cuckoo Search and Tabu Search Algorithm for Solving the Unit-Commitment Problem. *International Journal of Energy Optimization and Engineering*, *10*(2), 104–119. https://doi.org/10.4018/IJEOE.2021040105

Tüdeş, Ş., Kumlu, K. B., & Ceryan, S. (2018). Integration Between Urban Planning and Natural Hazards For Resilient City. In N. Ceryan (Ed.), *Handbook of Research on Trends and Digital Advances in Engineering Geology* (pp. 591–630). Hershey, PA: IGI Global. doi:10.4018/978-1-5225-2709-1.ch017

Ulamis, K. (2018). Soil Liquefaction Assessment by Anisotropic Cyclic Triaxial Test. In N. Ceryan (Ed.), *Handbook of Research on Trends and Digital Advances in Engineering Geology* (pp. 631–664). Hershey, PA: IGI Global. doi:10.4018/978-1-5225-2709-1.ch018

Valente, M., & Milani, G. (2017). Seismic Assessment and Retrofitting of an Under-Designed RC Frame Through a Displacement-Based Approach. In V. Plevris, G. Kremmyda, & Y. Fahjan (Eds.), *Performance-Based Seismic Design of Concrete Structures and Infrastructures* (pp. 36–58). Hershey, PA: IGI Global. doi:10.4018/978-1-5225-2089-4.ch002

Vargas-Bernal, R. (2021). Advances in Electromagnetic Environmental Shielding for Aeronautics and Space Applications. In C. Nikolopoulos (Ed.), *Recent Trends on Electromagnetic Environmental Effects for Aeronautics and Space Applications* (pp. 80–96). IGI Global. https://doi.org/10.4018/978-1-7998-4879-0.ch003

Vasant, P. (2018). A General Medical Diagnosis System Formed by Artificial Neural Networks and Swarm Intelligence Techniques. In U. Kose, G. Guraksin, & O. Deperlioglu (Eds.), *Nature-Inspired Intelligent Techniques for Solving Biomedical Engineering Problems* (pp. 130–145). Hershey, PA: IGI Global. doi:10.4018/978-1-5225-4769-3.ch006

Related References

Verner, C. M., & Sarwar, D. (2021). Avoiding Project Failure and Achieving Project Success in NHS IT System Projects in the United Kingdom. *International Journal of Strategic Engineering*, 4(1), 33–54. https://doi.org/10.4018/IJoSE.2021010103

Verrollot, J., Tolonen, A., Harkonen, J., & Haapasalo, H. J. (2018). Challenges and Enablers for Rapid Product Development. *International Journal of Applied Industrial Engineering*, 5(1), 25–49. doi:10.4018/IJAIE.2018010102

Wan, A. C., Zulu, S. L., & Khosrow-Shahi, F. (2021). Industry Views on BIM for Site Safety in Hong Kong. In J. Underwood & M. Shelbourn (Eds.), *Handbook of Research on Driving Transformational Change in the Digital Built Environment* (pp. 120–140). IGI Global. https://doi.org/10.4018/978-1-7998-6600-8.ch005

Yardimci, A. G., & Karpuz, C. (2018). Fuzzy Rock Mass Rating: Soft-Computing-Aided Preliminary Stability Analysis of Weak Rock Slopes. In N. Ceryan (Ed.), *Handbook of Research on Trends and Digital Advances in Engineering Geology* (pp. 97–131). Hershey, PA: IGI Global. doi:10.4018/978-1-5225-2709-1.ch003

You, K. Y. (2021). Development Electronic Design Automation for RF/Microwave Antenna Using MATLAB GUI. In A. Nwajana & I. Ihianle (Eds.), *Handbook of Research on 5G Networks and Advancements in Computing, Electronics, and Electrical Engineering* (pp. 70–148). IGI Global. https://doi.org/10.4018/978-1-7998-6992-4.ch004

Yousefi, Y., Gratton, P., & Sarwar, D. (2021). Investigating the Opportunities to Improve the Thermal Performance of a Case Study Building in London. *International Journal of Strategic Engineering*, 4(1), 1–18. https://doi.org/10.4018/IJoSE.2021010101

Zindani, D., & Kumar, K. (2018). Industrial Applications of Polymer Composite Materials. In K. Kumar & J. Davim (Eds.), *Composites and Advanced Materials for Industrial Applications* (pp. 1–15). Hershey, PA: IGI Global. doi:10.4018/978-1-5225-5216-1.ch001

Zindani, D., Maity, S. R., & Bhowmik, S. (2018). A Decision-Making Approach for Material Selection of Polymeric Composite Bumper Beam. In K. Kumar & J. Davim (Eds.), *Composites and Advanced Materials for Industrial Applications* (pp. 112–128). Hershey, PA: IGI Global. doi:10.4018/978-1-5225-5216-1.ch006

About the Contributors

Remya Lathabhavan is an Assistant Professor of Indian Institute of Management Bodh Gaya, India. Her research interests include Glass Ceiling, Corporate Social Responsibility, Human Resource Management, Data Analytics, Artificial Intelligence, Career Progression, mental health and psychology. She (co) authored many articles and book chapters in peer reviewed journals and books.

Nidhi Mishra completed her PhD in Organizational Behaviour from Indian Institute of Management Ahmedabad. Her research interests include Forgiveness, Mindfulness, Wellbeing, Resilience, Gratitude and Workplace Bullying, while her teaching interests are Qualitative Research Methods, Negotiations and Conflict Management, Mindfulness at Workplace and Organizational Behaviour. Apart from teaching and research, she has served as convenor of two International Conferences, and Program Directors for several MDPs, a FDP and a 11-month executive program at IIM Bodh Gaya. She is also the Chairperson of Samatvam, The Mindfulness Centre at IIM Bodh Gaya. She has published several research articles in International Journals and presented papers in National and International Conferences. Prior to pursuing her PhD, she did a B. Tech from NIT, Bhopal and has worked as Software Engineer in Accenture Services Pvt Ltd. She has more than 4 years of teaching experience and around 3 years of industry experience.

* * *

Aditya Amol Joshi is currently pursuing his Bachelors in Business Administration from the Indian Institute of Management Bodhgaya.

Zidan Kachhi is a counselling psychologist and an assistant professor. He has authored two books and published various papers in peer reviewed journals.

Kailashpati is a scholar at the Indian Institute of Management, Bodh Gaya(IIM BG), Mr. Kailashpati skillfully combines strategic entrepreneurship with his industrial engineering expertise. His multidisciplinary adventure began in Begusarai, Bihar, and has resulted in groundbreaking research influencing academia and industry. A new generation is motivated by his story to push boundaries and explore the limits of knowledge.

Jaspreet Kaur is currently working as an Assistant Professor in University Business School, Chandigarh University, Mohali, Punjab. She is a post graduate (MBA-H.R) from Panjab University, Chandigarh. She has also qualified UGC NET JRF in Human Resource Management/Labour and Social Welfare and has pursued PhD in Business Management from Chandigarh University, Mohali. She has over 8 years of experience in academic and administrative assignments. She also received "Best Teacher of the Department Award " in the year 2019 and 2021 in the field of imparting quality education. Her research interests include Employee Engagement, Management of Organizational Change and Organization Development. She has published several research papers and articles in reputed international and national journals and has presented papers in various national and international conferences. She also contributed one edited book and 10 book chapters on various topics.

Abha Kumari is a PhD scholar at the Indian Institute of Management, Bodh Gaya(IIM BG), and she completed her post-graduate(M.Com) studies at Banaras Hindu University. She has qualified UGC NET JRF in Commerce and UGC NET in Management. Her research interests include Corporate Governance, climate Finance and Corporate Finance.

Niveditha M is a driven professional with a recent PhD in organizational behavior from the Vellore Institute of technology, Vellore, and 7 years of valuable industry experience. Her research interests lie in the fields of Organizational Behaviour (OB) and Human Resource Management (HRM). Currently working at the National Statistics Office (NSO), Chennai Regional Office (RO).

Amrit Mund is a student in the Indian Institute of Management Bodh Gaya, pursuing Integrated Programme in Management. He has keen research interest in the field of Organisational Behaviour, Marketing, and Operations, and aims to contribute in these departments through valuable research.

Ashwini P is an aspiring researcher, who has eight years of experience in academic research on employee retention and human resources management in the healthcare sector. Her interests are General Management, Entrepreneurship, Organizational Behavior and Human Resource Management. She is presently pursuing her doctoral research at VIT Business School, Vellore Institute of Technology, Vellore, India

Prabir Chandra Padhy has more than 15 years of experience in teaching research, corporate training, and Industry consultancy. He has published 38 articles in journals of national and international repute. He has organized 3 AICTE-sponsored FDPs and 2 DST-sponsored WEDPs, 3 DST-sponsored FDPs, 2 MDPs, and many more. He provided corporate training in leading industries like Reliance Trends, JSB Technologies, Sysways, etc. He is presently working at VIT Business School, VIT, Vellore. His area of research interest in Entrepreneurship, Organisational Behavior, and HRM.

Dibyashree Panda is a student pursuing B.Sc Psychology (Hons) at PES University, Bangalore, India.

Smita Panda brings six years of academic teaching experience and over five years of scholarly research. Her academic interests encompass entrepreneurship, organizational behavior, and human resource management. Currently, she is pursuing her doctoral research at VIT Business School, VIT-Vellore, India. Additionally, she has contributed as a research assistant on an ICSSR-funded project. Smita has authored various research papers and book chapters, which have been published by esteemed publishers.

Archana Patro is an Associate Professor at IIM Bodhgaya in the Area of Finance & Accounting. She has done her Ph.D. (FPM) From the Indian Institute of Management Indore and have a Certificate of Specialisation in Finance and Accounting from Harvard Business School. She has around Ten years of Teaching and Research Experience. Prior to joining IIM BG, she worked as Assistant Professor at IIM Rohtak and IFMR Chennai. Over the span of her academic career, she was holding the important administrative position as Chairperson PGP, Chairperson PhD, Chairperson IPM, Financial Advisory and Investment Committee Chairperson, Chairperson Ranking and Outreach Committee, Chairperson Internal Complaints Committee (ICC) & Women Empowerment Committee etc. She has worked on various government projects and provided consultancy services for the Ministry of Consumer Affairs (Food & Public Distribution), National Women Commission, Food Corporation of India, State Finance Commission, GIZ Germany, Department of Tourism, Indian Department of Post etc. She has published her research in various reputed international and national journals. Her Papers were published in top journals such as Energy policy, International Review of Economics & Finance (IREF), Journal of Futures markets, Applied Economics Journal of Intellectual Capital etc. She was invited to present her research output on various platforms at National and international conferences. She has organised various National and International conferences as Convenor. She is the Programme Director for most of the long duration and short duration programmes of Indian Institute of Management and very active in providing training to Industry professionals through various executive education programmes and MDPs.

Rahul Raj is a student at IIM Bodhgaya.

Aiswarya Ramasundaram is a Professor in Human Resources, and specialises in Human Resources Development and Organizational Behaviour. She is the Associate dean for Student and Alumni Relations at LIBA. She has over 20 years of teaching, research, and administrative experience with some of the leading management institutions in India. She has published more than 50 research papers in national and international refereed journals.

Jenifer Arokia Selvi A. is a Research Scholar and currently pursuing PhD from Loyola Institute of Business Administration, (LIBA), Nungambakkam, Chennai on Emotional intelligence of leadership styles. Her area of research includes Ethical leadership, Green HRM Practices, Employees Sustainability and the Psychological Behaviour of Employees. She has published papers indexed in Scopus and Web of Science. She presented more than fifteen papers at various international conferences including IIM's and aspires to be a great researcher and academician in future.

Harsh Sinha is currently pursuing Ph.D. in Organizational Behaviour and Human Resource Management from IIM Bodhgaya. He has undertaken Research Work at Ministry of External Affairs (Central & West Africa Division) Government of India , IIM Indore and various institutions. He has done Bachelors in Marine Engineering from Indian Maritime University Kolkata and subsequently done his Masters in Hindi Literature.

Devaki V. is working as Assistant Professor of English, Vignan University. She has 4 + years of research and teaching experiences in the field of English Language Teaching and Applied Linguistics. she has cleared National Eligibility Test (UGC-NET). She did Master of Philosophy in English Language Teaching at Anna University, Chennai, and her Masters in Comparative Literature at Pondicherry Central University, Pondicherry. She worked as an Assistant professor of English at Vels Institute of Science and Technology (VISTAS) deemed University, Chennai from 2017 to 2019 and Rajalakshmi Institute of Technology, Chennai from 2022 to 2023. She received an Appreciation Award for the Best Utilization of Library Facilitates at the Vels University, 2018. Her area of interest is ELT; EAP,ESP, ERPP, ESL. Literature; LGBT, post-colonial literature, and modernism, literary theories, English Language teaching. She has published more than fifteen quality research articles in

International and National renowned peer-reviewed and refereed indexed journals. She has published five book chapters with ISBN. She has also presented research paper in International and National Conferences. She has been a reviewer in more than four International Journals in English Language, Literature & Culture. She also attended a One-month residential induction training program organized by Pandit Mandan Malvaliya National Mission on Teachers and Teaching (PMMNMTT), MHRD, Government of India from Nov to Dec 2017. She has received certificates for online courses through coursera from different international universities world-wide like University of Houston, Colorado, Wesleyan and Arizona State University.

Poondy Rajan Y. is a Doctoral Research Scholar and currently pursuing PhD from Loyola Institute of Business Administration, (LIBA), Nungambakkam, Chennai - 600034 on Leadership Qualities and Skills. His area of research includes Paradoxical leadership and HRM Functions. Having worked for eight years in prestigious universities and colleges, he has held positions as an administrator and lecturer. His main areas of interest include human behaviour and leadership in the area of human resource management. He has presented more than five papers at international conferences including IIM, his goal is to become a highly proficient researcher and professor in the future.

Shaheen Yusuf is an aspiring psychologist dedicated to understand the complexities of the human mind through academic exploration and real-world application.

Index

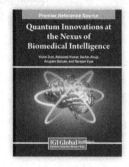

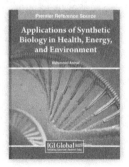

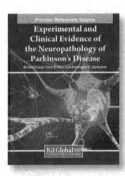
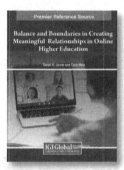

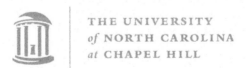

Printed in the United States
by Baker & Taylor Publisher Services

Printed in the United States
by Baker & Taylor Publisher Services